Report from
the Frontier

Report from the Frontier

The State of the World's Indigenous Peoples

Julian Burger

Zed Books Ltd.
London

Cultural Survival Inc.
Cambridge, Massachusetts

Report from the Frontier was first published in paperback in 1987·
by
Zed Books Ltd., 57 Caledonian Road,
London N1 9BU, UK,
and
Cultural Survival Inc., 11 Divinity Avenue,
Cambridge, Mass. 02138, USA

Cultural Survival Report No. 28.

Cover designed by Andrew Corbett.
Cover photo: *Quintik Ofong plays the 'Xumbing' bamboo jawsharp.
T'boli, Lam Delag, South Cotabato, Mindanao*. Reproduced by
courtesy of Filippijnengroep Nederland.
Maps by Andy Martin, unless otherwise stated.
Typeset by Format Photosetting, Bristol.
Printed and bound in the United Kingdom
by Biddles Ltd., Guildford and Kings Lynn.

Library of Congress Cataloging-in-Publication Number: 87-72334
US ISBN 0-939521-41-5. Pbk.

British Library Cataloguing in Publication Data

Burger, Julian
    Report from the frontier : the state of
    the world's indigenous peoples.
    1. Native races
    I. Title
    305.8   GN380

    ISBN 0-86232-392-4 Pbk

Contents

Tables

The tables of population rise are based on governmental and non-governmental sources. Census data on indigenous peoples is notoriously unreliable and the figures are estimated from general, often widely differing, sources.

Maps

Acknowledgements

I am grateful for the kind help and advice given to me by many people. I would particularly like to thank:

Robert Molteno of Zed Books for his enthusiasm and encouragement at the outset and during the writing of this book, and his colleague, Anna Gourlay, for her careful editing;

friends and colleagues at the Anti-Slavery Society for their support and indulgence;

Jeremy Swift for his comments on the typescript;

friends at the Copenhagen-based International Work Group for Indigenous Affairs, Survival International and the Workgroup for Indigenous Peoples in Amsterdam, for broadening my understanding;

and especially the numerous indigenous peoples from Australia, Bangladesh, Brazil, Canada, Chile, India, Peru, the Philippines, Thailand, the USA and many other countries – poor villagers, local activists and UN delegates – who have patiently described their conditions and aspirations.

The views expressed are those of the author.

1. Unwelcome Development

'We don't want a road, it will bring development,' called out an old man vigorously from the back of the meeting. Everyone nodded in agreement. The old man, a member of the Ho people – one of India's scheduled tribes, was adding his voice to those of many others in the village who did not want the government to build 10 more kilometres dirt road and bring their community closer to so-called civilization. Voices like this old man's cry out in many tribal communities all over the world: 'We don't want your development.'

The reasons for this unanimous rejection of the road were not difficult to understand. The village is set back in a band of thick forest which circles a small flat plain where the Ho grow paddy rice. A half a dozen other small tribal communities live in the forest and share the plain lands. Looking inwards from the village and across the fields of ripe, yellow paddy, towards the slopes of dark green forest, it is difficult to feel anything but satisfaction and contentment. Most years the rice they produce supplies all their staple food needs and the forest provides virtually every other necessity: meat, vegetables, fruit, forage, fuel, timber for building their homes and for making chairs, tables, beds and agricultural implements, leaves and berries for medicines, quiet groves for sacred contemplation, and a large playground which will never give up all its secrets for the village children.

The Ho village is about 20 kilometres from a main road joining two small market towns and is located on land owned by the Forest Department. Entry into the area is strictly controlled and vehicles must stop at a wooden barrier erected across the dirt access road. Near this control point there is a rather ramshackle bungalow where the forest officer lives with his family. Whenever a jeep arrives the official shuffles out and hands over a large, tatty book, such as might have been used for ledgers in Dickensian times, with a dozen columns requiring very precise information. The exact time of arrival is inserted, and both the driver and the visitor append their names. Only then does the man – still it seems with some lingering suspicion – officiously unlock the barrier and let the jeep through. It is reassuring to know that the forests are so well protected.

But 10 kilometres along the access road there is no sign of forest. There are no full-grown trees and only secondary vegetation – which might deceive a satellite but not the human eye – made up of low-lying bushes where the once flourishing sal trees have been cut down and are now coppicing in all directions.

Now and again the landscape is denuded of even these few bushes and already erosion is beginning to break up the land into small stony ravines. Where the road ends there is a desert panorama: arid and barren. It is only in the distance, and at two hours' walk, that the forest begins.

Ten years previously the whole area had been thick with trees under the protection of the Forest Department. Then came the access road. Shortly afterwards the big timber contractors arrived; they were given concessions to cut 1,000 trees and they felled 2,000. When they had had their fill, the small local contractors won concessions and took out what remained. Some of the cutting was legal – income generation for the Forest Department – and some was illegal, but within a decade the forest had disappeared. Finally, the tribal communities living in the area, deprived of their forest and the minor forest produce necessary for their survival, cut down any new growth and dug up roots to use for fuel or offer for sale, before they eventually gave up their struggle and moved away.

The village committee discussing the road-building plan were gathered beneath a tall, magnificent sal tree. All of those present knew that once the road was built, and the bribes flowed, the ancient tree which probably predated the founding of their community and provided shade at their meetings, would never survive the chainsaw of the contractors. This was why the old man was so vehement in his opposition to the road and looking beyond the perimeter of their forest at the dreadful wilderness created by the Forest Department in the name of development, it was easy to sympathize.

This book is about the present-day situation of the world's indigenous peoples. More particularly it is about the impact of development on these relatively self-reliant communities, for that is, perhaps, the single most harmful force affecting them.

Indigenous peoples live in what may be termed frontier land – deserts, tundras, forests, mountains and oceans. They may have always inhabited these regions or may have been forced to retreat there as other more powerful peoples have taken away their territory. But their comparatively quiet havens have come under renewed assaults in recent decades, as nation states seek to integrate and develop these hitherto marginal and neglected parts of their country. There is no denying that in the course of this spurious national development, thousands and perhaps millions of indigenous peoples have been killed. The development that is proffered so enthusiastically to them and to the world at large – the roads, settlements, ranches, mines and dams – is bringing about a destruction of these traditional societies which is at least as violent and as extensive as any in our history.

At the core of this impatient and rapacious exploitation is a myth. It is a myth whose two main components are that the land is empty of people and burgeoning with natural resources. The homelands of indigenous peoples are, more often than not, perceived as frontier lands. These lands are deemed wild, untamed, unknown, unowned and unclaimed and these qualities attract speculation and, of course, speculators. It is land both to conquer and exploit. For those contemplating its civilization, there is always the belief that some El

Dorado is waiting to be discovered and, for poor countries the vast mining project or multi-million dollar dam are the panacea for all economic and political problems.

But like all myths, the myth about frontier land contains only a modicum of truth. The land is underpopulated by comparison to other areas rather than empty, and the natural resources can provide long-term benefits only if carefully extracted and managed. In the effective development of these lands the indigenous peoples must be the partners and not the victims. Usually they are not even consulted; it is as if they did not exist.

However, such a myth serves a purpose for the ruling groups in the dominant societies because it provides a moral basis for colonization, displacement and exploitation. In 1975 the governor of Roraima in Brazil, irate with the internal and international protest about incursions on Yanomami Indian lands, put it this way: 'An area as rich as this, with gold, diamonds and uranium, cannot afford the luxury of preserving half a dozen Indian tribes which are holding up development.' Such a view may be seen as an extreme example of what is the overwhelming attitude of governments with respect to their frontier lands. Unhappily the last few decades have seen countless tragic examples arising from this single-minded pursuit of national development.

What follows is the story of the meeting of these two unequal societies: the one politically and economically powerful, welded to the world market and superpower rivalries; the other marginal to these international schemings, possessing a relatively self-reliant economy with a simple technology, low levels of production and nomadic land use (e.g. pastoralism, shifting cultivation, hunting and gathering) and a political organization which traditionally does not extend beyond the community. As the frontiers get pushed back and these two societies meet, the weakest are inevitably the losers. At least until recently they have been the losers, but in the last few years there has been a dramatic development. A great many indigenous organizations have been formed and there has been an increase of international support. While it would be premature to talk of a movement, there is certainly a growing sense of community among the various organizations and an interest in finding alternatives to the dominant development models. The action of this incipient indigenous movement is as much a part of this book as the conflicts which brought it about.

However, some general comments are necessary at the outset. To begin with, there is really no satisfactory term for the peoples whose conditions and lives are described, nor is there any acceptable definition. Anthropologists may certainly take issue over the peoples who are included under this umbrella expression, 'indigenous peoples'. It can only be hoped that by the end of the book, the reader will recognize that all the peoples mentioned, despite their differences, share some kind of common experience.

Furthermore, there is bound to be some dissatisfaction from specialists about the cursoriness with which important peoples and issues have had to be treated. Sometimes complex matters have had to be simplified for the sake of clarity or space. But the book is intended as a worldwide report and its intention is to illustrate the extent of the damage by present political and economic processes, rather than the details of important but particular cases.

Finally, this book is written not only in order to inform its readers of the present situation of indigenous peoples, but to provide some means for them to take action on their behalf. Nearly all writing is time-bound and none more than that dealing with contemporary political events. The indigenous movement here described is continually developing, achieving successes and experiencing setbacks. Development projects threatening untold grief today may never get implemented; peoples presently living in relative isolation may suddenly find themselves in an area designated for some new scheme which will totally destroy their traditional way of life. But though the events may change, the processes remain the same.

Fortunately, there are now numerous indigenous and concerned non-governmental organizations monitoring and resisting this kind of harmful development and questioning the process itself. This book is offered in the hope that an informed and active general public will no longer think of indigenous peoples as backward and passive, nor of their territories as empty lands of plenty.

2. Peoples at the Frontier

Indigenous peoples are survivors. They are scattered across the globe, often in remote and inhospitable regions, living what seem precarious existences. How these people manage in their harsh environments is a source of wonder to many in the West. Yet they do. The San bushmen survive the waterless wasteland of the Kalahari, the Amazonian Indians have successfully adapted to the complex ecosystem of the tropical rain forest and the Inuit (Eskimos) withstand the hard life of the Arctic and tundra.

There are other indigenous peoples who live in more accessible areas and have more familiar means of livelihood. They are the Native American peoples, the Aborigines of Australia, the Maori of New Zealand or the Quechua Indians of Peru; they inhabit special reserves or farming communities or else have drifted to the cities. Some may be almost indistinguishable in their appearance and way of life from members of the society which they have joined. But these peoples too are survivors. They have survived the often genocidal process of colonization and the long history of land dispossession.

Then there are other indigenous peoples who have not suffered genocidal colonization – as have the peoples of the Americas or Australasia – and who have not necessarily retreated to remote regions. Spanish occupation in the Philippines or British rule in India created identifiable tribal minorities out of peoples who shared a long common history with all the inhabitants of the area. The colonial process, by and large, left these peoples to their own devices and today they live in the mountains and forests of Asian countries, having retained many distinguishing cultural characteristics which set them apart from the mainstream. These peoples too are survivors because they have not been drawn fully into the political, social and economic life of the nation states of which they are a part.

Indigenous Peoples

The term indigenous peoples is used throughout this book because the designation is most widely accepted by the peoples themselves and has been adopted by the United Nations and other international organizations. Where alternatives are used, such as tribal peoples or national minorities, it is to avoid confusions or in accordance with common practice.

However, the term indigenous peoples has not met with universal acceptance, if only because, taken in its literal sense, most people are indigenous to their country. In the case of Africa the notion of indigenousness may even be misleading and irrelevant: some of the nomadic pastoralist peoples, for example, are comparatively recent inhabitants of the Sahelian region where they now live.

Nevertheless, alternatives to the term indigenous peoples have proved even less acceptable. Where once such peoples were referred to as primitive or backward, these are now considered inaccurate and pejorative descriptions. The word Indian as an all-embracing racial category ignores the heterogeneity of Native American societies. It also gives offence to Quechua, Aymara and other indigenous peoples of South America, being an epithet used by the invading Spaniards; certain Native American peoples reject its use because of its European origin. Many indigenous peoples of the Americas find the terms tribe or tribal people derogatory because they claim they are nations, while many peoples in Asia make no objections. In Australia the terms Aboriginal or Aboriginal people are used in preference to Aborigines by the indigenous peoples.

Writers who have sought alternatives have proposed native peoples, tribal minorities, national minorities, autochthonous peoples or Fourth World. The most neutral of these terms – Fourth World – has occasionally been used by indigenous peoples but it has also been adopted by writers to connote the expanding communities of lumpen proletariat living in slums around cities of Third World countries. Furthermore, there is a danger that in talking of First, Second, Third and Fourth Worlds, we fuel the notion that there is no common humanity, only peoples in conflict and competition with one another. Finally, governments with indigenous populations have themselves different terms. In Latin America the indigenous peoples are officially designated Indian notwithstanding the acknowledged racist connotations of the word; in the Philippines the indigenous people are described as national minorities and in India as scheduled tribes. But if there is disagreement about an acceptable term, a definition of what is meant by indigenous peoples has proved equally evasive.

Definitions

The United Nations has recognized the difficulties of drafting a universally acceptable definition and its formulation is lengthy and bureaucratic. The first part reads:

> Indigenous populations are composed of the existing descendants of the peoples who inhabited the present territory of a country wholly or partially at the time when persons of a different culture or ethnic origin arrived there from other parts of the world, overcame them and, by conquest, settlement or other means, reduced them to a non-dominant or colonial situation; who today live more in conformity with their particular social, economic and cultural customs and

traditions than with the institutions of the country of which they now form a part, under a State structure which incorporates mainly the national, social and cultural characteristics of other segments of the population which are predominant.

The second part of their working definition contains qualifications about isolated and marginal populations and reads:

Although they have not suffered conquest or colonization, isolated or marginal groups existing in the country should also be regarded as covered by the notion of 'indigenous populations' for the following reasons:

(a) they are descendants of groups which were in the territory of the country at the time when other groups of different cultures or ethnic origins arrived there;

(b) precisely because of their isolation from other segments of the country's population they have preserved almost intact the customs and traditions of their ancestors which are similar to those characterized as indigenous;

(c) they are, even if only formally, placed under a State structure which incorporates national, social and cultural characteristics alien to theirs.[1]

This working definition was adopted by the United Nations Working Group on Indigenous Populations, a subsidiary body of the Commission on Human Rights, when it was formed in 1982. It allowed the inclusion of the colonized native peoples of the Americas and Australasia and the tribal peoples of Asia whose claims to original occupation are more difficult to sustain.

The International Labour Organisation (ILO), the only other international body which has drafted a definition of indigenous peoples, describes the peoples which its Convention 107 protects as

members of tribal and semi-tribal populations in independent countries whose social and economic conditions are at a less advanced stage than the stage reached by other sections of the national community and whose status is regulated wholly or partially by their own customs or traditions or by special laws or regulations.[2]

The Convention which was adopted in 1957 sets out to protect and eventually integrate indigenous peoples into the mainstream of society. The more recent United Nations definition carefully avoids any of these paternalist aspects and does not imply, as the ILO Convention does, that indigenous peoples are socially or economically backward.

The definition adopted by the World Bank in 1982 with respect to indigenous peoples affected by development projects also contains paternalist and evolutionist elements. The Bank identifies various socio-economic factors as defining characteristics and most particularly notes that indigenous peoples are often geographically isolated, unacculturated, non-literate, often non-monetized and possess an economic base dependent upon a specific environment. As such, the Bank recognizes four main kinds of indigenous group according to the degree of isolation or acculturation, and its stated policy is to ensure the survival of uncontacted tribes and 'facilitate the development' of 'tribes at a more advanced stage of interaction within the nation'.[3] The assumption that there is only one line of development and that indigenous peoples benefit from following it is central to the World Bank's thinking.

Along with these international institutions, national governments tend to view their indigenous peoples as national minorities or minority populations requiring special treatment or consideration. They are a population recognized as different from the majority or dominant group, but implicitly a part of the total national identity. International organizations and national governments both carefully avoid referring to indigenous minorities as peoples because such a term carries with it the notion of self-determination.

Legal definitions by governments of their indigenous or tribal population vary considerably. In Australia an Aboriginal or Torres Strait Islander is defined as 'a person of Aboriginal or Islander descent who identifies himself as an Aboriginal or Islander and is accepted as such by the community with which he or she is associated.' An individual who declares himself Aboriginal on this basis may become eligible for special benefits. Most governments, however, do not define their indigenous population on the basis of self-identification and instead take into consideration criteria such as language, aboriginal descent, isolation and so on. In these situations the last word on who is indigenous is decided by the responsible minister in the government. By such means governments are able to keep control over the character and size of their indigenous populations.

For the purposes of administration this may be convenient but it can also lead to serious anomalies. In the United States of America, for example, bands, communities or individuals entitled to Bureau of Indian Affairs assistance must be enrolled and these groups constitute, as far as the administration is concerned, the total indigenous population. In fact, almost half of all Native Americans live in urban areas where they become ineligible for the Bureau's assistance. In New Zealand the Maori population is classified according to parentage, so that three Maori forebears and one white or *Pakeha* grandparent will constitute a three-quarter caste. But proofs of parentage are not required nor could they practicably be obtained in these cases. Individuals can, therefore, exercise choice depending upon whether they see themselves as part of the indigenous or the non-indigenous population.

Indigenous peoples have not accepted definitions proposed by non-indigenous peoples uncritically and, where they have offered their own, they have emphasized the notion of group-consciousness. The World Council of Indigenous Peoples, for example, has proposed that:

> Indigenous peoples are such population groups as we are, who from old-age times have inhabited the lands where we live, who are aware of having a character of our own, with social traditions and means of expression that are linked to the country inherited from our ancestors, with a language of our own and having certain essential and unique characteristics which confer upon us the strong conviction of belonging to a people, who have an identity in ourselves and should be thus regarded by others.[4]

The notion of belonging to a separate culture with all its various elements – language, religion, social and political systems, moral values, scientific and philosophical knowledge, beliefs, legends, laws, economic systems, technology, art, clothing, music, dance, architecture, and so on – is central to indigenous peoples' own definition. Indigenous peoples feel themselves to be different from the mainstream society of the modern nation state where they now find themselves included. Furthermore, the spokespersons of the indigenous movement that has developed in the last decade or two have no desire to be a part of the mainstream. 'Why join in the mainstream', commented one activist, 'when it is polluted?' The definition proposed by indigenous peoples implicitly contains the idea that their world-view is different. It sets them apart, and it confers on them the right to choose who is a member of their community and who is not. For certain indigenous peoples' organizations, indigenous peoples 'are not merely racial or national minorities' but 'constitute distinct and separate cultural, social and political entities, many of which have been historically and practically self-governing to some extent'.[5]

For the purposes of this book, a definition has been drawn from a group of overlapping criteria. An indigenous people may contain all of the following elements or just some. Indigenous peoples:

1. are the descendants of the original inhabitants of a territory which has been overcome by conquest;
2. are nomadic and semi-nomadic peoples, such as shifting cultivators, herders and hunters and gatherers, and practise a labour-intensive form of agriculture which produces little surplus and has low energy needs;
3. do not have centralized political institutions and organize at the level of the community and make decisions on a consensus basis;
4. have all the characteristics of a national minority: they share a common language, religion, culture and other identifying characteristics and a relationship to a particular territory, but are subjugated by a dominant culture and society;
5. have a different world-view, consisting of a custodial and non-materialist attitude to land and natural resources, and want to pursue a separate development to that proffered by the dominant society;
6. consist of individuals who subjectively consider themselves to be indigenous, and are accepted by the group as such.

The peoples discussed in the following chapters do not unequivocally fulfil all the criteria adopted in the definition. The Tuareg of Sahelian Africa, for example, are not indigenous in the sense of being the original inhabitants of the area; they are, however, a national minority and a mainly nomadic pastoralist people. The Mayan Indians of Guatemala are settled agriculturalists rather than nomadic peoples, but they are the original inhabitants by descent of a region overrun by a colonial power. The Quechua Indians of Peru, who prior to conquest were organized under a highly centralized Inca empire, now live in small, community-based groups (*ayllus*).

These defining criteria are not uniform even within a single indigenous community. There are Australian Aborigines who live according to their traditional way of life, others who are successful cattle ranchers and still others

9

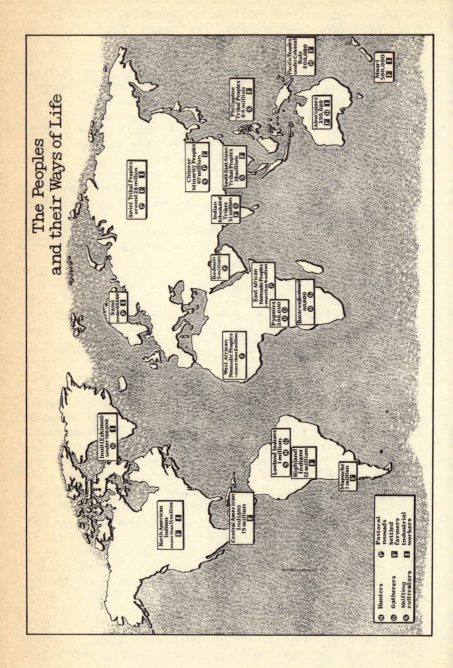

The Peoples
and their Ways of Life

Pacific Peoples
under colonial
Rule
500,000
Ⓟ Ⓗ

Maori
300,000
Ⓕ Ⓗ

Philippine
Tribal Peoples
6·5 million
Ⓢ Ⓕ

Aborigines
250,000
Ⓗ Ⓖ Ⓗ

Soviet Tribal Peoples
around 28 million
Ⓟ Ⓕ Ⓗ

Chinese
Minority Peoples
67 million
Ⓕ Ⓗ

South-East Asian
Tribal Peoples
18 million
Ⓢ Ⓕ

Indian
Scheduled
Tribes
51 million
Ⓕ

Bedouin
5 million
Ⓟ

East African
Nomadic Peoples
-more than 6 million
Ⓟ

Pygmies
200,000
Ⓗ Ⓖ

Basarwa(Bushmen)
60,000
Ⓗ Ⓖ

West African
Nomadic Peoples
-more than 8 million
Ⓟ

Sami
under 60,000
Ⓟ Ⓗ

Inuit (Eskimos)
under 100,000
Ⓟ Ⓗ

Lowland Indians
1 million
Ⓢ Ⓗ Ⓖ

Highland
Indians
12 million
Ⓕ

Mapuche
1 million
Ⓕ

North American
Indians
more than 1·5 million
Ⓕ Ⓗ

Central American
Indians
13 million

Ⓟ Pastoral
    nomads
Ⓕ Settled
    farmers
Ⓗ Industrial
    workers

Ⓗ Hunters
Ⓖ Gatherers
Ⓢ Shifting
    cultivators

in professional and manual employment in the cities. In most rich countries, significant numbers of indigenous peoples are settled in towns, but the links they maintain with their communities will differ widely. In a single village of scheduled tribes in India, for example, there can exist members who have an indigenous world-view – who dwell in the forest and have a symbiotic relationship with nature – and others who promote assimilation into the wider society and the adoption of 'modern values' as the proper development of their community. Like many definitions, that of indigenous peoples obscures as much as it clarifies.

In the last decade indigenous peoples have been claiming the rights to their own political, social, economic and cultural development and these claims are reflected in their own definition. Official definitions have largely ignored the demands of their indigenous populations to be treated as peoples and nations. While governments and international bodies continue to define such peoples as populations requiring special consideration within the context of the state, and indigenous peoples insist on their right to self-determination, definitions will receive little universal acceptance.

Who is indigenous?

Indigenous peoples number over 200 million and represent about four per cent of the global population.[6] They live in all the five continents: in First, Second and Third Worlds, in both East and West, in Communist and metropolitan capitalist nations, in populous countries like China and small islands like New Caledonia in the southern Pacific. Of the 161 member states of the United Nations about half have an indigenous population whose right to self-determination is being denied or restricted. To give some idea of distribution, there are about 2.5 million native peoples in North America, between 25 and 30 million indigenous peoples in Central and South America, 60,000 Sami (Lapps) in the Scandinavian countries, 240,000 Maoris in New Zealand and 250,000 Aborigines in Australia. The majority of the the world's indigenous peoples live in Asia: about 6.5 million in the Philippines, 11 million in Burma, 500,000 in Thailand, 51 million in India and 67 million in China.

Indigenous peoples are generally a demographic minority. The exceptions are Greenland, where the indigenous population accounts for 90 per cent of the total, and Guatemala and Bolivia where the indigenous people make up more than half the populations. Elsewhere indigenous populations are comparatively few: in Australia accounting for less than two per cent of the total population, in the United States of America around 0.5 per cent and in Sweden less than 0.1 per cent of the population. Even in China, where peoples belonging to national minorities number nearly 70 million, they make up only seven per cent of the country's population.

Indigenous peoples are the descendants of the original inhabitants of a territory which has been overcome by conquest. Most indigenous peoples, therefore, have a history of violence at the hands of settlers and invaders, although their experiences of colonial conquest are not uniform. In both North and South America the native population was decimated by the invading British, French, Spanish and Portuguese empires. The descendants of these settlers themselves eventually achieved independence from the motherland, but the Native Americans remained subjugated peoples. In Asia the colonial experience was different. The hill tribes of countries like Bangladesh or India faced subjugation at the hands of several invading peoples prior to occupation by the British, and some tribal peoples enjoyed greater autonomy under the Raj than at previous times. There were in any case no genocidal policies of the kind that so filled the colonial histories of the Americas. Indeed, it is since the Second World War and the advent of decolonization in Asia that numerous tribal and indigenous peoples have seen their comparative independence eroded at an alarming rate.

The most easily identifiable indigenous peoples are those engaged in nomadic or semi-nomadic economic activities. These peoples are often physically isolated and are living largely outside their national society and the world market. In fact indigenous peoples still pursuing what may be deemed their traditional lifestyle are in a minority. There are small groups of San bushmen, for example, who have no permanent settlements and have retreated to the less hospitable regions of the Kalahari desert where they survive by hunting animals and gathering roots and berries. There are a number of Amazonian Indian peoples living from hunting and gathering, planting temporary gardens and keeping on the move for half the year. Many more indigenous peoples practise different kinds of shifting cultivation (swidden agriculture). Shifting cultivation is a form of agro-forestry by which land is cleared of tree cover for one season, planted with a subsistence crop such as maize or rice, harvested and then left fallow for several years. The system allows complete regeneration of the forest if practised with sufficient time intervals. Numerous indigenous and tribal peoples in Asia and South and Central America practise shifting agriculture. Finally, there are societies whose main economic activity is herding animals, such as the Tuareg in Sahelian Africa or the nomadic pastoralists of the Mongolian People's Republic.

Large numbers of indigenous peoples are peasant producers. Indigenous peoples who are farmers producing on a small scale or at subsistence level can, therefore, be indistinguishable from the non-indigenous peoples living nearby. In India, for example, distinctions between scheduled tribes and non-tribal peoples cannot be made solely on the basis of economic activity. In the Peruvian Andes, the Quechua peoples farm like *mestizo* peasants. In such cases non-indigenous peasants and indigenous peoples produce the same crops with the same farming methods.

In the rich countries indigenous minorities are integrated into the national economy to a much greater extent. While some North American native peoples live on reservations and can exploit the natural resources of their land, nearly half live in cities where they are employed in industry, construction and the services. In general, the traditional economies of the original inhabitants of these countries have been substantially modified by capitalist development and continue to be so. Even in Norway, for example, although many Sami still retain some small interest in reindeer herding, it is the source of livelihood and income for only about ten per cent of them. On an individual basis there are often considerable overlaps. An indigenous person may retain some roots and economic stake in his ancestral land but derive the bulk of his or her income from work in the wider economy. Those more isolated indigenous communities like the Inuit (Eskimos) may for part of the year engage in activities outside their traditional independent economy – in the oil industry, for example.

When identification of indigenous peoples cannot easily be made on the basis of economic activity, it can generally be made on the basis of language, dress, custom and culture. Indigenous peoples will often possess a language of their own which is subordinated – by not being recognized by the state – to a dominant language. The identity of an indigenous people will depend on how successfully it preserves its language. A language distinguishes an indigenous people from the majority population and allows it to protect and pass on what is often an oral culture. In Latin America indigenous highland communities will trade at markets or sell their produce to local distributors with a minimum of communication, a fact reflected in their relatively poor understanding of the first language, Spanish. In many parts of Asia hill tribespeople not speaking the dominant language limit their contact with outsiders to the minimum thereby enhancing the differences between indigenous and non-indigenous peoples.

Other outward signals of indigenousness may be dress or choice of dwelling. Indigenous peoples live as communities and often this is expressed in the architecture of the village: there may be special houses for single men or, as in some indigenous communities in Borneo, long houses in which the whole village live. Indigenous peoples may also be distinguished by dress: the penis sheaths worn by some Papua New Guinea highlanders, the wooden mouth ornaments carried by certain Brazilian tribespeople or the *huipiles* or ponchos worn by Mayan Indians in Guatemala. Loss of tribal identity is often indicated by changes in architecture – for example, the decay of communal buildings or the demarcation of gardens around family houses, and by the adoption of the style of dress of the dominant society. Furthermore, while most societies practise one of the major religions, indigenous peoples are often animists or pantheists. Such traditional religions are often intimately bound up with a place. Thus, Australian Aboriginals, for example, regard certain natural features, such as rocks, pools or hollows, as sacred; in the Philippines ancestral burial grounds of many indigenous minorities are of vital spiritual importance: many forest-dwelling tribes in India will preserve for generations, sacred groves for worship and reflection. Traditional indigenous religions are much more directly related to the land than the majority religions.

Land and philosophy

It is probably in respect to land that indigenous peoples are most clearly distinguishable from non-indigenous societies. The struggle of indigenous peoples in the last decade or two has thus centred on land. Land contains their history and sense of identity, and it ensures their economic viability as an independent people. The importance of land to indigenous peoples has been expressed in this way by the Vice-President of the World Council of Indigenous Peoples:

> The Earth is the foundation of Indigenous Peoples. It is the seat of spirituality, the fountain from which our cultures and languages flourish. The Earth is our historian, the keeper of events and the bones of our forefathers. Earth provides us food, medicine, shelter and clothing. It is the source of our independence; it is our Mother. We do not dominate Her: we must harmonize with Her.
>
> Next to shooting Indigenous Peoples, the surest way to kill us is to separate us from our part of the Earth. Once separated, we will either perish in body or our minds and spirits will be altered so that we end up mimicking foreign ways, adopt foreign languages, accept foreign thoughts and build a foreign prison around our Indigenous spirits, a prison which suffocates rather than nourishes as our traditional territories of the Earth do. Over time, we lose our identity and eventually die or are crippled as we are stuffed under the name of 'assimilation' into another society.[7]

For indigenous peoples land has a sacred quality which is almost absent from Western thinking. Land is revered and respected and its inalienability is reflected in virtually every indigenous philosophy. Accordingly indigenous peoples see industrialized societies as those in which man seeks to be master of the earth. If he acquires a greater understanding of the natural order, it is to acquire dominion over it. For indigenous peoples the land is a living entity which can neither be claimed for oneself nor subjugated. The Australian Aboriginals see it as a 'vibrant spiritual landscape, peopled in spirit form by the ancestors who originated in the dreaming, the creative period of time immemorial'.[8] The International Indian Treaty Council, a non-governmental organization of indigenous peoples, has made this observation on the distinction between indigenous and Western philosophies:

> The philosophy of the indigenous peoples of the Western Hemisphere has grown from a relationship to the land that extends back thousands of years. It is founded on an observation of natural laws and incorporation of those laws into every aspect of daily life. This philosophy is profoundly different from the predominant economic and geopolitical ideology which governs the practices of the major industrial powers and the operations of transnational corporations. Its chief characteristic is a great love and respect for the sacred quality of the land which has given birth to and nourished the cultures of indigenous peoples. These peoples are the guardians of their lands which, over the centuries, have become inextricably bound up with their culture, spirits, their identity and survival. Without the land bases, their cultures will not survive.[9]

A spiritual rapport with the land is common in the philosophy of indigenous peoples, but it is at odds with the prevailing materialist notions of Western society. In their speeches and writings indigenous peoples identify a dichotomy between their values and those of the dominant culture. Land that is not owned by title deed, they argue, is regarded as unclaimed and seized; natural resources that are left untouched by indigenous peoples are considered as wasted and are exploited; economic activities which do not extract the greatest commercial benefits are judged inefficient and primitive. A common fate is shared by indigenous peoples with respect to their futures: non-indigenous majorities believe they can organize them better.

The common way of life of indigenous peoples – one that has a reverence for the land – is menaced by this overbearing attitude of cultural superiority and the material greed that accompanies it. As a consequence indigenous peoples all over the world face a similar struggle to protect their land, their culture and their way of life. Their antagonists may be governments, transnational corporations or even poor peasant colonists and the results of the contact between the two are often violent and far-reaching. In capitalist and Communist countries alike indigenous peoples are often deemed to live in a kind of physical and philosophical unclaimed territory which is up for grabs. Indigenous peoples are considered as merely inhabitants of frontier lands awaiting civilization. At an international conference on indigenous peoples in 1981, one delegate commented in this respect:

We live in a world where our tradition confronts contrasting ideas and practices. The oneness of the earth has been shattered by artificial entities called 'nations' that separate people from each other – even people sharing a common history, culture and tradition. The oneness of the earth has been shattered within those nations by other artificial boundaries dividing the open land into segments of 'private property'. The oneness of the earth has been shattered by commercial and industrial practices that poison air, land and water and the creatures dependent on them. The oneness of the earth has been shattered by the genocide unleashed upon us by exploiters who place profits before people, who do not stop with destroying the land but attempt to destroy also the people of the land, the indigenous peoples who live in harmony with the earth and her rhythms. In destroying Mother Earth and indigenous peoples, these exploiters of the land are also destroying themselves and unborn generations of plant, animal and human life.

We have seen this pattern of destruction repeated around the world by societies that base their way of life on excessive industrialization. We who have tried to take from Mother Earth only what we need, and to replace what we have taken with an offering to her, have had our land base eroded and stolen by industrial societies whose way of life seems at times to be a frenzy of destruction and consumption, whose greed causes them to fight with each other over the spoils of a spoiled earth. The industrialized superpowers and their allies are devastating the land, depleting its resources and engaging in a suicidal arms race, running towards a nuclear war from whose holocaust only death will emerge the victor.[10]

The pressures on indigenous peoples to assimilate into the wider society are now acute. Governments are set upon integrating their national minorities, and entrepreneurs, transnational corporations, development agencies and other economic forces are eager to exploit the minerals and natural resources located on indigenous peoples' lands. As has been noted, there is no very clear definition of which groups constitute indigenous peoples, but all the peoples referred to in this book face a systematic destruction of their cultures. It is this as much as anything which binds them together and makes of their problems a world issue. In both a physical and a cultural sense, indigenous peoples inhabit the world's remaining frontier lands.

Notes

1. United Nations Economic and Social Council, Commission on Human Rights, *Preliminary report on the study of the problem of discrimination against indigenous populations*, chapter 11, paragraph 19 (E/CN.4/Sub.2/L.566).

2. Convention No. 107 concerning the Protection and Integration of Indigenous and other Tribal and Semi-Tribal Populations in Independent Countries, International Labour Organisation, article 1.

3. World Bank, *Tribal peoples and economic development: human ecological considerations* (Washington, May 1982) p.5.

4. Cited in UN Commission on Human Rights, *Study of the problem of discrimination against indigenous populations*, submitted by the Special Rapporteur José R. Martinez Cobo, chapter V, p.5 (E/CN.4/Sub.2/1982/Add.6). The above contains a full discussion of the definition question. See also Rodolfo Stavenhagen, 'The indigenous problematique', *International Foundation for Development Alternatives* (Nyon, Switzerland) dossier 50, November/December 1985, pp.4-14.

5. Statement submitted by the International League for Human Rights and the Indian Law Resource Center to the United Nations Sub-Commission on Prevention of Discrimination and Protection of Minorities, 30 August 1983, Doc. E/CN.4/Sub.2/1983/NGO/13.

6. The World Bank estimates the global indigenous population at about 200 million. Cf. *Tribal peoples and economic development*, p.iii. This book provides tables based on official and unofficial sources in each of the regional chapters.

7. 'Rights of indigenous peoples to the Earth', submission by World Council of Indigenous Peoples to Working Group on Indigenous Populations, Commission on Human Rights, Geneva, 30 July 1985.

8. 'The Australian Aboriginal position paper on indigenous ideology, philosophy and land', submitted to International NGO Conference on Indigenous Peoples and the Land, Geneva, 15-18 September 1981.

9. 'Report to the Commission on Indigenous Philosophy', presented by the International Indian Treaty Council to International NGO Conference, September 1981.

10. 'Genocide in North America: the violation of the land and human rights of native peoples', presented by the International Indian Treaty Council to International NGO Conference, September 1981.

3. Life at the Bottom

In almost all countries indigenous minorities face discrimination and suffer disadvantage. They are more likely to be unemployed than the majority population, they will probably receive less remuneration than comparable workers and will almost certainly be concentrated, when they do find work, in the more menial and poorly paid occupations. Indigenous peoples, as they are integrated into the national life of the society, will usually take their place on the lowest rung of the ladder.

In other areas they are equally disadvantaged. They will receive less opportunity for schooling and non-academic training; they will have less access to medical care and other social welfare services; where they have moved to urban areas they will invariably occupy those suburbs or ghettos with the most rudimentary facilities and housing.

In these basic human provisions indigenous peoples may sometimes share their fate with other minorities or groups. In Latin America many impoverished peasants who have no Indian origins live in similar conditions; in India the scheduled tribes, as the indigenous population is known, encounter a similar marginalization to the scheduled castes or untouchables: ostracized and condemned to the most servile positions in society. Nonetheless, indigenous peoples consistently experience discrimination at work, in housing, in education and other amenities comparative to most other groups in society.

Employment

Attitudes towards indigenous peoples and their place in the labour force have been fashioned by the colonial experience. Indeed various labour practices that persist to this day in parts of Asia and Latin America have their roots in the institutions and social relations that were established by the colonists.

In Latin America, Indians were from the outset harnessed by the Spanish colonizers and used for the extraction of gold, silver and other resources. The mining activities of the conquerors led to extensive loss of life as Indians proved unfit for the task of this coercive labour and succumbed to disease and sickness. In Peru, for example, the Indian population was reduced to about one-quarter by the time of independence, and in Haiti, which was the first centre of Spanish

17

activity, the native population declined from an estimated 200,000 to 29,000 between 1492 and 1514.[1] The intervention of humanitarian missionaries and the wholesale destruction of life resulted in the abolition of Indian slavery in the mid-16th Century.[2] More resilient African slaves were subsequently imported to supply the labour force of the mines and plantations.

The abolition of Indian slavery in Latin America did not lead to real emancipation for these descendants of the Aztec, Inca and other kingdoms. They became virtually the goods and chattels of great estates under the proprietorial management of Spanish landowners. While the Indians on these *haciendas* were not technically slaves, they were nevertheless obliged to provide their labour free as domestics, gardeners and seasonal workers. In the course of the 19th Century, Indian communal land, which had been given some measure of protection, began to be acquired by large estates which required new land for a growing export agriculture. As a result many of these people became entirely dependent for their livelihood on these *hacendados*. Some of them became sharecroppers, returning one-third or one half of the harvest to the landowner; others gave their labour free in return for a home and a small garden on the estate; others became indebted to the landowner and found themselves unable to repay their debts and thereby bound to the estates. The rest joined the mass of landless peasants who provided seasonal labour on the great plantations and who in the last century have drifted to the big cities in the search for work.

In the Philippines, as in Latin America, a similar system prevailed. Tribal peoples were subjected to ruthless tribute payments and forced to render corvée labour. Just as in Latin America, native communal land was appropriated and incorporated into large commercial estates with the growth in demand for such crops as sugar and tobacco. The process of land concentration and an accompanying dispossession has continued ever since. Increasing numbers of tribal peoples are being reduced to subsistence farmers or migrating to the cities.

In North America and Australia, where colonization took the form of settlement rather than conquest and wealth extraction, there was little immediate requirement for indigenous labour. Certainly there was no systematic attempt to enslave the aboriginal population. Nevertheless, North American native peoples and Australian Aborigines were progressively denied their traditional land as the process of colonial expansion proceeded. Although the invading settlers were often successful in using indigenous labour for domestic service or specialist work connected with cattle or sheep-rearing, no compulsory labour system was imposed on the indigenous population in the manner of the Spanish colonies.

It is as well to note, however, that the way of life of some native peoples was not always the untainted paradise portrayed by the 19th-Century romantic novelists such as Chateaubriand. A number of Indian peoples of South America kept slaves and demanded tribute in labour, and slavery was practised by several Indian tribes in the Pacific North-West. On the Indian sub-continent the British colonizers encountered widespread slavery, a prevalent caste system and various other institutions of servility such as the *sutti* – the self-immolation of widows on their husband's funeral pyres. Destructive as they may have been in other respects, the British abolished slavery and such practices as the *sutti* within half a century after they had unified control. Colonial policy on such institutions as debt bondage and the rigid caste system was more pragmatic and no attempt was made to dismantle the landowning structure. As for the tribal population, this had already been pushed into the less hospitable forest and hill regions by Aryan colonizers in the 1500s. Long before the arrival of the British, these tribal peoples lived as shifting cultivators cut off from and peripheral to the dominant Hindu society. Later, under the British, missionary activity and commercial exploitation of the forests led to encroachment on to tribal land.

The colonial experience fashioned in the minds of the invaders the notion that the indigenous population was living in primitive ignorance and lethargy and was suitable only for forced labour. Accordingly these subjected minorities have been killed and enslaved without compunction or any sense of guilt. The atrocities that took place at Putumayo in the Peruvian Amazon at the turn of this century, for example, are just some of many in a long history of brutality against Indian communities. More recently a German film-maker, Werner Herzog, paid a local landowner a commission of 1,000 soles for every Indian he recruited for his film about the rubber baron Fermin Fitzcarrald. Four hundred Campa Indians were eventually contracted, of whom four died from food poisoning, others drowned in a boat accident and three were injured in a plane crash.[3]

The Putumayo Atrocities

Numerous acts of violence against the forest dwelling Indians of the Peruvian Amazon came to light in 1915. It was learned that entrepreneurs and certain British companies were extracting rubber through the use of Indian slave labour. The situation was investigated by Sir Roger Casement who presented his findings to a Select Committee of the House of Commons. He noted that the conditions existed not through neglect but through the positive assistance of the Peruvian government and the complicity of the companies concerned. There was an outcry at the appalling suffering inflicted on the Indians. One witness described the conditions to the Criminal Court of Iquitos as follows: 'I, Benjamin Saldaña Rocca, residing at 38, Calle del Prospero, beg to inform your worship that sentiments of common humanity on behalf of the unfortunate Indians dwelling on the Putumayo and its tributaries have forced me to denounce to your worship the celebrated malefactors, Victor Macedo and Miguel Loaiza. I charge them with having committed the crimes of swindling, robbery, incendiarism, poisoning and assassination, which are further aggravated by the infliction of the cruellest tortures by fire, water, the lash and mutilation.

The worst act that these two criminals are known to have committed occurred in 1903. In that year there arrived at Le Chorrera more than 800 of of the Ocaima Indians to deliver the produce they had gathered, and after this had been weighed and taken over, Fidel Velarde, the sub-manager of the section to which they belonged, picked out 25 of them on the ground that they were idle at their work. Victor Mazedo and his fellow scoundrel Loaiza thereupon commanded that a sack soaked in kerosene should be placed like a shirt over each of the Indians. This was then lighted, and the unfortunate Indians were seen running and shrieking in all directions . . .

Another of the hyenas of the Putumayo is one named Miguel Florez, who murdered so many men and women, as well as old persons and children, that Macedo, frightened lest Florez should depopulate the whole section, ordered the brutal Florez not to kill so many Indians for his entertainment, but only kill them when they failed to bring in rubber. Florez chastened by these orders of his superior, reformed himself, and in two months only put to death some 40 Indians.'

Cited in N. Thomson, *The Putumayo Red Book*, N. Thomson & Co, n/d, pp.59-60.

Instances of such slavery and ill-treatment are still being recorded among isolated indigenous groups. A report by the International Work Group for Indigenous Affairs, a non-governmental organization working on behalf of indigenous peoples, stated recently:

Chiquitano slaves are still found in the lowlands of Eastern Bolivia, at the service of rubber extractors. Today in the rubber forest in the northern parts of the provinces of Velasco and Ñuflo de Chávez, some 350 Chiquitanos are bound to their exploiters. The Indian lives in constant debt to his boss. His rubber production is paid for in merchandise worth much less than the rubber. On a shotgun, the capitalist can, after expenses, make over 1,300 per cent profit. It is impossible for the Indian to ever get out of debt as the employer has no scruples about using deceit, the whip, or even murder. The only alternative is escape. This is, however, feasible only in a few cases, since while the Indian is collecting rubber in the forest (for an average of seven months a year), his children are working for the employers at the main camp. If, in spite of obstacles, a Chiquitano succeeds in gathering his family and escaping with them, a hunt is usually organized. There are several cases in which entire families have been shot down.[4]

An Anti-Slavery Society report to the United Nations in 1978 noted that Aché Indians in Paraguay were being kept as slaves, and some had been sold for five or six US dollars to landowners for the purpose of land clearing. The report stated that 'most of the workers were paid in kind and overseen by military units' on the larger estates. 'The workforce', it concluded, 'was included in the valuation of the property and as recently as 1946 there were receipts for the sale of Amerindians. Not surprisingly Amerindians are still considered by some landowners to be part and parcel of their estates.'[5]

In 1982 an Indonesian daily newspaper, *Kompas*, gave information about the slavery-like work conditions being endured by the Asmat people, a tribal group living in West Papua, now the Indonesian province of Irian Jaya. They were being forced to fell timber for export.

In Ats sub-district, the people are forced to fell and load the logs on the ship, then ordered to go back and fell more logs to complete the cargo without being paid anything except a few packs of tobacco or an axe head as a labour bond and a debt voucher to be deducted when they are eventually paid. It is no secret that this kind of treatment and swindling is the lot of the Asmat people. They are powerless to resist openly, to demand higher wages or other improvements because they are constantly terrorised by officials who say, 'so, you want to oppose the government, do you?'[6]

Cases of extreme exploitation of indigenous and tribal labour may be found throughout Asia and the Americas. Many Andean and Central American Indians are the victims of the *latifundio* system reduced to scratching a living from subsistence plots, accepting inadequate wages or payment in kind and joining the growing mass of migrant workers dependent upon the vagaries of the plantation economy. A *New York Times* correspondent wrote of the Guatemalan Indians recruited as seasonal labourers in 1978 as follows:

For five months every year the nine huts of the El Baul sugar plantation, 65 miles south of Guatemala City, are home for 1,500 Indian cane cutters, their wives and their children. They sleep shoulder to shoulder on concrete floors sharing discomfort and disease. They use a stream as a washbasin and toilet. In cotton areas many are affected by the big doses of pesticides used by the farmers. In all areas they fall ill with tropical diseases for which their highland upbringing has not prepared them.[7]

Such migrant labourers are recruited after threats of violence by labour contractors working in close collusion with the armed forces. Often they are caught up in a cycle of debt which begins when the contractor offers an advance two or three months before the harvest at a time of shortage.

Slave labour and the Asian Games

The Asian Games in New Delhi in 1982 was the most expensive sporting event ever staged in India. It involved the building of stadiums, hotels and roads. An army of 125,000 workers, mostly landless peasants and many from the scheduled tribes, were drafted in to get the project finished in time. 'Scores of men and women, some recruited under duress, are known to have died or been badly injured at the sites,' wrote a journalist for *The Observer* (5 December 1982). A report prepared in 1982 by the Peoples Union for Democratic Rights, a New Delhi-based human rights organization stated that 'all the workers were getting less than the minimum daily wages fixed and some were leading a life of bondage without any right to quit and join some other work'.
The Other Face of ASIAD 82, Peoples Union for Democratic Rights, New Delhi, 1982.

The worst cases of abuse against indigenous populations occur in relatively isolated regions not subject to national jurisdiction where entrepreneurs can impose their own law. But in many cases governments are complicitous: in Indonesia the timber companies operating in Irian Jaya are owned by generals in positions of power; in Bolivia, Paraguay and Guatemala those same landowners who abuse Indian labour form part of the local or national ruling class. It is often an excuse tendered by governments that they cannot control individual violations in areas of their country where access is limited by geographical factors. Invariably, however, the perpetrators of these acts of violence are associated with governments and the economic interests supporting them.

Happily such appalling conditions are not universal for indigenous peoples. Governments have made efforts to provide assistance to these communities living in their territory. Their success is limited. Information about unemployment rates, income and working conditions shows clearly that, even where governments have provided special help, discrimination still persists.

In the case of the Sami, for whom work conditions are probably among the best for such groups, there is a tendency for them to hold unskilled jobs and to receive lower pay than the rest of Scandinavian workers. In Finland few Sami are employers and only four per cent of their population are engaged in professional occupations.[8] On the whole the incomes of the Sami are lower than the majority population.[9] While it is true that some Sami also carry on fishing and farming activities, some 90 per cent are involved in similar occupations to the majority of Scandinavians.

Indigenous peoples in the capitalist countries are the least advantaged group in society. In the United States of America the average per capita income for Indians is less than that for blacks, and half that of the white population. On the reservations average incomes are lower still because of unemployment. In 1970 unemployment reached 40 per cent of the workforce on many reservations, and some 18 per cent of those in work had only temporary seasonal jobs.[10]

In Australia the Aboriginal unemployment rate is estimated at five or six times the rate of the country as a whole; in Canada, unemployment rates on reserves reach nearly 50 per cent and on certain of these less than five per cent of the workforce had jobs; in New Zealand one in seven Maoris is unemployed against one in 30 whites.[11] In Japan the indigenous Ainu household receives a lower average income than the average Japanese family.[12]

Income disparities between the indigenous population and the rest of society prevail throughout Asia. In India the Commissioner for Scheduled Castes and Scheduled Tribes in a recent report noted that many tribal peoples were subject to debt bondage and that national and state governments were reluctant to enforce its abolition.[13] In the Philippines where many tribal communities have been forced off their land to make way for foreign-owned plantations, they have been obliged to accept pitiful wages. A Filipino worker for Castle and Cooke, a transnational company having a major share in the world's banana production, receives one-thirtieth of the salary of his counterpart in Hawaii.[14]

Although various governments have taken measures to protect their indigenous populations and increase their employment opportunities, discrimination persists. In certain cases the cause of the discrimination is the perception by employers that indigenous people are lazy and incompetent. The word *indio* in Latin America is often used pejoratively to denote good-for-nothing; in India the *adivasis* are considered by the caste Hindus as inferior, irreligious and uncivilized and referred to insultingly as *junglis* (forest-dwellers).[15] In Australia Aborigines are still considered by certain sectors of society as drunks and misfits. The Premier of Queensland, Bjelke-Petersen, commented on the Aboriginals in the state: 'If they don't want to live in our society they should go somewhere else. Go to the Northern Territory or New South Wales where the government seems to be foolishly pandering to them.'[16] Racist attitudes of this kind represent a major obstacle to indigenous peoples receiving fair treatment when they reach the job market and, in extreme cases, justify cruel and wanton exploitation.

Health

Indigenous peoples, like the rural populations of most countries in the developing world, have significantly less access to basic health care and social welfare provisions. These services tend to be concentrated in urban areas and one cause of the migration to the cities is the availability of medical care and other welfare benefits.[17] In many poorer countries health services are inadequate for the whole population. In Bangladesh, for example, it is estimated that in rural areas medical care extends to only 25 per cent of its predominantly rural population. Despite the already low levels of health care in these countries, that available to indigenous peoples is substantially smaller. This is reflected in higher infant mortality rates and lower life expectancy.

In Guatemala, Indians have a life expectancy about eleven years shorter than the *ladino* or non-indigenous population. Similar levels apply in Bolivia and Peru.[18] In Paraguay, infant mortality among some Indian communities reaches 50 per cent, while for the rest of the population it is under 10 per cent.[19] In the capitalist countries disparities between indigenous and non-indigenous sectors in health care are equally striking. In the United States of America malnutrition is more prevalent among Indians than among any other group and native people are eight times more likely to contract tuberculosis, for example, and 42 times more likely to suffer from dysentery than other Americans.[20] In Canada, infant mortality was two times higher among Indians than other Canadians. In Queensland, Australia, a medical report stated that in 1983 the death rate from infectious diseases was nine times higher on the reserves than in the rest of the state.[21]

On the whole governments have tended to make fewer provisions available for their more isolated indigenous populations. Indeed, in certain cases, governments maintain that the remoteness of their tribal communities rather than neglect is the cause of inadequate health care. In addition, indigenous peoples themselves are reluctant to make use of the services provided. Aborigines in Australia are often unhappy about being sent to hospital and thereby separated from the clan. Certain traditional cures are condemned by

Western-trained doctors. On matters of health practice there is often incompatibility between the two cultures.

But poor health among indigenous peoples is not due solely to inadequate medical care. A combination of factors such as unhealthy conditions of employment, poor housing and poverty lead to apathy and low nutritional intake. Nearly 97 per cent of Mexico's indigenous population is believed to possess no basic sanitary services such as drinking water and sewerage. Where pharmacists exist in many poor countries, strong and even dangerous drugs are sold without proper explanation, making this form of medical care hazardous. In the United States the low incomes of the Indian peoples mean they cannot afford medical insurance and must depend upon public health care which is deemed substandard.[22] Furthermore, only officially recognized Indians are entitled to comprehensive health benefits while the majority of non-federally recognized Indians are dependent on inadequate state services.

One conclusion that is easily drawn from the foregoing is that traditional health practices among indigenous peoples are not as effective as modern medical care. Measured by infant mortality or life expectancy rates this would certainly be true. But this is only one side of the story. Pre-contact communities may not enjoy health conditions comparable to modern Western societies, but conditions worsen considerably on contact. Epidemiological studies of newly contacted indigenous communities show that minor viral infections cause high death rates. Among the Yanomami of Venezuela, for example, epidemics of measles or whooping cough have been responsible for mortalities of up to 30 per cent in some communities and present diseases such as tuberculosis and malaria threaten them with extinction.[23] In Brazil in this century alone at least 87 Indian groups have become extinct as a consequence of contact with outsiders.[24]

In the past the decimation of indigenous populations has occurred as a direct consequence of colonial invasion. The invaders passed on to the conquered peoples diseases that were hitherto unknown; they also forced them off their land, denied them the products of that land and disrupted their economies. More than acts of war, such factors as disease and dislocation have caused the deaths of these peoples. Where relatively unassimilated tribal groups make contact with outsiders similar results take place. When the Xingu Indians of Brazil were forcibly relocated 25 per cent died from disease and homesickness. Most indigenous communities have developed no immunity to a number of diseases – parasitic, respiratory and deficiency based – that are relatively common in the world at large.

Furthermore, the nutritional habits of some of these communities before contact were better balanced than those that developed after contact. The introduction of processed foods into indigenous communities can have a disastrous effect on diets. It has been noticed, for example, that the Inuits of Canada have been badly affected by the change-over of eating habits, away from fresh meat and fish to unnutritious industrially produced foods. In Costa Rica the maize beer *chicha*, the traditional festive beverage of the Indian population, is being replaced by industrially produced spirits. *Chicha* has a high calorific value and is rich in vitamins, whereas the spirits replacing it have none of these qualities.[25] In Bolivia with the production of coca leaves severely restricted and controlled by the government in efforts to reduce cocaine production, their availability to the Indian people has become limited. The lethal, high-proof cane rum has taken their place. While coca leaves enable many Andean Indians to survive the rigours of hard work and small diets, rum in such circumstances leads to alcoholism and violence.

Poor health among indigenous communities is due to many factors beyond the scope of doctors or health administrators: poverty, unemployment, bad housing and so on. Indeed, poor health is really an indicator of the social position of these communities. Yet even if these conditions could be improved and health care made more available, there would remain a cause of concern. There remains a presumption that Western medicine is the most effective of all the medical practices. It is a presumption founded in the idea that all that is Western – its culture, its technology, its form of development, its laws – is best. It is worth remembering that some of modern medicine's most important discoveries – quinine, penicillin, opiates, anaesthetics – were derived from substances that had been used by indigenous communities centuries beforehand.

Education

The level of formal education of indigenous peoples is low. Compared to the majority, proportionately fewer indigenous peoples attend university, complete compulsory education or possess basic reading and writing skills. In the capitalist and underdeveloped countries alike this has been used by employers to justify paying low wages and discriminating against applicants for jobs and by governments to justify excluding indigenous minorities from public service. If it is noteworthy that these peoples are concentrated in those occupations paying the lowest wages and offering the least opportunities, then the low level of educational attainment must be recognized as a major obstacle to any improvement in conditions.

In the United States the average educational level of all Indians under federal supervision is five school years. Of the 40,000 Navajo Indians, one-third are estimated to be functionally illiterate in English. The drop-out rate of Indian children is twice the national average.[26] In Canada a similar drop-out rate exists among Indians and as few as three per cent actually finish secondary school.[27] In Australia the federal government has stated that 'until recently few Aboriginals have progressed through secondary school or entered tertiary education. Only a handful have qualified for open scholarships or bursaries.'[28]

In Latin America where levels of basic education are in any case lower than in the developed countries, illiteracy among Indians is high. In Guatemala, where three-quarters of the population is Indian, a UNESCO spokesman noted in 1978 that per capita investment in education was the lowest in the world; illiteracy among the rural Indian population is estimated at 82 per cent.[29] Generally speaking, among Andean Indians such high illiteracy rates are common. Few children have the opportunity of attending more than the first year or two of primary school and that often intermittently. The presence of Indians at university is rare. For the more isolated Indian communities schooling is almost entirely absent. In the Brazilian Amazon or the Paraguayan Chaco there are virtually no government-run educational projects.[30]

In Asia similar conditions prevail. In Indonesia primary schooling in isolated, tribal areas is sparse.[31] In India the literacy rate of scheduled tribes is 11 per cent, compared with 30 per cent for the total population.[32] In the Philippines, tribal regions like the Cordillera are provided with fewer teachers per head of population than elsewhere. In Malaysia, the tribal peoples (*orang asli*) receive little formal schooling.[33]

Low educational attainment is due in part to environmental conditions. For isolated indigenous groups, schools of any kind are often inaccessible. Many nomadic peoples could not in any case be served by the normal educational system and the static schoolroom is inappropriate to their way of life. Alternatives such as residential schools are rarely acceptable to indigenous peoples.

Basic education in most indigenous contexts is hampered by an absence of any *lingua franca*. In Brazil some 120 different languages are spoken by the Amazonian Indian peoples; in Guatemala there are 23 different languages spoken by the Indians; in India there are more than 400 tribal communities with distinctive languages; in the Philippines there are eight national minorities of half a million or more people speaking different languages. Any compulsory universal education in such countries must gain acceptance of the dominant language – Spanish, Portuguese, English or Pilipino. In the meantime governments have been reluctant to make any concessions about the language problem. Teachers are non-indigenous, often have no knowledge of the indigenous language and are obliged by law to teach in the dominant language. Thus, in Bangladesh the medium of instruction is Bengali although some half a million tribal people speak other languages; in Malaysia the tribal people (*orang asli*) are taught in Malay; in Chile the Mapuche Indians are taught in Spanish; in Paraguay the Guaraní-speaking Indians are offered rote-learning of entire Spanish sentences which they do not understand.[34] There are few countries in the world which accept an Indian language as an official medium of education and communication.[35]

Such formal education where it is available is often antagonistic to the traditions of indigenous peoples. It does not impart indigenous culture and few efforts are made to adapt it to the needs of indigenous communities. More often than not teachers come into the indigenous community with preconceptions; they view their own culture as superior. Such attitudes are communicated to the children who become demoralized and alienated from their own culture. In such situations children can become virtual outcasts: not fully acceptable to the dominant society and no longer fully able to play a part in their now derogated Indian culture.

In one important respect indigenous cultures differ from those dominant cultures alongside them. Indigenous cultures have an oral tradition and the

European cultures with their various oral roots – Greek rhetoric or Viking sagas for example – have long since given way to a primarily written culture. There is an assumption by dominant societies that indigenous people are culturally inferior because they do not give the written form the same importance as the spoken word. They may learn to read and write but not necessarily give pre-eminence to writing.

> . . . I detest writing. The process itself epitomizes the European concept of 'legitimate' thinking; what is written has an importance that is denied the spoken. My culture, the Lakota culture, has an oral tradition and so I ordinarily reject writing. It is one of the white world's ways of destroying the cultures of the non-white European peoples, the imposing of an abstraction over the spoken relationship of a people.[36]

More often than not education is seen as a means of gaining control of indigenous peoples and subverting their culture. Missionaries, teachers and governments have recognized that the way to 'civilize' their indigenous communities was to take a hold of the children before their parents could teach them the tribal way of life. By so doing they hoped to 'breed out' and finally eliminate indigenous culture. Throughout the colonizing process Spanish missionaries or English zealots have been so convinced of their own rectitude and the worthlessness of indigenous ways of life, that almost any method was permitted. History is strewn with the victims of these single-minded, evangelizing educationists.

Nor is the imposition of such damaging methods now absent from indigenous communities. The Summer Institute of Linguistics is the world's largest Protestant mission society and probably the largest single institution to concern itself with the plight of indigenous peoples.[37] Its primary objective is to bring the 'Word' to the bibleless before it is too late. Like similar organizations, the New Tribes Mission, for example, it is seeking instant conversions of Amerindians to Christianity and their adaptation to the Western, or perhaps more accurately, the American way of life. One report of the activities of the Summer Institute of Linguistics concluded:

> The pressures brought to bear on Indian societies have made political and humanitarian assistance for the indigenous groups urgently necessary. This has been the opening of organizations like SIL. The missionaries have exploited the situation to advance their own goals rather than improve the position of the Indians. Instead of calling attention to those policies which cause the resource crisis among the Indians, instead of trying to limit the penetration of exploitative trade and wage labour relations, SIL's Americanized Protestant Evangelicalism has individualized the solution and reduced the question to a matter of God vs Satan. In trying to solve the Indian problem SIL has become the Indian's problem.[38]

A boarding school for young Indians

The boarding school was opened for the education of the Yanomami and Yekuana Indians. After the school was constructed, it was necessary to fill it. So, Indians were enlisted, with scant regard for methods. The missionaries busied themselves, clothing the children and adolescents, putting flaps into their outfits; they were enticed into boats with sweets and dry cakes sprinkled with pepsi cola and promises of an easy future. That wasn't all. They went into neighbouring communities and came back with batches of naked children. The parents were not warned (what language could they use?). They tied up at the bank, and without entering the houses called the youngsters to come into the boats. The children thrilled at travelling in a motor boat didn't need to be asked twice. Off they went to an unknown destination. At the end of the long journey lay the boarding school. And here disillusion set in. Children cried for their parents, little brother or sister. Only busy adults, speaking an incomprehensible tongue, came to console them . . .

The young boarders are deprived of the natural activities to which they are accustomed. They are given foodstuffs which make them swell (maize flour, manioc, white bread, white rice and dough); although they have a false appearance of good health, in reality it is only tangible manifestation of their disturbance.

From the moment of their arrival the children are subjected to an intensive effort at deculturising. Everything Indian is devalued, scorned, set aside. The little Yanomami learn for the first time the word *indio*; at the same time, everyone points out that it has depreciatory connotations. Their hair is cropped – that beautiful shoulder length hair whose cut harmonises with the features of their faces. Even then, the sacrilege is not carried out by expert hands, but those of a clumsy, disdainful master. Their personal names are taken from them and replaced by ones they cannot correctly pronounce. Large stretches of their cultural universe are removed at a stroke: their names as a personal identity, their houses as a representation of the world, the kitchen as an expression of the gustatory values, as well as the meeting point between man and the environment, the family and the parents to which one's being is attached. A new and disturbing world surrounds the little Indian; a world marked by disturbing lacks and derisory signs. Surrounding the boarders are adults who are racist and hostile, or at best, paternalist.

Jacques Lizot, *The Yanomami in the face of ethnocide*, IWGIA, document 22, 1976.

Discrimination

In all countries there is discrimination in fact even when full equality may have been formally proclaimed in law. Both in their ratification of international conventions and their national constitutions, governments publicly declare their recognition of the right to equal protection under the law. In some cases, governments have even gone so far as to incorporate the concept of positive discrimination. Thus, for example, India, which has assumed responsibility for the protection and integration of the scheduled tribes has elaborated a series of measures to give them access to jobs, education and so on. Certain countries such as New Zealand, Canada and Australia have special ombudsmen to monitor acts of discrimination against their indigenous peoples. The United States has an Office of Indian Rights to enforce civil rights law for the benefit of Indians. Even in Guatemala, where Amnesty International and other human rights organizations have condemned the massive killing of Indians, articles 376 and 377 of the Penal Code state: 'Any person who commits any of the following acts with intent to destroy wholly or in part a national, ethnic or religious group, shall be guilty of genocide: (1) causing the death of members of the group; (2) causing injuries which seriously affect the physical or mental integrity of members of the group . . .'[39] It is a sad irony that in cases where the law is most explicit on human rights, the most flagrant violations occur.

The living conditions of most indigenous peoples stand in sharp contrast to the ideal proclaimed by the law. In addition, however, there is the notion, in most national legislation, that indigenous peoples are incapable of running their own affairs. This perception emerges most clearly in Brazil, where Indians live legally under a system of guardianship. The Civil Code of Brazil defines the Indian as incapable and under the guardianship of the Union whose delegated authority is the National Indian Foundation (FUNAI).[40] The Indian is defined as a ward who must be led 'progressively and harmoniously towards integration with the wider society'. Emancipation is gained by the petitioner showing to a court that he or she speaks Portuguese, can make a useful contribution to society and understands the customs of the national community. To date no Amerindians have been emancipated. This form of tutelage allowed the government of Brazil in 1980 to deny a passport to Mario Juruna, a Xavante leader, thereby preventing him from attending a meeting of the Russell Tribunal on the Rights of Indians of the Americas. Juruna like all Brazilian Indians is a minor for all legal purposes.

In nearly all countries which have an indigenous population, governments have created special agencies for their welfare. More often than not, however, these bodies serve as mechanisms of control over indigenous minorities and thereby compound the discrimination taking place elsewhere. In the Philippines, the Presidential Assistant on National Minorities (PANAMIN) – disbanded in 1985 – was the government agency charged with the welfare of minorities. Since its inception PANAMIN had been instrumental in the relocation of tribal peoples on reservation land; it was their policy to remove all the national minorities from their traditional land and settle them on reservations. Tribal peoples never had a representative in the leadership of PANAMIN and had no say in the formation of its policies. Instead, the head of PANAMIN, Manuel Elizalde Junior, and his close advisers were drawn from the ranks of businessmen involved in the exploitation of natural resources on tribal land.[41]

It is no exaggeration to say that governments have taken the view that they are part of a civilizing mission. They consider their role to be modernizing the indigenous economy and integrating the peoples into the mainstream of national life. Some lip-service will be paid to the idea of protecting the traditions of indigenous peoples but agencies, such as FUNAI in Brazil or PANAMIN in the Philippines, through their activities and programmes, do discriminate against the Indian or tribal way of life. It may be that this takes the form of relocating populations on new settlements or imposing a series of development projects on an unwilling people. However, under the guise of legality and ostensibly in the interests of indigenous peoples, governments have in certain cases discriminated against them.

Marginalization

Assimilation or partial assimilation of indigenous peoples has led to a concomitant despair at the loss of traditional social cohesion. This, coupled with an understandable disillusion with the opportunities offered by the wider, technologically advanced economy, has created serious problems among indigenous communities in urban areas or in reservations.

Violent and accidental deaths among indigenous peoples are often substantially higher than in the rest of society; crime and suicide rates are also high comparatively. Other problems such as alcoholism and prostitution tend to proliferate also. In Thailand, hill tribe girls are bought from their parents for 3,000 to 5,000 baht (about £100) by agents and sold to brothels in Bangkok and other tourist centres.[42] On Indian reserves in the United States as much as 95 per cent of the housing has been described as 'dilapidated, makeshift, unsanitary and crowded'.[43] Amazon cities like Manaus and Santarem are surrounded by the hovels of dejected remnants of tribal communities. It is sad evidence of how Indians are made marginal to the wider society once they accept assimilation.

A clear example of this marginalizing process exists in Australia where the forced removal of Aboriginal people from their traditional land and their settlement on reserves have served to undermine their way of life. The powerlessness to resist removal weakened the traditional authority of clan elders; unemployment and poverty have led to demoralization evinced by the excessive drinking, the incidence of prostitution and high rates of petty crime on reserves. Where Aboriginal communities have formed around mining towns or cattle stations, Aboriginal women have often been particularly vulnerable to the transient, white male population. The white employers have money and a high social status:

> The consequences of these relationships are invariable: they cause jealousy, tension and often violence between Aboriginal and white man; they disrupt the complex and important kinship patterns in Aboriginal society and they produce children who are neither a part of the traditional scheme, nor are they wanted or accepted as part of white society, yet it is the Aboriginal community which takes them and works them in and looks after them. Most alarmingly these encounters have introduced venereal diseases; only ten years ago, syphilis was virtually unknown in this region; it is now almost plague proportions and getting worse.[44]

More often than not the mere interaction of two cultures, particularly the interaction of a dominant and a non-dominant culture, leads to the imposition of the one and the destruction or emasculation of the other. What the dominant culture does is undermine the overt bounds of unity. The indigenous language disappears with the introduction of bilingual and then unilingual education; traditional dress vanishes as the raw materials become less available and as Western norms are imposed in schools and at the work-place; the oral tradition is spurned in favour of the written word; traditional land is taken away in the name of national development and the peoples must make their homes in unfamiliar environments of city or reservation; the means of livelihood based on the land are denied to indigenous communities, obliging men and women to enter an inimical job market. In the end these indigenous peoples find themselves caught between two cultures. Finally the indigenous culture disappears.

In such instances the marginalization of indigenous culture becomes cultural genocide or ethnocide. Ethnocide means that an ethnic group, collectively or individually, is denied its right to enjoy, develop and disseminate its own culture and language.[45] Where indigenous peoples do not face physical destruction, they may nevertheless face disintegration as a distinct ethnic group through the destruction of their specific cultural characteristics.

If there is one overwhelming and universal menace to indigenous peoples, it is that in time their culture will be eroded and that the world will be reduced to a wasteland of conformity and sameness. The complexities and differences will be eradicated as outdated obstacles to some narrow vision of progress and development. The prevailing condition of life of many indigenous peoples is a clear testimony to the fact that assimilation into industrial society has brought few benefits and many hardships. Indigenous peoples are situated well and truly at the bottom of the pile and there is little chance in the immediate future of their improving their position. What the future holds for many of these communities is the eventual loss of their cultural identity and their absorption into society as part of the growing mass of landless and under-employed poor.

Notes

1. Committee on Cooperation in Latin America, *Indians of the high Andes* (New York, 1946) p.8.

2. In Spanish America Bartolomé de las Casas and in Brazil the Jesuit António de Vieira are the best-known.

3. *Boletin Copal*, 11 May 1981, cited in *Survival International Review*, vol.6, nos. 3 and 4, p.107.

4. Jurgen Riester, *Indians of Eastern Bolivia: aspects of their present situation* (IWGIA document, Copenhagen, 1975) p.22.

5. Anti-Slavery Society, 'Paraguay: enslavement of Indians and the servile condition of peasants', Report to the United Nations Commission on Human Rights, 1978.

6. *Kompas* (Jakarta), 4, 6 and 7 October 1982.

7. *New York Times*, 27 March 1978; see also Anti-Slavery Society, 'Incidence of slavery and abuses against rural workers in Guatemala, 1976-1978', Report to the United Nations Commission on Human Rights, 1978.

8. Mervyn Jones, *The Sami of Lapland*, Minority Rights Group Report 55, 1982, p.9.

9. Information from the Nordic Sami Council.

10. James Wilson, *The original Americans: US Indians*, Minority Rights Group Report 31, 1976, p.5.

11. *New Internationalist*, July 1985, p.5.

12. George de Vos and William Wetherall, *Japan's minorities*, Minority Rights Group Report 3, 1983 edition, p.13.

13. *Report of the Commissioner for Scheduled Castes and Scheduled Tribes, 1979-81, Part I*, Twenty-seventh Report, New Delhi, 1981, p.26.

14. Anti-Slavery Society, *The Philippines: authoritarian government, multinationals and ancestral lands*, Indigenous Peoples and Development Series, 1983, p.59.

15. Dilip Hiro, 'The adivasis: the scheduled tribes of India', in Georgina Ashworth (ed.), *World Minorities*, vol.1, 1977, p.2.

16. *Observer*, (London) 5 September 1982.

17. In Guatemala, for example, over 80 per cent of doctors practise in the capital.

18. United Nations Economic and Social Council, Commission on Human Rights, *Study of the Problem of Discrimination against Indigenous Populations*, report submitted by the special rapporteur José Martinez Cobo, chapter XI, pp.14-15 (E/CN.4/Sub.2/1983/21/Add.5). Henceforward referred to as the Cobo Report.

19. Ibid., p.16. Information supplied by the Anti-Slavery Society.

20. Wilson, p.6.

21. *The Times*, (London) 19 April 1983.

22. Cobo Report, chapter XI, p.12.

23. Cf. Marcus Colchester (ed.), *The health and survival of the Venezuelan Yanoama*, ARC/SI/IWGIA document 53, 1985, pp.9 and 30.

24. Darcy Ribeiro, *Os Indios e a civilização* (Editora Civilização Brasileira, Rio de Janeiro, 1970) p.237.

25. Cobo Report, chapter XI, p.36.

26. Cobo Report, chapter XIII, p.21; see also Wilson, p.6.

27. James Wilson, *Canada's Indians*, Minority Rights Group Report 21, new edition 1977, p.24.

28. Cobo Report, chapter XIII, p.27.

29. El Instituto de Estudios Politicos para America Latina y Africa, *Guatemala: un futuro proximo* (Madrid, 1980), p.160.

30. Cobo Report, chapter XIII, p.15.

31. Ibid., p.15.

32. Cf. *Report of the Commissioner for Scheduled Castes and Scheduled Tribes, 1979-81, Part 1*, pp.162-207.

33. Cobo Report, chapter XIII, p.31 notes that improvements are under way.

34. Ibid., p.43.

35. In Peru Quechua is an official language with Spanish.

36. Russell Means, 'Indictment on industrial society', statement to the International NGO Conference on Indigenous Peoples and the Land, Geneva, 15-18 September 1981.

37. Soren Hvalkof and Peter Aaby (eds.), *Is God an American?* IWGIA/SI document, 1981, p.14.

38. Ibid., p.185.

39. Cf. Cobo Report, chapter VIII, p.24; see also Amnesty International, *Guatemala: a government program of political murder*, 1981.

40. Cultural Survival, *Brazilian Indians and the law*, Occasional paper 5, October 1981.

41. Anti-Slavery Society, *The Philippines*, chapter 6.

42. Cf. *Human Rights in Thailand Report* (Bangkok), vol.8, no.3, July–December 1984, pp.32-8.

43. Cobo Report, chapter XII, p.29.

44. *Survival International Review*, Summer 1978, p.14.

45. Cobo Report, chapter XV, p.16.

4. The Colonial Experience

For a long time the West perceived the history of the world it colonized as commencing from the moment of European contact. The colonial mind could comprehend only that the lands they were civilizing were being rescued from disorder, backwardness and obscurity. Everywhere throughout the Americas, the Spanish, Portuguese, Dutch, French and English invaders encountered only one people: Indians.

Whether it was in Africa, the British Raj, the Dutch East Indies or the Americas, the colonized peoples were there to serve a great European design. The lands in which these native peoples lived were seen as unproductive and unmastered and the Europeans saw themselves as a civilizing force. In order to fulfil this grand design, Africans were shipped in their thousands to work on the plantations of the Americas as slaves, and as slavery became increasingly repugnant to humanitarians and unprofitable to plantation owners, it was replaced by indentured labour from Asia. From time to time, colonizers wrote with admiration of the wonders of Hindu craftsmanship or the military skills of the Ashanti or Zulus, but for the most part there was little recognition of the great civilizations and complex societies which were being destroyed in the race for wealth, resources, new markets and political power. For the colonizing European powers, the peoples being subjugated could only benefit from contact with a technologically advanced and culturally superior race.

The history of colonialism varied enormously from region to region and from continent to continent. Throughout the Americas and Australasia the colonizing powers pursued policies of settlement which reduced the indigenous population dramatically so that now in most countries it is a minority. In Africa white settlement never reached such a scale and only South Africa and Namibia have yet to accept the process of decolonization. In Asia there was never any serious attempt at large-scale settlement and decolonization has left, as in Africa, a heritage of frontiers created to satisfy European requirements rather than reflect the natural boundaries between peoples.

For these various historical reasons, this book has identified as indigenous all the descendants of the original inhabitants of the Americas and Australasia, but only those peoples in Africa and Asia whose way of life is tribal and contains many points of comparability with the peoples of the Americas. If there are certain peoples from Asia and Africa who are included in this category, it is because they are today experiencing colonization of their homelands similar to that experienced by the Indians of the Americas or the Aborigines of Australia. Many of the attitudes and policies that prevailed in the Americas during the colonial period are, with only slight modification, a part of their contemporary world.

Pre-colonial peoples

The conquest by Cortes of modern-day Mexico was but a phase in the long history of man in Middle America. Previous great civilizations had flourished in the valley of Mexico and in the area now occupied by Guatemala, Belize, Honduras and the Yucatan peninsula. Archaeological evidence attests to the complexity of the social organization and the cultural achievements of early civilizations, such as the Olmec, Zapotec and Maya. These theocratic civilizations collapsed in the wake of new militarist powers like the Toltec, the Mexica and the Aztecs which imposed new religions, social and economic practices and political structures. By the time the Spanish landed on the mainland in 1519, the peoples of Middle America had enjoyed over 2,000 years of settled agriculture and organized political life and their land, with its cities, imposing temples and forts, was a testimony to their accomplishments.[1]

In Peru the Spanish *conquistadores* led by Francisco Pizarro encountered an equally extensive and complex society. The Inca empire of the high Andes was, according to most accounts, more benevolent than that of the Aztecs of the valley of Mexico, both in its conquests of neighbouring territory and in its social organization. Numerous Spanish chroniclers wrote enthusiastically about the cultural achievements of the Incas. Indeed one *conquistador* wrote to the King of Spain confessing profound guilt at destroying Inca society:

> His Catholic Majesty should understand that the said Incas had these kingdoms governed in such a manner that in all of them there was not a single thief, nor man of vice, nor idle man, nor any adulterer or bad woman; nor were people of loose morals permitted among them. Men had honourable and useful occupations; uncultivated lands, mines, pastures, hunting grounds, woods, and all kinds of employment were so managed and distributed that each person knew and held his own estate, and no one else took possession of it or deprived him of it; nor was there any litigation over it.[2]

The debate over the nature of Inca society, which has been described as socialistic by some and tyrannical by others, lies outside the scope of this chapter. However, important for our purposes is the fact that in both the valley of Mexico and the Andean highlands, the Spanish invaders encountered highly developed and successful civilizations which themselves had emerged out of a long human history on the continent. The invasion of the Spanish *conquistadores* and the subsequent settlement interrupted rather than began American history.

Yet not all peoples in the Americas or elsewhere belonged to militaristic empires. In North America, for example, the population at the time of conquest was probably around 12 million, in marked contrast, therefore, to the 25 million or so concentrated in Middle America. The autonomous Indian nations and societies, of which there were around 600 at the time of conquest, varied enormously in size and type. The Creek and Cherokee were farmers, the Apache were nomadic hunters, the Hopi in the south, influenced by the neighbouring Aztecs, lived in villages of adobe and practised a highly ritualistic religion. Furthermore, although there were rivalries and fighting among the Indian nations, no one nation had achieved pre-eminence. While it would be an exaggeration to say that the peoples of North America lived in harmony prior to colonization, all evidence suggests that they had adapted successfully to their environment. There existed in the Americas numerous strains of crops that were unheard of in Europe and vast herds of animals to support the hunting way of life of nations like the Oglala Sioux. All Indian peoples shared a common understanding of the natural world which was alien to the colonizing Europeans; for the Indian, man could only ever be the guardian of the land and never its owner.

In Australia prior to 1788, the Aboriginal people spoke over 500 different languages and lived in dispersed clans over the whole island. Although their livelihood depended upon hunting, gathering and fishing rather than farming, Aboriginals had developed successful techniques for thriving in their environment. They were able to enjoy full and complex spiritual lives based on the Dreamtime. The Dreamtime for Aboriginal people is the era when their ancestors travelled the country, engaged in adventures and created the natural features of the land and the code of life. The Dreaming has been passed down from generation to generation through myths, songs, rock and body paintings and dance; sites of former ancestral exploits are deemed sacred.

Pre-colonial life for Aborigines appears, therefore, to have been relatively harmonious; there are no legends of long internecine wars nor virulent epidemics before the arrival of the European settlers.

Effects of invasion

When Hernan Cortes and the 500 or so *conquistadores* who followed him embarked on their invasion, they faced only sporadic opposition and not concerted resistance. The Aztec empire had imposed its own tyranny on the people of the surrounding area, and with the arrival of the Spanish many rebelled. Cortes exploited the prevailing dissension and was able rapidly to achieve his objectives. Within two years of the invasion, the Aztec king was dead, the capital city captured and rebuilt and the subjugation of some 25 million Indian peoples begun.[3]

During the 1530s Pizarro began his conquest of the Incas with fewer men. But just as in Mexico, serious internal political problems beset the empire. The Inca lord, Huayna-Capac, and his heir had died prematurely and two claimants to the throne of a kingdom that extended along most of the length of the Andes had emerged. Pizarro cunningly exploited the civil war that ensued and with ruthlessness and multiple deceptions had succeeded by the end of the decade in capturing the capital of the Inca empire, Cuzco, and subduing a population of some seven million.[4]

In both Peru and Mexico, the Spanish invaders had come at opportune moments. Contemporary historians recognized that the survival of the small military forces that conquered these two great empires was nothing short of miraculous. On the other hand, however, the invading forces elsewhere were often welcomed warmly by the indigenous population. Columbus had remarked on the friendliness of the Caribs who lived on the island of Hispaniola, although it did not stop the eventual genocide of the entire native population. The Pilgrim Fathers who landed in present-day Massachusetts in 1620 and suffered in the first years, were greatly helped by the local Indians who supplied food and advised them on agriculture. In Tasmania, the invaders found the local Aboriginal community kindly and helpful: '. . . we could not walk on the dry grass without slipping every moment but these good savages to prevent our falling, took hold of us by the arm and then supported us.'[5] But wherever the invader reached he was ready to deceive and betray the native population whether it was friendly or hostile. In North America over 300 treaties were signed by the colonizers in the course of the migration westwards, many signed by the President of the United States, and all of them were broken.[6]

The effect of the invasion by Europeans on all these indigenous peoples was universally destructive. The Brazilian anthropologist Darcy Ribeiro estimates that the population of Latin America in 1492 was between 70 and 88 million and had been reduced to 3.5 million by the mid-17th Century.[7] Such figures are contentious and difficult to confirm, but contemporary accounts attest to the dramatic depopulation caused by the invasion. One commentator remarked of Peru:

> We cannot conceal the great paradox that a barbarian, Huayna-Capac, kept such excellent order that the entire country was calm and all were nourished, whereas today we see only infinite deserted villages on all the roads of the kingdom.[8]

The Aztec people and their subjects were reduced in little over a century from 15 million to two million. In North America Indians were able to retreat more successfully before the European invaders and the genocide was less dramatic. Nevertheless the native population of California in the thirty years between 1850 and 1880 fell from 120,000 to 20,000.[9] In Australia an Aboriginal population of 300,000 in 1788 on the eve of the invasion was reduced a century later to about 60,000. When the Spanish arrived in the Marianas Islands of the Pacific between 1695 and 1698 they forcibly concentrated all the Chamorro people living in the outlying islands on to Guam. As a result a population estimated at between 70,000 and 100,000 was reduced by 1756 to a mere 1,600.

Most destructive to these indigenous nations and communities was disease. The numerous ailments which had decimated Europe during the Middle Ages were brought over by the Spanish. In South America there were major outbreaks of epidemics of smallpox, typhus, measles and other diseases. The native population had no immunity to even less virulent sicknesses such as influenza and died in their millions. In North America and Australia disease also struck down Indians and Aboriginal people and was the single most destructive factor.

Notwithstanding the disastrous effects of imported diseases, indigenous societies faced continuous physical destruction from the colonists. The need to subjugate a numerically stronger people caused the settlers in the early years to institute reigns of terror. The Spanish practised kidnappings and wholesale massacres to instil fear. In North America extermination of entire Indian villages often occurred, of which the killing of 200 men, women and children of the Oglala Sioux nation at Wounded Knee in 1890 was only the last and best known. Colonel John Chivington reflected the attitudes of many army officers when he declared before shooting dozens of unarmed Indians at Sand Creek: 'I have come to kill Indians and believe it right and honourable to use any means under God's heaven.'[10]

The physical destruction of the autochthonous population was made morally possible by the prevalent racism of the colonizers. The Indians of the Americas were regarded by the Spanish and Portuguese as brute creatures and treated accordingly. Indeed it was not until 1537 that the Pope conceded that Indians were real people, capable of receiving the Christian faith. But such charity fell on deaf ears. The *conquistadores*, with few exceptions, continued to regard all Indians as animals suitable only for enslavement. In Australia the black population encountered similar attitudes among the invading whites: 'They do not understand exalted rank and, in fact, it is difficult to get into a blackfellow's head that one man is higher than another,'[11] wrote one observer in 1888. As they pushed westwards the pioneers of North America considered themselves bearers of civilization to a wilderness of savages described in 1867 by the Kansas newspaper, *Weekly Leader*, as 'A set of miserable, dirty, louse-infected, gut-eating skunks as the Lord ever permitted to live. Their immediate and final extermination all men should pray for.'[12]

From the first days of colonization, the European settlers pursued policies of extermination or assimilation. When the indigenous population did not encounter direct genocide, they faced instead enslavement, forced labour and menial work. In South America the native population became the means for the commercial exploitation of the New World. Indians were rounded up to build cities, dig mines and work the land. Although under the Aztec empire Middle American Indians had been subjugated to a limited form of slavery, the new Spanish masters considered their subjects an expendable resource. Many thousands lived and died as slaves in the silver mines. In Brazil until the large-scale importation of African slaves, Indians were used to work the sugar plantations. In the area around present-day Bahia, local Indians were hunted like wild beasts with the aid of bloodhounds and according to one source 'the better to train the bloodhounds for their work, they were fed on Indians assassinated for the purpose.'[13]

During the latter half of the 19th Century, South Seas islanders were lured away from their homes by false promises and trickery to work as indentured labourers on the cotton and sugar plantations of Queensland, Australia. Once there they worked in conditions of virtual slavery.[14]

In Australia, Aborigines were pacified and put to work for European society. The women usually became domestic servants and the men agricultural labourers. In North America few efforts were made to enslave the Indian population, but where Indians were assimilated by white society, they performed only the most menial tasks.

Where slaughter was condemned something almost as dangerous and more insidious emerged in the shape of a protective paternalism. The Reverend Bishop Hale writing of Australia's Aborigines expressed an opinion held by many in the 19th Century:

> Everyone who knows a little about aboriginal races is aware that those races which are of a low type mentally, and who are, at the same time, weak in constitution, rapidly die out when their country comes to be occupied by a different race much more vigorous, robust and pushing than themselves.[15]

The rapid expansion of European settlement in the colonies of the Americas and elsewhere profoundly disrupted the overall social and economic system and cultural traditions of the indigenous inhabitants. The colonizing forces destroyed the ruling elites and administrations of the Incas and Aztecs, causing a breakdown in food production and distribution. The introduction of cattle-rearing by the Spanish on arable land previously used for crops exacerbated the food shortages and caused famines. In North America the insatiable appetite for land remorselessly pushed the Indian peoples westwards. Herds of bison, on which peoples like the Apache were dependent, were wiped out indiscriminately. Out of an estimated population of 60 million bison in the 1850s, only ten (sic) remained by 1910.[16] In Australia white farmers rearing sheep occupied the best flat land and waterholes; imported livestock such as sheep, chickens, rabbits and pigs ate many of the local plants essential for the survival of Aboriginal people. 'I think altogether we die soon,' commented one Aboriginal, 'pig-pig eat him yams; plums fall down, wild pigs too much eat.'[17] In southern Africa there was a rapid decline in the population of Bushmen, from 200,000 at contact to 55,000 in 1921, at the introduction of capitalist pastoralism.[18]

Indeed, it is the alienation of indigenous land which has in the last centuries reduced tribal and indigenous peoples to such misery. In Central and South America colonists from Europe seized the best land and the Indian communities were left what remained or entirely dispossessed and forced to move to less hospitable areas. This was a pattern that emerged later in North America and Australasia. From the 16th Century until the early 19th Century there was a gradual transfer of land from indigenous to Spanish control. But in the 19th Century, as South and Central American countries achieved their independence, the power of the crown and the church was broken. Ecclesiastical properties and communal indigenous land were declared within the public domain and Indian communities lost land on a huge scale. Meanwhile the appetite of the great estates for new land grew as a result of the rise in demand for export crops like sugar and coffee. For most of the Indian population which, after the initial catastrophic demographic decline, had now grown in number, there was no means of livelihood. Their land had been taken away and the remaining communities were unable to absorb them. The *hacienda* (great estate) thereby became the only alternative economic and social institution capable of incorporating these people. The *hacendado*, having robbed the Indian of his land, now became his benefactor.

In fact, for many indigenous peoples the invasion by Europeans was not immediately seen as a threat. As one author says of the Aborigines of Australia:

> While conflict was ubiquitous in traditional societies, territorial conquest was virtually unknown. Alienation of land was not only unthinkable, it was literally impossible. If Blacks often did not react to the initial invasion of their country it was because they were not aware that it had taken place. They certainly did not believe that their land had suddenly ceased to belong to them and they to their land.[19]

In North America native peoples were at pains to understand the acquisitive nature of the settlers who seemed unwilling to share the earth's resources. As Cochise, an Apache leader, declared, 'Wars are fought to see who owns the land, but in the end it possesses man. None dare say he owns it for one day he too will lie beneath it.'[20]

On the whole the realization that the colonizers expected not to share the land with Indian peoples but possess it entirely came too late. They were forced to retreat and occupy only the hills, the forest and the deserts which no one wanted to farm or exploit. Their homelands, such as were left to them, were in regions of only marginal interest to the whole society.

Resistance

The invasion of the Americas and Australasia was not met with passive acceptance. Throughout the period of colonization the Aborigines of Australia, the Maoris of New Zealand, the native peoples of North America and the Indians of South America fought to defend their lives, territories and culture. In North America the Pueblo Indians successfully drove the Spanish off their land and across the Rio Grande in the 17th Century and won themselves over a decade of independence; the Iroquois Confederacy, the most powerful alliance of Indians, was able until the late 18th Century to protect its people from the full effects of colonization. During the 19th Century when the West was opened up by pioneers and brought under military control, numerous Indian peoples fought to defend their way of life and their land.

One of the most effective acts of resistance against encroachment by white settlers was made by the Northern Plains nations during the 1860s and 1870s. A series of uprisings by the Sioux and their allies led to a lengthy conflict with the United States Army. The Powder River War, as it was known, ended with the defeat of the government's forces and the signing of the Treaty of Fort Laramie, which provided for the continued independence of the three leading Northern Plains nations and legal title to a region occupying about half of South Dakota. Peace endured for four years and then in 1872 the Northern Pacific Railroad attempted to lay track across the territory reserved for the Indians. Despite this illegality, the federal government assisted the company in its efforts to get land concessions from the chiefs. The two prominent Indian leaders, Sitting Bull and Crazy Horse, rejected the offers. Then in 1874 General Sheridan decided to build a military base in the Black Hills, not only within Indian territory but also on an important sacred site. General Custer was sent to survey the site and at the same time confirmed the presence of gold. By the end of the year a gold rush to the Black Hills had been precipitated. Miners were attacked and killed in their hundreds by the Sioux but they were not discouraged. By 1875 the government determined to purchase the hills from the Sioux nation. The Sioux refused and by 1877 they had all been labelled hostile by the federal government and in a state of war against the United States. The army began a series of unsuccessful attacks on the Indian nations. First at Powder River and then at Rosebud Creek the army were driven off after suffering defeat. Then on 25 June 1876 over 200 soldiers under the command of General Custer were wiped out at Little Big Horn River. The defeat was a national humiliation and the federal government determined to launch a major assault on the Northern Plains nations. Within a year the United States army had overwhelmed any resistance, Indian leaders were killed and most of the population subjugated.[21]

In Australia such collective struggles were less common but there were many cases of local resistance. On the whole, conflict was not provoked by the Europeans using the land but by their determination to exclude Aborigines from it. In practice, as colonists took possession of the land and waterholes, Aborigines were denied the necessities of life. Conflicts, therefore, arose over access to land and these often ended in killings on both sides. But as in North America, the indigenous population was overwhelmed by numbers and by new weapons. The Aboriginal people were forced to adopt guerrilla tactics, stealing guns, attacking supply lines, property and animals, but eventually were forced to submit.

In Latin America uprisings were also prevalent throughout the period of Spanish occupation. Some indigenous groups, such as the Araucanians in southern Chile and Argentina, successfully held off the Spanish and later the armies of the independent republics until the mid-19th Century. In Peru in the 1770s and 1780s there were attempts to mobilize the Indian peoples and restore the Inca empire under the leadership of Tupac Amaru. In 1781 there was a major uprising and an attack on La Paz led by Tupac Katari.

On the whole, however, the Indian peoples of Latin America often found themselves mobilized by non-natives for political objectives which were not always in their interests. During the wars of independence against the Spanish crown in the early 19th Century, the Indians of Peru, Mexico and elsewhere were vital components of the liberation armies. Much the same happened in North America, where Indian peoples were recruited by French, English and Spanish alike during their own wars to secure hegemony. From 1689 until 1763 Europe transformed its new colonies into a battlefield, so that, according to one author, 'by 1763 most Indian groups east of the Mississippi had been affected by the long conflict and many of them had been destroyed.'[22] In the War of Independence which followed, Indians were mobilized with equal cynicism by both sides. Indeed, the recruitment of Indian peoples into national armies to fight for causes they do not really espouse has been a common theme in their history. The Indians of several countries in Latin America represent the majority of the army regular troops, but they are rarely found among the officers. During the two world wars North American Indians and Australian Aborigines were recruited and expected to fight alongside North Americans and Australians abroad, even though they were treated as second-class citizens at home.

Nevertheless, the experience over the years of repression, rebellion and manipulation has developed in indigenous peoples an ability to survive. In the brunt of colonialism they often physically retreated to protect their customs and way of life; other times, as among many Andean Indians, they have adopted a passive resistance to European society by withdrawal. The language, culture and strong sense of identity of a great many indigenous peoples have thus been kept alive. Indeed where such cultures have adapted themselves to the societies imposed upon them, they have often become stronger. During this century there has been a gradual reawakening of the political consciousness of Indian peoples. The revolution of 1910 to 1917 in Mexico was perhaps the clearest example of Indian participation in a major historical process, but it is not the only one. More recently in the Bolivian revolution of 1952 the majority Quechua and Aymara peoples played a vital role in promoting land reform and social justice. In Australia after the Second World War Aborigines began to organize themselves politically for the first time, staging a series of strikes in 1946, 1950 and 1951. In the 1960s the first Indian organization of Canada was formed, the Native Indian Council, which was able to represent their interests at the national level. In North America the National Congress of American Indians was created in 1944, open to all recognized tribes. In Norway, Finland and Sweden the first conference of Sami people took place in 1953, and three years later the Nordic Sami Council was formed. In India there were several rebellions and minor insurrections by tribespeoples during the 19th and early 20th Centuries, such as the Santal rebellion and Birsa Munda movement in Bihar.

Elsewhere in the world where indigenous peoples have organized – in Asia and the Pacific for example – it has been in support of decolonization. However, the withdrawal of direct rule by Britain of the Indian subcontinent, by the Netherlands of Indonesia and by the United States and later Japan of the Philippines, has created many subjugated national minorities and indigenous peoples. Since the 1960s throughout Asia these tribal and indigenous peoples have also been organizing themselves and demanding the right to self-determination.

The world-wide indigenous peoples' movement, as we shall see in the next chapter, has accelerated rapidly in the last two decades. It has taken many governments, who have assumed their indigenous population was a disappearing minority, by surprise and caused them to reappraise and readjust their policies. Yet although the consciousness developing among indigenous peoples is growing, the history of struggle is nothing new. The fight for survival of indigenous peoples began with the arrival of the first colonists.

Notes

1. On pre-conquest Middle America see G.C. Valliant, *The Aztecs of Mexico* (Doubleday, 1944) and Eric Wolf, *Sons of the shaking earth* (University of Chicago Press, 1959).

2. From 'Testamento de Mancio Sierra de Leguizamo, in Lewis Hanke (ed.), *History of Latin American Civilization*, vol.1 (Methuen, 1969) p.78.

3. The story is told in detail in William H. Prescott, *History of the conquest of Mexico* (London, 1889).

4. Cf. John Hemming, *The conquest of the Incas* (Sphere Books, London, 1973); William H. Prescott, *History of the conquest of Peru* (New York, 1847).

5. Cited in Henry Reynolds, *The other side of the frontier* (Penguin, Harmondsworth, 1982) p.24.

6. Russell Means in *Onaway*, Spring 1984, p.7.

7. Cf. Darcy Ribeiro, *The Americas and civilization* (Allen & Unwin, London, 1971) for impact of colonization.

8. Cited in Hemming, p.348.

9. James Wilson, *The original Americans: US Indians*, Minority Rights Group Report 31, 1976, p.16.

10. Cited in *Onaway*, Winter 1984, p.12; Dee Brown, *Bury my heart at Wounded Knee* (Picador, London, 1975) p.70.

11. Cited in Reynolds, p.151.

12. Cited in *Onaway*, Winter 1984, p.25.

13. Cited in G.E. Church, *The Aborigines of South America* (London, 1912) pp.72-3.

14. Cf. Edward Wybergh Docker, *The Blackbirders: the recruiting of South Seas labour for Queensland, 1863-1907* (Angus & Robertson, Sydney, 1970).

15. Revd Bishop Hale, *The Aborigines of Australia* (London, 1889) p.25.

16. James Wilson, p.17.

17. Cited in Reynolds, p.159.

18. Carmel Schire and Robert Gordon (eds.), *The future of former foragers: Australia and Southern Africa*, Cultural Survival Occasional Paper 18, October 1985, p.4.

19. Reynolds, p.65.

20. Cited in *Onaway*, Winter 1983, p.37.

21. Cf. *Onaway*, Summer 1983, pp.23-8.

22. James Wilson, p.14.

5. The Indigenous Movement Today

During the last two decades there has been a rapid increase in the number of organizations of indigenous peoples. Ethnic groups, however small, are now forming organizations to represent their interests both nationally and internationally. They are coming together more frequently to discuss issues of common interest and formulate united policies. Perhaps it is as yet premature to call it an indigenous movement because the organizations are so numerous and geographically and politically diverse that there is not yet a common programme. But there is little doubt, as the ensuing chapters will reveal, that the indigenous peoples' organizations are growing in both numerical strength and political importance. They are now a distinct new force in world politics and their struggles can no longer be considered marginal to the main concerns of governments and, more generally, mankind.

But what factors have contributed to this upsurge in the political activity of indigenous peoples? There are two fundamental developments of the last decade which have had significant repercussions on indigenous peoples. In the first place, there has been a massive explosion of demand for natural resources on the world market and this has stimulated vigorous exploration and exploitation. The search for new resources has brought governments, international development banks, transnational and national companies, entrepreneurs, speculators, big farmers, landless peasants and many others on to indigenous land. In the second place, the territories of indigenous peoples have increasingly become areas of strategic importance in the struggle for hegemony by the two superpowers. Where they are not subject to that wider ideological war, they are considered regions vital to the interests of national security of states without popular support. Such governments are often fearful of any peoples within their national boundaries with a strong claim to self-determination. In such situations indigenous peoples become a threat.

The search for new resources

Indigenous peoples live on what is deemed by mainstream society as frontier land, largely unclaimed, unowned and unexploited. The lands they occupy possess natural resources which until comparatively recently were deemed worthless or of little value and ignored. Yet in the last few decades these lands have been seen as locations of the earth's last undiscovered wealth and places where the enterprising can still get something for nothing. But these lands are not unoccupied nor can they give up their resources without serious environmental and human disruption. Furthermore, once the homelands of indigenous peoples have given up their material wealth for our consumption, there will be neither frontier land nor its inhabitants left.

The most seriously threatened habitat of indigenous peoples is the tropical rainforest. About seven per cent of the earth's land surface is covered with rainforest and it is the home of countless tribal communities and non-indigenous settlers. There are over one million forest-dwelling Indians in South America, and several hundred thousand Pygmies in the African forest; about 30 million tribal peoples in India depend upon minor forest produce, and hundreds of different indigenous communities live in the forests of Papua New Guinea, Borneo, the Philippines, Malaysia, Burma and Thailand. Only these peoples, after centuries of adaptation, have learned how to prosper in their environment without destroying it.

Yet in the 20th Century, and particularly in the last 20 years or so, the forests have been destroyed at an unprecedented rate. The United Nations Food and Agriculture Organization calculated in 1981 that if present levels of deforestation are maintained, one-fifth of the remaining tropical forest would be cut down by the end of the century.[1] In certain countries the destruction is far more rapid. The United Nations World Ecological Areas programme has estimated that in eleven countries – among them Thailand and Guatemala – tropical forests will virtually disappear by the year 2000. The present rate of cutting in Indonesia is 15,000 square miles per year and in Thailand 14,000 square miles per year.[2] In the Philippines nearly all the country's indigenous peoples live on public forest land which is disappearing at the rate of 650 square miles a year.[3] The world's largest rainforest in Brazil will be reduced by 53 million acres, one-sixth of its present size, before the end of the century.[4]

The tragic depletion of the rainforest has accelerated in recent years and shows every sign of continuing to do so. In Indonesia, for example, one of the world's leading timber exporting countries, 148,000 cubic yards were shipped abroad in 1961 but this had leapt to 25 million cubic yards by 1979. Overall, the industrialized countries imported 16 times as much tropical hardwood in 1984 as they did in 1950.[5] The four million tons imported by the West in 1950 will probably leap to a massive 100 million tons by the year 2000.[6]

Cattle-rearing has also been responsible for the felling of great swathes of tropical forest. In the Brazilian Amazon about 38 per cent of all deforested land in the period 1966 to 1975 was used for cattle ranches.[7] In the Central American region since 1960 nearly one-quarter of all forests have been destroyed to provide clearings for cattle ranches to produce beef, 90 per cent of which ends up as hamburgers or pet food on the US market.[8]

In many countries the forests appear to be uninhabited and unexploited wildernesses. Nothing could be further from the truth. All tropical rainforests sustain a human population of some kind and traditionally forest-dwelling peoples have developed an expertise as yet unmatched by scientists and other specialists. The forest provides for all their food, health and housing needs and also fulfils spiritual and cultural functions. While such peoples possess liberty to live on sufficient acreage of forest, neither they nor the environment will suffer. When, however, the forests are felled for timber and the tree stumps cleared to make way for cattle pastures, there are no long-term beneficiaries.

Replanting of trees in tropical rainforests has been largely unsuccessful, deforestation has brought about a rapid erosion of top soils, and crop yields from cleared lands decline rapidly. In areas of Brazil subjected to this kind of treatment, there are now only vast, barren, wastelands.[9] Where such land has been offered to landless peasants as part of a colonization programme, there has in most cases been unmitigated disaster. Sedentary farming on poor soils such as exist in tropical forests requires ever-increasing inputs of expensive fertilizers. Notwithstanding the use of fertilizers and pesticides, yields are unlikely to do anything but fall. In most cases the markets for cash crops are at a great distance, adding further costs to the producer. In Brazil where the colonization schemes have been on a grandiose scale, smallholders have been reduced to penury and drifted to frontier towns to eke out a precarious existence.

The greatest suffering caused by colonization, agro-industry and commercial logging has been to the forest-dwelling Indians. If they have had relatively little contact with outsiders, they are highly vulnerable to disease and a bout of influenza can decimate a tribe. As roads and timber-felling cut into and across indigenous territory, the self-sufficiency of a tribal community can be permanently damaged. Relatively unassimilated groups are then forced to choose between becoming dependent on non-tribal society or retreating on to an ever-diminishing and inadequate land base. In such instances, of course, Amazonian Indians have fought back, attacking settlers, road builders and logging operators.

However, by far the most destructive single activity by outsiders as far as indigenous peoples are concerned, is the hydro-electric project. The construction of a dam and the creation of a reservoir can create dislocation and damage on a vast scale. In the first place the reservoir submerges valley bottoms where the land is of good quality and where the major population centres are located. A Canadian environmental organization has described the effects of hydro-electric schemes in Third World countries in this way: 'Disease increases, farmers are forced to move to poorer quality land, food self-sufficiency diminishes, forests are either flooded or cut down by these hydro-evacuees in search for new land.'[10]

In Bangladesh where the Kaptai Dam was built in the Chittagong Hill Tracts region, 100,000 tribespeople were forced off their land, nearly one-quarter of the entire indigenous population of the district. The reservoir submerged about 40 per cent of the cultivable land. In the Philippines, where a series of dams are planned, an estimated 1.5 million indigenous and other peoples will be forced from their lands eventually and their rice terraces and communities will be destroyed. Such examples may be multiplied. About 5,000 Akawaio Indians have been moved off their land to make way for the Upper Mazaruni hydro-electric scheme in Guyana; about 40,000 Indians and poor peasants were removed because of the Itaipu Dam on the Paraguay–Brazil frontier; when the Bayano Dam was built in Panama the Kuna Indians lost 80 per cent of their reservation.

Now another gigantic dam is due to be built in Sarawak, Malaysia, at a cost of $US 4 billion. The Bakun Dam will flood 700 square kilometres of forests and more than 5,000 natives will be uprooted. In the Narmada River Valley in India there are plans to build over 300 large dams and relocate up to one million mainly tribal peoples.[11]

In the 1980s, 33 major dams are due to be completed, many on indigenous peoples' land. The World Bank expects to spend about $US 100 billion on hydro-electric projects up to the end of the century, so building dams is big business. If the present pattern persists, the indigenous peoples affected will be neither consulted nor compensated. The electricity produced will certainly not reach them either, since only six per cent of the Third World's rural poor can afford to use it.

The imposition of these dams has provoked protest and opposition. In some cases, indigenous communities such as the Bontocs and Kalingas in the Philippines have mounted successful resistance and forestalled the dam-building programme. In other cases the construction of a dam has led to the formation of alliances among indigenous peoples, environmentalists and urban-based political organizations. In Malaysia, for example, 14,000 tribal people were threatened by a dam in the Toman Negara National Park which was successfully opposed by the Malaysian branch of the Friends of the Earth and the local community.

The tribal peoples threatened with displacement by the Koel Karo Dam in Bihar, India, have successfully resisted the implementation of the project for nearly 30 years. Sami resistance to the Alta Dam in northern Norway resulted in the most serious outbreak of civil disobedience in the country in recent years.

The homelands of indigenous peoples have also attracted the attention of oil and mineral companies. In the United States of America, for example, 34 tribes are estimated to own one-third of all the surface-minable coal west of the Mississippi and 15 per cent of all national coal reserves, nearly 40 per cent of all uranium and four per cent of oil and natural gas deposits.[12] In Australia, the largest and least expensive to mine uranium reserves in the world are located on Aboriginal land.[13]

The potential wealth that can be extracted from indigenous land has brought together many major capitalist interests. The Great Carajás Programme in Brazil which will develop mining, hydro-electricity, agriculture, forestry and ranching is due to cover a site of 190 million acres. This massive project is receiving finance from the World Bank, the European Economic Community, numerous private North American and European banks, Japanese investors and as many transnational corporations as can get a piece of the action, including Rio Tinto Zinc, ALCOA, Bethlehem Steel, British Petroleum, Utah International, Elf Aquitaine and many others.[14] Within the project area are 20

Indian reserves and more than 13,000 tribal peoples whose interests, in the scramble for quick profits, are almost entirely ignored.

Despite occupying resource-rich land indigenous peoples rarely benefit when it is exploited. More often than not, tribal peoples are simply removed and relocated elsewhere without any compensation. Where there is some financial compensation it is usually well below any market evaluation and often in practice is it not fully paid out. Besides, resettlement sites are invariably located on poor soils where the self-sufficiency of the community is no longer possible. Even in the United States where indigenous peoples are well organized and familiar with legal procedures, they have had great difficulties in receiving a rightful share of wealth generated from their land. In 1981, for example, the Navajo received between 15 and 37 cents per ton of coal mined on their land, which the Peabody Coal Corporation were selling for $US 70 per ton, that is less than 0.25 per cent of the sale price. There are coal deposits valued at $US 10 billion on Navajo land but no work for the Indians: about 75 per cent are unemployed.[15]

Nor have indigenous peoples been ignored by the world's second largest export earner, tourism. In some countries, like Fiji, tourism represents about one-quarter of all foreign currency earnings. But even in countries where tourism is less important in the national economy, indigenous peoples are often offered as one of the attractions. Whether it is the rainforest Indians of Brazil or the heavily ornamented hill tribes of Thailand, indigenous peoples are considered exotic. Hotels and special lodges have been built on indigenous land and inevitably the values and requirements of the tourist clash significantly with those of the local inhabitants, turning the culture of the latter into a mere object for sale.[16]

In their bid to use and exploit indigenous land, governments, transnationals and speculators are causing widespread damage and, therefore, often facing increased resistance. When the Canadian Government and a consortium of oil companies attempted to construct a natural gas pipeline along the Mackenzie Valley through Dene land, they were successfully prevented by a special commission in 1977. The commission was established after determined protests by the Dene people and the public. Invasions on to indigenous land by outside interests are provoking opposition from not only the affected communities but also other sectors of society. The proposed development of five uranium mines in Saskatchewan on aboriginal land in 1983 has brought together indigenous peoples, churches, and the anti-nuclear lobby in a growing alliance of opposition.[17] In Panama where Rio Tinto Zinc attempted to open a copper mine on Guaymí land, it faced international protest and agreed to postpone the project.

Sometimes, however, the involvement of indigenous peoples in the exploitation of their land and their labour is more insidious. The raw materials for the growing and profitable drugs trade are produced for the most part on tribal land. The opium poppy of the golden triangle is cultivated by Shan, Hmong, and other hill peoples in Burma and Thailand. Coca leaves are produced in southern Bolivia and the forests of eastern Peru, Ecuador and

Colombia. In both the production of cocaine and heroin the indigenous peoples are as much victims as those in the rich countries who have become addicted. They often have no choice in whether they grow the crops. In Bolivia until recently senior army officers controlled all aspects of the cocaine business from the cultivation of coca leaves by indigenous and non-indigenous labour to its marketing in the United States. In Thailand the cultivation of the opium poppy is encouraged by narcotics dealers. It is still the only cash crop for which there is an almost limitless demand and the various United Nations and government crop substitution programmes have achieved only modest success.

Increasingly the exploitation of indigenous land has wider national and international repercussions. Deforestation is imparting permanent damage to the global environment; large-scale hydro-electric schemes have not only not fulfilled their stated objectives, but have drained away much needed foreign currency. The extraction of natural resources such as timber and minerals has taken place with little consideration for the long-term effects upon the local indigenous population and has not served in many cases the broader national interest. In such matters as uranium mining or the dumping of radioactive waste, the hazards extend well beyond the indigenous territory. In the Pacific the dumping of radioactive waste by Japan and the testing of nuclear weapons by France and the United States has provoked world-wide protest.

The search for resources and the exploitation of indigenous peoples' land by outside interests is bringing immense suffering and producing conflict on a world-wide scale. One writer has commented on the case of the United States, in the following terms:

> The motivation for the new Indian war is very similar to old wars. Indians sit on resources that America wants. America has reached a point of economic stagnation for which tribal resources may offer some relief. Corporations want to exploit the resources at the lowest possible cost in order to maximise profit.[18]

These words may well be broadened to include the rest of the world.

Post-war colonization

The political explanation for the rise in numbers and importance of indigenous peoples' organizations is related to the changes that have taken place in international relations since 1945. Until the Second World War, many of the peoples being considered by this book retained a high degree of political autonomy. This was particularly true of the tribal peoples of Asia. Others, such as the Indians of the Americas, had experienced several hundred years of colonization and had lost any strong sense of nationhood. The forest-dwelling Amerindians had been left to their own devices. Occasionally speculators flooded into Amazonia in search of profits and cheap labour, as in the rubber boom of the turn of the century, but by and large indigenous land was considered of no economic or political importance.

Just as a renewed search for resources took off in the post-war period, so also did a greater involvement of indigenous peoples in political affairs. Their involvement had two causes. Indigenous peoples both acted for themselves and were acted upon by outside factors. In the first place, in some countries, especially the rich ones, after a demographic decline, the post-war period saw a growth in population and an improvement in overall health. Many native Americans and Australian Aborigines had participated as regular soldiers in the war. Those who found work in industry were influenced by union and labour politics. The notion that indigenous peoples in the rich countries were not second-class citizens, which occurred at this time, paved the way for the contemporary movement to achieve wider rights to self-determination. Furthermore, the post-war process of decolonization and the international instruments developed by the United Nations provided a basis in law and in practice for the attainment of indigenous peoples' rights. Most importantly, the movement in favour of indigenous peoples' rights in North America that grew up in the 1970s was inspired by the successful political action taken by blacks during the previous decade.

But decolonization in the post-war period also created conditions which greatly affected indigenous and tribal peoples, particularly in certain Asian countries. In the newly formed East Pakistan, now Bangladesh, the tribal peoples of the Chittagong Hill Tracts lost all their former autonomy. The rights to exclude non-tribals from their territory and to appoint their own administrators and police force were abrogated by the new constitution. The hill people suddenly found themselves a minority population occupying land that was earmarked for settlement and development. The peoples of West Papua who had been, for the most part, left alone during the period of Dutch administration, found themselves the subjects of Indonesian rule. In order to guarantee the future of these territories within the Indonesian empire, transmigration programmes will bring settlers from the main island of Java. Before the end of the century the indigenous Papuan population will be a minority in their own land.

The European empires formed national frontiers which hardly reflected the traditional territories of the peoples within them. Throughout Africa, Asia and the Americas peoples were bifurcated on either side of country borders for no other reason than that one European power could expand no further or else simply to satisfy the whims of colonial administrators. Despite this, however, there was a certain amount of fluidity across frontiers. Throughout the British Raj, which stretched from present-day Pakistan to Burma, for example, there was freedom of movement. The subsequent nation states have struggled, often violently, to retain the territories and the peoples, however disparate, negotiated by them in the post-colonial period. Thus, Bangladesh fought a bloody war to achieve independence from rule by West Pakistan. The Karen and indeed most of the hill tribes are in open warfare against the Government of Burma; in north-eastern India the Nagas and the Mizos are still engaged, after more than 30 years, in an armed liberation struggle. Decolonization, therefore, raised the hopes of peoples who had experienced foreign domination. But instead of their aspirations for self-determination being fulfilled, they lost much of the autonomy they had enjoyed under their European masters. Decolonization in certain instances has, therefore, brought greater oppression, not more freedom.

The wider East-West confrontation has also brought indigenous and tribal peoples into struggles from which they had been largely exempt until 1939. The Second World War saw much of Asia and the Pacific pass from British to Japanese and then later United States control. The hill peoples of Indo-China were recruited by both the Communists and the French and North Americans. In Central America the Mayan peoples of Guatemala have been murdered by a military dictatorship which claims that all Indians are Communists and which receives uncritical support from the United States Government. In Nicaragua and Honduras, the Miskito Indians, who had been comparatively untouched by the atrocities of the Somoza dictatorship, are now embroiled in a war stage-managed in Washington.

The war against Communism has provided governments with justifications for massive defence expenditure and the suspension of civil rights in many countries in the Third World. Subversion and Communism have become catch-all misnomers for any form of popular opposition to the military dictatorships so prevalent in developing countries. In this political environment, indigenous peoples are perceived by governments as threatening. Their clear ethnic identity makes them easy targets. In Guatemala all Mayan Indians are considered enemies of the state, and in the Philippines tribal peoples are thought by the armed forces to be sympathetic to the Communist guerrilla force, the New People's Army. In Colombia the government and landowners refer to the Indian organization, the CRIC, as a subversive Communist group. Increasingly, indigenous populations are considered by governments ruling without a consensus of support – the majority in developing countries – as threats to national security or at the very least as peoples who require close control. It is no surprise that government agencies set up to assist indigenous peoples, like the National Foundation for Indians (FUNAI) in Brazil or the Presidential Assistant for National Minorities (PANAMIN) in the Philippines, have not only aided economic exploitation of indigenous land but have also been used as a means of political control. In the Philippines, for example, PANAMIN forcibly introduced a resettlement programme for the national minorities, and in Brazil FUNAI has for much of its history been directly under the Ministry of the Interior and run by army officers.

Among the more remote forest-dwelling tribes, evangelical organizations, like the Summer Institute of Linguistics (SIL), are actively engaged in neo-colonial missionary work. In practice such groups break down indigenous culture and promote, through schools and economic projects, Western and especially United States ideology. For the mainly white North American missionaries the liberation theology preached by some Catholic priests is against the gospel, and indigenous organizations are construed as pure satanism. The activities of the SIL and other North American evangelical groups have earned the hostility of indigenous peoples and, after widespread protests those missionaries have been banned altogether in some countries.

But the persistence of what have been called the new *conquistadores* is impressive. In Ecuador, for example, 90 Protestant sects have established themselves since 1981. The activities of the SIL are quite well recorded, but one of the largest and most insidious charities operating in Ecuador is World Vision, which began to expand its work after the expulsion of SIL. The organization is massively funded and run like a corporation from its headquarters in California. Funds are made available to local administrators who then arrange conversions through financial incentives. Local Indian communities have denounced their actions, because they have brought discord and conflict, and demanded withdrawal of World Vision from the country.[19]

Anti-Communist hysteria has been responsible for renewed assaults on indigenous peoples and super-power confrontations have turned many indigenous territories into war zones. In some instances indigenous peoples claim that they are already the first victims of a nuclear war. In the Pacific there have been deaths, serious sickness and pollution of land and sea as a result of the United States and French testing of their nuclear weapons.

When the political rivalries between East and West impinge upon indigenous and tribal peoples, there is really no other choice than to act politically in order to survive. It is that or disappear as a people.

Fighting back

Colonialism has always been resisted by indigenous and tribal peoples. Resistance has taken the forms of armed rebellion, civil disobedience and action through colonial institutions, such as parliament and the law courts. The North American Indian peoples fought with arms, lobbied presidents and signed treaties to protect their land. The South American Indian peoples rebelled against their Spanish conquerors, appealed to the church and protested peacefully to their colonial administrators to achieve social justice. Times have changed and the colonial situation is no longer as it was, but the strategies for survival remain unaltered. Today indigenous peoples are engaged in armed struggles and peaceful protest, in political lobbying and litigation. But in one important respect there is a difference in the opposition of the past and the political activity of the present. Indigenous peoples are no longer engaged in isolated acts of resistance but are now organizing at a national, regional and international level.

The international movement of indigenous peoples is a comparatively new phenomenon. It manifests itself through the several hundreds of indigenous peoples' organizations that have proliferated during the last decades. The movement grew out of a recognition of shared experiences and problems and has rapidly developed the beginnings of a common platform based on a different understanding of the past and an alternative vision of the future.

In the first place, a recognition has grown among indigenous peoples that they are part both of an exploited class and an oppressed people. The highland Indians of South America have been especially cognizant of the double discrimination they face as landless peasants and *indios*. Equally the Native American peoples argue that they are not only one of the poorest sectors in the United States but are also treated as second-class citizens because they are Indians. Many indigenous groups are examining the revolutionary and progressive struggles of the past and concluding that they did not achieve liberation for Indian and tribal peoples. This analysis has implications for the political programme of indigenous peoples.[20]

Russell Means, a leading activist in the North American Indian movement, has criticized capitalist and Marxist development. His radical critique is worth citing at length:

> Let's suppose further that we were to take revolutionary Marxism at its word: that it intends nothing less than the complete overthrow of the European capitalist order which has presented this threat to our very existence. This would seem to be a natural alliance for American Indian people to make. After all, as the Marxists say, it is the capitalists who set us up to be a national sacrifice. This is true as far as it goes.
>
> But, as I've tried to point out, this 'truth' is very deceptive. Look beneath the surface of revolutionary Marxism and what do you find? A commitment to reversing the industrial system which created the need of white society for uranium? No. A commitment to guaranteeing the Lakota and other American Indian peoples real control over the land and resources they have left? No, not unless the industrial process is to be reversed as part of their doctrine. A commitment to our rights, as peoples, to maintaining our values and traditions? No, not as long as they need the uranium within our land to feed the industrial system of the society, the culture of which the Marxists *are still a part*.
>
> Revolutionary Marxism is committed to even further perpetuation and perfection of the very industrial process which is destroying us all. It is offering only to 'redistribute' the results, the money maybe, of this industrialization to a wider section of the population. It offers to take the wealth from the capitalist and pass it around, but in order to do so, Marxism must maintain the industrial system. Once again, the power relations within European society will have to be altered, but once again the effects upon American Indian peoples here and non-Europeans elsewhere will remain the same. This is much the same as when power was redistributed from the church to private business during the so-called 'bourgeois revolution', European society changed a bit, at least superficially, but its conduct toward non-Europeans continued as before. You can see what the American Revolution of 1776 did for American Indians. It's the same old song.
>
> Revolutionary Marxism, as with industrial society in other forms, seeks to 'rationalize' all people in relation to industry, maximum industry, maximum production. It is a materialist doctrine which despises the American Indian spiritual tradition, our cultures, our lifeways. Marx himself called us 'precapitalists' and 'primitive'. Precapitalist simply means that, in his view, we would eventually discover capitalism and become capitalists; we have always been economically retarded in Marxist terms. The only manner in which American Indian people could participate in a Marxist revolution would be to *join* the industrial system, to become factory workers or 'proletarians' as Marx called them. The man was very clear about the fact that his revolution could occur only through the struggle of the proletariat, that the existence of a massive industrial system is a precondition of a successful Marxist society.

I think there's a problem with language here. Christians, capitalists, Marxists, all of them have been revolutionary in their own minds. None of them really mean revolution. What they really mean is a *continuation*. They do what they do in order that European culture can continue to exist and develop according to its needs. Like germs, European culture goes through occasional convulsions, even divisions within itself, in order to go on living and growing. This isn't a revolution we're talking about, but a means to continuing what already exists. An amoeba is still an amoeba after it reproduces. But maybe comparing European culture to an amoeba isn't really fair to the amoeba. Maybe cancer cells are a more accurate comparison because European culture has historically destroyed everything around it; and it will eventually destroy itself.

So, in order for us to *really* join forces with Marxism, we Indians would have to accept the national sacrifice of our homeland; we'd have to commit cultural suicide and become industrialized, Europeanized, maybe even sanforized. We would have to totally defeat ourselves. Only the insane could consider this to be desirable to us.

At this point, I've got to stop and ask myself whether I'm being too harsh. Marxism has something of a history. Does this history bear out my observations? I look to the process of industrialization in the Soviet Union since 1920 and I see that these Marxists have done what it took the English 'industrial revolution' three hundred years to do; and the Marxists did it in sixty years. I see that the territory of the USSR used to contain a number of tribal peoples and that they have been crushed to make way for the factories. The Soviets refer to this as 'The National Question', the question of whether the tribal peoples were an acceptable sacrifice to industrial needs. I look to China and I see the same thing. I look to Vietnam and I see Marxists imposing an industrial order and rooting out the indigenous tribal mountain peoples.

I hear a leading Soviet scientist saying that when uranium is exhausted, *then* alternatives will be found. I see the Vietnamese taking over a nuclear power plant abandoned by the US military. Have they dismantled and destroyed it? No, they are using it. I see China explode nuclear bombs, developing uranium reactors, preparing a space program in order to colonize and exploit the planets the same as the Europeans colonized and exploited this hemisphere. It's the same old song, but maybe with a faster tempo this time.

The statement of the Soviet scientist is very interesting. Does he know what this alternative energy source will be? No, he simply has faith. Science will find a way. I hear revolutionary Marxists saying that the destruction of the environment, pollution, radiation, all these things will be controlled. And I see them act upon their words. Do they know how these things will be controlled? No, they simply have faith. Science will find a way. Industrialization is fine and necessary. How do they know this? Faith. Science will find a way. Faith of this sort has always been known in Europe as religion. Science has become the new European religion for both capitalists and Marxists; they are truly inseparable; they are part and parcel of the same culture. So, in both theory and in practice, Marxism demands that non-European peoples give up their values, their traditions, their cultural existence altogether. We will all be industrialized science addicts in a Marxist society.

I do not believe that capitalism itself is really responsible for the situation in which we have been declared a national sacrifice. No, it is the European tradition; European culture itself is responsible. Marxism is just the latest continuation of this tradition, not a solution to it. To ally with Marxism is to ally with the very same forces which declare us an acceptable 'cost'.

There is another way. There is the traditional Lakota way and the ways of the other American Indian peoples. It is the way that knows that humans do *not* have the right to degrade Mother Earth, that there are forces beyond anything the European mind has conceived, that humans must be in harmony with *all* relations or the relations will eventually eliminate the disharmony. A lopsided emphasis on humans by humans, the European arrogance of acting as though they were beyond the nature of all related things, can only result in a total disharmony and a readjustment which cuts arrogant humans down to size, gives them a taste of that reality beyond their grasp or control and restores the harmony. There is no need for a revolutionary theory to bring this about, it's beyond human control. The nature peoples of this planet know this and so they do not theorize about it. Theory is an abstract, our knowledge is real. Distilled to its basic terms, European faith – including the new faith in science – equals a belief that man is god. Europe has always sought a messiah, whether that be the man Jesus Christ or the man Karl Marx or the man Albert Einstein. American Indians know this to be totally absurd. Humans are the weakest of all creatures, so weak that other creatures are willing to give up their flesh so that we may live. Humans are only able to survive through the exercise of rationality since they lack the abilities of other creatures to gain food through the use of fang and claw. But rationality is a curse since it can cause humans to forget the natural order of things in ways other creatures do not. A wolf never forgets his/her place in the natural order. American Indians can. Europeans almost always do. We pray our thanks to the deer, our relations, for allowing us their flesh to eat. Europeans simply take the flesh for granted and consider the deer inferior. After all, Europeans consider themselves godlike in the rationalism and science; god is the supreme being; all else *must* be inferior. Thus, the ability of Europe to create disharmony knows no limits.

All European tradition, Marxism included, has conspired to defy the natural order of all things. Mother Earth has been abused, the powers have been abused and this cannot go on forever. No theory can alter that simple fact. Mother Earth will retaliate, the whole environment will retaliate, and the abusers will be eliminated. Things come full circle. Back to where they started. *That's* revolution. And that's a prophecy of my people, of the Hopi people and other correct peoples.

American Indians have been trying to explain this to Europeans for centuries. But, as I said earlier, they have proven themselves unable to hear. The natural order will win out and the offenders will die back, the way deer die when they offend the harmony by overpopulating a given region. It's only a matter of time until what Europeans call 'a major catastrophe of global proportions' will occur. It is the role of American Indian peoples, the role of all natural beings to survive. A part of our survival is to resist. We resist not to overthrow a government or to take political power, but because it is natural to resist extermination, to survive. We don't want power over white institutions; we want white institutions to disappear. *That's* revolution.[21]

An indigenous vision of the future has been articulated which does not draw on Western models, either capitalist or Communist. One international indigenous organization, the Indigenous Peoples Network (IPN), has stated that its purpose is 'to achieve recognition of a world view distinct from the "left" and the "right".'[22] The precise nature of that world-view is still unclear, but already some key elements of a universal political platform are emerging. Indigenous peoples are claiming the right to recognition as nations, the right to determine for themselves their own future, the right to land and the rights to enjoy without interference their own culture, language and religion. It is little short of a programme of decolonization.

The Demands of Indigenous Peoples

(Extracts from a submission by the International Indian Treaty Council to the United Nations Working Group on Indigenous Populations, 29 July 1983)

II. Self-Determination

1. Indigenous populations are subject to an economic and/or political and/or social domination which is alien and colonial or neo-colonial in nature.

2. Indigenous populations are composed of nations and peoples, which are collective entities entitled to and requiring self-determination. The Working Group should, therefore, develop a definition of the ultimate goals of self-determination, appropriate to indigenous populations, and procedures for achieving those goals.

3. Indigenous nations and peoples who so desire should be granted the full rights and obligations of external self-determination.

4. Indigenous nations and peoples who wish to limit themselves to the exercise of internal self-determination only should be granted the freedom to do so. The rights of internal self-determination should include, but not be limited to, the right to:
    (a) control their own economies;
    (b) freely pursue their economic, social and cultural development in conformity with their traditional customs and social mores;
    (c) engage in foreign relations and trade if they so desire;
    (d) restore, practice and educate their children to their cultures, languages, traditions and way of life;
    (e) and the right to the ownership of land as the territorial base for the existence of indigenous populations as such.

5. In order to ensure that the self-government of indigenous populations is fully realized and to promote their release from alien and colonial or neo-colonial domination, the representatives and systems of governance, whether electoral, traditional or otherwise, should be those chosen by the members of the respective populations without the participation of or infringement by States, individuals, corporations or other entities.

6. All indigenous nations and peoples may, for their own ends, freely dispose of their natural wealth and resources without prejudice to any obligations arising out of international economic co-operation, based upon principles of full and informed consent, mutual benefit and international law. In no case

may any indigenous nation or people be deprived of its own means of subsistence.

7. Alternatively, all indigenous nations and peoples have the right to protect the environmental integrity of their territories by refusing to allow any form of development which, either directly or indirectly, threatens that integrity.

8. No State shall undertake or permit any form of development within the territory inhabited by an indigenous population without the full and informed consent, freely given, of a majority of the inhabitants.

IV. Treaties and Agreements

1. All treaties and other agreements entered into by indigenous nations and peoples, whether entered with States or with other indigenous nations or peoples, and whether denominated as treaties or otherwise, shall be recognized and applied in the same manner and according to the same international laws and principles as the treaties and agreements entered into by other States, in a manner consistent with the Charter of the United Nations.

2. Treaties should be construed as they were understood by the indigenous representatives who participated in their negotiation. Treaties entered between indigenous nations or peoples and States should be liberally interpreted, with ambiguities resolved in favour of the indigenous populations. Furthermore, these treaties should be interpreted in light of the conditions under which they were signed.

3. All rights enumerated within and implied by the terms of this set of principles shall apply with equal force to all indigenous nations and peoples whether or not they have entered into recorded treaties or agreements with any State. Nor shall any indigenous nation or people be deemed to have fewer rights or lesser status for the sole reason that the nation or people has not entered into recorded treaties or agreements with any State.

V. Jurisdiction

1. No State shall assert or claim to exercise any right of jurisdiction over any indigenous nation or people or the territory of such indigenous population unless pursuant to a valid treaty or other agreement freely made with the lawful representatives of the indigenous nation or people concerned. All actions on the part of any State which derogate from the indigenous population's right to exercise self-determination shall be the proper concern of existing international bodies.

2. No State shall claim or retain, by right of discovery or otherwise, the territories of an indigenous nation or people, except such lands as may have been lawfully acquired by valid treaty or other cessation freely made.

X. Land and Environment

1. No State shall undertake or permit any action or course of conduct with respect to the territories of an indigenous nation or people which will directly

or indirectly result in the destruction or deterioration of an indigenous nation or people through the effects of pollution of earth, air, water, or which in any way depletes, displaces or destroys any natural resource or other resources under the dominion of, or vital to the livelihood of an indigenous population.

2. Indigenous populations are the people of the land. This assertion follows from the fact that the way of life of many indigenous populations is based upon a profound respect for the natural environment, as evidenced by beliefs and practices which hold this sense of respect to be a primary consideration in the determination of the form of ownership and manner of use of the land. Therefore, the preservation of the society and culture of indigenous populations represents a means of protecting and preserving the natural resources of the earth, including the air, water, land, flora and fauna, and those natural ecosystems contained within the territories of the indigenous populations.

3. The viability of the indigenous approach to the use of land and the natural environment is exemplified by the fact that, where they have not been destroyed or grossly altered by conquering peoples, the socio-economic systems of indigenous nations and peoples are among the oldest, that is the most enduring and resilient, social structures to be devised by human kind. Thus, the preservation of the society and culture of indigenous populations provides a means of safeguarding a cultural resource from which other societies and future generations may learn techniques for the rational management of natural resources and for the promotion of a wise, harmonious and enduring relationship between human society and its environment.

During the 1970s numerous regional and internationally oriented organizations were created. In the USA the International Indian Treaty Council (IITC) was founded in 1974. Its declared purpose was to internationalize the struggles of indigenous peoples by building links with other groups and raising issues of concern at international conferences and meetings. In 1977 it received consultative status as a non-governmental organization (NGO) at the United Nations. In 1978 another North American group, the Indian Law Resource Center (ILRC) was formed. As its name implies, the centre is concerned primarily with action through United States courts and international bodies, such as the United Nations Commission on Human Rights.

The World Council of Indigenous Peoples (WCIP) also has its origins in North America. Founded in 1975 after an Assembly of the National Indian Brotherhood of Canada, it now incorporates indigenous organizations from all over the world. At the First Conference of the World Council of Indigenous Peoples in Canada it was estimated that in the region of 35 million indigenous peoples were represented through their delegates. Subsequent conferences of the World Council took place in Sweden in 1977, in Australia in 1981 and most recently in Panama in September 1984.[23]

At the Panama conference there were almost 300 indigenous representatives from 23 different countries. The situations of many peoples were debated: the

Sami of Scandinavia, the colonized peoples of the Pacific and the Indian peoples of the Americas; the issues included indigenous landholding systems, culture, self-determination, world peace and the arms race and genocide in Central America. On the key issue of policy to achieve the liberation of indigenous peoples, the WCIP resolved to educate the world about the injustices done to them through international tribunals and fora, make more use of the media and increase and make more effective the alliances with other indigenous and non-indigenous peoples. On the sensitive matter of armed struggles as a means of liberation, the conference had this to say:

> Where there is no justice, there will be violence. We decry the *need* to resort to violence. Those responsible for violence are not those who must resort to it as a last resort. The responsibility of violence rests upon the souls of those who deny justice. The resort to arms is justified, but *only* as a last resort, only after an appeal to reason is no longer available. But when a resort to arms becomes necessary, it should be done with pride and not with shame; it should be used with compassion and not with uncontrolled hate; it must be taken up always with a clear understanding that it is justified only for the sake of liberation of our people and not for the purpose of revenge or suppression of another person's right to life and liberty of self-determination.[24]

The regional organization for South America, the South American Indian Council (CISA), was established in 1980 at a conference at Ollantaytambo near the ancient Inca capital of Cuzco in Peru. The event had been preceded by the First Indian Parliament of the Southern Cone in Asunción, Paraguay, in 1974, and the creation of the World Council of Indigenous Peoples. Both these meetings impressed upon South American Indian organizations the need to build alliances and make links with indigenous groups. At the first conference CISA declared its ideology and objectives. It reaffirmed its adoption of 'indianism', with its notions of self-determination and self-management, and rejected 'indigenism' which made the state a benefactor of the Indian and which was, therefore, an ideology of oppression. Communalism, based on traditional Indian collective institutions, and different from Western, Communist or socialist concepts, was declared a guiding principle: 'We refuse the political tendencies copied from Europe, as none of them have the intention of liberating us,' one of the resolutions stated.[25] Three years previously, in 1977, the Regional Coordinator for Indigenous Peoples (CORPI) based in Panama was created to represent the interests of the peoples of Central America. Both CISA and CORPI are the regional representatives of the World Council of Indigenous Peoples.[26]

Although internationally based indigenous organizations have developed rapidly in the Americas, they are not confined to that region. In Australia the National Aboriginal Conference – disbanded in 1985 – the Federation of Land Councils and the National Organization for Aboriginal and Islander Legal Services represent Aboriginal interests and all have been active in the international arena. The Maoris of New Zealand were founding members of the World Council of Indigenous Peoples and have been mobilizing internationally on the nuclear issue and in criticism of transnational corporations. The Inuit

(Eskimos), who live below the Arctic Circle in Alaska, Canada, Greenland and the USSR, convened the first Inuit Circumpolar Conference in 1977 and a second meeting in 1980. The Sami (Lapps) of Sweden, Norway and Finland have also been active on the international scene, both at United Nations meetings and as founder members of the World Council of Indigenous Peoples.

Indigenous and tribal peoples of Asia have, however, been less visible at international gatherings. In part this may be because their past and present colonial situations are in certain respects quite distinct from those of the indigenous peoples of the Americas. There has been, to date, a disinclination by indigenous peoples in the Americas to recognize that tribal peoples in Asia share many of their demands. Equally, indigenous communities from Asia have not, in the recent past, brought their cases to international fora. Nevertheless, there are growing links: the oppression of West Papuan and East Timorese peoples by the Government of Indonesia, for example, is now firmly on the agenda of the World Council of Indigenous Peoples. The atrocities committed against indigenous minorities in the Philippines are also better known to the wider international indigenous movement. In 1980, in Antwerp, Belgium, at a meeting of the Permanent Peoples' Tribunal, a non-governmental body whose jury is drawn from a panel of internationally respected individuals, the Government of the Philippines' treatment of the national minorities was one of the major items of discussion.

The indigenous movement is now making use of the growing interest and support they have engendered among non-indigenous groups. One of the first important international meetings of indigenous peoples took place in Geneva, Switzerland, in September 1977. The International NGO Conference on Discrimination against Indigenous Peoples in the Americas was set up in response to the United Nations decade against racism which opened in 1973. Representatives of more than 60 Indian peoples from 15 countries took part and nearly 50 international NGOs attended.[27]

The 1977 conference was followed by a meeting of the Russell Tribunal in Rotterdam, the Netherlands, in November 1980 on the Rights of the Indians of the Americas. The tribunal assembled a jury of eminent scholars and lawyers from around the world. A total of 45 cases was submitted and 15 were presented in detail with witnesses and substantial documentation. In addition to statements about indigenous peoples in the Americas, there were also documents presented on other peoples, including the West Papuans and the Kurds.[28]

The following year, in September 1981, a second International NGO Conference on Indigenous Peoples and the Land took place in Geneva, organized, like the 1977 conference, by the Special NGO Committee on Human Rights. This time there were more than 130 indigenous delegates, more than at any previous international gathering. The NGOs attending represented a wider spectrum than previously, thereby reflecting a growing international awareness of the problems and demands of indigenous peoples. Four commissions were created to discuss land rights, indigenous philosophy, the effect of transnational corporations on indigenous peoples and the impact of nuclear arms. The conference strongly supported the formation of a working group on indigenous peoples as part of the United Nations Commission on Human Rights, and other action to improve and widen access of indigenous peoples to all UN bodies and specialized agencies and committees.[29] In 1982 the Commission acceded to this demand and established an annual Working Group on Indigenous Populations to gather information about the situation of indigenous peoples world-wide and make recommendations about future international laws to protect their rights.

The creation of a working group by the United Nations represents an achievement, albeit symbolic rather than actual, by the indigenous movement. The establishment of the World Council of Indigenous Peoples and regional organizations, such as the Council of South American Indians, are more practical actions to advance the interests of indigenous peoples at an international level.

There are, of course, still serious obstacles to international solidarity. Indigenous peoples are not undifferentiated wholes: there are many who remain unaware of the struggles for self-determination and land rights, and others who are attracted rather than repelled by assimilation into the mainstream. Most dramatically, there are still numerous tribal leaders who are given some nominal position or other privilege and, thereby, co-opted by governments. But although international solidarity is still tenuous and new it is an indication of the growing strength and political importance of the indigenous movement. Only time will tell whether indigenous peoples' organizations present a coherent and global picture of our human condition and an alternative strategy for confronting it.

Notes

1. Catherine Caufield, *In the rainforest* (Heinemann, London, 1985) p.38.
2. 'Forest destruction in Asia', *Balai* (Manila), vol.11, no.3, p.3.
3. Anti-Slavery Society, *The Philippines: authoritarian government, multinationals and ancestral lands* (London, 1983) p.64.
4. Caufield, p.38.
5. Ibid., p.151.
6. Patricia Adams and Lawrence Solomon, *In the name of progress* (Energy Probe Research Foundation, Toronto, Canada, 1985) p.63.
7. Caufield, p.40.
8. Adams and Solomon, p.64.
9. Cf. R. Goodland and H. Irwin, *Amazon jungle: green hell to red desert?* (Elsevier, New York, 1975).
10. 'The problem with large-scale hydro dams in the Third World' (Energy Probe, Toronto, Canada, June 1985).
11. *Survival International News*, no.7, 1984; for a critical look at dams in Africa see Henri Roggeri, *African dams: impacts in the environment* (Environment

Liaison Centre, Nairobi, 1985); a general study is E. Goldsmith and N. Hildyard, *The social and environmental effect of large dams* (Wadebridge Ecological Centre, 1984).

12. Joseph G. Jorgensen (ed.), *Native Americans and energy development II* (Anthropology Resource Center and Seventh Generation Fund 1984) p.7.

13. Al Gedicks, 'Lands for dreaming or mining?', *The Global Reporter*, vol.1, no.3, Fall 1983, p.13.

14. Robin M. Wright, 'The great Carajás: Brazil's mega-program for the 80s', *The Global Reporter*, vol.1, no.1, March 1983, pp.3-6.

15. Joseph Jorgensen, 'The political economy of the native American energy business', in Jorgensen (ed.), *Native Americans*, p.45.

16. Cf. 'The tourist trap', *Cultural Survival Quarterly*, vol.6, no.3, Summer 1982.

17. Robert Regnier, 'Grass roots alliance fights new mines', *The Global Reporter*, vol.1, no.4, Spring 1984, p.7.

18. Jorgensen, p.9.

19. Cf. Sabine Hargous, 'L'action de Vision Mondiale en Equateur', *Le Monde Diplomatique*, June 1985, p.12: for a thorough analysis of the Summer Institute of Linguistics' activities, see David Stoll, *Fishers of men or founders of empire?* (Zed Press/Cultural Survival, London, 1982).

20. For a typology of indigenous peoples' organizations see Richard Chase Smith, 'A search for unity within diversity', *Cultural Survival Quarterly*, vol.8, no.4, December 1984, pp.6-13.

21. Russell Means, 'Indictment on Industrial Society', presentation on behalf of the International Indian Treaty Council to the International NGO Conference on Indigenous Peoples and the Land, Geneva, 15-18 September 1981.

22. Cited in Alison Field, 'The Indigenous Peoples' Network', *Cultural Survival Quarterly*, vol.8, no.4, December 1984, p.67.

23. Douglas E. Sanders, *The formation of the World Council of Indigenous Peoples*, IWGIA Document no.29, 1977.

24. Cited in *IWGIA Newsletter*, no.40, December 1984, which contains a summary of the Fourth Assembly.

25. *Resolutions of the First Congress of Indian Movements of South America*, Ollantaytambo, Cuzco, Peru, 27 February to 3 March 1980, published by the Documentation Centre for Indigenous Peoples (DOCIP), Switzerland.

26. Roxanne Dunbar Ortiz, *Indians of the Americas* (Zed Press, London, 1984) pp.27-70 summarizes development of indigenous groups in the Americas.

27. *International NGO Conference on Discrimination against Indigenous Peoples in the Americas*, 20-23 September 1977, Geneva, Switzerland organized by the Sub-Committee on Racism of the Special NGO Committee on Human Rights.

28. The full reports of the Russell Tribunal are available from the Workgroup for Indigenous Peoples, Postbus 4098, 1009 Amsterdam, the Netherlands.

29. *International NGO Conference on Indigenous Peoples and the Land*, 15-18 September 1981, Geneva, Switzerland, organized by Special NGO Committee on Human Rights.

6. Indians in the Backyard: Central America and Mexico

In the centre of Mexico City stands one of the world's greatest anthropological museums. In its cool, airy splendour it houses room after room of artefacts which testify to the rich culture of the Indian peoples whose civilizations flourished in the centuries preceding the Spanish invasion. Throughout Mexico City and its environs there are many reminders of that pre-hispanic history, from the hugely-scaled temples and public buildings of Teotihuacan to the various mural paintings of Orozco and Diego Rivera commissioned after the Mexican Revolution. Mexicans are ostentatiously proud of that history.

In Mexico, Indians have achieved important political and commercial positions, including the presidency of the republic; a revolution has been fought in the name of Indian liberty; agrarian reforms have restored massive tracts of land to the Indians from whom they had been stolen during the previous four centuries; substantial public funds are available to safeguard Indian culture, languages and arts. Yet the present situation of the Indian reflects nothing of his glorious past nor his recent gains. He remains unquestionably at the bottom of the social ladder. 'Local political chiefs, landowners and the civil and military authorities of the region', testified a delegate from the state of Hidalgo, Mexico to the Fourth Russell Tribunal in 1980, 'keep the Indian population in a state of submission and almost colonial oppression.'[1]

The paradox is not unique to Mexico. Other countries with an indigenous population in Central and South America selectively revere their Indians' history and culture while relegating them to second-class citizen status. Such an ambivalent attitude may stem from the centuries of miscegenation. The majority population of Central America generally is *mestizo*, a mixture of Spanish and Indian. Little importation of slaves took place and the black percentage of the total population is correspondingly small. The majority *mestizo* population has identified itself with the dominant Spanish culture and demeaned its Indian lineage. Consequently the clearly identifiable Indian has been the victim of a process of internal colonialism, put upon by the *mestizo*, as this latter has been put upon by the white colonizers.

Yet whatever the relations among the various ethnic groups of Central America, divisions between *mestizos* and Indians are often unclear. In this chapter we identify about 13 million Indian peoples, approximately 14 per cent of the total population of the region, but double that figure would be possible and indeed has been suggested by other observers. (The indigenous Carib population of the Caribbean islands was almost entirely destroyed by the invading Europeans and their situation is omitted from the ensuing discussion.) Some of those identified are unmistakably indigenous because they continue to speak an Indian language or by virtue of their distinctive customs or their relatively isolated existence. But many other groups have lost most of the outward appearances of being Indian. They have been more or less assimilated and live side by side with non-Indian peasants who share with them the same poverty and hardships.

Generally throughout Latin America the prevailing land-holding system has created in the agricultural sector vast contrasts between the minority of owners of great estates, *latifundistas*, and the majority of peasants with subsistence plots of land, *minifundistas*. Despite attempts at agrarian reform in the 1960s land concentration has continued unabated and the land available to the poor has shrunk. As the average size of the subsistence plots has diminished, more and more peasants are becoming landless and, therefore, dependent upon the irregular, near starvation wages available on the large plantations.

The commercialization of agriculture resulting from improved marketing arrangements and technical inputs has brought about a growth of production of cash crops. Landowners have always favoured crops for export because they produce greater profits than food for the domestic market. The massive debts incurred by all the Latin American nations have served only to strengthen the exporting sector. There has been a consequent decline in the production of staple foods and a rise in their costs.

The unavailability of land and the difficulties of acquiring food in the countryside have exacerbated the crisis for all the rural population, indigenous and non-indigenous. But all efforts at the redistribution of land have met with fierce and violent opposition from the landowners, who are closely linked to local and national power structures. Peaceful efforts to achieve minimum wages through union action, and protect communal land and small holdings by legal means have been unsuccessful. More often than not such protests have been ruthlessly scotched by the police or the army. It is in this general context of hostility that the struggle by indigenous people for land and justice is currently taking place in Central and South America.

In El Salvador, parts of Mexico or Honduras where villages and *ejido* or communal land are shared by Indian and non-Indian alike, it is the mutual experience of deprivation and oppression that has bound them together in recent years. Although the problems faced by indigenous peoples in Central America are specific and different in many instances from those faced by rural peasants, the present wider struggle for social justice taking place in the region is providing a unifying focus for all poor peoples.

Table 6.1
Indians in Central America

Country	Numbers	% of total pop.
Belize	15,000	10
Costa Rica	20,000	1
El Salvador	960,000	21
Guatemala	3.6 million	50
Honduras	250,000	7
Mexico	8 million	11
Nicaragua	135,000	5
Panama	100,000	6
Total	*13 million*	*14*

Mexico

There are some eight million Indian peoples in Mexico, approximately ten per cent of the total population of the country. Although it should be remembered that since all statistics related to indigenous peoples are highly subjective they are also variable. The National Alliance of Associations of Bilingual Indian Professionals (ANPIBAC), for example, estimates that there are ten million Indians and 56 languages. They calculate that there are many millions who no longer speak an Indian language but who continue to live socially and culturally according to indigenous customs.[2] Indeed one writer has argued that since the entire population has Indian roots at least 16 million Mexicans can be counted as indigenous.[3]

Within Mexico's boundaries there are more than 100 ethnic groups. In the south of Mexico a number of different Mayan languages are spoken; in the states of Oaxaco, Hidalgo and Puebla one of the tonal Oto-Mangue language family is used by the indigenous population; in central and generally throughout Mexico the language of the Aztec empire, Nahuatl, predominates. There are entire states in central and southern Mexico where the Indian-speaking peoples exceed three-quarters of the population.[4] Furthermore, there are several peoples, the Yaqui and the Maya for example, who extend beyond Mexico's frontiers into the United States or Guatemala.

Landholdings in Mexico are of two kinds, private and communal. The latter type, the *ejido*, has its antecedents in the communal organization of land of Indian society before the conquest. Since the revolution of 1910 something in the region of one-quarter of Mexican territory has been restored to communal ownership.[5] However, despite this far-reaching agrarian reform former landowners or their heirs retained the best land and often control of water while poor-quality, unirrigated land was returned to the public domain. Indian communities and non-Indian peasants have been left with access to land which inadequately satisfies their basic subsistence needs. Many have, therefore, been forced to join the growing numbers of landless rural workers and become dependent on the large plantation estates. The resulting inequalities have been a cause of serious conflicts between landowners and the increasingly militant peasant organizations.

In 1982 in the state of Chiapas, for example, landowners with large estates producing coffee forcibly appropriated land held by Indian *ejidatarios*. Such acts are relatively common in Mexico where landowners are often the local political chiefs and can, therefore, use the judiciary and the police to support their claims. The procedure for legal action against the landowners is complex and expensive and most poor peasants and Indians are deterred from going to court in order to obtain their rights. In Chiapas, however, landowners were also paying below the legal minimum wage to the indigenous and non-indigenous labour force working on the coffee plantations. They had refused to register the union locally and had threatened and beaten union organizers and peasant leaders. In this instance the landowners had misjudged the mood of the local rural population. Instead of cowed passivity the union fought back and organized demonstrations and strikes.[6] This case is typical of confrontations taking place in the countryside between large estate owners and poor peasants. For the Indian peoples of Mexico the right to land and equal justice have always been two important concerns.[7] However, on these issues the Indian peoples of Mexico are united with poor non-Indian labourers in the countryside. The exploitation of their labour and the continuous appropriation of their land are central issues for all the rural poor.

In addition to these concerns which bring together Indian and non-Indian, there have developed a set of specific demands by indigenous organizations. The indigenous movement has criticized the paternalism of the state towards Indians as well as the national educational policy which it argues is eroding Indian languages and culture. The official body concerned with indigenous peoples, the National Indigenist Institute (INI), has been accused of making little contribution to the defence of Indian interests and even, in certain cases, in helping in the sequestration of Indian land.[8] Indian teachers have complained that there is little opportunity for them to participate in the national education system and hold executive or managerial posts.[9] In 1975 the National Council of Indigenous Peoples (CNPI), bringing together representatives of the 56 ethnic groups, and two years later the National Alliance of Associations of Bilingual Indigenous Professionals (ANPIBAC) were formed. The new generation of indigenous peoples organizations is highly critical of the *politica indigenista*, a policy made by central government for Indians, and are now seeking political power and the right to determine policy, what they term *politica indigena*.

Nevertheless, the growing consciousness among indigenous peoples in Mexico, while strengthening the indigenous movement generally, has been unable to prevent very serious damage being done to some of the more isolated groups and their land base. The Lacandón, for example, who occupy land in southern Chiapas have lost 13,000 square kilometres of forest since 1967. Traditionally these are Indians practising tropical agro-forestry in much the same way as their Mayan ancestors. Their methods, which include shifting cultivation of corn and vegetables and gathering of forest produce, were successful only while sufficient land was available. However, colonization, timber extraction and deforestation in preparation for cattle-rearing have seriously depleted their land resources and now, less than one-fifth of the community remain in the forest.[10] The tragedy with this commercialization of the forest, as with many such developments in tropical forests, is that the long-term benefits are extremely questionable. As one writer notes:

> Studies of pasture lands cleared from the montane rainforest of eastern Chiapas, where the soils are better than most in the region, demonstrate that the average yearly beef yield is 22 pounds per hectare. By contrast, the traditional swidden cultivation system [see p.12] of the Lacandon Maya, the area's indigenous inhabitants, produces up to 13,000 pounds of shelled corn per hectare per year and an equal amount of root and vegetable crops. Moreover, Lacandones produce these yields for five to seven consecutive years on a single forest plot before they allow the area to regrow for another cycle of food and forest five to ten years later. Even then, rather than abandon a harvested plot Lacandon farmers plant the area with tree crops – citrus, rubber, cacao, avocado, papaya – in a system of traditional agroforestry that both conserves the rainforest biome and enhances its regeneration as a renewable resource.[11]

The same writer concludes: 'Traditional food production systems practised by the rainforest's indigenous inhabitants are, without exception, more productive than the pastures that replace them.'[12] An observation that will be supported many times over in this book. As in other Central American countries, it is development with its apparent advantages that most threatens the traditional lands and subsistence economies of indigenous peoples. Even in a comparatively enlightened country like Costa Rica, the indigenous people are menaced by those who equate their own desires to make money with the national interest.

Costa Rica

Most of Costa Rica's population is white, non-*mestizo* and non-Indian. The indigenous population numbers about 20,000 in six main ethnic groups: the Guatuso, Cabécares, Bribris, Guaymí, Borucas and Térrabas. They make up no more than 0.1 per cent of the total Costa Rican population. A minority of the indigenous communities have retained their language and continue to practise their traditional customs. For the rest, close contact with the European settlers has led to a high degree of assimilation.[13]

Costa Rica unlike many of its Central American neighbours has enjoyed a relatively progressive government since a social-democratic revolution in 1948. However, dispossession of indigenous land has occurred with disconcerting rapidity. In 1960 the Boruca Indians, for example, had a reservation of 32,000 hectares which by 1975 had been reduced by 90 per cent to 3,200

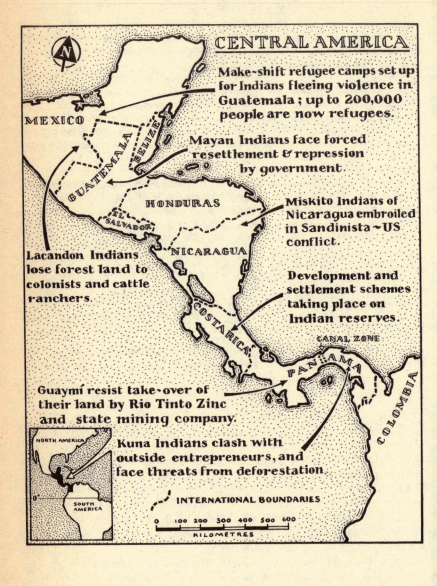

CENTRAL AMERICA

Make~shift refugee camps set up for Indians fleeing violence in Guatemala ; up to 200,000 people are now refugees.

Mayan Indians face forced resettlement & repression by government.

Miskito Indians of Nicaragua embroiled in Sandinista~US conflict.

Development and settlement schemes taking place on Indian reserves.

Lacandon Indians lose forest land to colonists and cattle ranchers.

Guaymí resist take~over of their land by Rio Tinto Zinc and state mining company.

Kuna Indians clash with outside entrepreneurs, and face threats from deforestation.

MEXICO

GUATEMALA

BELIZE

HONDURAS

EL SALVADOR

NICARAGUA

COSTA RICA

CANAL ZONE

PANAMA

COLOMBIA

NORTH AMERICA

SOUTH AMERICA

INTERNATIONAL BOUNDARIES

0 100 200 300 400 500 600
KILOMETRES

hectares. By the government's own admission the Guatuso Indians have lost 99 per cent of their land and 'will be completely wiped out in a few years time'.[14]

After long years of neglect, the Government of Costa Rica introduced pro-Indian legislation in 1973 and 1977. The *Ley Indígena* of 1977 established the rights of the indigenous population to defined reserves. Five areas totalling 100,000 hectares were designated and non-Indian people were forbidden access.[15] This indigenous land is inalienable and the Indian communities have the sole right to its forest and mineral resources.

In practice, however, the law remains inadequately enforced and ineffective. The government frankly admitted this in 1979:

> The life of the indigenous populations of Costa Rica is being seriously threatened by constant and arbitrary plundering of their lands; this phenomenon has increased alarmingly in recent years, even to the point where acts of violence have been committed.[16]

Since 1977 commercial logging, land invasions by non-indigenous settlers and various mining operations have occurred on the reserves. Oil exploration is currently taking place on Talamanca land, a hydro-electric project is planned on the Boruca reserve and with the growth of production of sugar cane and coffee, communal land is being claimed as within the public domain and being planted with cash crops. In 1983 the *Asociación Indígena de Costa Rica* claimed that a North American company had obtained a permit to develop 10,000 hectares of indigenous forest.[17]

The difficulties of guaranteeing indigenous lands against encroachment by non-indigenous settlers and other interests are well-recognized by the government. In a communication to the United Nations it stated that soon

> the above mentioned places of refuge will have ceased to exist altogether. This makes it urgently necessary to draw up and implement plans and programmes with a view to preparing indigenous persons to cope with this situation and to integrate, with as little effort as possible, into Costa Rican society.[18]

The enlightened concern shown by the government of Costa Rica has led it to draw conclusions which are antithetical to the interests of indigenous peoples. Daniel Rojas Maroto, the President of the *Asociación Indígena de Costa Rica*, has explained that it is the whole Western model of development which his people question:

> One of the attacks on our way of life is that of the capitalist system based on private property which tries to transform our system of community and communal production organization. The system of private property is encroaching more and more and almost encircles our areas, but it has not destroyed the Indian community spirit and group consciousness. Collectivism is not only possession of land but encompasses cultural and political questions, self-determination and control of the economy.[19]

Development on the Western model appears an attractive option to governments beset by severe economic problems. The massive scale of investment proferred by multilateral banks and transnational corporations is a great temptation to poorer nations trying to rid themselves of crippling debts and large deficits in balance of payments. It is a dilemma faced at the present time by Panama.

Guaymí versus the multinationals

Panama is a small country of 1.8 million people whose principal source of wealth is its canal. It is highly dependent on imports of food and consumer goods as well as capital equipment and, like other Latin American nations, is heavily indebted to the West. In recent years, therefore, Panama has looked for ways in which to diversify its economy through large-scale development projects.

In 1970 the Government of Panama and the state mining corporation, CODEMIN, granted a concession for exploration and feasibility to a Canadian company at Cerro Colorado, a forested mountain area in the west of the isthmus. The survey concluded that there were one billion tons of copper ore in the mountains which could be commercially exploited by open-pit mining. This made it one of the world's largest known reserves of copper. Ten years later, the London-based Rio Tinto Zinc Corporation took over the project.[20]

The proposed Cerro Colorado project is, however, on Guaymí land. There are approximately 80,000 Guaymí Indians in Panama and they live in the three western provinces up to and extending over the border with neighbouring Costa Rica. They live in dispersed settlements, often beside rivers, and practise swidden agriculture; some supplement their cash needs through work on the coastal plantations.

There has been a gradual encroachment on to traditional Guaymí land by settlers and plantation developers. The Guaymí, like all indigenous peoples, have retreated before these incursions and suffered a corresponding reduction of their swidden land and of course a decline in their standard of living. As the total land area available for slash and burn agriculture becomes smaller, indigenous communities are forced to shorten the fallow periods and reduce productivity. Among the consequences of this erosion of the economic base of the Guaymí has been to make the formerly well-managed subsistence system of agriculture inadequate for the needs of the community. There has been emigration from the indigenous area, increasing numbers of conflicts over land and serious deterioration in health and nutrition of the Indian population.[21]

The Cerro Colorado mining project is now an added threat to the future of these people. An estimated 330 square kilometres of land will be lost to the mine, 720 square kilometres have been designated as a concession for further exploration, various installations, like construction camps, will require land, and access roads will cut a swathe 100 metres wide and require up to 630 hectares.[22]

In addition to the loss of land, there will be a forcible relocation of a great number of indigenous communities. Five communities live directly within the mining area, seven are located on the site for the construction camp and three others will be flooded when a reservoir is built; the road from the port to the mine will pass through twelve Guaymí communities. All in all as many as 10,000 people, one-eighth of the Guaymí, will be affected by the project.

Fears have also arisen about the potential pollution likely to be caused by the Cerro Colorado project. During the construction period the main river systems will be silted and subsequently mine run-off will further pollute them. The dam and reservoir will alter the distribution of water and further affect farming and water requirements of the Guaymí communities.

The Guaymí have not been in favour of the project. If there are jobs created, they argue, they will certainly benefit the better-qualified non-indigenous Panamanians and not the Indian peoples. The influx of outsiders is expected to bring prostitution, gambling and crime into the region. Relocation will lead to the destruction of the community and many elders cannot be compensated with money or other land since their ties are with the village of their birth and the surrounding countryside. Besides which there is little suitable alternative land available for these Guaymí.[23]

The Guaymí have demanded a cessation of the project and a legal title to their traditional land. They are seeking a Guaymí *comarca* or territory and are presently negotiating with the government of Panama for such a guarantee. On the *comarca*, indigenous representatives would replace the national authorities and a Guaymí Congress will be recognized as the highest decision-making body. Disagreement at the present time arises over the rights to mineral resources on Guaymí land.[24] The government maintain that all natural resources should be exploited for the public good, a principle which, while sounding worthy, has been criticized by the Canadian Conference of Catholic Bishops in the following terms:

> Governments and corporations define the indigenous question as simply one of 'integrating' or 'incorporating' native peoples into a development model in which they have little or no say. The results are almost uniformly disastrous. The introduction of a new and dominant industrial economy (with its non-native work force, wage labour and related economic consequences) thoroughly disrupts the indigenous way of life and alienates native peoples from their own systems of economic, political, and social organization.[25]

At the moment the project is under review. Rio Tinto Zinc still retains an option to go ahead, but the government of Panama have made no firm decisions either way. In the meantime the Guaymí have been highly successful in mobilizing national and international protest against the mine, and support for a Guaymí *Comarca*.

The Kuna homelands

East of the canal, in the forested hills and valleys, and along the Caribbean coast from Colon to Colombia, live other indigenous communities. The largest indigenous minority in this area is the Kuna who number nearly 50,000 and are located in the San Blas district and on the small islands that litter the coast. The Kuna unlike the Guaymí enjoy a degree of political autonomy and have their own economic base. After an armed revolt against the Panama Government in the 1920s, an independent territory was established. The *comarca* of San Blas provides a legal guarantee of their right to land.

Both the constitution of the reserve and a subsequent law in 1953 give supreme authority to the Kuna General Council, which represents the 50 or so Kuna communities and meets half-yearly.[26] Land can be rented or sold only after approval has been granted by the council on two successive occasions. In practice, however, outsiders wanting to buy land or build on the *comarca* approach one of the three elected *caciques* or chiefs.

The Kuna continue to retain much of their own culture, including the women's special dress with its *mola*, a colourful tunic. Fine scenery, good swimming and the attractive local costumes have made the San Blas islands a tourist centre. HM Ambassador to Panama in a despatch in 1974 to the Foreign Office drew a sympathetic picture of the Kuna people: 'What could be more attractive than a society which has no word of its own for – and therefore no original conception of – time and money (curiously the imported words they use are English and not Spanish – watchi and moni).' But as the hotels sprang up and roads were constructed, as industries were set up and cash changed hands, he observed: 'Unless the Kuna can perform a miracle unique in our world, of teaching themselves to accommodate to and manage a 20th Century explosion of tourists, industrial development and cash nexus, it seems impossible that they will not be obliterated.'[27]

Since that time there have been a series of clashes between the indigenous communities and outside entrepreneurs. A number of tourist developments have proceeded but without permission from the General Congress. Where these developments have offended local customs, the Kuna communities affected have demonstrated and even burned down hotels in protest.

In a recent case, one North American tourist developer rented an entire island in perpetuity for US$ 200 a year from its Kuna owner. Although he had received permission from the *caciques*, the congress did not ratify the decision and asked him to withdraw. As the hotelier ignored repeated requests, dissatisfaction increased. Finally in 1981 a group of young Kuna Indians attacked the resort and wounded its North American owner. Further clashes took place between local villagers outraged by the attack on the American and some Kuna national guardsmen were sent in to restore order. Two of the guardsmen were killed in the riots and the Panama Government intervened and closed the resort.[28]

While the Kuna have a strong sense of identity and have achieved substantial legal guarantees from the government, some of the dispersed forest Indians of eastern Panama are more vulnerable. The southward path of the Pan-American highway presently being built through the Darien Gap with accompanying settlement and timber exploitation poses various threats to the 10,000 or so Chocoe and other nomadic peoples. Some 500 square kilometres of tropical forest a year are being cleared for pasture and with sad inexorability the homeland of Panama's forest-dwelling Indians is being torn open.

The Kuna people responded quickly by creating a 620-square-kilometre conservation area and now patrol their *comarca* in order to prevent encroachment on to their forest land. The Panama Government has created the Darien National Park so that some of the tropical forest will be protected from commercial exploitation. Such conservation measures include the designation of 'active cultural zones' for the indigenous groups of the forest. It remains to be seen whether the legally protected national park will be a sufficient defence against the rapacious interests of the businessman.

El Salvador, Honduras and Belize

No country in the Central American region has remained outside the present conflict centred on El Salvador and Guatemala. Refugees from both countries spill into neighbouring Mexico, Belize and Honduras as well as Costa Rica and Panama to escape the violence of civil war. Further to the south a new focus of confrontation has developed on the frontier between Nicaragua and Honduras. Since the Sandinista Front, in 1979, overthrew the Somoza family, one of Latin America's most repressive dynasties, counter-revolutionary forces have gathered in Honduras. Supported by the United States these have made frequent incursions into Nicaraguan territory to undermine the economy and destabilize the government.

For the United States the whole region is considered their backyard.[29] For most of this century they have exerted influence on Central American political life and intervened whenever it has been felt that forces antagonistic to its interests were growing too strong. In associating itself with entrenched dictatorships, the United States has shown itself hostile to all movements for social justice in Central America, interpreting trade unions, church, peasant and other popular organizations as subversive, Communist and threatening. The indigenous peoples of the region have consequently been caught up in a wider ideological and political struggle. They have been identified by the minority governments of Central America and the United States as the enemies in the backyard.

The indigenous peoples of Nicaragua have become the particular victims of the confrontationist politics of the region. The largest group, the Miskitos, are located in the north-east of Nicaragua and the south-east of Honduras. Some have been recruited by the counter-revolutionary forces after becoming disillusioned with the Sandinistas; other Miskito peoples have aligned themselves with the Nicaraguan Government. The experiences of socialist governments in developing a policy for their indigenous peoples are discussed more fully in chapter 11. The future of the Miskitos and other Indian peoples of Nicaragua will depend greatly upon the Sandinistas and their ability to defend their revolution and accept the multi-ethnic composition of the country.

Any estimate of the numerical strength of the indigenous population of El Salvador is bound to reflect the opinions of expert observers rather than the national census. As far as the national government of El Salvador is concerned there is virtually no Indian population while in the view of most experts at least 20 per cent or nearly one million people are Indian.[30]

While there are a few indigenous communities, like the Pipiles, which have retained some degree of cultural integrity, the majority of El Salvador's indigenous minority has been assimilated. Most of the Mayan Nahuatl communities lost their communal land and became landless labourers with the commercialization of coffee in the 19th Century. In 1881 and 1882 laws permitting expropriation of *tierras communales* or *ejidos* and their auction were passed. El Salvador, with its high population density, provided no other regions into which the Indians could retreat.

Then in 1932 following the collapse of the coffee market and the world depression, an uprising led by the Communist Augustin Farabundo Martí and others resulted in the occupation of several towns in El Salvador's coffee-growing zone. The authorities acted quickly and ruthlessly. During 1932, 30,000 Indians and peasants were killed by government troops. Just as in Guatemala today, the Indians in El Salvador were identified as subversives and Communists. They therefore faced the most violent repression. Traditional clothing was abandoned and the use of Indian languages was suppressed. These economic and political factors have de-Indianized the indigenous peoples of El Salvador. Those still speaking Nahuatl conceal the fact from the authorities for fear of being labelled Communists.[31]

But the present civil war in El Salvador has been provoked by many of the same injustices that existed more than 50 years ago. In the 1932 revolt Indians sought to maintain their communal land for subsistence crops and resist the encroaching coffee plantations. Today's war is being fought on much the same platform: a radical agrarian reform. Many identifiable Indian groups, like the Pipiles and Lencas, as well as those communities which retain the less obvious outward expressions of indigenous culture, actively support the Democratic Revolutionary Front (FDR).

Less than ten per cent of the total population of Honduras is estimated as Indian. Out of a population of nearly four million some 250,000 to 300,000 are Indian. A number of communities have remained relatively isolated, like the Chortis and Pipiles who live in the north-west of the country along the border with Guatemala and El Salvador, while the Lencas located in the south of the country are more or less acculturated. They may own communal land along the lines of the Mexican *ejido* system but if they do so they are often indistinguishable from *mestizo* peasants who have equal land rights. At the turn of the century some of the forest Indians in the east of the country received special treatment including freedom from tax and military service. Along the Atlantic coast up to and beyond the frontier with Nicaragua live Miskito communities numbering some 45,000, and a number of Sumu people.

The history of Honduras resembles that of its neighbours. In pre-hispanic times many of the peoples of the region shared a culture that was essentially

Mayan in origin; while generally Middle America was subjected to the domination of the expansionist Aztec state. The Spanish conquerors made no immediate political boundaries in the region, being content with extracting gold and silver from the main mining areas of Mexico and making expeditions throughout Central America for slaves to work the mines.

As Spain lost its grip on the Americas, the Federation of Central American Republics declared its independence in 1821. Within two decades the federation had split into separate republics and Honduras became independent in 1838. As frontiers became established and political differences grew, the indigenous population found their traditional lands straddling borders. The Miskito live in Nicaragua and Honduras, the Guaymí in Costa Rica and Panama, Mayan peoples live throughout Belize, Guatemala, southern Mexico and El Salvador.

Honduras is the archetypal banana republic. In the early part of this century this small country produced 25 per cent of the world's bananas and half of its cultivable land was owned by the North American giant, United Fruit (now United Brands). The company owned the ports, railways and ships and whenever political instability threatened the lucrative banana trade, the United States marines were deployed to intervene. (The marines invaded three times, in 1911, 1913 and 1924.) In common with other Latin American countries, Honduras experienced a wave of nationalism and reformism in the 1960s. This was followed by 18 years of military rule and it was only in 1981 that a civilian government once again took power in the country. The Sandinista revolution in neighbouring Nicaragua, however, has placed Honduras and part of its Indian population in the centre of the world stage.

Since the 1979 revolution Honduras has become the target in United States strategy for control of the region. The country is situated next door to Guatemala and El Salvador where highly developed guerrilla movements are based, and to the north of Nicaragua, whose liberation struggle was successful. In the last three years North American involvement in Honduras has grown. They now have an extensive military infrastructure and about 1,500 advisers there. In 1983, US troops undertook a massive and elaborate joint services exercise (Big Pine) along the coast with Nicaragua. In 1984 Michael Klare, the defence specialist, stated that: 'the US stands poised at the brink of the abyss of full-fledged intervention in Central America . . .'[32] Since then their involvement has grown. In their efforts to destabilize the present regime in Nicaragua, the United States Central Intelligence Agency have made use of the Miskito Indians living in Honduras. Many Miskito have been armed by the United States and have been recruited into the anti-Sandinista forces which are penetrating the north-eastern frontier of Nicaragua.

There are numerous Mayan communities in Belize. In the north, Yucatan Mayans work mainly on the sugar plantations and in timber extraction. In the south-west live Mopan Mayans, some of whom are relatively recent settlers, having fled the highlands of Guatemala in the 19th Century to escape oppression and poverty. In total some 16 per cent of Belize's population, that is some 30,000, are Indians.

The colonial government of Belize, formerly British Honduras, made grants of land and permitted local autonomy for the indigenous minority. In the 1950s an independence movement in the colony led to the granting of autonomy in 1964. Finally, on 21 September 1981, Belize was given full independence.

Today, in the opinion of the main Indian organization of the country, the Toledo Indian Movement of Belize, the indigenous minority faces discrimination and an erosion of reserve lands. Individual Indians have been persuaded to apply for private land title and this has strengthened the government's own policy aimed at eventual eradication of the reservations.[33]

But the Indian population faces perhaps a more serious danger: that of being drawn into the widening conflict taking place in Central America. Successive governments in Guatemala have laid claim to the territory and, sporadically, Britain is involved in negotiations concerning its ex-colony. On the whole Guatemala makes no secret of its desire to incorporate eventually the whole of Belize.

Early in 1983 Belize, Britain and Guatemala discussed a compromise that would have handed over one-sixth of the country, the province of Toledo, to the claimant. Since the majority of Belize's Indian population is located in the province, they would have found themselves under the jurisdiction of a government which brands all Indians subversive and is pursuing a policy denounced by many observers as genocidal.

By December 1983, however, the then President of Guatemala, General Mejia Victores, was urging Britain to keep its troops in Belize to defend the country's south-western border and provide a bulwark against the guerrillas.[34] One of Guatemala's three guerrilla armies is active in the region and might expect to find support among the Mayan peoples living in Belize. Britain and Guatemala discussed on the occasion the possibility of joint border patrols. President Reagan for his part has for some time been seeking to station United States troops in Belize.

Genocide and resistance in Guatemala

In the last few years no issue has concerned indigenous peoples more than the situation of genocide being endured by Mayan Indians in Guatemala. Guatemala is one of the few countries in the world where the indigenous population is in a majority. However, their standard of living, conditions of work and present political persecution are unparalleled anywhere; their suffering at the hands of successive military governments has brought unanimous condemnation from indigenous peoples from around the world.

Guatemala: Statement to the UN Working Group on Indigenous Populations by Francisca Alavarez, Guatemala: August 1983, Geneva

For some time, there have been denunciations against the systematic form and continuation of the violation of human rights against the Guatemalan populations, and against the indigenous population in particular. This situation is without doubt one of the most serious in all America, in which the Indians have been victims of massacres, torture, detention on a massive scale, had our homes and crops burned, our harvest destroyed, all of this aggravating the situation of violations of human rights that exist in Guatemala on a permanent basis, these extreme events being the result of a policy of genocide and ethnocide by the governmental regimes of our country, including past governments as well as the present one.

During the past year and a half, this policy has been carried out in a particularly cruel and brutal manner. Indigenous brothers and sisters have been found dead with their bodies horribly tortured, whole communities have been burned, women have been raped repeatedly by dozens of soldiers until they die. Especially targeted are pregnant women, and there have been reports of cases where government soldiers have eaten the liver of victims in front of the village, this being charged recently by Nobel Prize recipient, Adolfo Perez Esquivel. Other such testimony also exists. The tens of thousands of refugees in Mexico are testimony of these atrocities. In the present period, the Guatemalan government policy of genocide and ethnocide against the Indian peoples is in effect for three main reasons:

1. The Guatemalan military defends the interests of the small wealthy minority against the huge Indian and poor Ladino populations, who are forced to live in misery and as victims of exploitation, discrimination, oppression and repression. Indians are not considered to be human beings with basic rights. In response to the situation, the Indians, together with the rest of the people of the country, except for the small ruling minority, have organized on a massive scale to struggle for our rights. For this reason, the government considers us to be enemies, and each Indian is considered a real or potential subversive.

2. In Guatemala the Indians are the mass of the people, and with the Ladinos, have begun a process of social change on a massive scale, and for this reason we are objects of systematic campaigns of extermination.

3. The military seeks to destroy and shatter our cultural identity as Indians because the regime knows that our identity constitutes a part of our strength to resist and organize. The government knows that the land is sacred to us, so attempts to displace us from the land, and force us away from sacred sites preserved by our ancestors and by us today. They attack our communities and destroy our corn, which is our food supply and destroy our Indian clothing and all items that are Indian and reflect our identity. They systematically assassinate our elders who are the fountains of our oral tradition and for us are like books, libraries and universities are to the West. In this way, they are destroying our knowledge and our tradition, a repeat of what the Spanish invaders attempted 450 years ago. Worst of all, they kill our children in whom

lies the continuation of our culture. Our culture and our identity have permitted our survival over centuries of exploitation, oppression, discrimination and repression, and none of that has been able to take away our existence as Indians. For this reason we seek to destroy this regime which seeks to exterminate us.

Due to this conscious programme of the Guatemalan government to annihilate the Indian population of the country a number of aspects of human rights violations against the Indian people of Guatemala may be identified:

1. Violation of the right to life: not only are the Indians persecuted and massacred systematically, but also our people are forced into 'civil patrols' under the threat of death, and in that capacity are obliged to control and persecute our own indigenous brothers and sisters and non-Indian poor people.

2. Violations of economic rights: the government attempts to force submission of the people by destroying all food supplies and causing mass starvation, as well as preventing Indians from migrating to the coast to work for salaries.

3. Violation of cultural rights: the government campaign has created a rupture in all our traditions, particularly in relation to the land, and clearly we are persecuted for the simple fact of being Indian. Specific cultural targets are consciously hit by the military including our traditional elders.

4. Violation of religious rights: both Christian and traditional religious sites are systematically desecrated by the military, who use churches and sacred sites as latrines. Religious leaders, both Christian and traditional have been assassinated. The Bible is considered subversive.

5. Practices of forced labour: the Indian people have been forced, under the threat of death to join the 'civil patrols' which take them away from work. Also, the people have been forced to participate in programmes such as the one called 'a roof, a tortilla and work' which forces the Indians to do public work for the use of the military such as road building, and without receiving salaries or sufficient food to survive.

6. Practices of forced reconcentration and relocation of the population: Indians are forced to abandon their place of origin and relocate to distant 'model villages' (strategic hamlets as in the Vietnam war). These are actually concentration camps since they are enclosed and controlled totally by the military and the people may not come and go.

7. Denial of all political rights: The Indians are excluded by the army from taking on political responsibilities both at the national as well as the regional and local levels. Always before Indians have elected their own Mayors and leaders, and had our own organizations. These are now prohibited. Though the regime of Rios Montt named 10 Indians to the 'Council of State' with much fanfare of propaganda, these persons are not known to the Indian people, and they have been publicly denounced.

In conclusion, we Indians of Guatemala ask the following of the international community:

– That the Guatemalan regime (headed by whatever current military personage) be condemned for war crimes and genocide in the light of the continual and systematic violations of human rights of the people of Guatemala in general and

the indigenous majority in particular;
– That all governments in the world cease providing military assistance and sales to the Guatemalan regime and that commerce and travel cease;
– That all economic and financial assistance to this genocidal regime which could be used as a part of the military campaign of genocide cease;
– That it be recognized there exists in Guatemala a civil war, and that the full force of international law for the protection of civilian subjects and population be applied;
– That support be forthcoming for the terrible situation of thousands and thousands of Indians who are presently displaced within Guatemala (more than a million) and that humanitarian assistance be provided for them;
– That humanitarian assistance within Guatemala be provided by non-governmental organisms, such as the International Committee of the Red Cross and the Episcopal Conference of Guatemala without the interference or supervision of the Guatemalan military which uses such resources to control the population.

As in other countries subjected to Spanish colonization, the indigenous peoples of Guatemala had much of their land expropriated. The best agricultural land became concentrated in few hands and many Mayan Indians became tied labourers on large estates. Towards the end of the 19th Century the growth of demand for commodities drew Guatemala into the international market. In a short time Guatemala and its neighbour, El Salvador, became major coffee producers. While benefiting the *ladino* (non-Indian) élites enormously, the rise of the coffee plantation brought a new phase of dispossession of indigenous lands and a serious deterioration in the labour and living conditions of the Mayan Indians. Coffee exports increased eight-fold between 1870 and 1915 while in the same period one million hectares of public lands were sold or distributed to landowners, immigrants or merchants. Large areas of land traditionally occupied by Indians thereby fell into the hands of the *ladino* minority.[35]

Growth in coffee cultivation increased the demand for full-time and seasonal labour and, just as Indian land had been forcibly expropriated, so Indian labour was coerced into working for little or no recompense on the new plantations. On the eve of the great coffee boom, President Barrios declared the policy of his government towards the Indian population:

If we abandon planters to their own resources and do not give them strong and energetic support they will be unable to make any progress, for all of their efforts will be doomed to failure due to the deceit of the Indians. You should therefore, see to it: first, that the Indian villages in your jurisdiction *be forced* to give that number of hands to the planters that they ask for, even to the number of fifty and a hundred to a single planter if his enterprise warrants this number. Second, when one set of Indians has not been able to finish the work at hand in a period of two weeks, a second set should be sent to relieve the first so that the work may not be delayed. Third, that the two weeks' work shall be paid in advance by the mayor of the Indian town, thus avoiding the loss of time involved in paying every day. Fourth, above all else see to it that any Indian who seeks to avoid this duty be punished to the full extent of the law; that the planters be fully protected and that each Indian be forced to do a full day's work while in service.[36]

A series of laws to control Indian labour was passed and remained in effect until 1944. In 1877 the *Reglamento de Jornaleros* (Ruling for Labourers) obliged all rural workers to carry workbooks in which were recorded any debts incurred while working on the estates. Since labourers were forced by local political chiefs or by poverty to work the plantations and since landowners invariably ensured that their contracted workers fell into debt, the law created a legal framework for debt-peonage.[37] In 1884 a set of vagrancy laws compelled unemployed Indians to work 40 days a year on government projects and in 1934 and 1935, amendments to the law redefined vagrants as those who were not cultivating three hectares of corn in the highlands, thereby making eligible still greater numbers of Indians. Those without land or with too little were obliged by law to work on the plantations for between 100 and 150 days per year. Those who did not complete the required number of days could be imprisoned or forced to labour on the roads. Many thousands of highland Indians were by this means forced to work for the owners of the great estates. One observer in 1918 noted:

> The development of the peonage system has deprived them [Indians] of even the small measure of economic and political liberty which they once enjoyed, and by taking them away from their homes has almost entirely destroyed their old community life . . . Many of the Indian villages which once enjoyed a sort of independence from their white neighbours are now completely at the mercy of brutal local officials who are not content to exact money from the people under them by every conceivable pretext, but even make a regular practice of virtually selling into slavery those who are entrusted to their government.[38]

In 1944 the dictatorship of Ubico which had endured since 1931 was overthrown, and some of the feudal practices were dismantled. A new labour code and an agrarian reform programme were introduced. This progressive legislation also heralded a period of rapid organization of rural unions. For the Indians of Guatemala the brief period of progressive government brought certain benefits. The National Indian Institute was established, support was given to the traditional crafts, such as textiles, and education and health care promoted in Indian areas. However, the liberalization was short-lived. In 1954 a CIA-backed coup over threw the President, Jacobo Arbenz, and there followed until December 1985, 30 years of uninterrupted dictatorship.[39] Rural unions were made illegal, and repression – including the use of paramilitary death squads – has reversed any ameliorations achieved under Arbenz.

Today the rural population remains predominantly indigenous and is concentrated in the high plateau in the west of the country. The Indians of this area live on small plots of land now totally inadequate for their needs and are compelled by poverty rather than by coercive legislation to work on the plantations as seasonal labour. About 650,000 highland Indians make the annual migration to the coastal plantations.[40] There they live in appalling conditions, sleeping in open barns without facilities of any kind. The working conditions of these seasonal labourers has been described by one non-governmental organization as slavery-like. Their report for 1978 stated that:

> Many migrant workers did not undertake work voluntarily on the plantations, but were deliberately tricked into debts by contractors acting as moneylenders. Migrant workers who had originally undertaken seasonal labour in order to cancel debts, were often cajoled into further debts on the plantations themselves. The landowners in breach of the law might often maintain bars, gaming centres and brothels.[41]

In the aftermath of the 1976 earthquake which rendered one million people, nearly one-fifth of the population, homeless, many Indians returned to their homes to reconstruct. The resulting labour shortages led to contractors using force and threats to sign on workers for the plantations. Non-compliant labourers were denounced as subversives to the armed forces and community projects to increase domestic food production were suppressed to further drive them into the hands of the contractors.[42] In the last few years the climate of violence in the countryside has discouraged many Guatemalan Indians from travelling to work on plantations, but the estate-owners have found other sources from which to make up the shortfall, since the civil war in neighbouring El Salvador has caused many peasants to flee to Guatemala and seek the comparative calm of the plantation.

The dispossession of Indian land, a process that has been taking place since colonization, first forced the Mayan peoples to give up the more productive lowlands and cultivate the poorer soils of the highlands. Subsequently, with the growth of plantations, further incursions were made by private landowners on to communal Indian land, while the government ensured labour by coercive legislation. Later, labour contractors and the hostile government policy towards cooperatives, with their improved yields of staple foods, have further curtailed the freedom of indigenous labour and reduced the economic base of the Indian communities.

Such attacks on the Indian economy have been accompanied by persistent efforts by the ruling groups to undermine indigenous culture and sense of identity. Attempts to withdraw from contact with *ladino* society and preserve the independence of indigenous communities have been met by policies of forced assimilation. President Lisandro Barillas (1885-92) legislated against communal landholdings by recognizing only private title to land. Indians were conscripted into the national army and educated to despise their own people and culture. In today's atmosphere of violence and brutality, Indian recruits have been turned into an instrument of repression against their own people. One Indian recruit testified as follows:

> Each day they told us the same thing: a soldier should defend his country. The training was to beat us until we were bleeding This practice could reach a point when one of our own comrades was killed. One particular lieutenant Morales despised Indians and our customs. He taught us to change our families with the machine-gun and turn our girl friends into prostitutes. He taught us how to rape

women. When he asked, we would get women for him and when he had finished raping them he would hand them over to the other soldiers. In this way I went from being a soldier to the rank of sergeant.

They promoted me because I had guts enough to beat my own comrades and could stomach anything.

By such methods the Guatemalan army is able to convert thousands of Indian peasants into instruments of terror ready to carry out any kind of atrocity, completely disconnected from their people and families: literally an army of psychopaths, an army of dehumanized zombies.[43]

During the brief dictatorship of President Rios Montt, from 1982 to 1983, there was a concerted policy of repression of indigenous culture. Soldiers were instructed to destroy traditional clothing, especially the *huipiles*, and the hand-looms of the Indians; religious festivals were forbidden; the use of the various Indian languages was aggressively discouraged. Most importantly the army killed domestic animals and burned fields of maize, a crop that is not merely the staple food but also the basis of Mayan traditional beliefs.

Much of the state of violence directed by the governments of Rios Montt and his predecessor, Romeo Lucas García, against the Indian population has taken place against a background of popular resistance. Many Indians have joined with members of the non-Indian rural poor first in non-violent and now in armed struggle against the dictatorships. During the 1970s Indians began to play a greater role in the political opposition and in the 1974 election two were elected to the Guatemalan Congress. Four years later in 1978 the Committee for Peasant Unity (CUC) was formed which brought together *ladino* farm-workers and highland Indians for the first time. In 1980 over 100,000 plantation-workers, Indian and non-Indian, successfully came out on strike and brought about a near trebling of the wage rate.

The mobilization of Indians during the 1970s was to some extent assisted by the more progressive role of the church. The leadership of the Catholic Church in Guatemala had mounted an anti-government and anti-Communist campaign during the ten years of progressive rule from 1944 to 1954. Following the overthrow of Arbenz, however, there was a flurry of missionary activity among the Indians of the highlands to reassert orthodox values. The Catholics launched a lay catechist movement, *Acción Católica* (Catholic Action), and a number of Protestant churches also recruited substantial numbers of Indians as adherents.[44] The effects of these evangelizing activities were eventually in conflict with the original intentions of the church leaders. In daily contact with the social reality of Indians – their poverty, working conditions and the violence perpetrated by landowners, their agents, the police and the army – clergy became radicalized. In 1967 a group of missionaries from the United States was expelled.[45]

Since the late 1970s, the persecution of Indian lay-catechists and church personnel has proceeded unabated. During 1980-81 ten priests were murdered by the security forces and 64 nuns left the country after the death of a colleague and threats to their own lives. 'It was not until the late 1960s that the church began to shift its loyalties. And it was not until Lucas García came to power in

1978, that the Catholic Church was considered an enemy of the state,' writes Melville, one of the North American priests expelled in 1967.[46]

By the mid-1970s a number of guerrilla movements had become active: the *Ejército Guerrillero de los Pueblos* (EGP), the *Organización del Pueblo en Armas* (ORPA) and the *Fuerzas Armadas Rebeldes* (FAR). The EGP was particularly involved in defending Indian interests and mobilizing their communities and was successful in recruiting young Mayan Indians to its ranks. Support for the guerrilla armies from among highland Indians increased after 1976 when there was a marked escalation of violence by government forces in the countryside.

The killing of individual village leaders was followed by wholesale massacres of entire communities. On 29 May 1978 100 Kekchi Indians were murdered and a further 300 wounded in Panzos, Alta Verapaz. They were fired upon while in the town's main square where they were protesting to the mayor at attempts by local large landowners to evict them from their land, which they had lived on and worked for generations but for which they had no legal title. Both the President, Romeo García Lucas, and the Defence Minister owned large properties in the area.[47] The massacre, which occurred without provocation, became a symbol for the Indian peoples of Guatemala. It was perceived as an act of genocide and served to strengthen their resolve. Many began actively to support the guerrilla struggle and the Indian community became the real power base of the armed movement against the Guatemalan dictatorship.

In January 1980 a group of peasants from El Quiché province occupied the Spanish embassy in Guatemala City. They denounced· repression and disappearances but their protest was short-lived. On 31 January, the embassy was attacked and burned to the ground causing 30 deaths, including Spanish diplomats.

In March 1982, José Efrain Rios Montt seized power. A born-again Christian of the California-based Gospel Outreach Church, Montt launched a crusade against the Indian population all of whom he characterized as subversive. Over 10,000 troops were stationed in the main Indian departments of the highlands with orders to wipe out all bases of guerrilla support. A succession of massacres of Indian communities were perpetrated. On 20 July 1982 at Finca San Francisco in the department of Huehuetenango 302 Chuj Indians were killed – including women, children and elderly people – and only some 20 men from the community escaped because they were working in the fields at the time.[48] The massacre at San Francisco, however, was only one of a series whose main objective was to destroy any sources of supply to the guerrillas.[49] Amnesty International estimated that over 2,000 Indians and peasants had been killed by the armed forces in the first six months of Montt's government. The United States' human rights organization Americas Watch was less conservative and put the figure at nearer 10,000.[50]

Rios Montt attempted to destroy the indigenous communities of the highlands, not only with the use of genocidal attacks but also through a programme of forcible assimilation. The Montt government introduced into Guatemala the idea of model villages. Model villages or strategic hamlets were pioneered by the United States Government during the Vietnam war and their purpose was to remove physically an entire community from its traditional homeland, where it could act as a source of supply to the enemy, and place it in a rigorously controlled camp. Montt's objective was the same. He recruited Indian labourers for the construction work. These were paid well below the legal minimum wage or, in some cases, in exchange for inadequate equivalents in food. For many Indians the whole operation is perceived as a means of forcing them to build their own concentration camps. In the camps the army restricts free movement, dictates what crops are grown in the surrounding fields and determines the social and other activities of the villagers. The effect of this strategic hamletting is not merely to deny the guerrillas a base but to break up definitively the Indian community by dislocating them from their traditional farming and living areas and places of religious and cultural importance.

Coincidentally with the creation of strategic hamlets, Montt made all adult men eligible for Civil Self-Defence Patrols. In 1984 more than 800,000 men had been recruited, almost all of them against their will.[51] The patrols are used by the army to carry out routine duties in the controlled villages as well as take part in the anti-guerrilla cause. In one reported incident a village was threatened with bombing if it did not form a civil patrol and begin denouncing the guerrillas.[52] In this way Indians become unwilling victims and collaborators.

In August 1983 Montt was replaced by yet another military man, General Mejia Victores. Encouraging statements soon began to emanate from the United States Government suggesting that human rights violations against the rural population had now ceased. These were to some extent validated in a report prepared for the United Nations Commission on Human Rights by Lord Colville and presented in February 1984. Colville argued that army brutality in the past had been in response to guerrilla offensives and the new policy of President Victores should be given a chance since there were 'genuine reformers in the government'.[53]

Most observers disagree with the optimism expressed by the United States Government and in the UN report. One NGO (non-governmental organization) feared that since there was no real change in personnel or in fundamental policy 'the most recent military coup will bring about further repressive government'. The Inter-Church Committee on Human Rights in Latin America in January 1984 stated that 'Guatemala is the clearest example in Central America of genocide of indigenous peoples. Men, women, children and the elderly are tortured and murdered. Whole communities have been massacred.' The Americas Watch Committee in January 1984 described Guatemala as a nation of prisoners, declaring that 'the military rulers of Guatemala must be shamed before the whole world for their abuses'. The International Federation for the Rights of Man in February 1984 accused the government of being the authors of crimes against humanity and 'of acts of ferocious torture and multiple assassination against civilians'.[54]

Today, the highlands of Guatemala are devastated. Many villages have been razed to the ground. More than one million people are believed by the Guatemalan Conference of Bishops to have been displaced by the violence and are now internal refugees, while a further 150,000 to 200,000 have fled the country and now survive in makeshift refugee camps in Mexico, and other countries of Central America. Even there they are not safe from the Guatemalan army, as troops and helicopter gunships regularly make raids across the borders to attack the camps. For the Mayan peoples whose accomplishments in the fields of astronomy, mathematics and calendrics achieved during the first millennium AD were in advance of many European countries, their physical survival is now in doubt. They were able to resist and adapt to the violent contact with Spanish colonialism and survive the continuing dispossession of their lands after independence; today they face a government bent on their annihilation as a people. In December 1985 General Mejia Victores gave way to Vinicio Cerezo Arevalo, a Christian Democrat and first civilian president since 1954. However, the army still remains as powerful as ever. Any future they have now is linked to the union of opposition forces active in the country. The recently formed Guatemalan Patriotic Unity Committee (CGUP), which unites the four main guerrilla armies, has four Indians on its 26-strong committee.[55] As the majority population and the particular victims of army violence, the Indian peoples may be expected to play an increasingly important role in the politics of Guatemala. As one Quiché Indian stated in 1982: 'The revolutionaries are no longer something foreign to us. They are our own people.'[56]

Notes

1. Report of the Fourth Russell Tribunal on the Rights of the Indians of the Americas, *Non-selected cases: Central America* (Rotterdam, 1980).
2. Aurora Pérez, 'Mexico: bilingual-bicultural education', *IWGIA Newsletter*, no.38, July 1984, p.90.
3. Roxanne Dunbar Ortiz, *Indians of the Americas* (Zed Press, London, 1984) p.14.
4. Aurora Pérez, pp.90-103.
5. United Nations Economic and Social Council, Commission on Human Rights, Sub-Commission on Prevention of Discrimination and Protection of Minorities, *Study of the problem of discrimination against indigenous populations*, chapter XVII, p.12.
6. 'Mexico: indigenous organizations confront state authorities in Chiapas', *IWGIA Newsletter*, no.30, April 1982, pp.45-8.
7. Cf. 'Report on the Third National Congress of Indian Peoples in Mexico City, July 1979', *Survival International Review*, Spring 1980, pp.25-6; for a fictional account of the living conditions and revolutionary struggles of Mexico's Indians see B. Traven's Jungle Novels.
8. 'Mexico: new "conquistadores" rob land from the O'Otam people', *IWGIA Newsletter*, no.34, July 1983, p.78.
9. 'Mexico: ANPIBAC fights for a true bilingual education', *IWGIA Newsletter*, no.28/29, October/December 1981, pp.20-6.
10. Bruce Rich, 'Time running out for Mexico's last tropical forest', *Cultural*

Survival Quarterly, Spring 1982, pp.13-14.

11. James Nations and Daniel Komer, 'Indians, Immigrants and Beef Exports: Deforestation in Central America', in ibid., p.10.

12. Ibid., p.10.

13. Donald Rojas Maroto, 'Costa Rica: indigenous reality and the role of communication', *IWGIA Newsletter*, no.38, July 1984, pp.43-55.

14. United Nations, *Study of the problem of discrimination*, p.9.

15. David Stephen and Philip Wearne, *Central America's Indians*, Minority Rights Group, Report no.62, 1984, p.6.

16. United Nations, *Study of the problem of discrimination*, p.56.

17. 'Costa Rica: North Americans say they own Talamanca indigenous reserve', *IWGIA Newsletter*, nos. 35 and 36, October and December 1983, p.92.

18. United Nations, *Study of the problem of discrimination*, p.10.

19. Maroto, p.45.

20. See *El Pueblo Guaymi y su futura*, Centro de Estudios y Acción Social, Panama, 1982.

21. Up to 59 per cent of the active male population of Guaymí are emigrating to other parts of the country; in 1970, 85 per cent (twice national average) were illiterate; malnutrition among Guaymí due to low protein diet, few milk products available and meat eaten by less than half population more than once a month. Cf. *Dialogo social* (Panama, September 1982) pp.24-8.

22. Chris N. Gjording, *The Cerro Colorado copper project and the Guaymi Indians of Panama*, Cultural Survival Occasional Paper 3, March 1981, pp.23-6; *Survival International Review*, Summer 1979, pp.12-15.

23. Gjording, *passim*.

24. *IWGIA Newsletter*, no.33, March 1983, pp.40-1.

25. Bishop Remi de Roo et al., 'Canada and Cerro Colorado', mimeo cited in Gjording, p.39.

26. James Howe, 'Kindling self-determination among the Kuna', *Cultural Survival Quarterly*, Summer 1982, p.15.

27. Foreign Office, Summary to Panama Despatch of 10 July 1974 from HM Ambassador to Panama, Mr Dugald Malcolm.

28. Howe, p.17.

29. Cf. Jenny Pearce, *Under the eagle: US intervention in Central America and the Caribbean* (Latin America Bureau, London, 1982).

30. Cf. Richard Adams, *Cultural surveys of Panama, Nicaragua, Guatemala, El Salvador and Honduras* (Detroit, 1957), and Alejandro Marroquin, 'El problema Indigena en El Salvador', *America Latina*, 35(4), 1975, pp.747-71.

31. Judith Maxwell, 'Nahual-Pipil: "muy politica"', *Cultural Survival Quarterly*, Winter 1982, pp.17-18.

32. *The Nation*, 9 June 1984.

33. Cf. speech made by members of the Toledo Indian Movement at meeting of World Council of Indigenous Peoples, San Antonio, 20 April 1983 cited in *Native Peoples News*, London, Spring 1984, p.11.

34. *Guardian*, 3 December 1983.

35. Roger Plant, *Guatemala: unnatural disaster*, Latin America Bureau, 1978, p.68; Shelton Davis, 'The social roots of political violence in Guatemala', *Cultural Survival Quarterly*, Spring 1983, p.5.

36. Letter from President Barrios to department governors, 3 November 1877,

cited in J. Pansini, 'Indian seasonal plantation work in Guatemala', *Cultural Survival Quarterly*, Spring 1983, p.17.

37. Plant, p.68.

38. Dana G. Munro, *The 5 republics of Central America* (Oxford University Press, New York, 1918), cited in Shelton Davis, p.6.

39. Cf. Michael McClintock, *The American Connection, Volume Two: State Terror and Popular Resistance in Guatemala* (Zed Press, London, 1985); Richard Immerman, *The CIA in Guatemala: the foreign policy of intervention* (Texas University Press, Austin, 1982).

40. Philip Wearne, *Central America's Indians*, Minority Rights Group, no.62, 1984, p.12.

41. Anti-Slavery Society, 'Incidences of slavery and abuses against rural workers in Guatemala, 1976-1978', Report for 1978 to the United Nations Working Group on Slavery.

42. Ibid.

43. Oral testimony to the Permanent Peoples Tribunal on Guatemala, Madrid, 7-13 January 1983.

44. Gordon Willey, 'The Maya heritage', *Cultural Survival Quarterly*, Spring 1983, p.13.

45. Cf. M. and T. Melville, *Guatemala – another Vietnam* (Penguin, Harmondsworth, 1971).

46. T. Melville, 'The Catholic Church in Guatemala, 1944-1982', *Cultural Survival Quarterly*, Spring 1983, p.27.

47. *Guatemala 1978: the massacre at Panzos*, IWGIA Document 33, 1978, p.8.

48. *IWGIA Newsletter*, nos.35 and 36, October and December 1983, pp.106-10.

49. C.W. Nelson and K. Taylor, *Witness to Genocide, the present situation of Indians in Guatemala*, Survival International, 1983, pp.6-14; George Black, *Garrison Guatemala* (Zed Press, London, 1985).

50. Cf. Americas Watch Report, *Human Rights in Guatemala: no neutrals allowed*, Washington, 1982.

51. Statement by the Human Rights Commission of Guatemala (CDHG) to the UN Working Group on Indigenous Populations, Geneva, August 1984.

52. Americas Watch Report, pp.16-19.

53. Interview with *Wall Street Journal*, 30 April 1984, cited in Anti-Slavery Society, *Guatemala: UN whitewash?*, Special Bulletin, August 1984.

54. Ibid., p.iii.

55. Roxanne Dunbar, p.113.

56. Rigoberta Menchú, Intercontinental Press, 11 October 1982, cited in *Native Peoples News*, Winter 1982, p.3.

7. The Indians of South America

Throughout South America Indian peoples are under attack. The agrarian reform programmes of the 1960s and 1970s, which promised some modest redistribution of land in favour of the landless, have for the most part slowed up or halted altogether. In certain countries there has even been a renewed concentration of land into the hands of *latifundistas* in the last ten years. Land hunger among the rural population has led to poverty and suffering on an unprecedented scale. But instead of promoting land reforms, governments have chosen to confront opposition with repression and defuse especially volatile regions with promises of resettlement programmes. The land offered for colonization is in the vast area of Amazonia.

At the same time, governments have looked to the Amazon region not merely to solve their political problems, but also to provide economic solutions. Faltering economies and growing debts to private and multilateral banks have together caused governments to ponder on the riches of the Amazon and provided incentives for large-scale development projects. Roads have been built across thousands of miles of jungle, and millions of hectares have been granted to foreign and national companies as mineral and timber concessions. Swathes of tropical rainforest have been cut down and the land seeded for pasture for cattle ranching. The results of this costly speculation are becoming better known.

Massive profits have been made but little has yet accrued to the host nations; colonization schemes have been sponsored but many poor settlers live in as much misery as before; exploitation of the forest's natural resources has taken place but, almost without exception, this has brought irreversible environmental degradation. Most seriously of all, the human population which inhabits and has always inhabited these forests is suffering unprecedented destruction of its way of life.

The present situation of the indigenous peoples of the Andean highlands and the Amazonian lowlands is directly affected by the national political and economic development policies being pursued currently by South American states. By failing to resolve the issue of land reform, governments are causing increased hardships to highland Indians and peasants, and by promoting colonization and economic development in Amazonia they are destroying relatively self-sufficient indigenous communities.

Table 7.1
Indians in South America

Country	Numbers	% of total population
Argentina	350,000 (16 groups)	0.1
Bolivia	Lowland 80,000 Highland 4 million	66
Brazil	Lowland 200,000 (120 groups)	0.1
Chile	1 million Mapuche	9
Colombia	300,000 (60 groups)	1
Ecuador	Lowland 70,000 Highland 2 million	21
French Guiana	Lowland 4,000	4
Guyana	Lowland 30,000	4
Paraguay	Lowland 100,000 (17 groups)	3
Peru	Lowland 242,000 (39 groups) Highland 6.5 million	39
Surinam	Lowland 7,000	1
Venezuela	Lowland 150,000 (30 languages)	0.9
Total	*15 million*	6

Indian peoples of the highlands

The Indian peoples of the high Andes of Peru, Bolivia and Ecuador are the direct descendants of the Incas and their subjects. The Inca empire was based around Lake Titicaca and the valley of Cuzco and stretched at its height from Ecuador in the north to Chile and even Argentina in the south. Its population was estimated to be 15 million people. Today about the same number of Indian peoples speak one of the two main languages of the region. Between 11 and 14 million speak Quechua and about 1.5 million speak Aymara.[1]

These Indian communities are located in the numerous valleys that intersect the 2,000 mile long mountain range, often cultivating the poorer soils of the slopes. The richer soils of the valley bottoms have in most cases been occupied by large estates. While some communities still hold land, the bulk of the Indian peoples have become landless labourers or have some sharecropping arrangement with the local landowner; others have joined the mass of seasonal workers who migrate out of their homeland for employment. Indians are also an important part of the industrial labour force, particularly in mining in Peru and

Bolivia. Since the 1950s many Indian peoples have drifted to the towns to escape poverty and seek jobs and some of the welfare and educational benefits they believe are available. The majority of the population of La Paz is Aymara-speaking and increasingly the slums around Lima are filling with landless workers from Indian communities in the highlands.[2]

The history of the Indian peoples of the highlands of Bolivia, Ecuador and Peru is quite different from that of the indigenous population of the lowland regions. The Quechua and Aymara-speaking peoples have been in continuous contact with the non-native population since colonization. For generations Indians and *mestizos* have intermarried, and now, as in Mexico, clear racial distinctions are blurred. Furthermore, the conditions of non-Indian peasants and the autochthonous population are often indistinguishable in the countryside.

As in Central America, the communal ownership of land by Indians was permitted alongside private land during the colonial period. The *ayllu*, the system of land tenure developed by the Incas, was preserved under the Spanish crown through a system of *reducciones* or reserves. After independence in the early part of the 19th Century, however, all property was brought under a system of private ownership and the process of dispossession of Indian land escalated. In the Andean countries of Bolivia, Peru and Ecuador, the dispossession was less intense than in some of the Central American countries where pressures for land were greater, and many indigenous communities succeeded in retaining their traditional farming land.

> landowners certainly succeeded in expanding their domains, immense *haciendas* were formed, and millions of Indians ended up as debt-peons or serfs on these estates. But partly because the demand for seasonal labour was less acute, and partly because the available land area was so great, free Indian communities did survive in many areas.[3]

Resistance by Indian peoples in the highlands was also an important factor in successfully protecting their communities. The peoples of Inca descent have mounted a series of uprisings since colonization. In Colombia also, where communal landownership was abolished by law in 1850, fierce resistance by indigenous groups, particularly in the south-western Cauca province, achieved the protection of the *resguardos*, the Indian reserves created by the Spanish colonial authorities. It was not until early in this century that legislation once more recognized the legality of the Indian community. Changes to the laws and constitutions were effected in 1920 in Peru, in 1937 in Ecuador and in 1938 in Bolivia.

However, Indian revolts and state legislation have not prevented the general trend throughout South America towards a concentration of land into largely privately owned estates and the proliferation of ever smaller subsistence plots for the overwhelming majority. The *latifundio* system, which still dominates the agrarian structure of the region, made peons or dependent and impoverished sharecroppers of many in the countryside, non-Indian and Indian alike. The prevailing condition for most of the rural population in this century has been one of agricultural servitude. As one Peruvian writer has observed:

The inhabitants of the sierra have virtually no access to alternative forms of existence and of behaviour, a situation which prompts them to submit completely to the authority of those who control the key resources of the region.[4]

The alienation by powerful landowners of communal land occupied by the Indian has continued unabated for much of the second half of the 20th Century. On the whole, resistance has proved ineffectual because landowners hold political power locally and nationally throughout Latin America.

Nevertheless, there have been some partial, if short-lived successes. In Bolivia the indigenous population played a decisive role in the revolution of 1952. For the first time in the country's history a Quechua Indian was elected to the senate, and indigenous peoples participated actively in the revolutionary process. An agrarian reform programme was launched which permitted the recovery of land usurped from Indian communities and promoted land redistribution. On the whole the law favoured individual private ownership rather than communal production cooperatives, and in practice Indian communities were unable to repossess their traditional land. In 1964 the social revolution was abruptly halted by a military coup. But even in that decade, in which a favourable political climate reigned, only one-tenth of the agricultural labour force benefited in any way from the redistribution of land. Indeed, of the four million or so hectares of land redistributed only 16 per cent was actually cultivable.[5] A report by the Anti-Slavery Society commenting on the situation in Bolivia noted that

> by 1980 the average Indian was again reduced to the status of below-subsistence farmer or landless labourer, compelled to undertake regular migrant labour to commercial plantations, either in Bolivia itself or in the sugar plantations across the Argentine frontier.[6]

Agrarian reforms in the 1960s and 1970s in Colombia, Peru and Ecuador have experienced a similar history of stalling and obfuscation. In Peru, for example, ten million hectares of land were redistributed and large unproductive estates condemned, but accompanying legislation transformed the indigenous communities into peasant communities, thereby limiting their traditional forms of land tenure and denying them other special treatment. After 1975 and the fall of the nationalist government of General Velasco, land reform of any description was entirely halted.

In the last decade there has been a reversal of the redistributive land policies of the 1960s and a renewal of land concentration and consequent growth of landlessness among Indian and non-Indian peoples in the highlands. Characterizing recent developments, a 1984 International Labour Organisation report states:

> Agrarian reform as a goal has been abandoned throughout the Andean region. Peasants and Indians are being equally deprived of their lands, while their organizations and trade unions face a system of repression.

The same report continues:

Almost without exception, the settled indigenous communities are subject to severe fragmentation. They are not, like the reserves in certain American countries, relatively large areas of undivided land set aside for the exclusive use of indigenous populations. They tend rather to be small and often fragmented land plots, surrounded by the private properties of landowners who often make legal claims to the land, and exercise extra-legal forms of pressure, including violence, in their efforts to encroach on indigenous lands. The traditional occupiers of the indigenous communities now tend to be in urgent need of more and better lands, to stem the flight to the cities and curb the severe problems of rural landlessness.[7]

Despite reversals of the land reform programme and of the state protection of Indian land, indigenous communities have developed militant and increasingly effective organizations. There is, of course, a tradition of Indian resistance, and Indian peoples have spearheaded numerous revolts and revolutions in Latin America. However, the last ten or fifteen years have seen a strengthening of an indigenous movement that is independent rather than part of the wider liberation struggle led by the urban sectors.

In Colombia, where only some 500,000 of the total population of 20 million are Indians, there has been a determined struggle since 1971 when the Regional Indian Council of the Cauca (CRIC) was formed. Some 200,000 Paez and Guambiano Indians living in the south-west of the country in Cauca and Narino provinces have been fighting for the restitution of their traditional *resguardos* illegally occupied by landowners, some restitution of their local autonomy, including Indian governors and *cabildos* (Indian councils) and immediate steps to protect the Indian language. The CRIC itself has instigated numerous invasions of land which it claims is Indian. At the Sixth Congress of CRIC held in 1981, at which over 2,000 participated, it was stated that the organization was active in more than 50 different zones and had been involved in 32 land reoccupations.[8]

Such action threatens not only local landowners but the whole *latifundio* system. Accordingly the government and landowners have labelled CRIC subversive. Hundreds of Indians have been imprisoned and in 1981 Amnesty International confirmed that between 1973 and 1980, 48 CRIC leaders had been assassinated by hired gunmen.[9] In January 1984, a land invasion by 300 Indian men, women and children ended in violence when police attempted to expel them. Although the Indians were unarmed, the police shot and killed seven people and seriously wounded a further 18.[10] Individual killings had taken place during all of CRIC's history but such a large-scale massacre had not occurred in recent years. Within days over 1,500 Indians marched on the main town of the area, Popayan, to demand an investigation. The growing strength and confidence of CRIC has provoked a sharp escalation of police and, more generally, state hostility towards the indigenous communities.

In Bolivia, the *Movimiento Indio Tupac Katari*, MITKA, has been forced to function clandestinely since its formation in 1962 and has always faced persecution. MITKA has argued that Indians are exploited not only because of their class position but because of their race. 'The Indian is a whole people', has

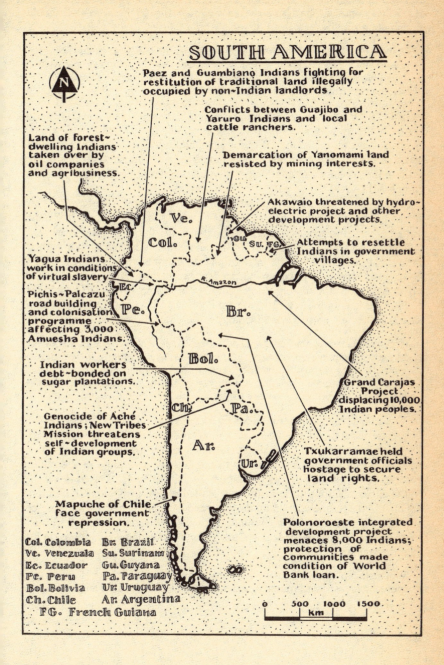

SOUTH AMERICA

Paez and Guambiano Indians fighting for restitution of traditional land illegally occupied by non~Indian landlords.

Conflicts between Guajibo and Yaruro Indians and local cattle ranchers.

Land of forest~dwelling Indians taken over by oil companies and agribusiness.

Demarcation of Yanomami land resisted by mining interests.

Akawaio threatened by hydro~electric project and other development projects.

Attempts to resettle Indians in government villages.

Yagua Indians work in conditions of virtual slavery.

Pichis~Palcazu road building and colonisation programme affecting 3,000 Amuesha Indians.

Indian workers debt~bonded on sugar plantations.

Genocide of Aché Indians ; New Tribes Mission threatens self~development of Indian groups.

Mapuche of Chile face government repression.

Grand Carajas Project displacing 10,000 Indian peoples.

Txukarramae held government officials hostage to secure land rights.

Polonoroeste integrated development project menaces 8,000 Indians; protection of communities made condition of World Bank loan.

Ve.
Col.
Ec.
Pe.
Br.
Bol.
Ch.
Pa.
Ar.
Ur.
Gu. Su. FG.
R. Amazon

Col. Colombia
Ve. Venezuela
Ec. Ecuador
Pe. Peru
Bol. Bolivia
Ch. Chile
FG. French Guiana

Br. Brazil
Su. Surinam
Gu. Guyana
Pa. Paraguay
Ur. Uruguay
Ar. Argentina

0   500   1000   1500
km

declared Constantino Lima, founder of MITKA, 'and not a single social class.' MITKA maintains that Indians are the majority in Bolivia and should implement an indigenous form of socialism.

> In the view of MITKA both the right wing and the left wing groups are interrelated since they are all imported from Europe . . . The Indian people itself is the left wing and fights for the restoration of the Mallcu-Inca type of socialism, based on cooperative Ayllu communities.[11]

In 1978 MITKA helped form the Popular Democratic Union (UDP) and has been able to play a central role in union and national politics. However, members have criticized the UDP for using and manipulating Indian support much as the revolutionary movement (the MNR) did during the 1950s. No independent political programme has yet been developed by the recently formed MITKA–1.

A new kind of political organization of Indians in Latin America with new demands has also taken place in recent years. In the first stage of the contemporary indigenous movement, marked by the first Inter-American Indigenous Congress in Mexico in 1940, Indians demanded recognition of their culture but accepted eventual integration into national society. At the eighth Congress at Merida, Mexico, an independent Indian movement was proclaimed which renounced the notion of integration.[12] In March 1980 the Council for South American Indians (CISA) was formed. At its first anniversary in 1981 it reflected this new and growing ideology among Indian peoples:

> In South America, the independent nation states which broke ties with the European Empires did not signify any achievement of liberty for us; on the contrary, they brought treachery and a great subjugation, plunder and slavery . . . As Indian peoples, we represent the collectivist option for the societies of the future . . . we are the only hope for a true socialism.[13]

The demand for self-determination by Indian peoples has been accompanied by greater assurance by indigenous communities about their political role.[14] There is certainly considerable disillusion about non-Indian political leadership and this is reflected in much of the recent activity and many of the public statements of indigenous organizations. In April 1984, a meeting of the National Council for the Co-ordination of the Indigenous Nations of Ecuador (CONACNIE) concluded that the indigenous struggle had to be directed towards the retrieval of communal and not individual land. A further confirmation of the independence of the Indian movement was expressed in the final statement:

> We see that in mestizo society there are sectors which are aware of indigenous peoples and respect us. But the great majority of mestizo society considers us as animals.[15]

The forest-dwellers

While the great majority of Indian peoples of South America are descendants of the Inca peoples and their subjects and live in the highland region of Peru, Ecuador and Bolivia, the lowland, forest-dwelling Indians occupy the vast area of the Amazon basin and adjoining lowlands and number more than one million in total (see table 7.1).

The Indians of the highlands are united historically, culturally and linguistically (speaking either Aymara or Quechua) but there are over 300 distinct ethno–linguistic groups among the lowland Indians. Furthermore, even though some languages are similar, the histories of the different tribal groups are highly varied. Some groups have a much longer contact with non-Indian society, while others have only recently been contacted. Even within large ethno–linguistic groups, such as the Amuesha of Peru, there are communities which have regular and established relations with non-natives and speak Spanish, and others which have remained isolated and have no knowledge of the outside. Indeed the great range of different Indian peoples, or in the case of the more numerous ethnic groups it might be more appropriate to talk of nations, and their geographical dispersal throughout a vast region almost half the size of the total land area of South America, might suggest that there can be no cohesive or unifying features. But this would be to misunderstand the numerous cultural similarities among lowland Indians and the importance of the great forces from outside now impinging upon their world.

The lowland Indians of South America are primarily forest-dwelling. They practise swidden cultivation, planting food crops in prepared clearings, harvesting and then replanting in new clearings to allow the tropical soil to lie fallow and restore itself naturally. Swidden cultivation, which also goes under the name of slash-and-burn agriculture, is neither haphazard nor destructive. It is part of a careful adaptation to the complex and highly vulnerable ecosystem of the tropical forest. It is a highly successful adaptation that has done no damage to the ecology of the rainforest, and always provided adequate and – supplemented by hunting and fishing and gathering – often substantial diets. Indeed, one authority on swidden systems has stated: 'Provided that no land shortage threatens the maintenance of an optimum cycle of cultivation and fallowing, swidden plots can yield as much or more than comparable fields under continuous cultivation.'[16] Contact with non-native peoples since colonization began, has modified some of these communities. Firearms or motor boats have been introduced, some nomadic groups have been sedentarized around missionary stations or cattle ranches and the introduction of money and the market economy has created various forms of dependency.

The future of the lowland Indians of South America depends on the protection of traditional territories so that the land can continue to satisfy their economic as well as their spiritual needs. The integrity of these forest communities has, since the conquest of the Americas and even prior to conquest, been threatened by outsiders. Sporadic invasions have occurred, prompted by the search for gold, diamonds and – at the turn of the century – rubber, and now oil and other minerals have been added to the list. But in the last two decades two significant factors have contributed to a renewed and more vigorous opening up of the Amazon region, thereby bringing the native communities into violent confrontations with advancing Western civilizations.

In the first place, the termination of all agrarian reform programmes in the region, leaving untouched wasteful and inequitable land tenure systems, created a politically dangerous land hunger in the populated highland regions of Peru, Ecuador, Colombia and Bolivia. Colonization of lowland regions appeared to governments as an attractive alternative to a radical redistribution of land in the productive highlands and coastal zones. A policy of resettlement offered opportunities to landless peasants to own land while doing nothing to dismantle the traditional political power of landowners. Since the 1970s poor peasants and highland Indians have joined the growing stream of settlers and brought them into direct conflict with forest Indians.

The other factor of significance is a combination of developments which has taken place in all South American countries, and led them into looking for economic expansion in their frontier zones. The Amazon region has always possessed the myth of El Dorado, and governments throughout South America are now willing to gamble millions of dollars in the search for economic salvation. In this they have been encouraged by the World Bank, the IMF and USAID as well as numerous Transnational Corporations (TNCs), commercial banks and private investors. Throughout the region, governments are selling off oil, mineral and timber concessions, selling great extents of forest for a few dollars a hectare to cattle-ranchers, and elaborating even more expensive and grandiose development schemes. The great burden of debt now borne by all South American countries, the ease of availability of international capital and the specific recommendations accompanying loans from multilateral banks all combine to make the Amazon rainforest region the focus of present development initiatives. Furthermore, in both the programmes for colonization and regional economic development, Indian people are rarely consulted and more often than not utterly ignored.

In the Peruvian Amazon, which occupies about 60 per cent of the surface area of the country, there live slightly less than 250,000 lowland Indians and 1.5 million non-Indians. There have been numerous forays since colonization by missionaries and prospectors into the Amazon region. Between 1880 and 1910, the first major assault to tap rubber affected Brazil, Peru, Bolivia and Ecuador and brought slavery and inhuman exploitation of the indigenous forest-dwelling population. According to one author 80 per cent of the native population of the Putumayo River was annihilated during the rubber boom.[17] Then in 1965 the civilian government of President Belaunde Terry instigated a road construction and colonization programme in the region. The stated aims of the project, which included resettlement and increased food production, were not attained. Instead, the access roads opened up the area to uncontrolled migration and resulted in numerous conflicts with indigenous communities.[18]

The area exposed to development was due east of the capital, Lima, and was occupied by about 4,500 Amuesha and 37,500 Campa Indians. Both groups responded rapidly to the invasion of their land. The Amuesha organized a Congress in 1969, the Campa in the 1970s and in April 1979 a Coordinating Committee of Native Communities of Amazonian Peru was formed. This latter was renamed the Inter-Ethnic Association for the Development of the Peruvian Selva (AIDESEP) and drew together about a dozen Amazonian Indian organizations. In 1979 a number of non-Indian organizations based in Lima joined forces with these Indian organizations and established the Committee for the Defence of Native Land.

From the fall in 1968 of the government of Belaúnde until the re-establishment of civilian rule in 1980 and the election once again of Belaúnde, Peru was governed by generals. General Velasco undertook a programme focusing on the nationalization of key agricultural and industrial sectors of the economy and redistributing land through agrarian reform legislation. For the forest-dwelling Indians of Peru there were two important changes. The Velasco government stopped promoting development in the Amazon region and, in June 1974, introduced the Law of Native Communities. The law gave official recognition to native communities, guaranteed the integrity of their territory and began a process of land titling. As one writer has commented: 'For the first time in Peru's history, some Indian settlements were given legal title to a small part of the territory on which they had lived for centuries or millennia.'[19] Nevertheless, despite these positive measures, by 1980 about 250 recognized Indian communities still held no title to land.[20]

In fact the pro-Indian legislation had a short life. In 1975 a new General had replaced Velasco and a halt was called on the programmes of nationalization and agrarian reform. By 1977 the implementation of the Native Communities Law had been suspended and in 1978 new legislation was in force allowing the government to grant land and forest concessions to private investors. In 1980 the new civilian president, Belaúnde Terry, began a massive programme for the conquest of the Peruvian Amazon. Once more the Amazon forest had become the panacea for the nation's ills.

In the Pichis-Palcazu special project a major highway, forestry development and colonization programme is currently being planned on land described as uninhabited by the government. In fact, some 10–15,000 people live in the valley destined for development of which 3,000 are Amuesha Indians. The plan calls for the settlement of 150,000 families but after a further study by USAID, who are part-funding the project, some changes were recommended. Most importantly, USAID recommended that measures should be taken to help the 13 Amuesha communities to adapt to the changes. More specifically the loan was made conditional on the creation of tribal lands with legal title. The Peruvian government responded by providing some land for the Amuesha but experts have since concluded that only one of the communities would receive sufficient agricultural land and none would have enough forest land to ensure survival.[21]

In July 1985 there was a change of government in Peru. Alan García was elected president and in his inaugural speech committed the government to the promotion of human rights. Despite this pledge human rights violations, particularly in the countryside where the guerrilla group Sendero Luminoso are active, continue unabated. Indigenous peoples in the highlands find themselves victims in the army's counter-terrorism. In the eastern lowlands, however, investment in colonization and development is likely to diminish.

Large-scale development projects are affecting other lowland Indians in South America. In Ecuador the frontier region has produced violent confrontations between settlers and Indians. Since 1968 Ecuador has become an important oil-producing country. Texaco-Gulf has established a base on indigenous territory in the east of the country and intercut tribal land with oil pipelines and numerous access roads. The present development strategy of the government is to promote large-scale farming of export commodity crops, such as tea, palm oil, and sugar, in the eastern lowlands and introduce settler families to provide cheap labour.[22]

In Venezuela serious conflicts have occurred in the savannah region between Guajibo and Yaruro peoples and local cattle-ranchers.[23] As the traditional areas of hunting and food-gathering are reduced by expanding farms, hunger has spread among indigenous groups. Cattle have been killed by Indians, and landowners have called for police intervention. On the whole, physical violence against indigenous communities by ranchers has been avoided and the last serious massacre of Indians took place in 1967. The major problem is the gradual appropriation of Indian traditional land and the inadequate response of the Government of Venezuela to provide some legal guarantees. As one writer puts it, 'official action is marked by ineffectiveness, bureaucracy and cynicism.'[24]

Such invasions by colonizing cattle-ranchers and other settlers of indigenous-occupied land are prevalent throughout the lowland areas. In Colombia the government has been actively promoting such colonization and according to one source 'of the sixty reservations established by INCORA (the Agrarian Reform Institute) there is not a single one which has not been invaded.'[25]

In Guyana the Akawaio are presently facing disruption from a proposed hydro-electric scheme in the Upper Mazaruni district. The area designated for the project is the home of 5,000 Akawaio and the dam will cause the flooding of 1,000 square miles of land and submerge all the cultivable land of the Upper Mazaruni.[26] Apart from the effect on the indigenous communities which will no longer have a land base and will be resettled in unfamiliar and unsuitable areas, there have been numerous other criticisms. The costs to Guyana of the project are considerable and the debt incurred likely to hinder other development activities of the government for years to come. The life expectancy of the dam has been estimated at forty years and specialists fear that without proper and costly supervision the reservoir created could stagnate and create an unhealthy marshland.[27] Such criticisms have perhaps raised doubts among planners in Guyana and the project has at the present time been put into abeyance. However, this has not brought any respite for the Akawaio since the government in 1984 signed a series of agreements with Canadian and other companies to undertake gold-mining in the region.[28] Similar projects are currently being planned on indigenous peoples' land in Venezuela.[29]

In French Guiana the small Amerindian population of 4,000 – reduced since the 1600s from some 30,000 – have attacked the government for its policies of assimilation. Top on their list of demands are the right to their traditional hunting way of life and a guaranteed land base.[30]

Most disturbing of all the effects of colonization and development in so-called frontier zones occupied by indigenous peoples is the loss of freedom experienced by tribal people. The appalling working conditions imposed upon Indians during the rubber boom at the turn of the century have been referred to elsewhere, but similar conditions have been recorded in recent years. One anthropologist working with the Amuesha population has stated:

> In the late 1960s when I first visited the area, 90 per cent of the adult male population was in debt to one patron or another and spent most of their productive time and energy working off their debts by clearing cattle pasture.[31]

In many areas of the Amazon, white or *mestizo* employers are able to impose a rigorous control over the indigenous labour force by monopolizing work, money, essential imports and services such as transport. Indigenous communities, their land base and, therefore, their independent livelihood taken away, are obliged to look to non-native settlers for survival. In Argentina, whose indigenous population number around 350,000, loss of land during the 19th and early 20th Centuries has left the Indians of the Chaco region without employment, living marginal existences on the outskirts of cities.[32]

In north-eastern Peru some 80 to 90 per cent of Yagua Indians are estimated to be caught up in the patron system. In this case the boom in the last ten years in 'white gold' – cocaine – has been responsible for enforcing bonded labour relations.[33]

Control over Indian workers is exerted by physical coercion as well as by endebtment. In the case of the Yagua, however, it is women who have faced particular exploitation. The demand for domestic servants in the frontier towns, such as Leticia, has grown as settlers and traffickers enrich themselves. To satisfy that demand masters are receiving young Indian girls as payment for debts and selling them to families.[34] The disappearance from Indian communities of marriageable girls can only have a most destructive long-term effect on the Yagua people.

In eastern Bolivia conditions of work of Indian peons are equally bad. A study in 1975 commented:

> Native labour is exploited in many ways . . . such as debt slavery and the servant system. Merchants acquire any surplus produced by the Indian communities by exchanging it for inferior and almost useless products such as alcohol and cheap cloth, on which they make enormous profits.[35]

Migrant Indian workers in the frontier zone south-east of Santa Cruz face similar treatment. Since the 1960s there has been a massive boom in sugar production as well as other crops and a consequent demand for cheap labour. Contractors are hired to endebt Indians and oblige them to work off their loans on the plantations. As many as 70 to 80,000 Indian and non-Indian peasants may well be affected by this form of exploitation.[36] The worker, while on the plantation, continues to incur separate debts at the local store, often owned by the landowner, and directly from the boss if for some reason the wages become inadequate. Thirty per cent of wages on one plantation were kept by the landowner as compulsory savings which in practice were rarely repaid, and acted as compensation to the employer if his men should fall ill or die. The whole system of remuneration is highly complex and open to manipulation by the landowner. As a consequence debts often exceed earnings by the end of the harvest and landowners are once again able to endebt peasants by advancing loans, thereby ensuring labour the following season. The labourers work 14 to 16 hours a day, and sometimes round the clock, and children as young as nine or ten are found on the plantations. Only the chewing of coca leaves makes such work endurable. As one report has stated: 'Strenuous labour, insufficient nourishment and indecent living conditions result in approximately 90 per cent of the harvesters, wives and children returning home ill.'[37]

In a statement made by the Anti-Slavery Society to the United Nations Working Group on Slavery in 1984 it was asserted that bonded labour had also been reported in locations throughout eastern Peru, and affected the Piro Indians of the Gran Pajonal area and the Yagua Indians.[38]

In Paraguay, where there live approximately 100,000 Indians, conditions are probably among the worst in all Latin America. In 1961 a Paraguayan zoologist wrote of the Guayakí or Aché Indians as follows: 'In the villages near the Guayakí (Aché) areas, there are slave traders who organize veritable man hunts for these aboriginals. They catch a Guayakí family by surprise, murder the parents, and carry off the children to sell them.'[39] Efforts by the government through its Office of Indian Protection, and later, the Native Affairs Department to eliminate slave-hunting and killing of Indians have proved largely ineffectual. A report in 1973 found the forest Aché close to extinction and still subject to capture and murder by colonizers seeking to occupy, unhindered, Indian land. Those Aché who had been brought to reservations were described as 'depressed, maltreated, tortured and in extreme ill-health.'[40]

A visit by the US lawyer Richard Arens in 1978 confirmed these findings. The reservations had been taken out of private hands and given over to various evangelizing Protestant missions but with little real improvement in conditions. He found all the children 'pathologically protein deficient'.[41] Of one reservation administered by the New Tribes Mission, a United States-based fundamentalist organization, Arens wrote:

> Everywhere I looked, I found the overcrowded make-shift hovels, wide open to the elements and cluttered with charred wood and offal, yes, and an occasional snake. Nowhere I looked were there sanitary facilities for Indians, and the place reeked of excrement. Everywhere there was a collective gloom of a people who had given up on life.[42]

As in other regions of South America being opened up for colonization and exploitation the indigenous populations often represent for governments and others a tiresome obstacle or else a potential cheap labour force. In Paraguay vast Mennonite colonies employ some 6,000 Indians, paying them only tokens redeemable at Mennonite-owned stores. Everywhere alcoholism, prostitution and cultural degradation prevail.[43]

The activities of fundamentalist church organizations such as the New Tribe Mission, the Summer Institute of Linguistics, and the UK-based South American Missionary Society, have often been highly damaging to Indian communities. Often engaging in forcible conversions, denigrating indigenous religions and customs, and even exploiting Indian labour, they have come under considerable criticism.[44] Nor have Catholic missions been exempt from such criticisms, although in the last decade or so the Catholic Church has taken a supportive and often courageous position vis-à-vis Indian rights. As one Jesuit missionary has commented:

> The problem of the indigenes has become difficult because we find it inconceivable to leave the Indians alone: to leave them alone on their lands, to leave them alone with their social and political customs, to leave them alone to decide for themselves what cultural traits should be preserved and which changed, to leave them alone so that they can go on being different. This does not mean passivity in the face of the problem of the indigenes but firm action to protect the Indian from ourselves, from the ranch owners, from the store keepers and perhaps from the missionaries.[45]

On the whole the fundamentalist missionaries have obstructed all self-help initiatives by Indian communities and consider the indigenous movement generally subversive. The penetration by hundreds of these evangelizing missionaries, while in certain cases providing improvements in health care, has also created dependence and undermined indigenous customs and traditional practices. In Colombia the New Tribes Mission has given gifts to Indians in order to force them into debt. In Paraguay, the New Tribes Mission in January 1979 used a group of reservation Indians to capture by force uncontacted members of their tribe.[46]

More often than not contact between missionaries and Indians provokes disaster unwittingly. The West Indies Mission, a Protestant mission based in Surinam, successfully settled one nomadic group in the south of the country in a series of villages during the 1960s. However, when they tried to extend the apparent benefits of village life to another nomadic group, the Akuriyo, the effect was disastrous. Within two years the entire population had lost a quarter of its members due to disease and changes in diet. According to one report 'the majority of women did not menstruate for more than a year' and 'a few just refused to live any longer'.[47] The author noted that the death toll utterly destroyed the network of social relations and left 50 per cent of children without one or both parents. There were twice as many young men as women but polyandrous unions were not allowed by the mission, further shattering social relations in the tribe.[48]

Although confrontations between Indian peoples and outsiders of all kinds – missionaries, colonizing farmers, prospectors and workers on development projects – occur regularly in the Amazonian region, indigenous organizations have also become stronger. There are organizations of lowland Indians in all South American countries and increasingly they are being supported by non-native organizations nationally and internationally. In Peru, Campa, Amuesha, Shipibo and Aguaruna all have their own councils. Defence committees and pro-Indian organizations exist in Venezuela. In Peru the Aguaruna forcibly evicted the German film-maker Werner Herzog from their land during 1979, after he brought in 400 Campa Indians to use in *Fitzcarraldo* and caused the death of four of them. In Ecuador the Shuar formed a federation in 1964 with assistance from Salesian missionaries. The federation was recognized by the government in the same year and has succeeded in reclaiming seven reservations and some control over educational policy in the area.[49] The Shuar also run their own radio station.[50] In September 1981 the first meeting on the Problem of Indian Populations in the Amazon Region was held in Quito.

The growth of indigenous organizations among the lowland Indians and the movement towards pan-tribalism is a result of the inadequate precautions and absence of consultation by national governments in South America in their development programmes in the Amazon region. As one writer has observed:

> Events have shown that the Indians cannot rely on the state to fulfil its legal and moral duties towards them and, in the final analysis, only they can solve the problems they face. The existence of the Indian movement is a clear sign that they are well aware of this and that the goals of survival and self-determination are their own.[51]

The Mapuche of Chile: an experiment cut short

There are several small indigenous groups in Chile: Aymara, Quechua and Atacama Indians in the north, Fuegian Indians in the extreme south and Polynesian peoples on Easter Island. The Mapuche, however, are an important minority and number about one million, nearly ten per cent of the country's total population. They are located in the rich temperate agricultural provinces in the south of the country where in some areas they constitute the majority of the rural population.[52]

The Mapuche are the original inhabitants of most of present-day Chile and one of the few peoples in the region who were not conquered by the Incas. They fiercely defended their independence during the early years of Spanish occupation and by the Treaty of Quillan in 1641 retained a territory of some ten million hectares south of the river Bío-Bío. It was only in the 1880s that the independent Chilean state successfully crushed Mapuche resistance and incorporated their lands. The Mapuche were settled on numerous small reserves which were separated from one another and an influx of European settlers took over the better-quality land in between.

From a homeland which on the eve of the Spanish invasion had covered a territory of over 30 million hectares, from Antofagasta in the north to the island of Chiloé in the south, the Mapuche lands had, by 1929, been reduced to

525,000 hectares distributed in 3,078 separate reserves. Even these reserve lands were whittled down by local landowners who also exerted control on government. Earlier laws which had protected the communal ownership or occupation of land by the Mapuche were undermined. Then in 1927 the government began to issue titles of individual ownership. The legislation ensuring the inalienability of Mapuche land was allowed to lapse between 1943 and 1947 and 100,000 hectares, one-fifth of the Mapuche land base, was acquired by non-Mapuche landholders.

The decline in Mapuche land ownership continued until the 1960s when a limited agrarian reform programme was introduced by the Christian Democrat Party. The reform was directed at the large landowners and aimed to expropriate and redistribute the land of the great estates. In fact, less than one-third of the targeted large estates were expropriated. In the same period, however, the Mapuche themselves were growing more politically active and in 1961, for the first time, the Mapuche joined forces with other peasant organizations.

In 1970 the Popular Unity government led by President Salvador Allende won power. The new government supported a programme of radical agrarian reform and the progressive restitution of lands formerly owned by the Mapuche people. The Mapuche had not benefited greatly under the early agrarian reform programme and put strong pressures on the new government for the restoration of their lands, even, when necessary, invading and occupying large estates. As a consequence, although between 1960 and 1970 land restored to the Mapuche amounted to only 1,443 hectares, in the three years of the Popular Unity government (1970–73) 70,000 hectares were returned to the indigenous communities.[53] Legislation was also passed to allow communal ownership and consolidation of Mapuche land. An Institute for Indigenous Education was created in 1972 which increased the grants available to Mapuche children, and improved literacy – in Spanish and the Mapuche language, Mapudungun – and schooling programmes to the communities. A new government agency, the Directorate of Indigenous Affairs, was formed to promote the interests of the Mapuche people.

The Allende period opened up to the Mapuche opportunities to participate in national affairs in a way which would have been unthinkable under previous governments; it also created possibilities for the development of indigenous culture and organizations.

The coup instigated by the Chilean armed forces under the leadership of General Pinochet in September 1973 reversed the programmes of agrarian reform and for the restoration of indigenous lands. Mapuche who were involved in political organizations or took part in land invasions faced imprisonment, torture and death at the hands of the armed forces, police and paramilitary death squads. The expropriation of large estates was halted and a dismantling of the agrarian reform of the previous decade was set in motion. The Mapuche began again to lose land to the powerful landowners who had backed the coup. Decree Law No. 2568 for the 'Indians, Indian lands, the Division of the Reserves and the Liquidation of the Indian Communities' of 1979 purposefully aims at the destruction of the Mapuche. It allows anyone living in a Mapuche community, irrespective of whether he or she is Mapuche, to demand that land traditionally held in common be divided. Once divided the lands are no longer deemed indigenous, nor the people Indian. As a result of the decree the number of Mapuche communities has fallen from 2,066 in 1979 to 655 in 1985.[54] Mapuche lands amount to only 350,000 hectares, a little over one per cent of their original territory. The government has also approved special tax incentives for communities that divide their land and penalties for those that do not.[55]

The national organization of Mapuche, ADMAPU, has brought together the communities to resist the programme of the government and is allied to other organizations working for democracy in Chile. But ADMAPU's combativity has attracted persecution by the police and right-wing death squads, and Mapuche leaders and activists have been murdered, imprisoned and sent into internal exile.

ADMAPU brings together 1,350 communities and aims to maintain the culture and identity of the Mapuche people. At its third National Assembly in January 1983 ADMAPU approved the Alternative Project for the Mapuche People whose principal objectives were as follows:

> *We declare ourselves*:
> ● For a new society, just and democratic, in which we can participate as a people with equal rights vis-à-vis other social sectors of the country. We believe that a new democracy without the participation of the Mapuche people cannot be a democracy.
> ● In favour of the development and progress of society, participating in the strong unions of peasants and workers in our country. Our historical place is to be together with those participating actively in the process of social, economic and political transformation of society.
> ● For the autonomy and self-determination of our people in as much as we should be managers of and protagonists in our own process of development
> ● Finally, and with what has gone above, we demand participation in the drawing up of a new political constitution which reserves and guarantees our rights and cultural heritage in accordance with our existence as an ethnic population.[56]

Two decades ago, in the 1960s, the Mapuche played a limited role in the political transformation of their country. They were passive recipients of change. Today in Chile, as in other parts of Latin America, the indigenous people are an essential part of the alliance of forces struggling for national liberation.

Brazilian Indians in the path of development

Although there are only some 225,000 Indians in Brazil, a little over 0.1 per cent of the total population, three-quarters of them are located in the Amazonian region.[57] There they have lived in relative isolation for centuries, largely unaffected by developments elsewhere in the country. In recent years, however, Amazonia has been earmarked for intensive capitalist development and increasingly their world is being impinged upon by outside forces. Initially, these indigenous communities were easy prey to the imported diseases and judicial dissimulation of the colonizers; they were, as Shelton Davis has argued, victims of the great economic miracle about to be performed in the Amazon.[58] But in the last few years the Indians of Brazil have created their own organizations, won the support of large sectors of Brazilian society and are now actively defending their rights and their homelands. They have now entered into a struggle for land.

The development of the Amazon region has long been on the agenda of Brazilian politicians. This area, some 30 times the size of England, is the largest frontier zone in the world and is thought to possess large mineral and potential land resources. In the past there have been sporadic incursions into the region in order to extract gold or diamonds and, at the turn of the century, rubber. Prospectors have always penetrated the region, as have settlers escaping poverty and landlessness; but until recently there has been no national policy for the development of the Amazon region.

In the 1890s the Brazilian Government attempted to learn more about the region and commissioned Candido Mariano da Silva Rondon to carry out a survey and establish basic telegraph services. In 1910 an Indian Protection Service (SPI) was formed and some of the first efforts to pacify the indigenous population were made. Then in 1940 the President of Brazil, Getulio Vargas, announced his own desire to conquer the waters and forests of the Amazon and the first colonization schemes were organized in the states of Pará and Mato Grosso.

Since the early 1960s, however, the Government of Brazil has made the opening up of the interior of the country a priority in its development policy. A military coup in 1964 brought to power a government allied to foreign, and especially United States, business interests. The mineral codes of 1934 and 1954 which had limited the freedom of outside mining companies were abrogated and various international companies were given exploration rights within the region. Further changes to tax laws governing profit remittances allowed the development of large-scale ranching by Brazilian and foreign entrepreneurs. 'Operation Amazon' was launched by the government in 1966 and an administrative body, SUDAM – the Superintendency for the Amazon – charged with its implementation. The whole project was underwritten by massive inflows of foreign capital and multilateral loans.

The process of development was reinforced in 1970 with the creation of a new overall programme: the PIN, a Plan for National Integration. The new plan included a massive road-building programme, with a highway crossing from Santarém in the north to Cuiabá in the south, and from Paraíba in the east to the Peruvian border on the west. In total over 15,000 kilometres of roads across some of the most densely forested and difficult terrain in the world were planned. Accompanying the road-building programme was to be an equally ambitious scheme for the colonization of the areas either side of the highways. An expected five million landless peasants were to be relocated, each family with a plot of 50 hectares or more. The colonization programme was the responsibility of INCRA, the Institute for Colonization and Agrarian Reform.

What has been the effect of this massive programme of development upon the indigenous communities of Brazil? Since 1970 various tribal groups have been decimated, and the major cause of the decline of numbers has been disease. The Indians of Brazil are highly vulnerable, as indeed are all the indigenous peoples of the Americas, to imported diseases. Ailments such as chickenpox, measles, tuberculosis and influenza have spread rapidly and mercilessly through whole tribes and proved fatal. Contact by colonizers without proper measures to immunize the Indian communities continues to take place. One extensive study in 1972 reported it found some demographic improvements as a consequence of the medical activities of the National Indian Foundation, FUNAI, and the Christian missions. Other reports continue to place the absence of medical services among Indians and the devastating effects of contact between outsiders and Indians as a principal source of serious epidemics among the tribes.[59] The great numbers of settlers coming into the Amazon region constitutes, therefore, a threat to all indigenous communities which have remained relatively unassimilated.

Development projects which include road construction, hydro-electric schemes, mineral exploitation, timber-felling and deforestation for cattle-rearing have taken place on land inhabited by indigenous peoples. A study in 1981 identified seven hydro-electric projects either planned or in progress, threatening between 32 and 34 Indian areas and flooding or causing the expropriation of at least 100,000 hectares of land.[60] Tucuruí Dam in the state of Pará flooded 2,000 square kilometres of forest, part of which comprised land officially recognized in 1975 as the territory of the Parakanás.

The major roads through the Amazon have all passed through indigenous land. The BR-808 passed through the Xingu Park in 1970 and caused the removal of several groups of Txukurramãe; in the same year, the Transamazonian Highway passed through Parakaná land and the resulting contact with non-Indians led to 40 deaths of Indians from influenza; the Cuiabá-Santarém road brought contact between the Kreen-Akrore and settlers which resulted in the death of as much as 80 per cent of the tribe; the northern perimeter highway which passes through Yanomami land has brought with it serious epidemics of measles, malaria and other imported diseases. At least six road systems are presently cutting through indigenous land and bringing sickness and conflict in their wake.[61]

In the agribusiness sector various massive sales of public land have taken place to foreign and Brazilian corporate interests. The United States shipping millionaire, Daniel Ludwig, bought 1.5 million hectares of virgin forest for timber extraction and ranching on which were located nine Indian villages. Volkswagen of Brazil own a ranch of over 140,000 hectares in the state of Pará, part of which is on traditional Indian land. Numerous transnational corporations, including US Steel, Bethlehem Steel, Rio Tinto Zinc and ALCOA, have been or still are involved in mineral extraction projects on land recognized by the federal government as indigenous.[62]

In 1981, the Brazilian armaments firm Capemí and a Japanese company called Agromax, used toxic defoliating agents, supplied in part by US multinational Dow Chemical. The defoliants – principally a refined version of Agent Orange, the chemical used in the Vietnam War – were dropped over an area of nearly 2,500 square kilometres to clear a site for a hydro-electric station. Some 7,000 people, including two entire Indian tribes, are alleged to have died as a direct consequence.[63]

Funding for many of these projects has been raised from the World Bank, USAID, the Export–Import Bank, and the EEC as well as private banks and financial institutions. The pillage of the Amazon has attracted international speculation on a grand scale. The fate of the vulnerable Indian communities standing in the wake of such powerful forces, however, has been incidental to the deliberations of planning bodies and outside investors. One of the most grandiose schemes planned on Indian land is the Polonoroeste project. The Polonoroeste is an integrated development project including road-building, colonization and agricultural production in the west of Brazil and covering an area of nearly 160,000 square miles – not far short of the surface area of Sweden. An estimated 25 Indian groups with a total population of about 8,000 are affected.[64] In 1981 the World Bank approved a loan of US$ 300 million for the project. In its 1981 evaluation the Bank stated:

> The principal conclusion of the present report is that the Northwest has the potential to become an important agricultural and timber producing region of Brazil, and a place where migrants from other parts of the country may be productively and permanently settled on small-scale farms.

However, it went on to describe the project as possessing 'a higher-than-normal degree of risks'. More particularly, the report warned that

> the government should be prepared to accept some of the negative effects frequently associated with accelerated development in frontier areas. Included among these negative effects are likely to be: (1) continued conflicts over land-related issues, including some invasions of Indian lands . . .[65]

In the event, a special project to protect the Indian population was made a condition of the loan by the World Bank and additional funds were made available to FUNAI, the National Indian Foundation. FUNAI was, under the agreement, charged with demarcating the 13 areas of Indian occupation and ensuring their protection. However, by 1984 only three of the thirteen had been legally demarcated, and two of these only partially. On the Igarapé Lourdes reservation, for example, which is the homeland of the Gavião and Arara Indians, 350 settler families had invaded and set up small farms. In another area of the Polonoroeste project, one of the roads passes through the land traditionally occupied by four Nambiquara groups. The Nambiquara, one of the most vulnerable of Brazil's indigenous minorities because of their susceptibility to imported diseases, were largely uncontacted until 1970.[66]

In Pará and Maranhão another massive project is underway. The Greater Carajás project is on an even grander scale than the Polonoroeste and has attracted numerous TNCs (transnational companies) as well as EEC and World Bank support. In the project area are major deposits of iron ore, bauxite, nickel, manganese and gold and there are some ten million hectares of land thought suitable for large-scale agribusiness. In 1981 of some US$ 30.6 billion of direct investment 30 per cent was to be met by foreign businesses and banks. For the indigenous communities of Gavião, Guayajará and others as well as the many non-Indian settlers, the project is a potential disaster. Some 100,000 people will be dispossessed of their lands and join the already vast labour reserve; 10,000 Indians living in the zone will be displaced. Their forests are the last in the entire state of Maranhão. Once these have disappeared, there will be no means for them to survive.[67] The French oil company Elf-Aquitaine, after public pressure, finally offered the paltry sum of 300 million Cruzeiros ($136,000) to the Satere-Maue Indians as compensation for the destruction of their lands.

Projects like those of Carajás and Polonoroeste are only the larger-scale of many exploration and exploitation schemes in the whole Amazon region. The building of roads and the generally favourable atmosphere for foreign companies have led to growing investment and speculation which in turn have precipitated small-scale and even individual prospecting for gold and other minerals. In the rapid development of the region the Indian peoples have been largely ignored. While it may be possible to argue that the government can in no way control the activities of individual colonizers and prospectors, it has itself initiated integrated programmes for the economic development of certain zones without carrying out adequate social impact studies or ensuring that the Indian peoples likely to be affected are protected from incursions on to their land. Indeed, certain government officials have plainly stated their attitudes towards the Indians. In 1975 the governor of Roraima in the north of Amazonia declared as noted earlier that 'an area as rich as this, with gold, diamonds and uranium, cannot afford the luxury of preserving half a dozen Indian tribes who are holding back development.'[68] The area so coveted by the governor was the Yanomami Park, the land of over 4,500 Indians, which had been 'interdicted'.[69] In fact, the interdiction has meant little in practice as the Yanomami land continues to be invaded by mining companies and illegal settlers. Only the final demarcation can provide a strong legal basis for excluding these people, since the interdiction represents little more than a declaration of intent on behalf of the government. In the case of the Yanomami the reluctance to create a Yanomami reservation is particularly dangerous. Many Indians of the region are uncontacted and have, therefore, not been vaccinated, making them highly vulnerable to the imported diseases carried by outsiders.

Of course the overall impact of these multitudinous and largely uncontrolled development projects in the region has not been fully assessed. While it is clear enough that many indigenous communities are threatened, there are also other possible problems associated with these developments. The dependency on outside finance and investment for most of the projects has been criticized by Brazilian scientists and economists.[70] Loans have had to be raised on the international market which can only exacerbate the debit crisis crippling Brazil. The projects in the Amazon, attractive as they appear to be on the surface, grossly distort the Brazilian economy, diverting precious funds and expertise away from neglected regions like the north-east in favour of the spurious benefits of the Amazon. Furthermore, the general ecological deterioration – the indiscriminate logging of rainforest, the deterioration of the soil quality, the effects on water tables and the general impact on the ecosystem – is now causing international concern.

After the Transamazonian Highway was built and INCRA, the Agrarian Reform Agency, began its colonization programme, it took only five years for the scheme to collapse ignominiously. Soil fertility declined rapidly after the plots were cleared, crop failure was common and there were no proper means for commercialization. By 1977 over one-third of the original settlers had abandoned their plots.[71] According to one environmental specialist the Polonoroeste project may lead to the irreversible loss of nearly 40,000 square miles of intact ecosystem.[72]

On the political level, land conflicts have increased not only between settlers and Indians, but between settlers and large landowners ready to evict them to create large ranches. Just as elsewhere in Brazil, the systems of land tenure – with large estates and small subsistence plots – soon re-establish themselves. As one observer has noted: 'As always occurs on the frontier, the small fish kill one another, while their larger brethren take part in the war from a distance.'[73] If one of the rationales of the opening up of the Amazon is to provide land for poor peasants, it has been to date almost universally unsuccessful.

Yet Brazilian law guarantees the rights of the Indian peoples to their own land. The Indian Statute of 19 December 1973 contains a provision which guarantees 'the Indians and native communities, in the terms of the constitution, permanent possession of the land they inhabit, recognizing their right to exclusive usufruct of the natural wealth and all the utilities existing on that land' (Act No. 6001, Art 2, Para IX). Furthermore, the Act authorized the demarcation of Indian land within five years and ensured its legal protection.

However, despite what appears to be a clear constitutional safeguard for indigenous land, the same statute left the government a number of loopholes. Article 20 gave the Union the right to expropriate Indian land and relocate Indian communities elsewhere in the interests of national security or development.[74]

Notwithstanding the legal loopholes of the Indian Statute, even the demarcation of Indian land was not implemented within the prescribed timetable. In 1973 although there were some two dozen reserves in existence, only Xingu Park was for the exclusive use of Indian peoples. The others were partially invaded by non-Indian colonizers and had been afforded no protection by FUNAI. By 1978, less than one-third of the territories had been demarcated.

More recently in 1983 a succession of government measures have attempted to reduce the legal status of the Indian. A revision of the Civil Code proposed that Indians should be defined as 'absolutely incapable before the civil law' and made completely subject to the authority of FUNAI. At present Indians are considered as 'relatively incapable' and, therefore, require the assistance of the Indian Foundation, FUNAI, to which they can express their wishes. The new law would take away this channel of communication. In the same year a further and contradictory amendment was proposed which would completely emancipate the Indians and make them ordinary Brazilian citizens. Although appearing well-intentioned, the amendment would effectively deny Indian communities any communal land base and take away the minimal protection provided by FUNAI. It was, therefore, strongly rejected by the Indian peoples themselves.

Other legislation in 1983 facilitated mining on Indian land by granting to FUNAI the responsibility of granting concessions to companies on a case by case basis. The Presidential Decree of November 1983 opened the floodgates and within one month 300 requests had been received from mining companies. While the November 1983 decree forced FUNAI to act as an intermediary for mining interests, an earlier decree in February took away from the agency its responsibility in defining Indian land. The February decree gave to an interministerial working group the job of identifying Indian land and thereby allowed various state bodies not concerned with indigenous rights a say in land demarcation.

FUNAI, the National Indian Foundation, has not had an unequivocal history. Set up orginally as the Indian Protection Service (SPI), its name was charged after allegations of corruption and abuse of Indians were confirmed in the 1950s. FUNAI is a department of the Brazilian Ministry of the Interior, its director is appointed by the President, and it is, therefore, subject to political pressures. Its policies are determined by national considerations which at the present time favour economic development of the Amazon region and integration of its native inhabitants. On the whole, FUNAI acts as a mediator for the state; its senior staff have often been completely ignorant of the condition and problems of Indian peoples. However, FUNAI has also recruited dedicated and skilled field workers and achieved modest success in programmes of medical welfare. Indeed, Jurandy Marcos da Fonseca, President of FUNAI, was removed from office by the government because he opposed mining on Indian land and refused to sign the enabling decree of November 1983. But on the key issue of demarcating a territorial base and ensuring its full protection, FUNAI has almost completely failed.

Yet until recently, the Indian peoples of Brazil have offered only sporadic resistance to the incursions on to their land. Settlers, prospectors and missionaries have from time to time been killed by small groups but it was not until a decade or so ago that a broad-based organization of Indians undertook to act concertedly against the threat to their land. During the 1970s meetings of chiefs began to take place and in 1978 23 leaders representing 13 different tribes met in the capital, Brasilia. There they held discussions about the general problems faced by indigenous peoples in Brazil and agreed to unite to demand land. In April 1980 nine Indian leaders came together and formed the Union of Indian Nations (UNI) and by September of that year some further 30 leaders had joined. The objectives of the new union were to represent member indigenous nations and promote cultural autonomy, self-determination and mutual collaboration. The union also planned to work towards the recovery of their lands and laws to protect their inviolability. In December 1980, at an assembly of over 200 Indian representatives, one of the delegates expressed the spirit of the new militancy of the indigenist movement: 'Those who feel the problem of the Indians are Indian, and those who have to solve those problems must be the united indigenous peoples.'[75]

Coincidentally the church began to support the efforts of the nascent indigenous movement. Throughout the military dictatorship, from 1964 to 1985, individual priests had played a vital role in the defence of human rights. As the military regime turned its attention to the exploitation of Amazonia, many priests found themselves the only spokesmen for the Indians. The church established an organization, the Indigenist Missionary Council (CIMI), which brought together priests and missionaries working in Indian areas; CIMI also produced a bi-monthly newspaper, *Porantim*, which actively defended the Indian cause. Unlike many missionaries evangelizing in South America, CIMI is committed to Indian self-determination.

Support has also come from other non-indigenous quarters. In 1980, 80 employees of FUNAI, dissatisfied by its policy, set up the Brazilian Society of Indigenists which gave direct assistance to the indigenous movement. A number of opposition members of parliament also formed a pro-Indian group. On specific issues, such as the creation of the Yanomami Park in Roraima, the Indian movement has been able to get the support of a wide section of Brazilian society. The pro-Indian groups have been joined by a distinguished group of scientists and academics who are concerned about damage to the overall ecology of Amazonia.[76]

In 1983 the first Indian was elected to congress. Mario Juruna, a Xavante Indian representing Rio de Janeiro, immediately put in motion a number of new initiatives. Most importantly, Juruna sought to change FUNAI. He succeeded in getting approval for the creation of an Indian Commission which had the right to investigate allegations of mistreatment of Indians, to propose pro-Indian legislation and investigate the implementation of existing Indian legislation.[77]

While the indigenous movement has been active at the national level, there have been several Indian groups which have taken direct action. On 23 March 1984, for example, a group of Txukurramãe took over a ferry linking one of the major trans-Amazonian roads and seized several hostages. The incident arose from a longstanding dispute over land in the Xingu Park. This park had been established during the 1960s and the Txukurramãe relocated within it. In 1970, however, a major road cut across the park's northern sector and the Txukurramãe were asked to move again. Half refused to leave and remained in the isolated northern sector which was invaded by settlers who believed the area was uninhabited. Conflicts between settlers and the Txukurramãe flared up continuously.

In 1976 two workers were killed and in 1980 a further eleven were murdered. The violence did not stop further incursions on to land which the Txukurramãe properly felt was their territory.

The Txukurramãe, impatient with waiting for a solution to their dispute, seized six employees of FUNAI, including the Director of the park. Three officials subsequently sent to negotiate with the Txukurramãe were also kidnapped. The Indians were demanding the resignation of the FUNAI director as well as proper safeguards for their land. Other Indian groups in the park supported the action and declared that they were ready to fight if necessary. Meanwhile in Brasilia the new Indian deputy, Mario Juruna, raised the issue both in congress and with the Minister of the Interior. On 30 April 1984, a delegation of Indians went to Brasilia to again put their case. The resulting political lobbying and direct action at last reached a successful conclusion. The head of FUNAI was dismissed, an agreement was reached on demarcating the disputed territory and the hostages were released.[78]

In April 1984 the Second National Convention of Indian Peoples took place in Brasilia and brought together 450 representatives from 85 Indian groups as well as delegates from other countries. It was the largest meeting of Indians in the history of the movement. A National Indigenist Council was created and the Union of Indian Nations (UNI) was subdivided into five regions. Delegates declared that important tasks for the future were to train Indians in administration and restructure the Indian agency, FUNAI, so that it reflected more accurately the concerns of Brazil's indigenous peoples.[79]

UNI, is however, a fragile organization and highly dependent on financial support from church and aid agencies outside Brazil. Its leadership is composed of younger, activist Indians, who may not always receive the support of community elders. But scepticism from the traditional leadership of the communities is breaking down as the necessity of all Indian peoples to join forces to combat land alienation becomes more evident. UNI remains the only pan-tribal voice for Brazil's indigenous peoples and put up candidates for the state and federal elections in November 1986.

In 1985 Brazil elected its first civilian president, Tancredo Neves, since 1964. Neves had expressed interest in giving the indigenous population a fairer deal but his death on the eve of taking office cut short any positive new programme. His successor, President José Sarney, has shown more caution in his dealings with the Indian peoples. Major decisions concerning the demarcation of Indian land have been placed in the hands of an Inter-Ministerial Working Group responsible to the Minister of the Interior and the Minister of Agrarian Reform (INCRA). Meanwhile, FUNAI, the government Indian agency, has been decentralized and now has six regional offices whose superintendents are appointed by local politicians. Under such an arrangement it is likely that local political interests will prevail over Indian concerns. The prospect for a just land rights programme for Brazil's indigenous peoples seems no nearer, despite the changeover to civilian rule.

The indigenous inhabitants of South America have successfully forged regional and continent-wide organizations. There is a clear sense of identity, particularly among the forest-dwelling peoples whose lands are being taken over by multinational corporations, big ranchers and colonizers. Those same economic and political forces are at work in Asia as well, but the indigenous peoples are for the most part struggling against them in isolation. There have not developed so far any regional organizations representing peoples from different countries in Asia nor are there even organizations which bring together distinct peoples of the same country. In India, whose tribal population is greater than the aggregate of all the indigenous peoples of the Americas, there are virtually no independent organizations representing their interests. However, this situation is now changing and tribal peoples who have passively moved aside when faced with development programmes on their land are now challenging their governments.

Notes

1. Centro Antropológico de Documentación de America-Latina, Mexico, cited in *Le Monde Diplomatique*, March 1982, p.17.

2. Eric Sabourin, 'Des liens renouvelés avec les campagnes', *Le Monde Diplomatique*, March 1982, p.19, notes that of the 2 million or so living in the slums of Lima, half are Indian; in La Paz a majority of Indian women are domestic slaves, working from 5 in the morning until midnight, according to *Wiñaymarka* (La Paz), November 1983, p.8.

3. Anti-Slavery Society, 'The land rights of Latin American Indians', report to International NGO Conference on Indigenous Peoples and the Land, Geneva, 15-18 September 1981, pp.5-6.

4. Julio Cotler, 'Traditional haciendas and communities in a context of political mobilization in Peru', in Rodolfo Stavenhagen (ed.), *Agrarian problems and peasant movements in Latin America* (Anchor Books, New York, 1970) p.536.

5. Antonia García, 'Agrarian reform and social development in Bolivia', in Stavenhagen, p.314.

6. Anti-Slavery Society, p.6.

7. International Labour Organisation, 'Indigenous and tribal peoples and land rights'. Note by International Labour Office, 1984, pp.29 and 31.

8. *IWGIA Newsletter*, no.27, June 1981, p.61.

9. *IWGIA Newsletter*, no.25/26, March 1981, p.42.

10. *IWGIA Newsletter*, no.38, July 1984, pp.37-42; Survival International, 'Indian massacre in Colombia', Urgent Action Bulletin, February 1984.

11. *IWGIA Newsletter*, no.19, June 1978, p.16.

12. Cf. Marie-Chantal Barre, 'De l'indigénisme à l'indianisme', *Le Monde Diplomatique*, March 1982, pp.18-19.

13. Cited in *IWGIA Newsletter*, no.27, June 1981, p.7.

14. Cf. Yves Materne (ed.), *The Indian awakening in Latin America* (Friendship Press, New York, 1980).

15. *IWGIA Newsletter*, no.38, July 1984, p.58.

16. David Harris cited in Norman Whitten, *Amazonian Ecuador: an ethnic interface in ecological, social and ideological perspectives*, IWGIA Document 34, 1978, p.52.

17. Stefano Varese, *The forest Indians in the present political situation of Peru*, IWGIA Document 8, 1972, p.4.

18. Richard Chase Smith, *The dialectics of domination in Peru: native communities and the myth of the vast Amazonian emptiness*, Cultural Survival, Occasional Paper 8, October 1982, for full discussion of project.

19. Stephen Corry, 'Cycles of dispossession: Amazonian Indians and government in Peru', *Survival International Review*, no.43, 1984, p.52.

20. Ibid., p.57.

21. Survival International, 'Peru: Amuesha land threatened', Urgent Action Bulletin, November 1983.

22. Whitten, p.54.

23. Esteban Mosonyi, 'The situation of the Indians of Venezuela. Perspectives and solution', *The situation of the Indian in South America* (World Council of Churches, Geneva, 1972) pp.43-55.

24. Ibid., p.51; see also Walter Coppens, *The anatomy of a land invasion scheme in Yekuana territory, Venezuela*, IWGIA Document 9, 1972, and Nelly Jiménez, *The dynamics of the Yecuana political system*, IWGIA Document 12, 1973.

25. Adolfo Triana, 'Indian groups in Colombia', *Survival International Review*, vol.6, nos.3 and 4, Autumn 1981, p.8.

26. Cf. William Henningsgaard, *The Akawaio, the Upper Mazaruni hydroelectric project and national development in Guyana*, Cultural Survival Occasional Paper 4, June 1981; Gordon Bennett and Audrey Colson, *The damned: the plight of the Akawaio Indians of Guyana*, Survival International Document VI, n.d.

27. Bennett and Colson, p.7.

28. *Survival International News*, no.6, 1984, p.3.

29. Cf. *Survival International Review*, vol.7, no.2, Summer 1982, pp.4-19.

30. Eric Navet, *Camopi, commune Indienne? La politique 'Indienne' de la France en Guyane en 1984*, Diffusion Inti et Geria, Paris, June 1984.

31. Richard Chase Smith, p.51.

32. The majority of indigenous peoples in Argentina live in the Chaco region in the north-east of the country; some 10,000 Araucanian Indians are estimated to be living in Nequen province in the south-west. On Argentina see Nemesio Rodriguez, *Oppression in Argentina: the Mataco case*, IWGIA Document 21, 1975.

33. It is estimated that 40 per cent of the regional Amazon economy rests on narcotics trafficking. For discussion on effects of the cocaine boom on indigenous peoples, see Antonil, *Mama Coca* (Hassle Free Press, 1978).

34. Jean Pierre Chaumeil, *Between zoo and slavery: the Yagua of Eastern Peru in their present situation*, IWGIA Document 49, 1984, p.17.

35. Jurgen Riester, *Indians of Eastern Bolivia: aspects of their present situation*, IWGIA Document 18, 1975, p.53.

36. Brigitte Simón, Barbara Schuchard, Jurgen Riester and Barbara Riester, *I sold myself; I was bought*, IWGIA Document 42, 1980, p.8.

37. Ibid., p.66.

38. Anti-Slavery Society, 'Bonded and forced labour in Peru and India', Report for 1984 to the United Nations Working Group on Slavery.

39. L. Miraglio cited in Mark Munzel, *The Aché Indians: genocide in Paraguay*, IWGIA Document 11, 1973, p.7.

40. Munzel, ibid., p.24; see also R. Arens, *Genocide in Paraguay* (Temple University Press, 1976).

41. R. Arens, *The forest Indians in Stroessner's Paraguay: survival or extinction?*, Survival International Document IV, 1978, p.3.

42. Ibid., p.6.

43. Luke Holland, 'Holy smoke: Protestant Missions and the Indians of Paraguay', *Survival International Review*, no.43, 1984, pp.36-44.

44. Eg. Soren Hvalkof and Peter Aaby (eds.), *Is God an American?* (IWGIA/SI, 1981); David Stoll, *Fishers of men or founders of empire?* (Zed Press, 1982).

45. Bartolomeu Meliá, *Accion* (Asunción), November 1970, cited in Hugh O'Shaughnessy, *What future for the Amerindians of South America?*, Minority Rights Group, no.15, 1973, p.14.

46. *Survival International News*, no.2, 1983.

47. Peter Kloos, *The Akuriyo of Surinam: a case of emergence from isolation*, IWGIA Document 27, 1977, p.21.

48. Ibid., p.22.

49. Cf. Ernesto Salazar, *An Indian federation in lowland Ecuador*, IWGIA Document 28, 1977.

50. Louis-Jean Calvet, 'Ecoles radiophoniques chez les Shuars', *Le Monde Diplomatique*, March 1982, pp.16-17.

51. Stephen Corry, p.68.

52. On the Mapuche people see Bernardo Berdichewsky, *The Araucanian Indian in Chile*, IWGIA Document 20, 1975 and Kenneth I. Taylor, 'A report on the situation of the Mapuche Indians of Chile', *An end to laughter? Tribal peoples and economic development*, Survival International Review, no.44, 1985, pp.125-35.

53. Berdichewsky, p.24.

54. 'Human rights violations against the Mapuche of Chile', Report for 1985 to the United Nations Working Group on Indigenous Populations presented by the Comité Exterior Mapuche.

55. Kenneth Taylor, p.132.

56. Cited in Patricia González, 'Chile: a history of dispossession and discrimination', *IWGIA Newsletter*, no.42, June 1985, p.56.

57. According to the Indigenist Missionary Council (CIMI) 180,000 are in permanent contact, 30,000 are integrated (of whom 10,000 live in and around Manaus) and 15,000 are uncontacted.

58. Shelton Davis, *Victims of the miracle* (Cambridge University Press, 1977); see also R. Goodland and H. Irwin, *Amazon jungle: green hell to red desert?* (Amsterdam, 1977) and Darcy Ribeiro, *Os Indios e a civilização* (Rio de Janeiro, 1970).

59. Cf. Edwin Brooks et al, *Tribes of the Amazon Basin in Brazil 1972*, report for the Aborigines Protection Society (Charles Knight, London, 1973); Alcida Ramos and Kenneth Taylor, *The Yanoama in Brazil, 1979*, ARC/IWGIA/SI Document, no.37, 1979, pp.123-7.

60. Paul Aspelin and Silvio Coelho dos Santos, *Indian areas threatened by hydroelectric projects in Brazil*, IWGIA Document, no.44, 1981, pp.3 and 5.

61. *IWGIA Newsletter*, no.34, July 1983, pp.20-30.

62. *Opinião*, No.128, 18 April 1975, cited in Anna Presland, 'Reconquest', *Survival International Review*, vol.4, no.1, Spring 1979, pp.21-3.

63. *Morning Star*, London, 7 December 1984.

64. Survival International, 'Brazil: Polonoroeste development threatens Indians', Urgent Action Bulletin, October 1983.

65. World Bank, *Brazil: integrated development of the northwest frontier*, Washington DC, 1981, cited in Cultural Survival, *In the paths of Polonoroeste: endangered peoples of western Brazil*, Occasional Paper 6, October 1981, p.13.

66. Cf. Cultural Survival, ibid.

67. Iara Ferraz, 'Os Indios pagam primeiro e mais caro', *Ciencia hoje*, November/December 1982; on the project see also Centre de Recherche et

d'Information pour le Développement (CRID), *Brésil: le projet Grand Carajas*, January 1983.

68. Cited in Robin Wright, 'The Yanomami saga', *Cultural Survival Quarterly*, vol.6, no.2, Spring 1982, p.29.

69. In Brazilian law interdiction is a provisional first step. After interdiction the land is delimited, i.e. boundaries are surveyed, and then demarcated, i.e. physically marked out.

70. Cf. *Raw Materials Report*, vol.1, no.2, Winter 1982.

71. Cultural Survival Special Report, *Brazil*, December 1979, p.45.

72. Robert Goodland, 'Brazil's environmental progress in Amazonian development', paper submitted to 44th International Congress of Americanists, Manchester, 6-10 September 1982.

73. *IWGIA Newsletter*, no.34, July 1983, p.24.

74. For discussion of Indian law see Anna Presland, Cultural Survival Special Report, *Brazil*, December 1979.

75. *IWGIA Newsletter*, no.27, June 1981, p.48.

76. Jean Eglin and Hervé Théry, *Le pillage de l'Amazonie* (Maspero, Paris, 1982) pp.160-5.

77. Cf. *Porantim*, June/July 1983, p.13; for Juruna's maiden speech see *Porantim*, May 1983, pp.8-9.

78. Survival International, 'Brazil: Xingu Indians take hostages as land conflicts escalate', Urgent Action Bulletin, April 1984.

79. *IWGIA Newsletter*, no.38, July 1984, pp.23-5.

8. The Colonization of Asia's Tribal Peoples

The great majority of the world's indigenous and tribal peoples live in the Asia region. In the area from the Red Sea to the Pacific Ocean, including what was once named Asia Minor and the immense Asian territories of the Soviet Union there may be as many as 150 million people in this category. But such figures need qualification.

The recorded history of the region is long and complex. Great empires, such as the Mughal or the Chinese Han, have been born, expanded and declined before the European powers established their colonies. As a consequence of this turbulent history peoples have fled in the face of menacing expansionist kingdoms and other peoples have settled and remained behind at their decline. Some peoples, particularly the Chinese, have travelled and traded extensively. With all these movements and migrations most countries in Asia today have numerous ethnic groups within their boundaries. As one authority has commented on India:

> It will be appreciated that in an ancient racial melting pot like India, no sociologists, historians or anthropologists are in a position to say with any degree of certainty that the scheduled tribes of India are the only indigenous populations. Further, there is no certainty as to who displaced whom and which of the races in India are today descendants of the conquered or the conquerors.[1]

The question of who is indigenous in Asia is less obvious than in countries like the United States or Brazil where there is a clear history of colonization.

What distinguishes these peoples is not that they can be readily identified as the original inhabitants of a designated territory, even though in certain cases this may be so, but that they are experiencing many of the features of colonization: racial discrimination, religious persecution, economic marginalization and political oppression.

Many of the indigenous and tribal peoples of Asia have a distinctive minority language and a separate culture from that of the mainstream. They inhabit isolated or relatively isolated regions such as forests, hills or deserts where they hold land in common or in accordance with some form of customary ownership. Until comparatively recently these peoples have been able to exist more or less independently of wider national political developments. In the period of colonial administration their natural resources were systematically exploited.

117

However, since the withdrawal of the European powers from the region following the Second World War, there has been a rapid escalation of economic exploitation of tribal land and a growing determination by the independent states to incorporate the territories and assimilate the peoples that formerly had enjoyed some degree of autonomy.

It will be clear that a single chapter on the tribal peoples of Asia must omit considerable detail. There will be no reference to the ten million or so Kurds living in Iran, Iraq, Turkey, Syria and Soviet Armenia, or national minorities such as the Armenians or the Palestinians who all have homelands and may legitimately lay claim to independent nations of their own.[2] The situation of the tribal peoples of the USSR and China is discussed in Chapter 11 and that of the five million or so Bedouin in the Arabian peninsula is referred to in the section dealing with nomads in Chapter 9. This chapter makes only cursory reference to the tribal peoples of Iran, Afghanistan, Pakistan, Taiwan, Sri Lanka, Indo-China and Burma, many of whom have been caught in the destructive history of super-power politics of recent years. Longer sections examine the situation of tribal peoples in India, Bangladesh, Indonesia, Malaysia, Thailand and the Philippines.

Table 8.1
Tribal Peoples in Asia

Country	Numbers	% of Total Pop.
Afghanistan	6.7 million Pathan	
	300,000 Baluchis	
	3 million Koochis	
Bangladesh	600,000 (official figures)	
	1.5 million (estimates)	1
Burma	11 million (11 main groups)	30
India	51 million, over 200 groups	7
Indonesia	1.5 million (300 ethnic groups)	1
	(government figure)	
Laos	800,000	23
Malaysia	Peninsula 71,000	Peninsula 4
	E. Malaysia 500,000	E. Malaysia 50
Pakistan	2.5 million federally	8
	administered	
	5.2 million provisionally	
	administered	
Philippines	6.5 million	16
Sri Lanka	2,000	
Taiwan	310,000 (10 main groups)	2
Thailand	500,000 (6 main groups)	1
Vietnam	800,000	2
Total	*85 million*	

Tribal peoples in recent history

The Indo–China wars, the Vietnam war, the Soviet invasion of Afghanistan, the Islamic Fundamentalist revolution in Iran, and the socialist revolution in Burma have all had profound effects on the local tribal populations. Indigenous peoples themselves have been engaged in independence struggles throughout the Asia region: in West Papua since 1962, in East Timor since 1974, in the south of the Philippines since 1972 and before, in Burma since 1949 and in Bangladesh the tribal minorities have fought for autonomy since 1972. It would not be an exaggeration to say that for many tribal groups the last four decades have been one long fight to establish the right to exist as an independent people.

This would certainly be true of Burma. The Karen struggle for independence in Burma is one of the most long-standing rebellions in Asia by indigenous peoples. Like the Nagas in India, the Karen demanded statehood in the run-up to British withdrawal from its colonies in Asia. During its occupation of Burma, Britain had imposed its administration on the Burmese population of the plains but had left the hill people to their own devices and officially classified their homelands as 'Excluded Areas'. When the Japanese invaded Burma, they did so with the collaboration of Burmese nationalists, but the fiercest resistance to this new invasion came from the hill tribes and especially the Karen. The Karen took the brunt of the reprisals during the Japanese occupation and perceived the Burmese nationalists allied to them as enemies. When discussions concerning independence took place between the British Government of Clement Attlee and the Burmese Nationalists led by Aung San, the Karen were formally excluded.[3]

About one-third of the Burmese population of 34 million is composed of ethnically distinct hill people. They consist of eleven main groups of which the largest are the Karen, Kachin, Shan, Chin, Palaung and Burmese Naga. In 1948 the Panglong Agreement gave the Kachins, Chins and Shans semi-autonomous status within the Union of Burma with the option to secede at the end of a ten-year period. No plebiscite was taken in 1958 and in 1962 a military dictatorship under General Ne Win was established. In 1974 a new constitution created centrally controlled administrative divisions and formally dismantled the minority states.

The socialist government of Burma has confronted the Karen independence movement since 1948, and in the 1960s it faced insurgency from the Shan, Kachin, Arakanese and Chin. For many years these peoples fought their separate wars against the Government of Burma. Indeed, there were rivalries even within the ethnic groups themselves. In Shan State, for example, there were at one time as many as 15 different armed groups, some fighting politically and others under the control of warlords involved in the profitable opium trade.

The six million Karen, for their part, however, have a well organized military and political structure. They have an army of about 20,000 under the leadership of Major General Bo Mya, and a parallel political organization consisting of a Prime Minister, a committee of Karen elders and ministers of state. The present

Karen State (Kawthoolei) although not officially recognized by the Burmese Government has its own taxation system and an annual budget of about US $2 million.[4] Its principal source of income comes from smuggling and trading goods between Rangoon and Thailand. The Karen population, however, is widely dispersed and the majority continue to live in the delta region of the Irawadi and not in the liberated hills.

However, the cost of the war which has now endured nearly 40 years is high on the civilian population – as many as 300,000 are thought to have died as a result of the war since it began in 1948. Burmese offensives into the hills occupied by the Karen have brought countless deaths and acts of savagery. Karen and other hill peoples are considered backward and inferior and are often drafted forcibly as porters. Villagers are considered automatically as insurgents, and arrested, beaten and killed.[5]

In 1976 the military and political organizations of the nine main ethnic groups formed the National Democratic Front, whose objective is the establishment of a federal union of Burma providing political, social and economic rights to all the indigenous minorities. The growing unity of the main ethnic groups has coincided with a more aggressive military policy by the Burmese armed forces. Since early 1984 the Burmese Government has escalated its military activities and increased the number of attacks on civilian villages, accusing villagers of supporting the Karen National Liberation Army. The violence has resulted in massive flights of Karen and other minorities into neighbouring Thailand where they have settled in refugee camps. By mid-1986 there were an estimated 18,000 refugees externally and a further 100,000 people are believed to have fled their villages and now live a precarious existence in the jungles. Individuals from ethnic minorities are treated as virtual slave labour by the Burmese Army. An independent report to the Anti-Slavery Society described the treatment of porters as follows:

> The Burmese army uses porters to carry food and supplies in most of the rugged, minority states of Burma where mules and other forms of transport are of little use. In theory the porters are 'volunteers' and should receive pay, but in practice the system of recruitment is widely abused by local Burmese army commanders. Since in many areas villagers run away at the first sight of the Burmese army, local commanders press into service or 'conscript' any villagers they can find. For large scale operations the numbers thus press-ganged can run into hundreds. It would appear that army commanders show little discrimination in who they take – anyone they come across would appear to be fair game. Allegations of poor treatment are many; porters often receive little or no food and no medicine. Sick porters are regarded as shirkers and are beaten and left behind. Many porters thus run away at the first chance they get though they run the risk of being shot. On occasion it is alleged porters are sent ahead of Burmese army troops in areas where rebel attacks are expected or mine-fields are suspected. And at the end of a 'tour of duty' when pay is due to the porters, unscrupulous army officers will leave the porters in the jungle or encourage their 'escape' so as to avoid payment. Soldiers then pocket the porters' pay.
>
> These allegations were made both in areas where there is active insurgency (Karenni, Karen, Mon states) but also in Arakan where there are few insurgents

today. Second-hand reports made the same allegations for the Shan and Kachin states. In all cases one of the underlying problems is the attitude of Burmese army officers to local minority villagers as peoples whom they consider 'suspect' as insurgents.[6]

The tribespeople of Burma have to a great extent remained unaffected by the super-power conflicts affecting South-East Asia. The same cannot be said for the hill tribes of Indo-China whose populations have been decimated and driven into exile by the devastation of full-scale war.

The tribespeoples of the hills of Vietnam and Laos were relatively unaffected by the movements of peoples from India and China in previous centuries. The Montagnards of south Vietnam and the hill peoples of Laos were brought into the wider history of the region in the 19th Century when the French began their occupation. Following the Second World War the Viet Minh, the nationalist Vietnamese, and the colonial French authorities both recruited the highlanders. Subsequently, with United States involvement in South-East Asia, the Montagnards were drawn into the Vietnam war.[7]

In Laos the Meo hill people were recruited by the CIA as part of its clandestine army to fight the Communist Pathet Lao. At the height of the war some 70,000 Meo were in arms and fighting the Communists; other Meo were recruited by the Communists. In 1967 the US-backed army was defeated by the Pathet Lao and the Meo homelands came under attack. The war caused permanent disruption of the traditional way of life of many highlanders. An estimated 200,000 Meo refugees fled the violence and now live in scattered communities throughout the United States, in France and in refugee camps in Thailand.[8]

Since its formation in 1975, the new Communist government in Vientiane has pursued a policy of assimilation for the hill tribes. Many have been taught Lao for the first time. Model villages have been built and health and educational facilities made available. The massive displacements and the disruptions to the social organization of Meo peoples in Laos caused by the war make any return to the self-contained life of pre-colonial time impossible.

To the west, in the arc of crisis as it has become known, in Iran, Afghanistan and Pakistan, two tribal peoples have been affected by dramatic events of the last years. The Baluchis and Pathans between them have homelands which stretch across all three countries. The Baluchis are not a homogeneous group; some tribes have become sedentarized and assimilated while others retain their distinctive, semi-nomadic way of life. The Pathans are equally heterogeneous, the highlanders most strongly guarding their traditional culture, and the farmers of the plains more closely linked to the national government.[9] In total there are more than five million Baluchis living in Iran and Pakistan and some 20 million Pathans inhabiting northern Pakistan and Afghanistan.[10]

In the period of the British Raj the Baluchis and Pathans fiercely defended their independence and were never brought under direct colonial rule. In the new Pakistan both groups retain their autonomy but equally play little part in national political life. Baluchis and Pathans, for example, hold few top

121

government or civil service posts. During the Bhutto government in the 1970s a major tribal rebellion by the Baluchis broke out. The government claimed that the insurrection was started by tribal chiefs trying to guard their traditional feudal privileges, but Baluchis maintained that Bhutto was seeking to increase state control over tribal areas. Whatever the causes, the rebellion was bloodily suppressed and since that time all minority populations are viewed with considerable suspicion. The military dictatorship of General Zia has only increased central government intervention in tribal areas. As one author has suggested:

> The likelihood diminishes that the government of Pakistan, faced with a rapidly mounting population and enormous pressures on limited land and other resources, will sacrifice control over any part of the national economy to the wish for genuine tribal autonomy.[11]

But likely to be most disruptive to the way of life of the tribespeople is the Soviet invasion of Afghanistan. Many hundreds of thousands of tribespeople have fled into Pakistan as refugees and Pakistan has become an asylum for the largest concentration of refugees in the world.[12]

In Afghanistan itself the three million or so nomadic and semi-nomadic Koochis have been affected by the civil war. Described as Afghanistan's 'silent minority', they are now much restricted in their movements within the country and across borders, and many have fled into Pakistan.[13] In Iran the Baluchis on the southern border have confronted the Khomeini government on numerous occasions since 1979.

The great political changes of this century have also affected the 300,000 or so indigenous Taiwanese, living in the mountains as rice cultivators and hunter-gatherers. The ten main tribes speak languages similar to the indigenous minorities of the Philippines. They retreated before the first wave of colonization from the province of Fukien on mainland China in the 17th Century and onwards. The mainland Chinese were fleeing the destruction caused by the war between the Ming dynasty and the Manchus. A second, more recent wave of migration, occurred when the Nationalist Chinese Army under Chiang Kai-Shek made Taiwan their headquarters. Both migrations have reduced the indigenous minority to only about three per cent of the total population. The Fukien Chinese make up well over three-quarters of the population and control much of the business activity, while the nationalist Chinese maintain their political grip of the country through their control of one of the world's biggest armies. The indigenous minorities have little access to the political system and do not benefit from the economic prosperity of the country.[14] Furthermore, intermarriage between Chinese men and aboriginal women – partly because of the lower bride price – and the drift to the cities by the indigenous inhabitants in search of work, is resulting in a rapid process of assimilation.

One of the smallest tribal groups in Asia is the Vedda of Sri Lanka. The Vedda are the island's original inhabitants. When the Indo-Aryans invaded around 500 BC, they were driven to the eastern forests. There are now only about 2,000 Vedda living in small groups as hunter-gatherers and swidden cultivators. Since the early 1980s the little land they still occupy has become threatened. In 1982 the World Wildlife Fund launched a campaign to save the elephant by creating a conservation park on Vedda land. The Vedda are now forbidden to enter the area. Then, in 1983, a major irrigation project was authorized, affecting indigenous territory. The consequence of both these projects has been to seriously disrupt the Vedda way of life and lead to the removal of all but one of their communities.[15]

The scheduled tribes of India

About 51 million people in India, seven per cent of the total population, are tribal. But to call them indigenous is to invite debate, for the long history of migrations of peoples in the subcontinent makes it impossible for any single group to claim antecedence. Nevertheless, if the scheduled tribes, as they are designated by the government, are not indisputably India's original peoples, they are certainly among the country's earliest inhabitants. Today, however, they are the most isolated and marginalized of all the different populations living in India. One author has dubbed them a 'subterranean civilization'.[16] Another has described tribal India as an internal colony exploited by Hindu India.[17]

There are more than 200 tribes speaking more than 100 main languages scattered throughout India. Some tribal groups are numerous. The Gonds and Santals, for example, have populations of over two million but others can be measured in hundreds. They are located in large numbers in the north-east, in the States of Arunacchal Pradesh, Mizoram and Nagaland where they are the majority population, and across the centre of the country, in the states of Bihar, Madhya Pradesh and Orissa. About 85 per cent of India's scheduled tribes live in the central states, but in none of these states do they account for more than a quarter of the population.

Although these tribal groups are distinct from one another in many respects, they share a number of common features. Most *adivasis* (tribespeople) live in remote hilly or forested areas. Less than ten per cent practise shifting cultivation but more than half depend upon forest produce for a livelihood; only three per cent live in towns. Their level of socio-economic development is low; incomes are lower than for any other group in Indian society, fewer attend schools, fewer read and write and fewer have access to health facilities. In the state of Andhra Pradesh, for example, the scheduled tribes have incomes of only 34 per cent of those of non-tribal people and the literacy rate is 11 per cent against an all-India rate of 29 per cent.[18] The report of the Commissioner for Scheduled Castes and Scheduled Tribes for 1979-81 stated that the majority of tribal communities survived below the poverty line and were among the country's poorest 30 per cent of the population.[19]

Until the period of British administration the tribespeoples of India were mainly forest-dwellers living in isolated communities practising shifting

Tribes of India

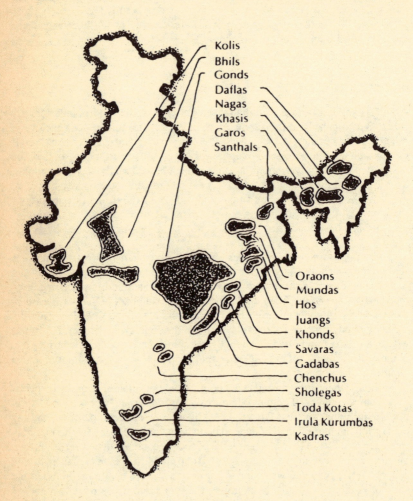

Kolis
Bhils
Gonds
Daflas
Nagas
Khasis
Garos
Santhals

Oraons
Mundas
Hos
Juangs
Khonds
Savaras
Gadabas
Chenchus
Sholegas
Toda Kotas
Irula Kurumbas
Kadras

Source: *The State of India's Environment, 1984-85*

cultivation and hunting and gathering. Colonialism had a profound effect upon these tribal communities. In the search for resources tribal land was opened up, and to further their exploitation the forests were protected and access to them controlled. The introduction of the institution of private property created possibilities for outsiders to acquire land held communally by tribespeople. The alienation of tribal land by non-tribals and the state appropriation of the forests caused various, often serious, uprisings: in 1831-2 the Kol rising in Bihar, in 1855 the Santal rebellion, in 1895 a revolt by the Mundas. There was a state of almost continuous rebellion in the north-east, in the Naga hills and Assam. But resistance was not directed only against the British. Non-tribal money-lenders, traders and labour contractors were quick to follow in the wake of the commercialization of tribal land and these brought unfamiliar forms of exploitation to the indigenous inhabitants. In an effort to reduce the conflict both between itself and the tribes and between the tribes and mainstream Hindu society, the British designated certain areas as scheduled districts to try to segregate and protect the many tribal communities.

Nevertheless, by the time independence was achieved in 1947 large numbers of *adivasis* were landless and many migrated from their traditional homelands to find work. The authors of the constitution of India recognized the extreme poverty of the tribal communities and the discrimination they faced. The new constitution endeavoured both to protect their cultural identity and provide mechanisms for their eventual assimilation. Article 46, for example, states:

> The State shall promote with special care the educational and economic interests of the weaker sections of the people, and in particular of the scheduled castes and scheduled tribes, and shall protect them from social injustice and all forms of exploitation.

Seats are reserved for scheduled tribes in both national and state parliaments. In the 1981 election, for example, 40 out of a total of 542 seats were held for the tribes in the *Lok Sabha* (the national parliament). Similar provisions existed in the state legislatures and in the 1980 elections 315 seats out of a total of 3,821 were reserved for the scheduled tribes. Several states have also passed laws prohibiting the alienation of tribal lands.

Countless other laws exist protecting the rights of scheduled tribes and discriminating in their favour. There are provisions for representations of the scheduled tribes in most parts of the public services and even private enterprise. Special programmes for economic development have been established in tribal areas, including provisions for rural credit, education and training and small-scale industry. Both national and state laws prohibit the sale of tribal land to outsiders. Yet despite a plethora of laws protecting the scheduled tribes of India, few are effectively implemented. Indeed, instead of their position being in any sense advanced, the present condition of the tribespeople is one of increasing oppression and pauperization.

Most menacing for the scheduled tribes are the national and state policies relating to forest land. About 50 per cent of scheduled tribes inhabit or are dependent upon forest produce. In 1952 the New Forest policy permitted the union and the states to grant concessions to outside interests. Subsequently a programme of commercial forestry has forced many forest-dwellers into a state of landlessness and unemployment. As one journal has commented, 'the depletion of forests and their increasing commercial use have progressively eroded the traditional rights which local (mainly tribal) people enjoyed.'[20]

Since the 1970s a policy of afforestation has been established. Vast areas of mixed forest have been felled by outside logging companies and the deforested areas planted with fast-growing varieties of eucalyptus and pine. While these trees satisfy the needs of the paper mills, and rayon and plywood factories, they take away a source of livelihood from those who reside in the forests. The State of India Report in 1981 pointed out that:

> besides food, the forest also supplies the tribals with their requirements of building materials, fuel and fodder. In addition, minor forest products like gum, honey, mahua flowers, bidi leaves etc., are collected and sold to earn cash. Hence, denial of tribal rights over forests or destruction of forests upsets their entire lifestyle.[21]

The destruction of forest land in the Himalayas and the hills of the north-east have brought disaster not only for the indigenous inhabitants but also for the non-tribals living in the plains. The cutting of trees has caused soil erosion on the slopes, landslides and the silting of rivers. Down-river this often brings floods. The high-water mark of the massive Brahmaputra River, for example, has gradually risen for the last 40 years and since 1960 has never dropped below the danger level.[22] In 1981 the National Commission on Floods estimated that 1,181 people died as a result of flooding.[23]

According to the State of India report a possible one million hectares of forest per annum are being destroyed. The government for its part has reacted to the indiscriminate deforestation with ever more draconian measures against the *adivasis*. The New Forest Bill of 1980 gives wider powers to the forest officers, increases the punishments and still further extends the minor forest produce outlawed. An *adivasi* could face a prison sentence of six years if he collects food or fuel to permit his family's survival. The large-scale commercial exploitation of forests has not been curtailed and profits still attract state governments and entrepreneurs.

However, tribal communities have not remained passive in the face of the despoliation of their homelands. In 1972, for example, villagers from the Chamoli district in Uttar Pradesh discovered that the government had sold their annual allocation of trees for tool-making and building to a sporting goods manufacturer. The ash trees were due to be used in the manufacture of cricket bats and tennis rackets. The villagers protested unsuccessfully and finally embraced the trees to prevent them being cut down. This time the government withdrew the concession. This first action began a successful non-violent movement to save the forests. The Chipko movement, as it became known, spread to many communities concerned about the forests throughout the Himalayas.

Such actions were motivated not only by a concern for the environment; they arose from a fear of the future without forests. One of the leaders of the movement declared: 'Saving the trees is only the first step in the Chipko movement. Saving ourselves is the real goal. Our future is tied up with them.'[24]

In the central Indian states the forests have been devastated with equal ferocity, but resistance by tribespeople has taken a less non-violent, Gandhian form. In the state of Bihar the scheduled tribes have organized a major revolt. The Bihar Forest Development Corporation has been replacing the native sal trees with teak, which has only a commercial use. The indigenous peoples of the region satisfy a range of basic needs from the sal tree and planting teak is seen as a threat. When in 1977 the reforestation programme began in earnest, tribespeople petitioned. But, unable to get any results, they began raiding teak nurseries and destroying saplings. Public protests were met with harsh police repression. In 1980, 13 tribespeople were shot dead by the police and over 200 arrested in the town of Gua. Since then tribespeople have felled teak trees and denied access to officials to many parts of the forest

Industrial developments have also detrimentally affected the scheduled tribes, particularly those living on the Chotanagpur Plateau. The Chotanagpur Plateau lies at 500 to 1,000 metres above sea level in the southern part of Bihar and extends into part of West Bengal, Madhya Pradesh and Orissa. It is a geographically and culturally distinct area, once entirely forested, and traditionally the homeland of several tribal groups and other forest-dwelling peoples. The district is sometimes referred to as Jharkhand or Forest Land by the indigenous inhabitants. The Chotanagpur Plateau is one of India's major industrial belts and there are rich deposits of coal, copper, bauxite, iron ore, uranium and other minerals; the plateau contributes about 45 per cent of the country's present production of minerals and holds about 35 per cent of its known reserves. Some 85 per cent of state revenue emanates from the region but only 18 per cent is returned in the form of rural development. The peoples of the Chotanagpur Plateau regard their region as a colony of the rest of India exploited for its wealth but receiving no benefits from development.[25]

In the last three decades industrial development on the Chotanagpur Plateau has accelerated. In the course of establishing factories, mines, dams to supply electricity, and urban centres to accommodate the expanded workforce, the indigenous peoples of the region have been uprooted and deprived of their land with little or no compensation and virtually no attempt at rehabilitation. Each time the local inhabitants have had to give way to the exigencies of national development. The report of the Commissioner for Scheduled Castes and Scheduled Tribes acknowledges these negative aspects of the process of development:

> The alienation of tribal lands to non-tribals, specially in the tribal areas which have been opened up as a result of the establishment of industrial and mining complexes and other development processes, is still widely prevalent, in spite of the legislative and executive measures taken by various state governments to prohibit transfer of their lands. In nine states for which information was available nearly 400,000 cases of land alienation had been registered in 1979-1980

and . . . there may be a large number more such cases which have yet to be identified.[26]

Despite the expansion of industrial activity in the area, indigenous peoples have not benefited greatly. Senior posts and the permanent, skilled labouring jobs are taken by *dikus* or outsiders, and the local people are left with poorly paid employment as casual labourers or else join the swelling ranks of street-dwellers. In the main industrial town of Jamshedpur, tribal people who ten or 15 years ago owned their land, are now obliged to take casual work in the local steel industry. If they get work it is often a result of bribing the labour agents, and accepting the loss of up to 50 per cent of the official wage.[27]

Forestry policy and the dispossession of tribal land by industrial interests have forced many scheduled tribes on to the labour market. Here they join India's very poorest and most discriminated-against sectors, landless peasants and scheduled castes – the untouchables. Many fall victim of the system of debt bondage, a condition arising from the pledge by a debtor of his labour or that of his family as security for a debt. Once money-lenders or landowners have obtained such a pledge, they trap a worker and his family into virtual slavery for life. According to the Commissioner's report interest can be as high as 200 per cent per annum.[28]

Debt bondage has been unlawful in India since 1947 but it is still widely practised. Some five million and perhaps as many as 20 million people may be working in such conditions. In the state of Orissa, the National Survey on the Incidence of Bonded Labour estimated that nearly one-fifth of the agricultural labour force were bonded labourers. The same report maintained that 87 per cent of bonded labourers were from the scheduled castes or tribes.[29]

In India there is a general failure to implement the law and protect the rights of scheduled tribes. Local landowners and entrepreneurs are the main transgressors but they are also the backbone of the Congress (I) Party. The scheduled tribes on the other hand have little economic or political power and little influence over state and local officials. Consequently government funds available for tribal development are far outweighed by the value of the resources extracted from tribal areas.

The scheduled tribes have reacted variously to their exploitation. Some have joined the urban poor, others have migrated to other states to find work and others have organized trade unions or cooperatives. The Chipko movement in the Himalayas is only one of the many actions taken by the indigenous peoples in India.

On the Chotanagpur Plateau tribal peoples formed their own political party, the Jharkhand Party, shortly after independence. The party called for the creation of a new tribal state. In the 1950s it became the main opposition party in the state legislature and held over 30 seats; it also had five MPs in the national parliament. It has since suffered splits and no longer has the same political influence.

In Bihar where tribespeople have been the most active, the police have also been at their most repressive. Numerous killings and beatings of tribal protesters and activists have occurred. In 1979, in its investigation into acts of police repression in Singhbhum district, Bihar, an Indian human rights organization concluded that:

> police firings and lathi charges were unwarranted and premeditated. The police actions were not advised by the competent officers on the spot, necessary precautions were not taken and warnings not given, innocent people were arrested without warrants, and the administration concocted charges after the event. The law and order machinery seemed to be confident that Adivasis and poor peasants deserved this treatment. High government officials also seemed to condone these police actions. A Senior Janata party member summarised: 'No minister thought it necessary to visit the place of firing because adivasis were killed.' In no case were the victims given compensation or rehabilitation.[30]

In the north-east of India the hill peoples of Nagaland, Manipur and Mizoram have been fighting a war against the government since the 1950s. At Independence the Nagas had also sought their independence but had achieved only a state within the Union of India. The Mizos were incorporated into the state of Assam and since 1966 have been fighting for secession. The National Socialist Council of Nagaland, the Mizo National Front and the People's Liberation Army of the Meetei people of Manipur are all actively engaged in guerrilla warfare. For these ethnically distinct hill peoples, as *India Today* put it, 'India represents only a brown colonialism that replaced the white colonialism of the British.'[31] The Indian Army for its part has encountered various severe, if minor, defeats, and atrocities on both sides are not uncommon. 'The Northeast has turned into a veritable police state. Out of the country's 72 battalions of the Central Reserve Police Force (CRPF), 37 are posted in the Northeast.'[32] However, subjugation of the hill tribes seems unlikely. They have a long martial tradition and a strong sense of identity. As one Naga villager has stated: 'We do not believe we can ever live under Indian rule, we only hope the struggle will be resolved peacefully.'[33]

The peoples of the Chittagong Hill Tracts of Bangladesh

The indigenous peoples of Bangladesh account for less than one per cent of the total population. In the recent past, many of the tribal groups – such as the Garo or Santal – have been to a large extent assimilated into Bangladeshi society and lost their identity as a separate people. On the whole, these peoples now occupy the lowliest positions, in a country where poverty and landlessness predominate, and are treated by many Bengalis as social outcasts.[34] In the Chittagong Hill Tracts region of Bangladesh, however, the indigenous population has managed to retain a separate identity and way of life. It has not as yet been forced to join the mainstream of Bangladeshi life and is now fighting for the right to autonomy within Bangladesh.

The Chittagong Hill Tracts is a region of forested hills and ravines in the south-east of Bangladesh and is bordered by the Indian states of Tripura and

Mizoram in the north and by Burma in the south. There are 600,000 or so tribespeople living in the tracts who identify themselves as hill people, in contrast to the Bengali population from the plains. In every respect they are distinct from the majority peoples of Bangladesh. They are of Sino-Tibetan descent and physically resemble the hill people in neighbouring Burma; the majority are Buddhist and not Muslim; their languages and their way of life and customs are different from the majority of Bengalis in Bangladesh.

The hill people of the Chittagong Hill Tracts are composed of 13 main tribes, of which three – the Chakma, the Marma and the Tripura – make up nearly 90 per cent. These peoples remained independent until the middle of the 17th Century when the tracts were annexed by the Mughals. Although they paid a trade tax to the Mughals, the Chakma and the other tribespeoples retained their traditional authority over the region. When the region was ceded to the East India Company and subsequently administered by the British there was little change in the relationship. Indeed the British administration formalized the autonomy of the region with the promulgation of the Chittagong Hill Tracts Regulation of 1900 which strictly controlled the entry and residence of non-tribals. Although ultimate authority resided in the British-appointed deputy-commissioner, the political institutions of the hill people were unaffected, and tax-collecting, policing and many aspects of criminal and civil law were administered by the tribal chiefs. Indeed, until decolonization following the Second World War the hill people enjoyed a wide degree of independence and protection from the intrusion of Bengali settlers from the more populated plains.

Traditionally, the hill people practise shifting cultivation, known locally as *jhuming*, by which a mixture of food crops, and commodities such as cotton, are grown in prepared clearings. As with all shifting cultivation, a period of time, in this case about seven years, was required while the land was left fallow and the soil given time to regenerate. Although the British protected the political authority of the tribespeople, they introduced policies which seriously affected the successful application of *jhuming* cultivation. During the 1870s they banned *jhuming* from about a quarter of the forest land, and as the remaining land had to be farmed more intensively, soil deterioration occurred. In 1947, on the eve of British withdrawal from the Indian subcontinent, the hill tracts faced a difficult economic and political future.

At the time, there was a movement for complete independence for the region within a confederation of tribal states consisting of Tripura, Cooch-Behar and parts of Assam, but it did not prevail. The hill tracts became a part of the newly created East Pakistan and almost at once the peoples of the hill tracts began to lose much of their traditional autonomy. The indigenous police force was disbanded and Bengalis were brought in as replacements. The special status of the hill tracts and the protection afforded by the 1900 Regulation were circumvented by the 1962 constitution. In their turn, the tribal chiefs and their traditional administration were bypassed by a new centralized system. In all these areas, central government became supreme. The creation of Bangladesh, following the civil war of 1971, brought further diminution of the independence of the tribespeople. A deputy-commissioner now doubles as district magistrate,

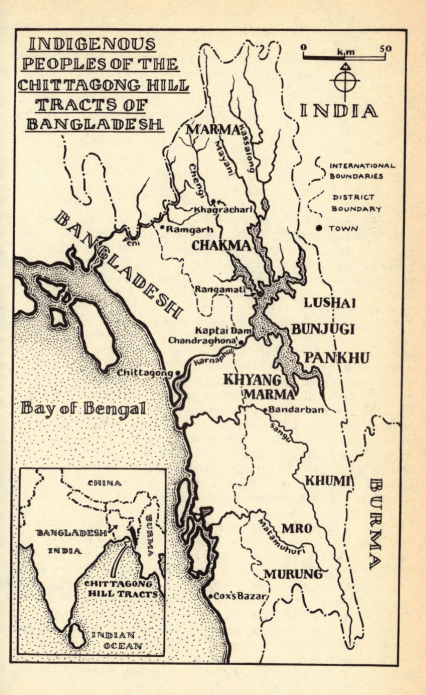

INDIGENOUS PEOPLES OF THE CHITTAGONG HILL TRACTS OF BANGLADESH

INDIA

INTERNATIONAL BOUNDARIES

DISTRICT BOUNDARY

● TOWN

MARMA

Kassalong

Mayani

Chengi

Khagrachari

● Ramgarh

Feni

CHAKMA

Rangamati

LUSHAI

BUNJUGI

Kaptai Dam

Chandraghona

PANKHU

Karnaphuli

● Chittagong

KHYANG
MARMA

● Bandarban

Sangu

Bay of Bengal

KHUMI

BURMA

Matamuhuri

MRO

MURUNG

● Cox's Bazar

CHINA

BURMA

BANGLADESH

INDIA

CHITTAGONG
HILL TRACTS

INDIAN
OCEAN

and is in charge of all revenue collection as well as being co-ordinator of all development programmes taking place. Indeed, there is hardly any activity he does not control and his powers are virtually unlimited.[35]

Following the abolition of the special status of the Chittagong Hill Tracts in 1964, however, another serious threat was posed to the hill people. Restriction on entry and residence now lifted, many Bengalis began to settle in the district. At first the settlement was on a small scale but in 1979 the President of Bangladesh, Ziaur Rahman, put in motion a major programme of colonization. Some 100,000 Bangladeshis were to be settled in the first phase of the scheme. Land was allocated to each family and grants were provided to help the settlers through their first year. In 1982 a new phase of settlement began during which a further 250,000 Bengalis were to be transferred to the district. It is thought that about 30 per cent of the total population are now Bengali, and that by the end of the decade the indigenous peoples of the hill tracts will be in a minority.

The justification for the settlement is a familiar one for many indigenous peoples: the land they inhabit is deemed unoccupied and unexploited. In the case of the hill tracts neither assumption is true. The hill slopes traditionally belong to tribal society as a whole, and as in most societies which practise shifting cultivation, a system of allocation of land exists and village headmen carefully ensure that land is not over-cultivated. Bengali settlers have, therefore, been given land which belongs to tribespeople to whom no compensation has been made. Furthermore, in most cases the land is not suitable for permanent cultivation. According to a study by a team of Canadian consultants, only 800,000 acres, a little over 20 per cent of the district, is suitable for horticulture or rice cultivation.[36] The landless peasants settled in the hill tracts have no knowledge of hill farming and the rate of failure is high. Unable to survive after the initial modest priming from the government, these Bengali settlers have encroached on tribal-owned wet rice lands and taken over gardens and hill land successfully farmed by the tribespeople. As a consequence, tribespeople in the hill tracts have been forced from their lands to occupy less hospitable areas. The settlement programme has been unsuccessful in attaining any of the stated economic benefits and can be understood only as a means for internal colonization. There can be no doubt that once the numbers of Bengalis living in the hill tracts exceed those of the indigenous tribespeople, the case for autonomy will be weakened.

Not only have the tribespeople of the hill tracts been the victims of a policy of neo-colonization, but they have also been impoverished by a succession of development projects. In the early 1960s the Kaptai Dam was built across the main river of the hill tracts, in order to provide hydro-electric power for the industrializing and urbanizing East Pakistan. The reservoir submerged 650 square kilometres of prime agricultural land, about 40 per cent of the cultivable land of the tracts. One-sixth of the total indigenous population was displaced and the majority received no compensation of any kind. Those displaced were forced to cultivate the already overpopulated hill slopes and this caused further depletion of soil fertility. For most of the tribespeople the hydro-electric project has made matters worse. Virtually all electricity produced by the scheme supplies urban centres outside the tracts. A survey carried out in 1979 indicated that 93 per cent of tribespeople felt that economic conditions were better before the building of the Kaptai Dam.[37]

Other development schemes have had equally adverse effects on the indigenous population. A road-building programme assisted by the Australian Development Assistance Bureau (ADAB) was criticized by tribespeople because it was wider than needed for commercial use and allowed access by the Bangladeshi armed forces. In early 1981 ADAB pulled out of the district. A reforestation programme assisted by the Swedish International Development Authority (SIDA) was criticized on the grounds that it would deprive tribespeople of more than half their traditional land. In 1981 SIDA also pulled out of the district and stated the main reason for their decision 'was the inability to give the programme such a direction as to benefit the ethnic minorities in the area'.[38]

The recent economic and political changes affecting the tribespeople of the hill tracts have been met with growing hostility. In 1972 a tribal resistance force was formed called the Shanti Bahini. The Shanti Bahini claim to have 1,000 armed guerrillas, but many more supporters, and have control in parts of the tracts. They demand autonomy within Bangladesh and a separate legislature, the restitution of all lands taken by Bengali immigrants since 1970 and a ban on further immigration. The Shanti Bahini also seek amendments to the constitution which will protect their indigenous culture and identity.

However, their political demands have gone unanswered and successive governments in Bangladesh have responded by increasing the military forces in the region. In 1980 an estimated 30,000 regular and paramilitary troops were stationed in the hill tracts and the number of police stations doubled in the four years from 1976 to 1980. Inevitably the presence of the armed forces in such large numbers has provoked conflicts. Tribespeople feel intimidated by the armed presence and with good reason. Since 1975 numerous killings, beatings and attacks on property have taken place. On 25 March 1980 about 300 unarmed tribespeople were killed by troops and Bengali settlers in the small village of Kaokhali Bazar. In June 1981 riots by Bengali immigrants, supported by government soldiers, caused the deaths of approximately 500 tribal men, women and children in the area around Matiranga. Since April 1986 there has been further violence against tribespeople. During May of that year more than 100 tribal people were reported to have been killed in the Khagrachari-Panchari area and in villages near Matiranga.

In addition to the attacks on tribespeople and their property, there have also occurred numerous instances of violence against Buddhist monks and desecration of temples. Religious persecution and the widespread racism of the majority population of Bangladesh against the tribal minorities, have created such an atmosphere of terror in the hill tracts that many have fled across the border into India. In 1981 *The Times of India* (5 October 1981) estimated that about 40,000 refugees were living in various Indian border states. On 5 May 1986 *The Times of India* reported the renewed flight of refugees into Tripura state following the escalation of military activity in the hill tracts.

But although the picture appears bleak there have been attempts by the Government of Bangladesh to find a political rather than a military solution. Towards the end of 1983 an amnesty was declared for all Shanti Bahini fighters with an offer of land, jobs and cash. Nevertheless, despite the apparent generosity of the government rehabilitation programme, there were few takers. By the deadline there were fewer than 100 Shanti Bahini who had surrendered. In January 1984 they had undertaken a dramatic kidnapping of three Shell employees and were demanding a reported £200,000 ransom. The Shanti Bahini accuse the government of making no efforts to discuss their demands. The Bangladeshi Army, for their part, have imposed a virtual state of war in the tracts. Road blocks are everywhere and movement is strictly controlled and severely restricted. While the Government of Bangladesh remains stubborn in its determination to annex the hill tracts for Bengali settlement and the Shanti Bahini continue to fight for the return of local autonomy, the tribespeople will go on suffering the full brunt of the undeclared war.

Orang Asli in Malaysia

The federal state of Malaysia was proclaimed in 1963 and comprises the former British colonies on the Malay peninsula, excluding Singapore, and the two eastern states of Sarawak and Sabah on northern Borneo. Malaysia is a multi-racial society with an indigenous Malay population and two important non-indigenous groups, the Chinese and the Indians.

The tribal groups of Malaysia are the descendants of the oldest inhabitants of the region. On the Malay Peninsula they are known as the Orang Asli, the original people. There are 19 Orang Asli tribes in three main groups. The Negritos inhabit the hills and jungles of southern Thailand and the northern parts of the Malay peninsula and live as hunter-gatherers in small nomadic bands. The Sengoi inhabit the central highlands and practise shifting cultivation. Both groups speak different languages related to the Mon-Khmer group. The Proto-Malays are less distinctive than the other two groups and have been partially absorbed into Malay society.[39]

The Orang Asli were largely ignored both by the British during their administration and by the Malay sultans who had little interest in exploiting the highlands and saw the tribal inhabitants only as potential converts. During the Communist revolution and the British anti-insurgency campaign in the 1950s, the Orang Asli became caught in the crossfire. The Communists recruited them to their guerrilla army, while the government attempted to impose upon them a programme of forcible resettlement. The policy proved a disaster and was resisted by the tribespeople. In 1953 attempts were made to improve the well-being of the Orang Asli through health, education and other welfare activities. Since the defeat of the Communists, and independence, the Orang Asli have enjoyed a measure of legal protection and state assistance. The welfare of the Orang Asli is now the responsibility of the Malaysian Department of Aboriginal Affairs. However, recent economic developments in the peninsula threaten the livelihoods of many of the more isolated groups.

In one area of the central highlands, for example, the homeland of 300 Batek tribespeople is being deforested. These mainly nomadic peoples depend upon forest produce and fish and game for their livelihood. By 1980, however, one-third of the forest traditionally occupied by the Batek had been cut down by the commercial logging companies and a further one-third had been sold as timber concessions. One author maintains that 'it is not unreasonable to suppose that the entire area will be deforested by the end of this decade.'[40] The consequences for the Batek according to the same source are likely to be a decline in living standards, possible malnutrition and inevitable demoralization.

However, while the Orang Asli are a small proportion of the population of the Malay peninsula – they number only some 70,000 – there are about half a million tribespeoples in eastern Malaysia, comprising 50 per cent of the population of these states. The most numerous are the Iban (or sea Dayak) with a population in the state of Sarawak of over 300,000. Other tribal groups include the Bidayan (or land Dayaks), Kayan, Kenyah, Kelabit, Murut and Punan. Most of these groups have migrated from other parts of Borneo and span the state and national boundaries that now divide the island. Most of the tribespeople are non-Muslim and are physically distinct from the Malay peoples. Despite the variations existing among the different tribal groups, they share certain common features. Most live in the hills and forests and more than half of Sarawak's tribal population is engaged in shifting cultivation and rice production. As in other regions where swidden agriculture is practised, the success of this agricultural system depends upon the availability of sufficient forest lands to ensure an adequate fallow period. The traditional way of life then is both highly dependent upon the forest and closely integrated with it.

Tropical rainforest covers approximately 75 per cent of the land area of Sarawak and is the state's most important natural resource. For the peoples who dwell there, the forest provides virtually all their needs, but for the Government of Malaysia, it is an unexploited wilderness which can be harnessed in the cause of economic development. In the last two decades timber exports from Malaysia, particularly from Sabah and Sarawak, have accelerated. According to the *State of the Malaysian Environment 1983/4*, timber companies are stripping forests at the rate of 15 hectares every hour.[41] The Director of the Forestry Research Institute of Malaysia stated that the country's forests would disappear by 1990 at the present rate of exploitation.[42]

As far as the government is concerned the forests are state-owned. The Sarawak Government is able to make concessions to logging companies in return for which it receives royalties on the volume of timber, export duties and various other administrative fees. For the logging company, extracting timber is a highly profitable and low-capital enterprise, and a certain source of foreign exchange for the government. However, the tribespeople have suffered.

In the Baram district, for example – an area of 8,000 square miles with a tribal population of 50,000 – there are over 40 logging camps. 'The once forested district of Baram has been reduced to bare patches of eroded, barren and useless land. Tribal communities which once depended on the forests as their main source of food, medicines, building material and income are now faced with an uncertain future.'[43] Tribal communities seeking concessions themselves are refused because they have no political power and can offer no bribes. 'Timber is politics' declared one tribesperson, 'if you support the right man, you get a timber area.'[44]

The serious threats to the livelihoods of the indigenous peoples of Sarawak and Sabah are causing conflicts with logging operators. In an incident in March 1983, ten villagers threatened to burn down a logging camp after compensation was refused. One Punan community in the Baram district refused compensation saying they needed the land and forest much more.[45] On other occasions local people have sabotaged machinery and blocked access roads. In 1981, 400 tribespeople in the Baram district visited a logging camp and removed tractor parts and halted work in protest against the granting of a concession to an outside company. The various indigenous communities in the area had submitted an application for a timber concession in 1967. The concessionary favoured by the Sarawak Government was the son of the former governor.[46]

In 1985 another threat to indigenous peoples in Sarawak emerged, this time in the shape of a massive hydro-electric project. The federal government plans to build a dam at Bakun at a cost of $4 billion, flooding 700 square kilometres and displacing about 5,000 Kenyah and Kayan tribal people. The Bakun Dam is destined to become one of the biggest of its kind in South-East Asia and is Malaysia's most expensive development project ever. The indigenous peoples living in the area have organized a Residents' Action Committee to fight the dam. 'Our land is our survival and to flood it would mean the extermination of our peoples,' they have written to the Prime Minister's Office.[47] 'Money is nothing to us,' one tribal leader has declared, 'even if we were paid millions of dollars, this money cannot guarantee our survival. Money can be printed, land cannot be created.'[48] The group have urged the government to spend more money on building roads and improving educational and health services. They have also asked for a fairer price for their farm products and an ending of damaging logging operations in the area. The economic and environmental viability of the project is also being questioned by other groups in Malaysia, and the indigenous peoples find themselves with important allies in their resistance to the dam.

The tribespeople of Malaysia do not face the almost genocidal policies recently enacted in Bangladesh but they do face an uncertain future. The Government of Malaysia like most in Asia is bent upon rapid economic development through the exploitation of its natural resources. Inevitably the indigenous populations who are the traditional users of these resources will suffer.

Thailand's hill tribes

The hill tribes of Thailand constitute only a little over one per cent of the total population and number about 500,000. There are six main ethnic groups – the Karen, Lisu, Hmong, Yao, Lahu and Akha – and numerous smaller ones, including Chinese traders. The hill tribes are ethnically and linguistically distinct from the majority Thai population and practise various other religions. The Thais are Buddhist, and the hill tribes predominantly animist, although some, like the Karen, have been influenced by Christianity.

The hill tribes inhabit scattered remote villages in the highland provinces of the north. They live at altitudes above 2,000 feet, the Lisu and Hmong at higher elevations and the Karen at the lower. Although there are some who are migratory, most of Thailand's tribal peoples live in settled communities and practise swidden cultivation. The valley bottoms have long since been occupied by Thai farmers growing wet rice.

Until the mid-19th Century the hill tribes existed with a high degree of autonomy, only paying tribute to the various semi-autonomous principalities that then composed Thailand. In return the hill tribes received official title to their land and referred to the Thai princes when resolving conflicts. The unification of Thailand in 1873 reduced the power of the northern Thai princes and replaced it by rule from Bangkok. In the course of the 19th Century and early 20th Century, the Kingdom of Siam consolidated its control over the lowland districts of the north. The uplands were at this moment mainly ignored by the new central government and remained largely unaffected until recently.

Table 8.2
The distribution of Thailand's hill tribes

Tribe	Total population	Population in Thailand	Other countries
Hmong (Meo)	6,000,000	58,000	China, Vietnam, Laos
Karen	3,000,000	200,000	Burma
Yao	800,000	19,000	China, Vietnam, Laos
Lisu	400,000	10,000	China, Burma
Lahu	200,000	18,000	China, Burma, Laos
Akha	100,000	9,000	China, Burma, Laos
Kha Htin		23,200	
Kha Mu		4,150	
Lawa (Lua)		8,000	

Source: Tribal Research Centre, Chiangmai.

Significant developments took place in the 1960s which seriously affected the hill people. Demographic growth and expanding agribusiness in Thailand led to an influx of peasants into the northern hills in the search for land. Many of those unable to settle in the valleys, because land was already owned by Thai farmers, moved up on to the hill slopes where no such private title existed. The group most immediately affected was the Karen.

The Karen are the largest tribal minority, number some 200,000 or more, and inhabit the north-western region contiguous with the Burmese frontier. On the other side of the border in Burma live another 3.5 million Karen with their

own army engaged in a struggle for an independent Karen state. There has never been a Karen nation but they have one of the oldest histories of occupation of the region.

The Karen like other hill tribes in the region are shifting cultivators, and have no legal rights to the lands and forests they use. Land over 600 metres (2,000 feet) is deemed to belong to the King and, therefore, may be sold or leased as any other public land. Thailand, unlike many countries with tribal minorities, has no system of reservations. Thai farmers have moved on to traditional land farmed by the Karen and acquired individual title to it. Indeed, in some cases rice terraces built and cultivated for generations by Karen have been claimed and occupied by Thais. Karen land has also been taken over by tribespeople from higher altitudes and other countries who have themselves been displaced by the Indo-Chinese wars.

The Thai Government has pursued a forestry policy which has further reduced the economic base of the Karen and other minorities. When forestry reserves are created, minorities can find themselves illegal squatters and may be removed; they are denied access to the forest, the use of its products and the cultivation of swidden plots. In practice, forest officers have taken a particularly aggressive position in relation to the hill people and driven them forcibly and often with considerable violence from the forest reserves. Official government policy is to reduce and eventually eliminate shifting cultivation and sedentarize the hill tribes in order to protect the forests. But in fact by establishing forest reserves, the government has only succeeded in increasing the number of shifting cultivators on the remaining land. Further environmental destruction has been caused by inexperienced and inept Thai farmers attempting swidden cultivation because it is the only system that is successful in the forest ecology.

But by far the greatest threat to the land base of the Karen and other hill tribes has been caused by the opening up of the area for economic development. A network of roads was built in the 1960s prompted not only by the desire to gain access to exploitable resources but also to reach into the highlands and combat insurgency. Thai and foreign mining and logging companies were established in the wake of the road construction further impinging upon tribal land.

An incidental side-effect of these developments has been the deterioration in the highland ecosystem. Road construction, mining and commercial logging as well as the pressures on land use created by the influx of Thai farmers have affected watersheds, caused pollution of streams and rivers, and led to soil erosion.

The shrinking economic base has led to poverty and malnutrition among many of the hill tribes and especially the Karen. Many communities do not produce enough rice for their own needs and the young men have drifted to the mines and tea plantations for work or become wage-labourers on the Hmong opium plantations where they are known as 'nowhere men'. Some of the young women have also been forced to leave the village and look for employment in the towns and a great many have become prostitutes in one of Thailand's burgeoning industries, sex tourism.[49]

When the Karen and other hill tribes move into Thai society they are discriminated against, paid the lowest wages and expected to carry out the most menial tasks. A sense of demoralization affects many Karen, a fact that is pointed up by the high levels of opium addiction among many communities. Five times as many hill people are addicted to opium as lowlanders and in certain Karen villages as many as half the population are addicts. A report for USAID in 1978 noted that most hill tribes were part of the poor majority, that non-opium producing highland families lived below the poverty line and that in terms of living standards and career opportunity almost all families would be classified as disadvantaged.[50]

The Thailand Karen, unlike the Hmong, the second-largest tribal group, have been less able to resist cultural and economic deterioration. They were converted to Christianity by the American Baptist Missionaries at the end of the 19th Century and, unlike the Karen on the Burma side, have not developed any strong political consciousness or tribal organization. The Hmong, on the other hand, have retained a strong cultural identity, practise pantheism and have a long musical and oral tradition. The Hmong also produce an important cash crop, opium, which has enabled them to survive better the impact of outside forces such as those that menace the Karen with assimilation or extinction as a people.[51]

The Hmong, the Akha, Lisu and Lahu inhabit the golden triangle at higher altitudes than the Karen and are all involved in the cultivation of the opium poppy. The largest of the groups, the Hmong, who number about 50,000 in Thailand but over five million in China, are recent arrivals having migrated there during the last hundred years.

The Hmong grow opium for a variety of reasons, partly because it is a cash crop with a guaranteed market and partly for cultural and medicinal reasons. But the large scale of opium production and its persistence despite the ban must rest with forces outside the control of the Hmong. The world market creates a demand on an unprecedented scale and provides to the middlemen involved enormous profits. Many Thai officials charged with suppressing the opium business are integral to its continuation and depend upon rake-offs to supplement their comparatively low salaries. Furthermore, the hills of Thailand and neighbouring Burma are the homes of armed warlords, traders and remnants of the Kuomintang, the Chinese National Army, which fled after the success of the Chinese Revolution – all of whom intimidate the Hmong and ensure their involvement in poppy cultivation. The Western-backed Thai Government has tolerated the Kuomintang because it fulfils a counter-insurgency role and, therefore, turns a blind eye to its principal source of income.

For the Hmong, however, the internationalization of the opium business and their involvement as producers since the 1960s have brought mainly persecution upon their communities. Government and United Nations programmes to substitute other crops for the opium poppy have largely failed because of official complicity and the vested political and economic interests involved. There have also been technical and marketing problems associated with crop substitution which are only now being addressed by the Public Welfare Department responsible for tribal development.

The hill tribes of Thailand have also been caught up in the almost continuous military and ideological conflict since the Second World War. In 1953, the Royal Thai Government formed the Border Police Patrol (BPP) to prevent Communist infiltration from neighbouring Laos and Burma. As the Indo-Chinese war developed it embroiled more of the region in the conflict. The hill people were often labelled Communists and treated with suspicion. The BPP built up contacts with tribal communities and with a judicious mix of tools, medicines and propaganda, endeavoured to counter Communist influence. In the late 1950s Communists from Laos recruited tribesmen from the hills and provoked a small-scale war between the Thai Army and the Hmong and other hill peoples. The 1967 Red Meo War, as it is known, created many thousands of refugees and brought hill men into conflict with each other.

For many Hmong, however, their involvement in rebellion against the government was not due to any strong sympathies with Communism. The pressures on available land because of migrations into the area had been worsened by government policies to restrict opium cultivation and limit tribal access to the forests. Government programmes to date have tended to exacerbate rather than improve the situation of most tribespeople.[52]

In the case of the Hmong, despair led to revolt in the late 1960s, but most other tribespeople have been unwilling to take such actions. The majority of the tribespeople of northern Thailand continue to be treated as potentially hostile or as second-class citizens and their economic base is shrinking every year as economic development and geo-political considerations bring further incursions into the hills. Many tribespeople would probably desire little more than to have enough land to grow rice and to be left alone to develop in their own terms. But the strategic importance of the border area to the east and west, and the insatiable demand for opium from the rich countries, make the realization of such a hope highly unlikely.[53]

Victims of Indonesian empire

Indonesia is probably one of the most culturally diverse nations in the world with over 13,000 islands and more than 300 ethnic groups speaking about 240 languages. It is also among the poorer countries of the region and despite abundant natural resources, the per capita income of its 160 million population is only about £400 per annum. Widespread poverty and the lack of a homogeneous national identity are factors that have given Indonesia a turbulent post-colonial history. Since 1965 a military dictatorship under President Suharto has dominated the country, killed and imprisoned many hundreds of thousands and is combating secessionist struggles in the South Moluccas, East Timor and West Papua.

The South Moluccas, once known as the Spice Islands, are situated more than 1,500 miles to the east of Indonesia's capital, Djakarta. The people are

Melanesian, speak their own language, Amboinese, and are predominantly Christian. To a large extent they have preserved their community-based culture. When the Dutch colonial powers withdrew from Indonesia in 1950, the Republic of South Moluccas declared its independence, but it was short-lived. Within the year Javanese troops had invaded the islands and taken power. Nationalist leaders were killed and exiled but a guerrilla war continues. Since the 1950s the Government of Indonesia has settled about half a million Javanese on the islands, and alienated 168,000 hectares of ancestral (*adat*) land. The more than one million South Moluccans face an intensive programme of Islamicization and Javanization: intermarriage between the two distinct peoples is promoted, traditional dress and the indigenous language are scorned, and Christian men are reportedly forced to wear black Muslim caps.[54]

The Indonesian armed forces overwhelmed the peoples of the South Moluccas and never really faced serious opposition, but in East Timor the story has been different. East Timor is located at the eastern end of the Indonesian archipelago. It was a Portuguese colony from 1702 until 1974, when the Salazar dictatorship in Portugal collapsed. In November 1975 the Fretilin government declared independence and established the Democratic Republic of East Timor. In a little over a week Indonesian troops from the neighbouring province of West Timor invaded, and a bloody war, resulting in the deaths of 200,000 people – about one-third of East Timor's population – has endured ever since.[55]

Indonesia recognizes 1.5 million tribespeople officially, with the eastern province of Irian Jaya (West Papua) the most heavily populated, followed by Kalimantan (Borneo), Sulawesi and Sumatra. The tribal peoples are described in the 1945 constitution as those communities inhabiting remote areas 'whose social life, economic performance and level of civilization are below acceptable standards'. The Directorate for the Development of Remote Communities is charged with their upliftment. Some of the initiatives of the Indonesian Government have been welcomed by the tribal minorities: schools, roads, health centres and improved communications. Indeed in 1985 a 29,000 hectare forest was made over to a nomadic tribe of Kubu people. Other programmes, especially those of transmigration of Javanese settlers to outlying islands, have been rejected. Transmigration had taken place under the Dutch, but it was only after 1965 that it became more structured. In the first five-year plan (*Repelita* 1) from 1969 to 1974 the government moved about 25,000 families; from 1974 to 1979 a further 60,000 families were moved; from 1979 to 1984, and from 1984 to 1989, the government plans to move a total of one and a quarter million families, or nearly six million people.[56] Transmigration is the greatest single threat to the futures of the indigenous peoples of Indonesia.

Transmigration is central to the political programme of the Indonesian Government which is contained in the notion of *Wawasan Nusantara*, the Indonesian Archipalegic Outlook. According to this view all the ethnic minorities form part of the national unity. On 9 March 1983 the People's Consultative Assembly (MPR) confirmed that Indonesia with its numerous distinct ethnic groups was one political, economic, cultural and defence unit. Such a policy has not allowed the government of President Suharto to accept even modest claims to self-determination; the distinct peoples of Kalimantan, South Moluccas, East Timor or West Papua must either conform to the Javanese notion of the state or disappear.

Of all the menaces to indigenous peoples in the world, few can be as poignant or as urgent as that threatening the one million or so Melanesian people of West Papua. It is possible with legitimacy to talk about genocide elsewhere – the Mayan Indians in Guatemala, the Aché in Paraguay, the Chakma and other tribal peoples in Bangladesh – but even in the context of such violence the destruction of the West Papuan people has few parallels. More particularly since until very recently the Papuans have had relatively little contact with invading powers and are now experiencing a particularly aggressive and racist colonization from Indonesia. The tragedy is compounded because history is repeating itself so evidently. The invasions of the Americas and especially Australia are being reborn in West Papua, only this time aided by the United Nations and the general assembly of nation states. Few indigenous peoples have such a clear right to nationhood.

West Papua, the western half of the island of New Guinea, was colonized only in the early 19th Century. The Dutch established a fort in 1828 and for more than a century did little more than maintain a presence on the island. Some resistance, often in the form of millenarian movements, was mounted to end forced labour and taxation but it was suppressed. In the early years of this century as Dutch and other foreign interests began to explore for oil, the movement against colonialism became clearly focused.[57] Then during the Second World War, West Papua was occupied by the Japanese until they were defeated by the Allied Forces under General MacArthur in 1944. The Dutch returned to administer their colonies in 1945 but very soon found themselves fighting a movement for Indonesian independence. Furthermore, the dominant view among nationalist leaders was that all the Dutch-administered territories in the region including West Papua should be part of the new Republic of Indonesia. Discussions about the fate of the Papuan people continued throughout the 1950s and 1960s, the Dutch on the whole favouring eventual independence, the Indonesians arguing for incorporation and the multinationals who had now discovered copper and gold, as well as oil deposits, privately lobbying for a quick settlement in favour of Indonesia. At no time were the Papuans consulted, even though the United Nations debated the issue on numerous occasions.

Finally, in 1962, the United States of America brought the two sides together and produced the New York Agreement which was ratified by the United Nations General Assembly. The Agreement provided for a brief interval of United Nations stewardship to be followed by Indonesian administration, and an Act of Free Choice – a referendum on independence – six years later. The ensuing years until 1969 were characterized by successive revolts by the Papuans and increased military involvement and repression. The day following the transfer of power to Indonesia, thousands of school textbooks

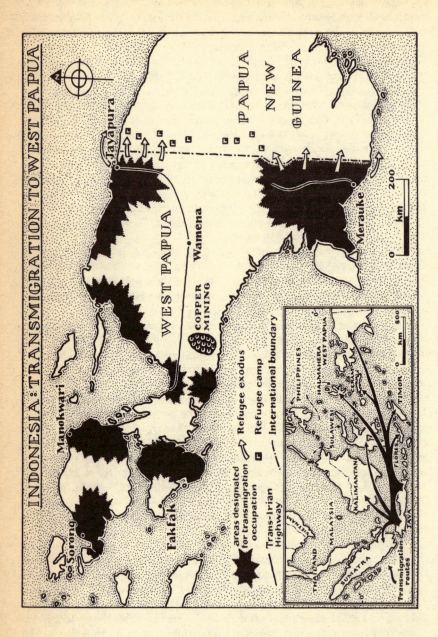

INDONESIA: TRANSMIGRATION TO WEST PAPUA

about Papua and Papuan flags were publicly burned.[58] One day later the Papuan Parliament, the New Guinea Council, was dissolved; and in the same month laws were passed banning all political activity, including publications and meetings. In the same year an Anti-Subversion Decree provided the armed forces with a *carte blanche* to arrest and imprison anyone considered to be acting against the interests of the state. In 1965 the first major revolt against Indonesian rule was launched by the Free Papua Movement (OPM) and other uprisings quickly followed.

When the Act of Free Choice was held West Papua was already in the throes of virtual civil war. There was no implementation of a plebiscite on the basis of 'one man, one vote' and instead 1,025 representatives were appointed to express the will of the Papuan people. Under threat of imprisonment and even death these representatives voted unanimously in favour of remaining a part of Indonesia. In November 1969 the United Nations approved the implementation of the Act of Free Choice and accepted its result. The diplomatic note of disquiet expressed by the United Nations observer was completely ignored: 'I regret to express my reservation regarding the implementation of Article XXII of the Agreement, relating to "the rights, including the rights of free speech, freedom of movement and of assembly of the inhabitants of the area",' he wrote in his report to the Secretary-General. 'In spite of my constant efforts, these important provisions were not fully implemented and the [Indonesian] Administration exercised at all times a tight political control over the population.'[59]

For the majority of Papuan people the occupation by Indonesia is an act of colonization. The Papuans are ethnically distinct from the Javanese and other Indonesian peoples. They speak numerous languages unrelated to Indonesian and are a mixture of animists and Christians, so do not share the Islamic religion with their colonizers. Three-quarters of the population live in scattered rural communities throughout the highlands, and many practise shifting cultivation. Those inhabiting the coastal plains live off sago plantations and some depend upon fishing. For the Indonesian immigrant population coming from rice-growing areas in Java and Sumatra, the food production systems of the Papuans appear alien and primitive. The gulf dividing the two populations, Indonesian and Papuan, is widened by their different customs and costumes: much of the rural population of Papua decorate their bodies and wear ornaments, such as penis sheaths. The Indonesians have nothing but contempt for the indigenous population of the island, whom they regard as virtual savages and treat with scorn.[60]

The colonization by Indonesia of West Papua was prompted in part by a vision of imperial greatness, recalling the expansion in the 14th Century of the Hindu-Buddhist state of Mayapahit. But West Papua has another attraction beyond that of fulfilling a long-lost dream of empire: it is resource-laden. Rich deposits of oil have been discovered in the western tip of the island, including Indonesia's highest-producing oil well. Most of the major petroleum companies – Shell, Conoco, Texaco, Total and Chevron – have important drilling concessions. Nickel, cobalt, tin, copper, silver, molybdenum and gold have all been found in significant quantities. The Freeport Mine in the highlands is the site of one of the world's largest outcrops of copper mixed with gold. Predictably multinational corporations – US Steel, Philips, ICI – have interests in mineral extraction on the island. Finally the timber resources of West Papua are exceeded only by those on Kalimantan (Borneo), and an area of over 30 million hectares, three-quarters of the land area, is forested. By 1980 there were 68 separate logging concessions, mainly Indonesian and Japanese, laying claim to more than 60 per cent of the country's forest resources.[61]

The exploitation of West Papua's resources has had the most disastrous impact on the indigenous population. Oil exploration and mineral extraction have created virtually no employment opportunities for Papuans. In the oil industry only some 20 per cent of the workforce are Papuan and none are in supervisory posts. According to one source: 'local employees were subjected to intimidatory treatment by the Indonesian authorities and more than two-thirds of the Papuans' pay was taken by the military.'[62] At Freeport Mine the majority of workers are Filipinos, Indonesians, South Koreans and technicians from Australia and the United States.[63] The Papuan villagers in the immediate area have been intimidated and attacked and 100 square kilometres of their traditional land wired off. In the 1970s the local Amungme tribespeople made numerous protests but there were no offers of compensation or modification of the mine's policy. In 1977 a series of acts of sabotage were staged, including cutting the main copper slurry pipeline, but the Indonesian armed forces replied by spreading terror throughout the region. Papuans were reported to have been shot just for approaching the mine, and nearby villages were indiscriminately mortared by the army.

Where Papuans have been able to get work it has sometimes been under conditions of virtual slavery. In one of the main timber extraction areas, the Asmat tribespeople have been compelled by local Indonesian officials to cut and transport trees. The workers drafted into this system of forced labour fear that if they refuse employment, they will be tagged as subversives. The low wages offered are withheld or often not paid at all. Furthermore such illegal logging practices bypass state taxes intended for subsequent disbursement to the Papuans affected.

Concessions by the Government of Indonesia of vast tracts of land to foreign companies and national entrepreneurs have a far-reaching effect on the economic base of the Papuans. Communal land rights are ignored by the Indonesian authorities since the forests are regarded as unoccupied and unutilized. However, as the United Nations recognized, such an interpretation 'fails to recognize the complete dependence of the local people on the forest; not for timber perhaps, but for shelter, protection, food and minor products and, above all, the maintenance of fertility of garden areas.'[64]

The Papuan people, however, are now faced with an even more serious threat to their land and livelihood. Population pressures on the main island of Java led the Government of Indonesia, on the advice of the United Nations and the World Bank, to relocate Javanese landless peasants on the less populated islands. In their five-year plan (1979-84) the government began transmigration programmes on Sumatra and Kalimantan, but since 1984 the government has selected West Papua as a location. Between 1984 and 1989, 500,000 to one million Javanese are due to be settled on the island, thereby making the Papuans a minority population in their country. As the former Papuan governor stated despairingly: 'By the year 2,000, Papuans will be like the Aborigines of Australia, the Indians in America or the Maoris in New Zealand. All pushed out by newcomers.'[65] The transmigrant population are settled on the more fertile land and Papuans who have been dispossessed have received little or no compensation.

But overpopulation in Java – Java holds 90 million people or 60 per cent of the population on seven per cent of the land area – is not the only concern of the Indonesian Government. Transmigration serves an important political function. Transmigrants have been settled in areas of local opposition and along the border with Papua New Guinea, which is crossed regularly by Papuan guerrilla fighters. The massive influx of Javanese will create an important source of pro-Indonesian sentiment and diminish the possibility for West Papuan independence.

Since the mid-1960s there has been armed opposition to the Indonesian occupation of West Papua. The Free Papua Movement (OPM) built up substantial support in the period preceding the Act of Free Choice in 1969 and in 1977 and 1978 launched a series of offensives against the Indonesian armed forces and economic targets. In 1984 the OPM briefly took over the centre of Jayapura, the capital of the province, and raised the West Papuan flag. However, the military strength of the OPM is relatively meagre. Although there are claims of 30,000 organized in the OPM, there are very few arms. The Indonesian Government for its part has installed an occupying army, including commando units hardened by the fighting in East Timor; they have sophisticated weaponry and helicopter gunships. On paper it is an unequal struggle but the OPM maintain that only about ten per cent of West Papua is controlled by Indonesia.

The effects of militarization have been devastating for the indigenous population. Tens of thousands of tribespeople have been killed by the Indonesian Army and villages bombed and strafed. Papuans are arrested, detained, tortured and executed without reference to any judicial procedure. Since 1984 when the Indonesian Army renewed its efforts to defeat the OPM, there have been swarms of refugees fleeing into Papua New Guinea. By the end of the year more than 6,000 men, women and children had sought refuge and nearly all the villages in the border region had been emptied; and by the end of 1986 this figure had more than doubled.

The Philippines' national minorities

There are approximately 6.5 million people in the Philippines belonging to over fifty indigenous minority groups. Until recent years they successfully retained their lands, and cultural and political independence. The Igorots,

Kalingas and Bontocs of Northern Luzon are the largest groupings and cultivate wet rice terraces but most other minority groups practise swidden farming. Today there are few tribes subsisting entirely by hunting and gathering and most, such as the Negritos, have been forced to withdraw into less hospitable mountainous areas and have experienced severe population decline. The Negritos and Aetas, for example, lost over 50,000 hectares of their traditional land to the United States Clark Air and Subic Naval bases. For all tribal minorities the idea that the land they consider to be their physical and spiritual environment can be claimed by outsiders, is incomprehensible.[66]

The tribal minorities of the Philippines were formed during the Spanish occupation (1521–1896). Until colonization the principal social unit was the *barangay*, a community of 100-500 people. As the Spanish subjugated the islands some groups resisted, like the Muslim Moros in the south and the tribes of the Cordilleras in the northern island of Luzon, while others retreated into the hills and forests. When the Spanish left, there were thus two fairly distinct groups, a Filipino majority which had been thoroughly assimilated, and numerous indigenous minorities which had retained their cultural identity and economic independence.

Spanish colonial rule was immediately replaced by that of the United States. North Americans were, however, more successful in alienating land from the tribal minorities. A series of land laws made whole areas of communal land part of the public domain and, therefore, available for private or corporate acquisition and exploitation. The traditional owners were driven from their land by deceit or by force and increasingly great estates of sugar cane, bananas and pineapples were created. Tribal Filipinos retreated before the onslaught and by the eve of the Second World War the Philippines economy and particularly its agricultural exports were dominated by the United States.

In the late 1960s and 1970s the commercialization of agriculture intensified. The absence of further frontier land meant expansion by agribusiness could take place only at the expense of smallholdings growing food for the domestic market. More than 23,000 hectares of land were acquired for sugar cane production by the Bukidnon Sugar Corporation (BUSCO) in two years from 1974 to 1976 and thousands of Manobo peoples cheated of their communally held land. The expansion of fruit production such as bananas and pineapples dominated by three United States Corporations, Del Monte, Castle and Cooke, and United Fruit, has occurred at the expense of various national minorities. On the island of Mindanao families of tribal minorities have been removed from their land by legal chicanery and often by force. They have been turned from self-sufficient farmers into impoverished plantation workers or part of the mass of unemployed continually expanding the slums of the cities.

Britain's own development bank, the Commonwealth Development Corporation, has participated in this process of land alienation and rural pauperization. A loan of £6.4 million was advanced to the Philippines National Development Corporation and the Malaysian-based Guthrie Corporation to plant oil palm in an area around Agusan del Sur. Originally the land granted by the Philippines Government for plantation projects on the island of Mindanao

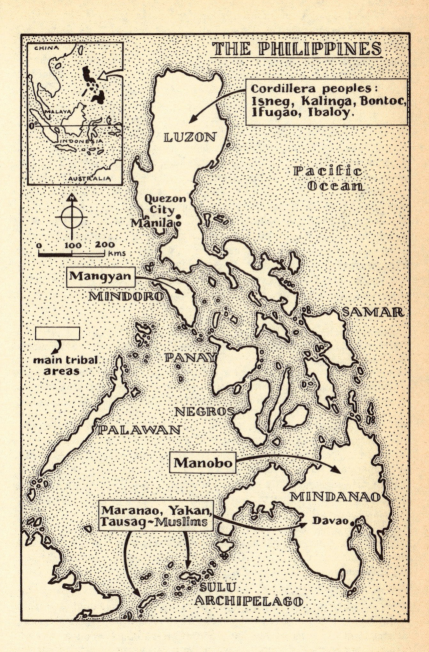

THE PHILIPPINES

CHINA

Cordillera peoples:
Isneg, Kalinga, Bontoc,
Ifugao, Ibaloy.

LUZON

MALAYA

INDONESIA

AUSTRALIA

Pacific
Ocean

Quezon
City
Manila

0   100 200
         kms

Mangyan

MINDORO

SAMAR

main tribal
areas

PANAY

NEGROS

PALAWAN

Manobo

MINDANAO

Maranao, Yakan,
Tausag~Muslims

Davao

SULU
ARCHIPELAGO

totalled some 40,000 hectares. In the case of the CDC-funded venture about 8,000 hectares will eventually be cultivated. In granting the land the government took no account of the resident population and in the first phase of the project over 3,000 people were forcibly evicted of whom about half were tribal Manobos. The evictions were accompanied by no less than 30 murders and hundreds of acts of violence and intimidation by a paramilitary force, the Last Command, employed by the NDC and Guthrie.[67] Such acts of violence and intimidation, while well-documented in this instance, are common practice in the Philippines and because the indigenous peoples have no recognized title to the land they are particular victims of such abuse.

More than half of the Philippines is deemed forest land and within the public domain and virtually all the country's indigenous peoples live in those designated areas. For the minorities it is their ancestral land, but for successive governments in the Philippines it is land that is unexploited and unclaimed. Since the 1960s the forests have been logged at a rate virtually unparalleled elsewhere. More than one-third of the Philippines' forests has now been felled, mostly for export by United States and Japanese corporations and with no programme of reforestation planned. The only government initiative has been to deny use of the forest to its traditional indigenous occupants whose swidden cultivation, it is claimed, is responsible for the loss of trees. But, as one report maintains, the tribal minorities have successfully managed the forests for generations:

> Among the Ifugaos of Kiangan, for example, high quality trees planted in the forest by far-sighted Ifugaos in the past have been alienated to the State and then to logging companies. Those trees were planted for their aesthetic qualities, as a protection of vital watersheds, or as a future source of high quality timber or fuel to be used by direct descendants of the planters. Now these heirs are barred from even a share in the profit from their legacy.[68]

In the early 1970s one logging company, the Cellophil Resources Corporation, was awarded concessions of nearly 200,000 hectares in an area of Northern Luzon. The logging company operation threatened the livelihoods of five separate minority groups – the Tinggians, Bontocs, Isnegs, Kalingas and Kankanais – inhabiting the mountain provinces. A total population of about 150,000 are already or will in the near future be affected by the concession. The forests are integral to the economy of the peoples of this region. Although rice grown on irrigated terraces is the main subsistence food, the forests provide supplementary proteins such as game or swidden plots for cattle, and timber for fuel. The logging pursuits carried out on Tinggian land have already disrupted the economic base of the community and provoked widespread opposition. In a resolution passed in 1979 the Tinggian Community stated:

> The entry of the Cellophil Resources Corporation into our municipalities and barangays will destroy our watersheds critical to our water supply for drinking and irrigation; water for our cattle; and will result in the pollution and drying up of our rivers and brooks in which we catch fish and crabs for our daily subsistence;

The cutting of trees from our steep mountains will cause erosion and destroy our fields and farms thereby depriving us of our livelihood as well as the destruction of the natural beauty of our forests;

The entry of Cellophil Resources Corporation in our municipalities will decimate the culture, traditions, customs and other such vital interests of our people;

The operation of the Cellophil Resources Corporation in our municipalities will ruin the strong unity and harmony of our tribal communities which are held together by an extensive peace pact.[69]

One of the most serious threats to the indigenous minorities of the Philippines is, however, the ten-year energy programme which began in 1979. The programme includes the building of 31 dams, nearly all of them on lands presently occupied by minorities. Inevitably the best agricultural land on the valley bottoms will be submerged and the watersheds above the dam will be protected. If the full programme goes ahead an estimated 1.5 million people would lose their homes, land and livelihoods and need to be relocated elsewhere.

In the Kalinga area, for example, although the average household cultivates only about 0.5 hectares of rice, the yield is more than three times the national average and sufficient to satisfy basic needs.[70] But the valley environment is also a heritage protected by the living and of great cultural and spiritual importance to the minority people.

The advantages of the energy programme for the wider national society are equally questionable. The costs were estimated at US$ 6.5 million in 1979, much of the work and consultancies will be contracted from outside the Philippines and the electricity produced, if the present pattern of distribution is maintained, will benefit primarily foreign-owned industrial enterprises, and not the rural and urban poor. USAID, the Asian Development Bank and the World Bank have all underwritten the massive expenditure and numerous commercial banks have advanced loans to the Philippines Government as well.

Nevertheless, despite this alignment of great capitalist interests, the programme has met with effective resistance from tribal peoples and had to be modified or partially shelved. In the Chico River basin in northern Luzon where four dams were scheduled, the local Kalinga and Bontoc inhabitants organized mass meetings and acts of civil disobedience. The government brought in troops to quell the opposition but repression only pushed the Kalingas and Bontocs into supporting the New People's Army (NPA), the armed wing of the Philippines Communist Party, which was operating in the area. Unable to ensure the safety of the survey and construction teams, the World Bank withdrew its support for this part of the programme.[71] But while this was a reprieve for the tribal minorities upstream, those downstream still face the same threat. Indeed, the government has attempted to implement its energy programme against the will and often without the knowledge of local communities throughout the islands of Mindanao and Luzon.

The government agency responsible for the national minorities of the Philippines was – until its disbandment in 1985 – the Presidential Assistant on

National Minorities (PANAMIN). There was no representation of tribal people in the leadership of PANAMIN and most board members were leading businessmen, often with commercial interests in indigenous areas. The head of PANAMIN, until he died in 1985, Manuel Elizalde Jr, came from one of the Philippines' wealthiest families with holdings in mining and logging companies. Other board members were stockholders in major national companies and closely associated with foreign multinational corporations.[72] From 1977 the most important part of PANAMIN's work and the major expenditure was on its counter-insurgency drive in minority areas. The agency was responsible for relocating communities in special government reservations to make way for development projects. In practice those removed received no title to land and had no control over their economic or other activities. From tribal elders, the power in the community was transferred to the PANAMIN officials. Between 1977 and 1985 some 2.5 million Filipinos – according to PANAMIN – were confined to such reservations. In 1985 President Marcos closed down PANAMIN and created the Office of Muslim Affairs and Cultural Communities (OMACC). Following President Aquino's election, moves are under way for separate Ministries for Muslim Affairs and National Minorities.

The economic policy of the government of the Philippines was to promote large-scale commercial agriculture, export-oriented industry, foreign investment and major infrastructural developments. It was a policy which, while finding favour in the boardrooms of the International Monetary Fund and the World Bank, brought misery to the majority of the population. Political opposition grew not only in the countryside and in the factories but also among large sectors of the middle class. The militarization, the suspension of trade unions and civil rights and the climate of oppression and violence brought to the attention of the world's press in 1984 with the assassination of the opposition leader Benigno Aquino, all served to bring about widespread opposition to the Marcos dictatorship. For the tribal peoples of the Philippines the existence of a national movement is of growing importance. In the struggle to prevent the dam projects in the Chico river, tribal minorities ceased to organize on a village basis and came together with other communities and other tribes to form *bodongs* or peace pacts.

'Even if the dam is not built here in our area but is built further down river among the Kaluga, we shall be just as concerned,' it was declared at one meeting. 'For we are all one people with them.'[73]

The Cordillera peoples of the island of Luzon have come together under the Cordillera People's Alliance and are now demanding an Autonomous Cordillera Region.

PACT OF THE CORDILLERA PEOPLE'S ALLIANCE FOR THE DEFENSE OF THE ANCESTRAL DOMAIN

Preamble

We, the indigenous people of the Cordillera, met in June 1984 in Bontoc, Mountain Province, and organized the Cordillera People's Alliance for the Defense of the Ancestral Domain.

Aware of the problems which are perpetrated by the State, the ruling elite, and the imperialists against us as national minorities: the violation of our right to our ancestral domain and its natural wealth; the aggressions against our culture, our indigenous political systems, and our life:

Conscious of our right to self-determination, which for us means: the right to our ancestral domain; to autonomous management, disposition, utilization, and development of its resources; to respect for our culture and for our political integrity as a people;

Convinced that we can win genuine recognition of these rights only through a broad, united, and militant struggle;

Mindful that this struggle can be successfully waged only in conjunction with the over-all Filipino struggle for national freedom and democracy;

We pledge hereby to work in unity and earnest in upholding the provisions of the Pact.

ARTICLE I
THE INDIGENOUS PEOPLE OF THE CORDILLERA AND THEIR ANCESTRAL DOMAIN

This Pact shall cover the Cordillera Mountain Range which is the ancestral domain belonging to its indigenous inhabitants by historic right. The ancestral domain comprises the land occupied by the Igorot people: Bontoc, Ibaloy, Ifugao, Isneg, Gaddang, Kalinga, Kankanaey, Tinggian, Bago, Balangao, Kalangoya, Karao, Kataguan, Mandek-ey, Atta Negrito, Pugot; the rice terraces, swidden farms and orchards; the mountains, forests, waters and minerals; the pasturelands and hunting grounds; the burial sites and sacred grounds; and the sky above.

ARTICLE II
DECLARATIONS OF RIGHTS AND POLICIES

Section 1. On the violation of our right to our ancestral domain. – As original inhabitants of the Cordillera, we possess the inalienable and primary right to our ancestral domain. We have the right to defend this ancestral domain, and to recover and regain control over lost territories and resources.

In order that this right be guaranteed, the Cordillera ancestral domain shall be constituted as an autonomous region within the democratic coalition government. The coalition government shall guarantee that the Cordillera ancestral domain be the perpetual and inalienable collective property of our people.

Section 2. On the violation of our ancestral proprietary right to our natural resources. – We, the people of the Cordillera, have the ancestral proprietary right to the management, disposition, utilization, and development of all natural resources within our ancestral domain, prior to national and other constituencies.

All existing and foreign-controlled industries within the Cordillera shall be nationalized, but with just compensation for the communities displaced, and indemnities for all past injuries caused by the operations of such industries.

Henceforth, further exploitation of resources within the ancestral domain by national and other constituencies shall require democratic consultation with and approval by the people of the autonomous region. Just compensation and a share in the beneficial returns shall be allocated to the people of the autonomous region.

We have the right to the conservation of the natural resources necessary for environmental protection and improvement, industries shall have corresponding measures for more beneficial, longer-term, and ecologically-sound utilization of natural resouces.

In areas where big landlords have usurped large tracts of land, depriving farmers, the land shall be apportioned to those who have been deprived, and to those who have actually tilled the land.

Appropriate adjustments shall be made to take into consideration the economic rights of non-indigenous inhabitants of the Cordillera.

Section 3. On the violation of our right to economic prosperity and genuine social development. – We, the people of the Cordillera, have the right to all-rounded, socio-economic development.

Historical and current political processes and the exploitation of the Cordillera natural resources for the benefit of outside interests have placed many of our people in a marginalized situation. We therefore have the right to receive more economic benefits in the form of State allocations and social welfare services for an accelerated development towards social and economic prosperity.

Any economic development program should be within the framework of social justice, the broadest possible participation of the people in the entire development process, adaptation of indigenous forms and systems of collective labor and cooperative management, and self-reliance.

All development efforts should begin with development education, so that our people may gain a full understanding of the implications and consequences of such efforts, and so that we can direct programs or choose alternatives which best suit our needs and interests.

Section 4. On the violation of our right to respect for our indigenous culture, and to pursue our cultural development. – We, the people of the Cordillera, have the right to maintain the integrity of our indigenous culture, and to pursue cultural development.

Indigenous cultural institutions shall be recognized and treated with respect. We have the right to maintain our indigenous belief systems, value systems, learning systems, and practices in freedom and for so long as these are meaningful and viable for us. We shall neither be forced to abandon nor be encouraged to artificially maintain these for the benefit of outside interests. We have the right to freely innovate upon these, and to utilize these as the venue for developing a progressive and scientific worldview.

Indigenous rituals, customs, and artistic traditions shall be treated likewise, and shall be protected from vulgarization or exploitation for commercial ends. The freedom to make creative, meaningful, appropriate, and progressive innovations upon these is our people's right.

There shall be institutional rectification of all discriminatory and incorrect ideas and beliefs about our people. The mass media, schools, churches, and other institutions involved in the processes of information-dissemination, opinion-moulding, and socialization shall transmit only correct and truthful ideas regarding the national minorities.

In the autonomous region, these institutions shall be given the task of cultivating among our people a proper knowledge, understanding, and appreciation of themselves, their culture, and their historical experience.

The growth of a united Cordillera consciousness shall be encouraged, provided that ethnic differences shall be recognized and respected.

Mutual understanding and respect between the people of the Cordillera and the other peoples of the Philippines shall be cultivated. Appreciation of Filipino nationalist culture and the development of a Filipino national language shall also be encouraged in the Cordillera, provided that these do not prejudice our appreciation and development of our own culture and languages.

The people of the Cordillera shall be encouraged to write their own history and culture.

Section 5. On the violation of our right to political integrity, and on the non-recognition of our indigenous political systems. – We, the people of the Cordillera, have the right to political integrity through the establishment of an Autonomous Cordillera Region consisting of the defined Cordillera ancestral domain.

The Autonomous Cordillera Region shall have an autonomous government which shall truly represent our interests as indigenous national minorities: in recognition of our political integrity as one people with a common geography, historical experience, culture, and current situation; in due respect for our indigenous socio-political systems; and in consideration for our particular needs, problems, and demands.

All government authority within the Autonomous Cordillera Region shall come from the indigenous people of the Cordillera. We have the right to manage our own internal affairs according to the will of the majority of our people without undue external interference. We have the right to democratic participation in determining policies, programs and projects which may affect our lives and future.

Regional autonomy shall be established within the framework of a national democratic coalition government. The Autonomous Cordillera Region shall be an inalienable part of the Philippine State. As such it shall enjoy the right of representation and participation in the coalition government and in all other organs of the State.

Our people shall have, without discrimination, the same rights and duties as other citizens of the Philippine State. We shall participate on equal footing with the rest of the Filipino people in all aspects of public life.

Regional autonomy shall not impair, but rather contribute to, the territorial integrity and political unity of the entire Filipino nation.

(a) *Organizational structure of the Autonomous Cordillera Region*:
We, the people of the Cordillera, have the right to determine our form of

self-government in consideration of political systems we are already practicing.

The smallest political unit shall conform with existing indigenous socio-political structures like the clan, *dap-ay, ator, bodong, kalon*, or whatever system the people choose as appropriate to them.

All sectors, indigenous ethnolinguistic groups, and/or provinces in the Cordillera shall be given proper representation in any higher organs which shall be created, based on the organization, population, and area of these groups.

The rights of non-indigenous inhabitants of the Cordillera shall be accorded due considerations in the political system to be established.

Organs at all levels shall exercise certain rights of self-government.

(b) *Legislation*: A regional legislative body shall be established in the Autonomous Cordillera Region. It shall enact specific rules and regulations according to the political, economic, social and cultural characteristics of our people. Custom laws which are currently in effect or in practice among the various ethnolinguistic groups in the region shall be respected and considered in the formulation of regional policies and legislation. These shall be carried out all in accordance with the will of the majority of our people.

A Regional Charter shall be drafted, defining democratic participation of the Cordillera people in all regional autonomous organs, and defining the relations of the Autonomous Cordillera Region with the national government.

The Cordillera people shall have the right to be represented in national legislative bodies.

The national Constitution shall provide for equality and unity between the Cordillera people and the rest of the Filipino nation. National laws shall likewise be enacted prohibiting discrimination against national minorities.

(c) *The Judiciary*: The Autonomous Cordillera Region shall have the right to set up its own judicial system based on the laws of the Cordillera legislature. The courts to be established shall be responsible, among other functions, for obtaining indemnification for all victims of State abuse in the Cordillera.

(d) *Fraternal Relations*: In the spirit of solidarity and internationalism, the Autonomous Cordillera Region shall promote fraternal relations with other national minorities, sectors, and regions in the Philippines, and with other indigenous peoples in the world.

Section 6. On militarization and State repression. – We, the people of the Cordillera, have the right to a life of peace and order. We have the right to utilize our own indigenous systems or establish freely our own means of maintaining peace and order in the Cordillera, without military intervention and State repression of our civil and political rights.

Civilian authority shall at all times reign supreme over military authority.

In March 1986 Mrs Corazon Aquino, the widow of the opposition politician assassinated by Marcos supporters, was swept to power with popular acclaim following an election campaign in which she championed the cause of the poor.

The future of the national minorities in the Philippines is now to be determined by the complex of alliances grouped around the new president, whose members represent radical political movements, business interests and some residual supporters of the Marcos dictatorship.

The Bangsa Moro struggle

The two million or so Bangsa Moro people of southern Philippines have suffered since independence in 1946. Their homeland is in the south of Mindanao and the collection of islands of Sulu, Basilan and Palawan. Even during Spanish colonization of the rest of the Philippines, the Moros defended their land and were, as a result, in a state of war for over 300 years. When the United States replaced Spain as colonial masters they also tried to subdue the mainly Muslim peoples of the south but were equally unsuccessful. With decolonization after the Second World War the Moros sought independence but their aspirations were unfulfilled and the region and its people became a part of the new Philippines.

Since then, successive governments have sought to incorporate the territory into the Philippines. Communally held land was declared within the public domain and national resources were thereby made accessible to outside exploitation. Many poor Moros were dispossessed of their land to make way for settler schemes. In 1972, the Marcos dictatorship began a full-scale war against the Moros which has brought about the deaths of around 90,000 civilians and the destruction of 250,000 homes and other buildings. For its part the Bangsa Moro people have a political organization, the Moro National Liberation Front (MNLF), and an armed wing, the Bangsa Moro Army (BMA), with some 16,000 combatants. The MNLF have shown themselves quite capable of resisting the Philippine Army but unable to win a decisive victory. Accordingly, the struggle in the south of the country has become one of Asia's most bloody secret wars.[74]

The new civilian government of President Corazon Aquino which came to power in 1986 brings hopes of a peaceful solution, not only to the Moro struggle but to those of other national minorities in the Philippines. President Aquino has publicly expressed concern for social justice for the poor, and tribal peoples are very often the poorest of the poor. But vested political and economic interests continue to retain a grip on many key adminstrative posts, so change, if it takes place at all, is likely to be slow.

The indigenous peoples of the Philippines, like those of other countries in Asia, occupy land over which governments wish to assert their sovereignty. The independent nations of the region which have come into being since the Second World War have themselves begun their own colonization process. Indonesia has forcibly annexed East Timor, West Papua and the South Moluccas; Bangladesh occupies the formerly autonomous hill tracts region with an estimated one-third of its regular armed forces; in India the tribal parts of the north-east have been designated no-go areas for outsiders as Union troops keep the lid on various secessionist movements; in Burma, all the main ethnic minorities have been fighting the government virtually since independence because they do not want to be incorporated into a centralized Burmese state; in the Philippines, tribal peoples have been removed from their homelands to make way for logging companies, agribusiness, mines and hydro-electric schemes, and when they have protested they have faced the army's guns. It would not be an exaggeration to say that most tribal peoples in Asia are in conflict with their governments, merely because they seek to remain a distinct people with some political and economic independence. As the European powers have withdrawn from the region, the tribal peoples of Asia have become the victims of a new foreign domination: that of the majority populations under whose tutelage they now live. The rights to self-determination of peoples have not been achieved with the demise of European colonialism – as will be seen in the next chapter on Africa – and there are still indigenous peoples seeking to determine their own futures.

Notes

1. Government of India, 'Comments and observations with regard to the country monograph on India', statement to the United Nations Working Group on Indigenous Populations, August 1983.

2. See for example Minority Rights Group reports on *The Kurds* (1984), *The Palestinians* (1984) and *The Armenians* (1981).

3. Hugh Tinker, 'Burma: separatism as a way of life', in Georgina Ashworth (ed.), *World Minorities*, vol.I (Quartermaine House, 1977) pp.31-42; see also Martin Smith, 'Politics of opium', *Inside Asia*, London, no.5, September–October 1985, pp.7-9.

4. Sterling Seagrove, 'Karen rebels in Burma', *Soldier of Fortune*, April 1984, p.66.

5. Documents submitted to the Anti-Slavery Society from the Human Rights Committee for Non-Burman Nationalities, Thailand.

6. 'Human Rights Violations in Burma, 1985', report of the Anti-Slavery Society, 1985; this picture of human rights violations was confirmed by the author in his own interviews with Karen refugees in Thailand during June 1985.

7. Cf. Gerald C. Hickey, 'Some aspects of hill tribe life in Vietnam', in Peter Kunstadter (ed.), *Southeast Asian tribes, minorities and nations*, vol.11 (Princeton University Press, 1967) pp.745-69.

8. 'The Meo of Laos', in Ashworth (ed.), *World Minorities*, vol.1, pp.110-14.

9. Robert G. Wirsing, *The Baluchis and Pathans*, Minority Rights Group Report, no.48, 1981.

10. Ibid., p.6.

11. Ibid., p.16.

12. *Refugees magazine*, no.2, January 1983.

13. Wendy Kahn, 'The Koochis of Afghanistan', in Ashworth (ed.), *World Minorities*, vol.II, 1978, pp.61-4.

14. Sarah Jane Hawthorne, 'The Taiwanese (Formosans)', in Ashworth (ed.),

World Minorities, vol.II, pp.124-33; Carl Goldstein, 'The crumbling culture of Taiwan's aborigines', *Far Eastern Economic Review*, 29 May 1986, pp.46-9.

15. Cf. Wiveca Stegeborn, 'Sri Lanka: The Veddas – a people under threat', *IWGIA Newsletter*, no.42, June 1985, pp.166-80.

16. Centre for Science and Environment, *The state of India's environment, 1982* (New Delhi, 1982) p.120.

17. Communication by the Anti-Slavery Society to the United Nations cited in *Study of the problem of discrimination against indigenous populations*, chapter XVII, p.157.

18. Steve Jones, 'Tribal underdevelopment in India', *Development and Change*, vol.9, no.1, January 1978, pp.45-6.

19. Government of India, *Report of the Commissioner for Scheduled Castes and Scheduled Tribes*, Part 1, 1979-81, p.3.

20. *Frontier* (Calcutta), 15 January 1983, p.9.

21. *State of India's Environment, 1982*, p.121.

22. Ibid., p.46.

23. Centre for the Society of Developing Societies, *Goa's forests* (Delhi, 1982) p.5.

24. Gerald D. Berreman, *Himachal: science, people and progress*, IWGIA Document 36, Copenhagen, 1979, p.31; see also Gerald D. Berreman, 'The movement to save the Himalayas', *The Global Reporter*, vol.1, no.4, Spring 1984, p.16.

25. Julian Burger, 'Tribal Minorities in Asia: the indigenous peoples of the Chotanagpur Plateau, India', report to Coopération Internationale pour le Développement et la Solidarité, Brussels, February 1986, p.40.

26. *Report of the Commissioner*, pp.143-4.

27. Julian Burger, p.26.

28. *Report of the Commissioner*, p.331.

29. National Survey on the Incidence of Bonded Labour (Final Report 1981) cited in Anti-Slavery Society, 'Bonded Labour in India', statement to the United Nations Sub-Commission on Prevention of Discrimination and Protection of Minorities, August 1982.

30. *Repression in Singhbhum*, report of the fact-finding committee of the People's Union for Civil Liberties and Democratic Rights, Delhi, March 1979, pp.2-3.

31. *India Today*, 31 October 1982, p.81.

32. *Probe India*, September 1982, p.54.

33. *India Today*, 31 October 1982, p.91; on the Nagas see also Neville Maxwell, *India and the Nagas*, Minority Rights Group Report No. 17, 1973 and IWGIA, *The Naga nation and its struggle against genocide*, Copenhagen, July 1986.

34. A good description of the daily life of rural communities in Bangladesh is provided by Betsy Hartman and James Boyce, *A Quiet Violence* (Zed Press, London, 1984).

35. Anti-Slavery Society, *The Chittagong Hill Tracts: militarization, oppression and the hill tribes* (1984) p.39.

36. Forestal Forestry and Engineering International Ltd, *Chittagong Hill Tracts, soil and land use survey*, report 1967 cited in Anti-Slavery Society, *The Chittagong Hill Tracts*, p.17.

37. M.Q. Zaman, 'Tribal integrity and national integration: the Chittagong Hill Tracts case', paper prepared for a seminar on Tribal Cultures of Bangladesh,

University of Rajshahi, 28 to 30 March 1980.

38. Anti-Slavery Society, *The Chittagong Hill Tracts*, p.39.

39. Gordon P. Means, 'The Orang Asli of Malaysia', in Ashworth (ed.), *World Minorities*, vol.II, p.89.

40. Kirk Endicott, 'The effects of logging on the Batek of Malaysia', *Cultural Survival Quarterly*, vol.6, no.2, Spring 1982, p.20.

41. Robert O. Mathews, 'SAM: environmentalism in Malaysia', *The Global Reporter*, vol.1, no.4, Spring 1984, p.17.

42. Cited in 'Tribal peoples in eastern Malaysia', report for the Anti-Slavery Society, 1982, unpublished.

43. 'Malaysia: tearing the heart out of a tribe', *IWGIA Newsletter*, no.39, October 1984, p.90.

44. Ibid., p.93.

45. Ibid., p.92.

46. Anti-Slavery Society, 'Tribal peoples in eastern Malaysia'.

47. Letter to the Prime Minister from the Bakun Residents' Action Committee, 4 February 1986.

48. Cited in *Sarawak Tribune*, 5 February 1986.

49. Cf. *Human Rights in Thailand Report*, vol.8, no.3, July–December 1984, pp.32-7.

50. Gerald C. Hickey and Jesse Wright, *The hill people of northern Thailand: social and economic development*, USAID, June 1978, pp.3-5.

51. Julian Burger, 'Tribal minorities in Asia: the Karen of Thailand', report to Coopération Internationale pour le Développement et la Solidarité, Brussels, September 1985.

52. There is now some evidence of success, especially since the government began to use less coercive methods. According to one source Thai opium production was 145 tonnes in 1966 and reduced to 35 tonnes in 1984. Cf. Yoyanna Sharma, 'Fighting drugs through development', *Development and Cooperation* (Bonn) no.3, May–June 1984, pp.22-3.

53. Nic Tapp, *The Hmong of Thailand – Opium People of the Golden Triangle*, Anti-Slavery Society, 1986.

54. Information from submission to the United Nations Working Group on Indigenous Populations, July 1985, by Republic of South Moluccas, Homeland Mission.

55. For a full story of the struggle in East Timor see Carmel Budiardjo and Liem Soei Liong, *The War against East Timor* (Zed Books, 1984) and Torben Retboll (ed.), *East Timor: the struggle continues*, IWGIA Document 50, Copenhagen, October 1984.

56. Mil Roekaerts, 'Land rights of tribals in Kalimantan, Indonesia', report to Coopération Internationale pour le Développement et la Solidarité, Brussels 1985 (draft).

57. Cf. Peter Worsley, *The trumpet shall sound: a study of cargo cults in Melanesia* (New York, 1968).

58. TAPOL, *West Papua: the obliteration of a people* (1983), p.24.

59. Ibid., p.32.

60. Ibid., p.66.

61. Anti-Slavery Society, *Plunder in Paradise: the struggle of the West Papuan peoples*, 1986 (forthcoming).

62. *Newsweek*, 18 February 1974, cited in TAPOL, p.37.

63. Anti-Slavery Society, *Plunder in Paradise*.

64. FUNDWI, 'Role of forest-based industries in West Irian', cited in Anti-Slavery Society, *Plunder in Paradise*.

65. TAPOL, p.54.

66. The Anti-Slavery Society, *The Philippines: authoritarian government, multinationals and ancestral lands*, 1983, p.23.

67. Catholic Institute for International Relations, *British investment and the use of paramilitary terrorism in plantation agriculture in Agusan del Sur, Philippines*, August 1982; cf. also Parliamentary Human Rights Group, *The CDC and Mindanao*, report of a visit to the Philippines by Alf Dubbs MP and Colin Moynihan MP, 21 September to 1 October 1983.

68. Anti-Slavery Society, *The Philippines*, p.73.

69. Cited in ibid., p.85.

70. Ibid., p.90.

71. Walden Bello, David Kinley and Elaine Elinson, *Development debacle: the World Bank in the Philippines* (Institute for Food and Development Policy, San Francisco, 1982) pp.56-8.

72. See chapter 6 of Anti-Slavery Society, *The Philippines*, for details of business interests of board.

73. Cited in Bishop F. Claver, 'The progress of the people at the nozzle of a gun', *Southeast Asia Chronicle*, Issue 67, October 1979, p.32.

74. Cf. 'Appeal of the Bangsa Moro people to the Permanent People's Tribunal', an appeal to the Permanent People's Tribunal, Antwerp, Belgium, October 1980. The war has created two million refugees; 535 mosques and 200 schools have been demolished, and 35 cities and towns have been wholly destroyed; cf. '400 year war – Moro struggle in the Philippines', *Southeast Asia Chronicle*, Issue 82, February 1982, p.3.

9. The Threatened Peoples of Africa

The colonization of the Americas brought about an irreversible change in the conditions of life of the indigenous populations. Their numbers were drastically reduced and today in most countries they are a physically and culturally oppressed minority. In Africa as in parts of Asia, however, the indigenous peoples proved more resilient to European invasion. The result is that in Africa nearly all the present-day states are controlled and peopled by the original inhabitants. The exceptions are South Africa and Namibia which are ruled by a white minority population.[1] It may seem curious, therefore, to include the continent of Africa in a report examining the state of the world's indigenous peoples. But the motives for doing so are simple enough, for decolonization has not liberated or provided equal rights and privileges for all ethnic groups. This chapter considers the situations, not of the indigenous inhabitants as such, but of certain national minorities whose relatively independent and self-reliant way of life is threatened by recent developments.

Africa's most threatened peoples are those living in remote areas, where the land, whether desert, semi-desert or tropical forest, is unsuitable for settled agriculture. They are peoples like the Tuareg of the Sahel region or the Masai of East Africa who are nomadic pastoralists; or else they are peoples like the San (Bushmen) or the Pygmies who depend in part upon hunting and gathering. In all events they are peoples who have achieved a masterly adaptation to what are perceived by most outsiders as inhospitable environments. Their special skills and culture have helped them survive and sometimes prosper but there are growing pressures both upon the peoples themselves and the environment in which they live. They are increasingly being forced to give up their nomadic existence and become settled farmers or seasonal workers. In some cases this process of sedentarization has been actively promoted by African governments as part of a programme of rural development. The forests are also being cut down to make way for cattle ranches and plantations, and the savanna contiguous with the Kalahari and Sahara deserts is subjected to intensive overgrazing. The changes wrought upon these fragile ecosystems are seriously, and perhaps irrevocably, affecting Africa's hunter-gatherer and pastoral peoples. This is not to suggest that government policy alone is responsible for the dramatic changes to the lives of these peoples. As one writer has commented:

Many of the influences now profoundly changing traditional pastoral and hunter-gatherer societies in Africa and elsewhere have their origin in colonial conquest and organization, and are continued today by economic processes originating in the western developed world, often helped by development programmes conceived and executed largely by foreign specialists.[2]

The colonial heritage

Africa today is a product of European colonialism. The slave trade emptied Africa of millions – some believe as many as 100 million in the course of its operation – of young, able-bodied men and women. The loss of so many farmers and craftsmen contributed to the distortion and stagnation of the African economy.[3] When the slave trade gave way to the physical occupation of Africa by rival European powers, new kinds of destruction were worked on the continent. The longstanding political entities which governed in various parts of Africa were overwhelmed. The Muslim states of Dahomey and Western Sudan, the Zulu nation, the kingdoms of Madagascar, of Egypt, of the Asante, of Benin, of the Yoruba and many more all disappeared and their territories fell under the control of whichever European power reached them first. Peoples sharing the same language and culture found themselves subject to French, British, German or some other foreign administration according to how frontiers were negotiated far away in Europe. At the Berlin Conference in 1884-85 the imperialist powers agreed to spheres of interest and areas of proposed occupation, and by 1901 fairly precise borders were defined. Topographical and cultural features in Africa were given no consideration.

The colonial powers also brought important changes to the African economy, most notably to indigenous agriculture. In West Africa, European trading companies buying such cash crops as palm oil were established, and African farmers increasingly adapted to and grew dependent on the new markets. As Europeans settled in East, Central and Southern Africa more and more of the best land was taken over and turned to cash crop production. African peasants either became labourers on the new estates or else moved on to more marginal lands. In certain extreme instances foreign concession companies were given rights to huge tracts of land as well as labour by the colonial powers. King Leopold of Belgium, for example, owned a territory more than half the size of Europe and with the use of a brutally administered system of forced labour extracted profits from rubber production. As a consequence of these changes, domestic food production in Africa declined and well-established land-use patterns were disrupted.[4]

As the new nation states emerged in Africa following the Second World War, frontiers were left virtually unchanged. At a meeting of African heads of state in 1964 it was ruled that 'the borders of African states on the day of independence constitute a tangible reality' and member states of the Organization of African Unity (OAU) pledged themselves to respect 'borders existing on their achievement of national independence'.[5] By adopting such a position and retaining European-imposed frontiers, the majority of African states now consist of what one author described as 'a loose assemblage of different ethnic groups or tribes'.[6]

Self-determination

There are few states in sub-Saharan Africa which are not made up of peoples from numerous ethnic groups. In Nigeria, for example, there are some 400 different linguistic groups and 200 tribes; in Ghana there are nine main ethnic groups; in Tanzania about 120 tribal groups. In most countries often one ethnic group has achieved some pre-eminence to the detriment of the rest. In Ghana the Akan occupy most professional posts; in Kenya the Kikuyu are the best educated and wealthiest group though they make up less than ten per cent of the country's population; in Uganda where there are over 40 ethnic groups several of the Nilotic-speaking groups benefited under President Milton Obote only to face persecution under President Idi Amin; in Zimbabwe there is continuing friction between the majority Shona people who support the prime minister, Robert Mugabe, and the Ndebele people, supporters of Joshua Nkomo.

Although there are some successful examples of powerful ethnic groups accommodating lesser groups, such as is the case of the majority Bemba people of Zambia in their dealings with the Lozi of the western province, serious inter-tribal conflicts have also occurred. Whereas in some countries such tribal rivalries may eventually disappear and give way to a new sense of national unity, in other countries, serious conflict is already underway and shows no sign of diminishing. In Chad, for example, a civil war broke out only five years after independence in 1960. Although the present fight is between Muslim factions, at the heart of the 1960 conflict were the traditional rivalries between the mainly Muslim nomadic tribes of the north and the Christian tribes of the south which had settled as agriculturalists along the rivers and around Lake Chad.[7] In Western Sahara, the indigenous Sahrawis have been fighting for nationhood since 1976 when the Spanish colony was ceded to Morocco. As in other parts of the world – the example of West Papua springs readily to mind – the inhabitants were not consulted and a powerful neighbour seized the territory by force. Since that time the Council of Ministers of the Saharan Arab Democratic Republic (SADR) have achieved diplomatic recognition and its armed wing, the *Frente Polisario*, has waged a war of independence.[8] Recent history in Africa suggests that where there is a conflict, governments incline towards authoritarian solutions. Of the 40 sub-Saharan governments, only five allow opposition parties; the rest are divided between one-party states and military dictatorships.

In the Horn of Africa the issue of self-determination has been obscured in recent years by the greater world attention which is focused on the drought and widespread famine in the area. At the centre of the dispute is Ethiopia. Towards the end of the 19th Century, Ethiopia under Menelik II undertook a vast programme of conquest to the south. The predominantly orthodox Christian

Amhara people took over and settled in the territories inhabited by some 80 different tribes. Under Menelik II and later Haile Selassie the predominantly Oromo population of the south were forcibly converted and assimilated. Today, though they are by far and away the largest single ethnic group in Ethiopia, making up over 50 per cent of the total population of the country, their language is banned in schools and public institutions and many are conscripted into the ranks of the army against their will. The Amharic people who make up only 15 per cent of the total population dominate all government positions and constitute 109 of the 123 members of the country's ruling Central Committee.

Discrimination and oppression have driven many Oromo to join together to fight the Ethiopian Government. Although there was no original Oromo nation, the Oromo people share a similar language and cultural characteristics such as the *gada*, a system of age and generation grading. In 1974 the Oromo of the south defined their territory and formed the Oromo Liberation Front.[9] But their struggle is made more complex by the fact that present-day Somalia does not incorporate the traditional territories and Somali people of what was Somaliland. Many Somalis, the majority nomadic pastoralists, occupy the Eastern Harer Province of Ethiopia. These tribespeople are distrusted by the Ethiopian Government and have experienced similar kinds of discrimination to the Oromos, and they too have offered resistance. In 1977 a fully fledged war flared up in the Ogaden desert. Since then two movements have developed: the Western Somali Liberation Front (WSLF), which does not favour unification with Somalia, and the Somali Abo Liberation Front (SALF), which receives Somali Government backing.[10]

To the north, Eritreans and Tigrayans are both engaged in liberation struggles against the government. For most of the last 500 years Eritrea has been subjected to only temporary and partial occupation. The Italians ruled from 1894 until 1941, when the area fell under British administration. In the 1950s the United Nations General Assembly declared Eritrea an autonomous unit within a federated Ethiopia. In the ensuing years the autonomy of Eritrea was subverted and repression of popular protest and local leaders grew. In the early 1960s fighting broke out and large areas of the province have since been brought under the control of the Eritrean People's Liberation Front.[11] Tigrayans have united in the Tigray People's Liberation Front (TPLF) but despite many similarities with the Eritrean movement, its objective is autonomous status within Ethiopia, not independence.[12]

The Government of Ethiopia has responded to these numerous ethnic conflicts by greatly expanding its armed forces – there are now some three-quarters of a million men in arms – and relocating dissident populations on a massive scale. By 1986 an estimated 1.5 million people are due to be removed from their homelands and settled in the western provinces, many of them against their will.[13]

The situation in Ethiopia is not exceptional – it merely provides a more exaggerated example of the problems of self-determination faced by a number of African countries. In one sense decolonization has not resolved these questions but instead has pushed the issue of self-determination of the many

Table 9.1
Threatened Peoples in Africa

Nomadic pastoralists:
          14 million
  (+ about 5m in Arabia)

San (Bushmen):
  Botswana   25,000
  Namibia   29,000
  Angola   8,000
  Total: *62,000*

Pygmies: 200,000

distinct ethnic groups into abeyance. At the heart of the matter is the inflexible Western model of the nation state which appears not to suit a continent where large numbers of people are nomadic and semi-nomadic and where many often hold clan rather than national allegiances. Such peoples have a long history of coexistence with other groups as well as complex and highly adaptable concepts of territorial rights. Perhaps in time a way will be found to retain the present political configurations with their ethnic diversity while also satisfying the demands for self-determination. However, for the three peoples examined in this chapter – the nomadic pastoralists, the Pygmies and the San (Bushmen) – that time is fast running out and with it the strategy they have developed for survival in the harsh environments they have made their homelands.

The nomadic pastoralists

There are some 14 million pastoralists in Africa and a further five million desert-dwelling peoples in Arabia. In Africa they live primarily in the Sahelian region of the Sahara – the belt of land stretching from Senegal and Mauritania in the west to Chad in the east between the desert and the rich grasslands further south – and the East African countries of Kenya, Tanzania, Uganda, Sudan, Ethiopia and Somalia. Pastoral peoples occupy and successfully exploit zones of poor productivity with only desert scrub and seasonal grass, and characterized by low irregular rainfall. Pastoralists form a minority of the Sahelian population – in the region of 10 to 15 per cent of the population in most countries. Although in Somalia more than three-quarters of the population are nomadic pastoralists, and in both Somalia and the West African state of Mauritania they are in government. Despite their numerical importance the pastoralist way of life is becoming more difficult to pursue and may be in danger of disappearing altogether. Of the Sahelian nomads one writer has commented that their situation is 'increasingly desperate and hopeless', and of the pastoralists of East Africa another has written: 'the future of the traditional pastoralists is at risk. By the end of the century they may belong merely to memory'.[14] In recent years African pastoralists have faced growing discrimination from their governments and have had to bear the brunt of two savage droughts and the extensive deterioration of their environment.

Nomadic pastoralism is a highly flexible way of life suited to fragile marginal scrublands. Pastoralists range from purely nomadic groups who travel across the Sahel more or less continuously, locating pockets of pasture and trading, to the semi-nomadic peoples who move their cattle between two regions. During the dry season pastoralists will use the pasture around a base well, taking care not to overgraze, and with the wet season they will move away allowing the grazing to recover. Some pastoralists move their cattle south to the harvested fields of settled farmers. There the cattle can graze on the stubble during the dormant season and manure the ground, thus ensuring its fertility for the following year. Pastoralist society is based on animals – cattle and sometimes camels, sheep and goats – and grazing rights. The former are the private wealth of the individual and the latter the common and shared heritage of the tribe or community.

By their successful adaptation to the conditions of the semi-desert regions and their reciprocity with local settled farming communities, pastoralists were able in the past to survive long periods of drought and withstand famine. The pastoralist way of life, far from being an inefficient and primitive mode of production, has proved to be a most effective system for survival and even prosperity. One agricultural adviser has made this comment about the present economic system:

> The only form of life which does not threaten the Sahelian environment is nomadism. The continuous movement of men and animals allows vegetation to replenish itself and does not threaten water resources and the grazing land around them.[15]

Yet today the nomadic pastoralists must face serious problems on various fronts. Their grazing lands are being reduced, their traditional rights to the land and water resources are being eroded, the control of herds, pastures and water is increasingly falling into the hands of outsiders and their political power is diminished as they find themselves for the most part a minority people within states dominated by urban élites. Finally, since the early 1970s the Sahel and the semi-arid regions of East Africa have been hit by long periods of drought and a dramatic ecological deterioration. The worst affected have been the nomadic pastoralists, many of whom have lost their entire herds and been forced into what are becoming permanent refugee camps where they must survive on handouts.

The demise of the pastoralist way of life coincided with the colonization of Africa by the European powers. As the African economy was remoulded to suit the interests of the European market the symbiotic relationship that existed between the settled agriculturalists and the pastoralists was broken. Subsistence farmers in the French West African colonies, for example, were taxed and forced, occasionally with the additional fillip of army coercion, to change from the cultivation of millet and rearing of domestic animals to cash crops such as groundnuts. The land quickly became exhausted and farmers cleared new land thereby impinging upon the common pasturelands of the herders. This trend continues today.

Yet it is pastoralism that is deemed an unsuitable economic pursuit and considered damaging to the environment by most African governments. The collectivist and politically independent qualities of most pastoralist peoples have been seen as antagonistic to the proper implementation of Western models of development. Since the 1950s development efforts have, therefore, sometimes focused on the sedentarization and monetization of these formerly self-sustaining communities. National economies requiring ever-increasing exports of livestock and crops to pay back debts and satisfy the requirements of aid donors have led African governments to adopt policies harmful to the interests of pastoralists.

The result of these policy orientations has been to introduce a succession of projects to increase and manage livestock and encourage permanent crop-farming through the use of irrigation and fertilizers. The Sahel has been seen as an area which could become a beef-exporting zone if only large-scale ranching and centralized fattening and butchering facilities could be established. Little heed has been paid, until comparatively recently, to the views of the peoples who had herded animals successfully in the region for many thousands of years. Herdsmen in Niger, for example, asked the government in vain not to sink more new wells in their traditional lands because outsiders were being attracted and the nearby pastures overgrazed.[16]

The improvements to water resources in the Sahel instead of benefiting the pastoralists inadvertently brought newcomers into the area and increased competition for water and pasture. When governments attempted to regulate water rights, they failed to recognize the already existing and highly flexible rights of access developed by pastoralists and conflicts and overgrazing often resulted. Other efforts to improve stock-rearing in order to fit in with the needs of a high consumption and export economy were equally unsuccessful. Between 1975 and 1982, for example, nearly US$ 11 billion of foreign aid was poured into the Sahel of which a quarter was for agriculture. Yet of the 29 major agricultural projects surveyed by the Club du Sahel, a group made up of the aid donors, only two were considered effective.[17] Nomadic stock-rearing, which suits the changing rainfall and pasture patterns of the Sahel, has proved difficult to replace.

There have also been a number of prestigious dam and irrigation projects funded in these arid zones – in the Awash Valley in Ethiopia and on the Senegal River at Diema and Manital – but they have rarely justified the massive investment. In the Awash Valley development, Afar pastoralists lost most of their grazing lands to commercial farms of cotton and sugar, and were denied access during the dry season. A number of the concessions were sold to foreign investors and the nomadic pastoralists received no compensation for their loss. When the 1972 drought hit Wollo Province where the project was based, the herds were decimated and many Afar starved to death.[18]

Misconceived development policies have only exacerbated the already serious deterioration of the Sahel. The arid and semi-arid lands contiguous with the world's main deserts are increasingly threatened with desertification. The United Nations Conference on Desertification (UNCOD) estimated in 1977 that 6.9 million square kilometres of land in Africa south of the Sahara are severely menaced in this way.[19] Indeed, according to one writer over 650,000 square kilometres of the Sahel – the 7,000 kilometre long and 500 kilometre wide zone south of the Sahara – have been turned into desert in the last 50 years.[20] The causes of desertification are now believed to be overcultivation, overgrazing, deforestation and poor irrigation practices and it is man's influence rather than any climatic changes, such as drought, which is responsible for the deterioration of the land and the resulting crises of famine.[21] 'Drought triggers a crisis, but does not cause it,' one writer has commented;[22] another has noted: 'Governments do not see desertification as a high-priority item. Rangeland deterioration, accelerated soil erosion and salinization and waterlogging do not command attention until they become crisis items. Lip-service is paid to combating desertification, but the political will is directed elsewhere. There seems to be little appreciation that a major goal of many developing nations, that of food self-sufficiency, cannot be attained if soil and plant resources are allowed to deteriorate.'[23] Consequently, in 1980 only 1.4 per cent of aid money in the Sahel region went to forestry and ecology projects and barely five per cent to livestock-raising.[24] The bulk of foreign aid is directed towards infrastructural and urban-based development programmes which benefit African élites, rather than the rural poor who have little political power. The human victims of these inappropriate and short-sighted land-use policies are the nomadic pastoralists.

In the 1973 drought thousands of herdsmen had to move to camps for food aid, no longer able as in the past to survive. There they often faced discrimination and humiliation. In Niger, Tuareg nomads found themselves in refugee camps administered by the settled majorities from the south. In Mali, for example, the French newspaper, *Le Monde*, alleged that Tuaregs were deliberately starved by the authorities.[25]

But why are governments so hostile to nomadic pastoralists? There are historical and political reasons. The Sahelian nomads controlled the trade routes across the desert and, thereby, dominated the settled farming communities to the south. The change in fortunes exacerbated by colonization and then decolonization, left these fiercely independent peoples politically and economically weakened. When the French gave up their colonial possessions in West Africa the nomadic pastoralists became minorities split up among six independent nation states, and like many minorities they became scapegoats for post-independence problems. 'Saharan governments resent our lack of nationalistic sentiment,' declared a Tuareg, as 'we do not consider ourselves Algerians, or Malians or Mauritanian, but first and foremost Tuaregs owing more allegiance to a fellow tribesman on the other side of the border than to any national government.'[26] Of course, such sentiments, though applying to close kin, may not necessarily extend to the Tuareg people as a whole.

Today nomadic herders have increasing difficulties in crossing borders because of the growing customs restrictions and sometimes deliberate bureaucratic obstructions. If territorial disputes occur, nomads of the same tribe may be denied movement even to visit their family on the other side of the frontier. Gross violations have taken place where pastoral peoples have been viewed by the authorities with distrust. In April 1983 a group of nomadic Bororo herdsmen of the Central African Republic migrated with their cattle to neighbouring Zaire to escape oppressive administrative controls. They were admitted into Zaire but, after protests by the Central African Republic, were expelled and their animals confiscated. On their return many of the Bororo were imprisoned, and others who attempted to retrieve their cattle killed as they crossed the frontier into Zaire. In early 1984, about 4,000 Somali herders were rounded up in northern Kenya, tortured and beaten, many of them to death. As many as 1,400 people may have been murdered in this way. The causes of the massacre are still unclear. The Kenyan authorities claimed that local inter-tribal rivalries were responsible for the violence, while Somali herders maintained they were victims because they were considered sympathetic to the secessionist movement in the district.[27]

There are also economic roots to the general discrimination against pastoralists by African governments. In Somalia, for example, where herders constitute the majority of the country's population, and where livestock is the major export, 150 or so large and medium-scale merchants control virtually the entire industry. In the last decades the independence and living standard of the individual pastoralist producers have been seriously eroded.[28] In Mali, outsiders have managed to get an even tighter hold of the traditional pastoralist economy. In some parts of the country up to 50 per cent of the cattle are owned by non-nomads, such as merchants and civil servants, and nomads are employed as herders and receive only the animals' milk in payment.[29] In African countries where there are pastoralist minorities, ownership of livestock is increasingly falling into the hands of a new class of non-pastoralists, and cattle are merely entrusted to the care of pastoralists. Furthermore, the range lands themselves are passing out of the hands of their traditional users and being nationalized or privatized.[30] As with tribal peoples in other countries of the world, customary title to land is not recognized.

Pastoralists have also suffered as a result of government-sponsored conservation and tourism. Large areas of Masailand in southern Kenya have been turned into national wildlife parks. Masai are excluded from these national parks – formerly their homelands – which are maintained ostensibly for the worthy preservation of fauna, flora and threatened animal species, but more pragmatically to attract rich tourists vital to the Kenyan economy.[31]

Without an adequate and secure land base pastoralists cannot expect to survive and thrive, and without pastoralist skills and practices applied to these dry, marginal lands, there is likely to be further ecological deterioration. However, for the most past, the urban-based élites who now dominate African countries have a vested interest in pursuing their present policies, particularly with the massive food aid now pouring into the continent. Until pastoralists organize themselves more effectively to defend their way of life, or unless the crisis of food shortages, desertification and impoverishment in Africa becomes too acute, there is unlikely to be significant change.

The San of Southern Africa

The nomadic pastoralists are not the only group in Africa finding their land base reduced and their traditional skills unwanted. The San or Bushmen are the original inhabitants of the present republic of South Africa and much of southern Africa.[32] Some 2,000 years ago they came into contact with Bantu-speaking peoples from the north and in the middle of the 17th Century European settlers arrived and began to seize their lands from the south. As their traditional territories were taken and the game herds depleted, the San often turned to cattle-raiding. The white colonists responded by organizing raids on the San communities, killing many and forcing the rest into the less hospitable desert and semi-desert regions. Others moved north to the Bantu area and became settled agriculturalists. Today there are an estimated 62,000 San living in the Kalahari desert of Botswana, Namibia and Angola, but none survive in South Africa itself.[33]

The San speak a distinctive language with predominant click sounds and share a way of life which is geared to survival in one of the world's harshest environments. As with many indigenous peoples their self-sufficient hunter-gatherer economy and independent social organization are seen as antithetical to the interests of the modern state. In recent years, therefore, there have been strong pressures on the San to intermarry with Bantu-speaking peoples and become settled farmers.

The traditional San economy is based on the hunting of animals and the collecting of fruits, vegetables, roots and nuts. San live in small bands, occupy a territory which can cover as much as 4,000 square kilometres, recognized by other groups, and hold no notions of private property either in regard to land or belongings. The San acquire other goods by exchanging animal skins or by working as herdsmen for neighbouring Bantu.[34] But although San communities have successfully adapted to their environment and are capable of survival, they are under increasing pressures as vital land and water resources fall into the hands of individual cattle-ranchers.

Already the numbers of entirely unassimilated San may be measured in hundreds rather than thousands. Probably between 2,000 and 5,000 still live by hunting and gathering.[35] In Botswana, San foragers live in only four areas and in the largest of these, the Central Kalahari Game Reserve, the resident population has declined from 6,000 in 1960 to 1,000 in 1984. The Central Kalahari Game Reserve was established to conserve an environment with sufficient land and game reserves to allow the San way of life to persist.[36] However, the San are increasingly facing competition from farmers living on the periphery of the reserve. Cattle eat the precious wild foods, such as the drought-resistant tsama melons, which are a source of water and nourishment to the San during periods of no rainfall.

171

As settled agriculturalists and livestock-owners take over the land and water resources and join in the hunt for game, the San have often had no alternative but to find work as day labourers, drift to the small towns without work or join the government settlement schemes. The disintegration of their traditional way of life has brought social problems and many have turned to 'begging, piecework and stocktheft for survival' and are left demoralized and apathetic.[37] In one town in Namibia where the population has grown from 25 to more than 900 in the last few years, 'alcoholism, violent crime and prostitution prevailed among the Bushmen who had migrated there'.[38]

In Botswana official policies, such as the Tribal Grazing Land Policy and the Remote Area Development Programme, are implemented within a wider context of competing interests. Botswana at independence in 1966 was one of the world's poorest countries and had relatively few agricultural resources. The government has invested heavily in rural development, especially since the mid-1970s, and encouraged cattle ownership and beef production for export. The majority of Tswana people have responded to these government initiatives by increasing their herds, fencing large areas of land for ranches and taking over scarce water resources. Inevitably the nomadic life of the San and the mobility of the wildlife population have been affected. The San are often left little choice but to become herders of Tswana-owned cattle.

On the other hand the Government of Botswana has introduced the Bushmen Development Programme 'to foster the self-reliance and development of Bushmen citizens, and enable thereby their greater adaptation to the socio-economic changes taking place in Botswana'.[39] Indeed, Botswana is one of the few governments in the world which has tried to give hunting and gathering minorities some say in the decision-making process.

But whether the San are able to survive as a people with a distinct language and culture is open to question. A former co-ordinator of the Bushmen Development Programme, Liz Wily, has observed that

> access to land was an underlying intention of the Bushmen Development Programme. This required the politicization of the San and their involvement in determining their own future, under the umbrella of the more acceptable concept of promoting self-reliance.[40]

But there is a reluctance by the government to recognize traditional headmen, and equally, difficulties for the egalitarian San to accept the idea that a spokesperson or committee can make decisions on their behalf.

In Namibia, however, the San must face other more serious threats to their future. Since 1974 San have been recruited by the occupying South African army and there are now two Bushmen battalions consisting of about 850 men.[41] The South African Government has successfully exploited the traditional suspicion of the San towards the majority pastoral Ovambo population, and persuaded skilled San trackers to help hunt down SWAPO guerrillas.[42] In southern Angola, where the South African Army has regularly made incursions, local San and other hunter-gatherer peoples have been caught in the crossfire.[43] According to one assessment there are probably less than 300 San continuing to live a more or less traditional, self-sufficient lifestyle in Namibia and even these are due to be removed from their territory as the Department of Nature Conservation extends the nature reserve.[44]

Pygmies

Pygmy populations exist in many areas throughout Western and Central Africa.[45] They inhabit the rainforests and possess a unique subsistence culture based on hunting and gathering. Today, there are probably some 200,000 Pygmies but increasingly they are mixing with the dominant Bantu societies surrounding them. Their future, like many peoples indigenous to the rainforest, is linked closely to the speed with which the trees are felled to make way for roads, settlements and plantations.

Pygmies are people of the forest. 'The forest is the father and the mother to us and like a father or mother it gives us everything we need – food, clothing, shelter, warmth and affection', writes Colin Turnbull recording the words of one Mbuti Pygmy.[46] Pygmies are the original inhabitants of the forest but not its only ones. Bantu and Sudanic-speaking slash-and-burn agriculturalists have lived in the Ituri forest of Zaire, for example, for at least 2,000 years.[47] But for them the forest is a place of evil and danger and a force to battle against. However, the great gulf that exists between the Bantu villagers and the nomadic Pygmy communities has led to the development of a relationship of mutual convenience. In the Ituri forest, where one of the largest and least assimilated groups of Pygmies live, there are about 40,000 Mbuti. These hunt in bands of between ten and 70 people.[48] Traditionally, each band develops a close relationship with a particular village and receives cultivated foods in exchange for forest produce such as game or honey. Villagers will also help their Pygmy band in dealing with authority. Sometimes Mbuti women will work in the villagers' gardens to acquire foods not available in the forest.[49]

In its traditional form this relationship of reciprocity is mutually beneficial. But it should be noted that villagers consider Pygmies as inferior and try to achieve their subjugation by putting Pygmy boys through initiation rites and thereby binding them to the village.[50] While Pygmies can return at will to the forest such patron–client relationships are unable to develop a strong hold on the band. But when such an option is not available, Pygmies can find themselves incorporated into a system of cultural subordination and exploitation. In Cameroun, for example, where the tropical forest has been greatly depleted, Pygmies have found work on plantations but receive a monthly salary of one-fifth that paid to even the lowest-paid Camerounian labourer.[51]

Discrimination is found at many levels and particularly in marriage. Bantu men can marry Pygmy women, who are considered obedient and hard-working, but Pygmy men are not allowed to marry Bantus. By such a union Pygmy women will find their role much depreciated. For Bantu villagers, a woman is a labourer in the fields and takes few economic decisions, 'but for Pygmies,' Colin Turnbull writes, 'a woman is more than a mere producer of wealth. She is an essential partner in their economy.'[52] In some cases Bantu farmers have accepted young Pygmy brides in settlement of debts. It is not unusual, in areas where the process of assimilation is well advanced, to find Pygmy communities emptied of marriageable girls, obliging young men to live with older women no longer able to bear children.[53]

The threat to the Pgymy way of life comes more from the growing commercial exploitation of the forest than any direct exploitation of indigenous labour. In Central Africa, deforestation has affected many indigenous Pygmy communities, reduced food resources available through hunting and gathering, and forced many to become cheap labour on Bantu farms and plantations. Even in the Ituri forest in Zaire, which covers an area of 70,000 square kilometres, deforestation is becoming more widespread with the expansion of coffee plantations. The clearing of land for coffee production has effects which extend well beyond the plantation itself. Migrant workers flock to the area, attracted by the prospect of employment, and clear their own parcels of land to grow subsistence foods and a small coffee crop. According to one calculation 'for each 100 hectares of forest cleared for a plantation, approximately 700 hectares are cleared for subsistence gardens and small coffee holdings.'[54]

Although offering some short-term advantages to the Pygmy communities, by enlarging the demand by the new settlers for forest produce, there are inevitable long-term consequences. Already many areas of the Ituri forest are depleted of game, and Mbuti Pygmies have been forced either to retreat to less populated parts of the forest or become agriculturalists or plantation-workers.[55]

Yet despite the depletion of unassimilated Pygmies throughout Central and Western Africa and the disadvantages of life in the dominant society, there has been no organized protest or resistance. Nor has there been any evidence of conflict between the forest-dwellers and the new settlers, as has been the case in rainforests in other regions of the world – perhaps because so long as the forest exists, the Pygmies will always have somewhere to retreat to.

Notes

1. This chapter does not discuss the situations in South African and Namibia, which are extensively examined in many other publications.

2. Jeremy Swift, 'The future of African Hunter-Gatherer and Pastoral Peoples', *Development and Change*, vol.13, no.2, April 1982, p.161.

3. Cf. Walter Rodney, *How Europe underdeveloped Africa* (Bogle-L'Ouverture Publications, London, 1983) chapter 4.

4. Cf. Barbara Dinham and Colin Hines, *Agribusiness in Africa* (Earth Resources Research, London, 1983).

5. James Mayall, 'Self-determination and the OAU', in I.M. Lewis (ed.), *Nationalism and self-determination in the horn of Africa* (Ithaca Press, London, 1983) p.77.

6. I.M. Lewis, 'Introduction', in Lewis, p.13.

7. Cf. Eric Rouleau, 'Guerre et intoxication au Tchad', *Le Monde Diplomatique*,

September 1983 and Gérald Galtier, 'Comment reconstruire l'état tchadien', *Le Monde Diplomatique*, November 1984.

8. John Gretton, *Western Sahara: the fight for self-determination* (Anti-Slavery Society, London, 1976); Tony Hodges, *The Western Sahara*, Minority Rights Group Report no.40, London, 1984. Fifty-eight countries now recognize the SADR, of which 29 are African.

9. Paul Baxter, 'The problem of the Oromo', Lewis, pp.129-49.

10. Michael Reisman, 'Somali self-determination in the Horn', Lewis, pp.151-73.

11. David Pool, *Eritrea: Africa's longest war* (Anti-Slavery Society, London, 1982); Mary Dines, 'Eritrea's War for Liberation', *Cultural Survival Quarterly*, vol.8, no.4, December 1984, pp.54-7.

12. In addition to these movements there is also an Afar Liberation Front active in Wollo Province.

13. Survival International, 'Ethiopia: the resettlement programme, an evaluation', n.d.; see also Jason Clay and Bonnie Holcomb, 'Politics and the Ethiopian famine 1984-1985', Cultural Survival Occasional Paper 20, December 1985.

14. Patrick Marnham, *Nomads of the Sahel*, Minority Rights Group Report no.33, London, 1979, p.15 and Neville and Rada Dyson-Hudson, 'The structure of East African Herds and the future of East African Herders', *Development and Change*, vol.13, no.2, April 1982, p.213.

15. Fouad Ibrahim cited in Chris McIvor, 'Nomads of the Sahara – a Vanishing Tribe', *Development and cooperation*, no.3, June 1985, p.26.

16. Alan Grainger, *Desertification* (Earthscan, London, 1984) p.69.

17. *The Economist Development Report*, April 1984, p.8.

18. 'Lessons to be learned: drought and famine in Ethiopia', Oxfam Public Affairs Unit, July 1984, p.5. In the 1970s a similar large-scale development project along the Baro River in Ethiopia led to the eviction of several Anuak communities. Protest and resistance were met by force and several hundred people were killed. Cf. *Survival International News*, no.8, 1985.

19. Grainger, p.8.

20. Fouad Ibrahim, 'The fight against the desert', *Development and Cooperation* (Bonn), no.6, November/December 1983, p.9..

21. Grainger, p.10.

22. Ibid., p.33.

23. Harold Dregne cited in Anders Wijkman and Lloyd Timberlake, 'Is the African drought an act of God or of man?', *The Ecologist*, vol.15, no.1/2, 1985, p.12.

24. Grainger, pp.48-9.

25. *Le Monde*, 6 February 1974, cited in Marnham, p.9. See also Jonathan Derrick, 'The great West African drought', *African Affairs*, October 1977.

26. Cited in McIvor, p.27.

27. Cf. Statement by the Anti-Slavery Society to the United Nations Sub-Committee on Prevention of Discrimination and Protection of Minorities, 6-31 August 1984; see also *IWGIA Newsletters*, nos.37 and 38, May and July 1984.

28. Cf. Dan R. Aronson, 'Pastoralists: losing ground in Somalia', *ARC Newsletter* (Boston, USA) vol.6, no.1, March 1982.

29. *The Economist Development Report*, April 1984, p.8.

30. Swift, pp.171-2.

31. Colin Deihl, 'Wildlife and the Maasai', *Cultural Survival Quarterly*, vol.9, no.1, February 1985, pp.37-40; see also *IWGIA Newsletter* nos. 35 and 36,

October and December 1983, pp.182-4 and Kaj Arnhem, *The Maasai and the State: the impact of rural development policies on a pastoral people in Tanzania*, IWGIA document, no.52, 1985.

32. David Stephen, *The San of the Kalahari*, Minority Rights Group Report no.56, 1982.

33. Botswana: 25,000, Namibia: 29,000, Angola: 8,000.

34. For a description of the traditional life of the San, see Elizabeth Marshall Thomas, *The Harmless People* (Secker & Warburg, London, 1959).

35. *International Herald Tribune*, 19-20 February 1983 cited in *IWGIA Newsletter*, no.33, March 1983, pp.116-18.

36. Robert K. Hitchcock, 'Foragers on the move', *Cultural Survival Quarterly*, vol.9, no.1, February 1985, p.32.

37. Liz Wily, 'A strategy of self-determination for the Kalahari San', *Development and Change*, vol.13, no.2, April 1982, p.292.

38. *International Herald Tribune*.

39. Wily, p.306.

40. Wily, pp.305-6; on the prospects for the San see also Carmel Schire and Robert Gordon (eds.), 'The future of former foragers', Cultural Survival Occasional Paper 18, October 1985.

41. David Stephen, p.14.

42. Simao Souindola, 'Angola: genocide of the Bosquimanos', *IWGIA Newsletter*, no.31-2, June-October 1982, pp.66-8.

43. Souindola and correspondence with the author.

44. *Survival International News*, no.8, 1985.

45. Eg. Zaire, Rwanda, Cameroun, Central African Republic.

46. Colin Turnbull, *The Forest People* (Book Club Associates, London, 1974) p.87.

47. Robert Bailey, 'Development in the Ituri forest of Zaire', *Cultural Survival Quarterly*, vol.6, no.2, Spring 1982, p.23.

48. Ibid., p.23.

49. Nadine Peacock, 'The Mbuti of Northeast Zaire: women and subsistence exchange', *Cultural Survival Quarterly*, vol.8, no.2, Summer 1984, p.15.

50. Cf. Turnbull's description of Nkumbi rites, in *The Forest People*, p.196.

51. Agence France Presse, *Bulletin d'Afrique*, 18 May 1983.

52. Turnbull, p.186.

53. AFP, *Bulletin d'Afrique*.

54. Robert Bailey, p.23.

55. Ibid., p.25.

10. Indigenous Peoples in Rich Countries

Colonialism in North America, Australia and New Zealand followed a different pattern to the system imposed on other regions of the world. The original inhabitants were less numerous than their counterparts elsewhere, they occupied large, seemingly unexploited, territories and in the first years were not hostile to the European settlers. Settlement developed rapidly, the indigenous population declined correspondingly and those remaining were pushed on to less and less fertile land. Often they were forcibly removed on to reserves or mission stations where until comparatively recently they experienced a slow diminution of numbers and lowering of morale. In the early part of this century the indigenous peoples of the rich countries were judged by the dominant society to be facing eventual assimilation and disappearance.

Today, however, such an observation appears wildly inaccurate. The indigenous peoples of the rich countries have experienced demographic growth and a renewal of cultural pride, and have formed effective political organizations. In many respects they are the most dynamic sector of the international movement of indigenous peoples even though they number only some two per cent of their total.

What has brought about such a reversal? Certainly the improved health and welfare condition of indigenous peoples has made an important contribution, notwithstanding their continuing deprivation when compared to the rest of society. The civil rights movement among Blacks provided an example of how oppressed peoples in the United States of America could improve their situation. Indigenous peoples in rich countries had much greater freedom to organize than those living in poor countries. Native American peoples and Aborigines have made use of the courts, the press and the availability of financial support within the country, not only from church and other institutions, but also from their respective governments. It has been easier for them to publicize their case and attract the support of the Marlon Brandos and Robert Redfords, as well as the solidarity of some sectors of Western progressive opinion, such as the church, trade unions and students. The non-materialist and caring ecological beliefs practised by indigenous peoples also found sympathy among a disillusioned younger generation in those most materialist and environmentally destructive cultures.

Probably the single most significant event for indigenous peoples in the rich countries in the last two decades has been the acceleration of mining and other resource exploitation on the residual and apparently valueless areas of the country left in their hands. The 1960s saw an expansion of Western industry and a consumer boom and this in turn sent the great multinational corporations on a world-wide hunt for cheap minerals. They first turned to the forests, mountains and deserts of their own countries.[1] Vast untapped oil, coal, uranium, natural gas and hydro-electric resources existed on the lands of indigenous peoples. Soon dams were being built on Cherokee and Cree homelands in North America, oil was being extracted from Aboriginal land in Australia and Inuit (Eskimo) territories in Alaska, open-cast mining for coal was taking place on Dine and Crow reserves and uranium was being produced from Lakota, Dene, non-status Indian and Meti lands in the United States and Canada.[2] In 1981 the World Council of Indigenous Peoples identified transnationals 'as the most immediate and serious threat to the survival of the Indigenous Nations of the Fourth World'.[3]

Table 10.1
Indigenous Peoples in Rich Countries

Country	Numbers	% of population
Australia	250,000	2
Canada	Status 326,000 Non-status 250,000–800,000 Inuit 25,000	4
New Zealand	300,000 Maoris	10
Pacific Colonies	500,000	
USA	1.5 million	0.5
Japan	Ainu 50,000	
Inuit Peoples	Alaska 30,000 Canada 25,000 Greenland 42,000 USSR 1,500	
Sami Peoples	Finland 4,000 Norway 35,000 Sweden 17,000 USSR 2,000	
Total:	*3.4 million*	

This chapter looks at the effects of this renewed invasion of indigenous people's land in rich countries, shows how it has threatened once again the survival of certain groups and how it has also precipitated a resurgent resistance. The citizens of Australia, New Zealand, the United States and

Canada enjoy standards of living among the highest in the world, yet the original inhabitants are often as poor as the most deprived of Third World countries. Numerous indigenous islanders in the Pacific continue to live in colonial situations and exercise virtually no control over their future. The movement of these peoples for self-determination in the leading capitalist nations is today exerting an influence out of all proportion to their numbers.

Ainu in Japan

One of the smallest indigenous populations in any capitalist country is that of the Ainu. The Ainu are the original inhabitants of the northern island of Hokkaido in Japan and they were conquered and brought under military control as early as the 9th Century although the region was not formally annexed until 1869. Nevertheless, the Ainu retained many of their distinctive features, and for their part, the Japanese behaved with discrimination towards them. Today the Ainu are referred to in government documents as 'former aborigines' and are considered outsiders by the mainstream of Japanese society.

There are about 50,000 Ainu but few are now full-blooded, having intermarried with Japanese families over many generations. Their economic and social position is notably lower than that of most Japanese. Since the 1970s, however, a growing sense of cultural pride and sense of history has been generated, particularly by the young, better-educated Ainu. This resurgence expressed itself politically in 1977 when an Ainu stood for election and gained 55,000 votes, although not sufficient to win a seat. Some tribal lands have been restored to the Ainu, but not adequate to form an economic base for their long-term survival. More often than not, where reserves have been created the Ainu have become objects of curiosity for camera-clicking Japanese tourists.

Since 1984 an Ainu organization, Hokkaido Utari, has been demanding local representation, the teaching of the Ainu language in schools and universities, and some small concessions on land rights. Of all the indigenous peoples of rich countries, however, the Ainu are perhaps the least organized and the least likely to survive as a culturally distinct community.[4]

Sami of Scandinavia

By contrast the Scandinavian Sami have experienced a renaissance of their culture and reinvigoration of their political influence. Their total population is estimated at 58,000 with the majority living in northern Sweden and Norway and only about ten per cent inhabiting the Arctic regions of Finland and the Soviet Union.[5] The territory they occupy is covered with forests which give way, in the extreme north, to tundra. The climate is predominantly cold with temperatures falling to $-50°C$, although there may be short warm summers. The Sami have developed a unique way of life after many centuries of adaptation to this harsh environment. Traditionally they are hunters and fishermen and this nomadic existence was combined with small-scale agriculture. Land was always collectively owned and its distribution and use, as indeed other aspects of life, were determined by the *sii'da* or community.

The process of colonization, the intervention of missionaries and the exploitation of the region's natural resources have wrought significant changes on the Sami. Most Sami are now employed in industry or administration and fewer than 20 per cent earn their living from reindeer-farming which, in earlier times, was the main source of livelihood. The area available for reindeer has progressively diminished since the turn of the century and the costs involved in herding have increased. The Sami have, therefore, been forced to look for a future in the wider society where they are severely disadvantaged. On the whole Sami are more likely to be unemployed than other Scandinavian peoples and they are more likely to be employed as unskilled or semi-skilled labourers. Their standard of living is comparatively lower than that of non-Samis.

There are also immediate threats to what remains of the Sami homeland. Major hydro-electric projects in Norway in particular but also in Sweden and Finland have interfered with reindeer migrations, flooded farmland and disturbed river fishing. Since the 1950s more than 100 of the northern rivers have been dammed at a cost to Sami land. When the Norwegian Government moved forward with its plan to dam the Alta River in 1982, however, it faced widespread demonstrations from Sami and non-Sami supporters. Protesters chained themselves together and lay in the paths of the bulldozers in sub-zero temperatures and more than one-quarter of Norway's police force was transported to the north to overwhelm them. Norwegians were shocked at such a confrontation in a country where justifiable pride is taken in its progressive civil rights position.[6]

Although the events at Alta focused international attention on the comparatively unknown situation of the Sami, their struggle for self-determination was not new. The Nordic Sami Council had been formed in 1956 with representatives from Norway, Sweden and Finland. Within each of these countries independent organizations, like the Sami Union and the Sami Youth Movement, have developed. Since the late 1970s the Sami have also been active at international meetings: in 1976 joining the World Council of Indigenous Peoples and in 1978 participating at the United Nations. At a meeting of the UN's Working Group on Indigenous Populations in August 1983, Lars-Ande Baer, a representative of the Nordic Sami Council, stated:

> We, the Sami, are the indigenous people of Sámi-Aednan (Samiland). Yet the Samis are a people in four countries, the people and the land has been divided up over the course of history by the states of Norway, Sweden, Finland and the Soviet Union. Despite this fact, we Sami consider ourselves as one people and as a cultural, linguistic, economic and political unit.

He went on to demand:

> (1) that Sami people receive legal protection as an indigenous people in each Nordic country;
> (2) that we receive legal protection for our traditional land and natural resources

in each Nordic country;

(3) that the traditional livelihoods of Sami people be protected and laws be accordingly amended in each Nordic country;

(4) that the Sami language be recognized by law as an official language;

(5) that the Sami language and culture be preserved and developed as a living language and living culture;

(6) that Sami society and representative bodies be officially recognized;

(7) that according to our common traditions we are able to maintain and support efforts on behalf of world peace.[7]

The governments of Norway and Sweden, to their credit, have responded more openly than most Western governments to the demands of their indigenous populations. They have also promoted, as have Australia and Canada, the issue of indigenous peoples' rights at the United Nations and other international fora.

Inuit of the Arctic

The determined efforts being made by the Sami to defend their culture and homelands are echoed by another northern people, the Inuit (Eskimos). There are about 100,000 Inuit peoples in four countries: 30,000 in Alaska, 25,000 in the North Western and Yukon Territories of Canada, 42,000 in Greenland and 1,500 in the USSR.[8] Like the Sami they inhabit the tundra region and traditionally live from fishing, hunting and small-scale farming in small, scattered communities. The Inuit of all countries share a way of life and culture and have comparable colonial histories. Recognition of their common condition was expressed by the first Inuit Circumpolar Conference in 1977 and a second meeting in 1980 at which land rights and the preservation of Inuit culture were identified as paramount aims.

In certain respects, however, the situations of different Inuit communities varies. Greenland has been self-governing since 1979 and Inuit make up 85 per cent of the population of the island. While criticisms may justifiably be made of Danish exploitation in the 19th and early 20th Centuries, in recent years the government has supported the Greenland economy substantially.[9] The small numbers of Inuit in Siberia in the USSR have successfully retained their traditional identity and language, although they are under increasing pressures to assimilate.[10]

The North American Inuit communities are facing major changes as a consequence of the colonial policies of the United States and Canada. The native Alaskans, which include Aleut Islanders and Alaskan Indians as well as the larger Inuit group, make up less than one-eighth of the total population; in the North-West Territory and the Yukon of Canada, Inuit and other Indian peoples, such as the Dene and Metis, are in a minority.

In the 19th Century northern Canada attracted speculators of the Hudson Bay Company looking for furs and in the 1880s and 1890s discoveries of gold, silver and copper brought more prospectors; in the 1920s oil and gas were discovered in the Mackenzie Valley in North-West Territory and in 1968 in

Alaska. The waves of settlers, workers and entrepreneurs accompanying these discoveries have wrought massive changes on the Inuit. From a relatively self-sufficient, semi-nomadic existence they have had to adapt to a modern capitalist economy.

Since the 1960s the Inuit have developed a growing consciousness of their identity and their rights. Most Inuit recognize that a return to the old way of life is now no longer realizable, so they are demanding a greater share and control of the wealth produced from their lands. In 1969 COPE, the Committee for Original People's Entitlement, was formed to try to achieve these objectives. In 1977 a national organization of Inuit, the Inuit Tapirisat of Canada, was established. Both organizations proceeded to enter into negotiations with the government.

In Alaska, the Federation of Alaskan Natives had succeeded in negotiating a land settlement act in 1971 which made over 40 million acres, about 11 per cent of the land surface of the state, to native title and provided for nearly US$ 500 million of compensation. In 1984 COPE managed to reach an agreement with the Canadian Government which gave the Inuvialuit Inuit groups living in the Western Arctic region title to 91,000 square kilometres of land and compensation totalling over 50 million Canadian dollars. The Inuit communities would have no rights to any gas, oil and minerals on about 85 per cent of that land. The agreement effectively extinguishes any claims on other areas outside the settlement region occupied by Invialuit Inuit.[11]

Negotiations are also now progressing on another scheme which could split the North-West Territory and create in the north-eastern area of Canada an Inuit state which would be called Nunavut (our land). A campaign initiated by the Inuit Tapirisat of Canada led to a plebiscite within the North-West Territory in which the majority voted for a division. In 1982 the Minister for Indian and Northern Affairs, John Munro, agreed in principle to the idea. At the same time the Nunavut Constitutional Forum was created, bringing together elected members of the North-West Territory Legislative Assembly and elected Inuit leaders with the aim of preparing a Nunavut constitutional act. Unlike many other land settlements which have given indigenous peoples a territory and denied them real political power, the Nunavut Constitutional Forum will create a state within federal Canada where Inuit are a majority. The Chairman of the Forum, Dennis Pattersen, has stated 'what we need is a political framework in which economic development can take place with the full involvement of our people.'[12]

The following sections look at how indigenous peoples of other rich countries are trying to achieve political as well as economic control over their own futures.

The Aboriginal people of Australia

The Aboriginal people number about 250,000, a little over one per cent of the total population of Australia.[13] The majority live in rural communities in the northern and central areas of the country. Queensland has the largest Aboriginal population and in Northern Territory Aborigines make up about one-quarter of the total population of the state.[14] Some Aborigines continue to live on the reserves established in the latter part of the 19th Century and often organized by missionaries; others, probably as many as one-third of all Aborigines, live in camps on the outskirts of small towns as fringe-dwellers; and about ten per cent of Aboriginal people now live in the cities of Australia. Aborigines living in rural areas remain a vital part of the labour force on many cattle stations.

The majority of Aboriginal people have been forced to adapt themselves to the dominant European culture, although some have managed to retain their own culture, to continue to speak their own languages and to pursue a nomadic or semi-nomadic lifestyle despite the artificiality of the reserves. In recent years there has been a movement of Aboriginal people to re-establish their own communities independently. The outstation movement has taken place mainly in northern and central Australia and there are now over 150 homeland centres for about 4,000 people.

Employment opportunities for Aborigines in the mainstream economy are limited. The unemployment rate among Aboriginals is six times higher than that for Australia as a whole. In rural areas Aborigines without work may exceed 80 per cent.[15] In other respects living conditions of Aborigines are well below those for the rest of society. Ninety per cent of Aborigines are believed to live below the poverty line.[16] On cattle stations Aboriginal stockmen are often paid far less than their white colleagues and are more likely to be laid off.[17] Those who are unemployed rarely receive the full benefits and welfare payments to which they are entitled and on one settlement at Yuendemu near Alice Springs only 12 people out of a population of 400 mostly unemployed Aboriginals were receiving unemployment benefit.[18]

The health of Aborigines is often below average and in certain cases compares badly even with poorer developing countries. The lifespan of Aborigines, for example, is about 20 years shorter than that of white Australians. Poverty, malnutrition and the poor medical facilities available in many Aboriginal communities affect children in particular. About 25 per cent of Aboriginal children were estimated to be chronically malnourished in Sydney in 1977, and according to one source 'an Aboriginal baby is four to five times more likely to die than the child of a white Australian.'[19]

The Director of the National Trachoma and Eye Health Programme, Professor F.C. Hollows, has reported that Aborigines are eight times more likely to become blind than white Australians.[20] A report published in 1983 in the *Medical Journal of Australia* revealed that 'the death rate from infectious diseases among Aborigines in large reserves in Queensland is nine times higher than the state average.'[21]

Discrimination against Aborigines is also widespread. The Victoria Aboriginal Legal Service has reported that Aborigines in Victoria were 45 times more likely to go to prison than whites, and on Groote Eylandt, an island in the Gulf of Carpentaria where the majority population is Aboriginal, the

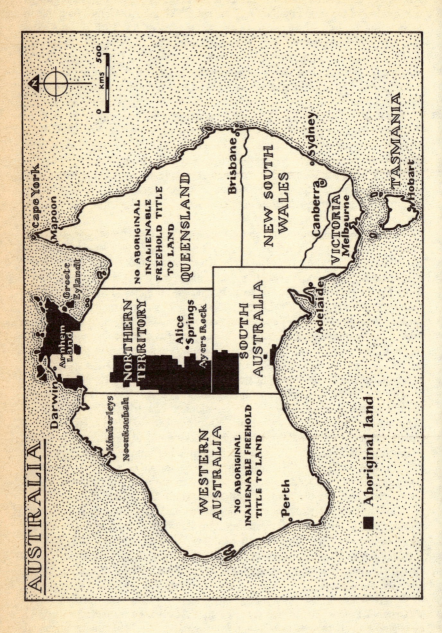

imprisonment rate is 25 times the national average.[22] Racist comments have come from the Premier of Queensland, Bjelke-Petersen, and from a leading mining tycoon, Lang Hancock, who in 1981 favoured putting all Aboriginals together in a remote area of north-west Australia, then 'dope the water so that they would become sterile and breed themselves out'.[23]

Racial discrimination, poverty and deprivation were the background to the Aboriginal resistance that began in the 1960s. At about this time the invasion of mining companies on to the last reserves of land occupied by Aborigines was the spur to action. They began to recognize that their survival would depend upon their capacity to organize for self-determination and land rights.

However, one of the first actions of the new Aboriginal movement took place not on mining land but on a cattle station. In 1966 a strike by 200 stockmen of the Gurindji tribe at Wave Hill Station in Northern Territory owned by the British Vestey family developed into a wider demand for land rights in the form of capital to set up their own cattle ranch. As the strike developed, white trade unionists and progressive sectors of Australian society were made aware of the low wages and poor living conditions on the station; they also learned that the Vesteys held over 20,000 square miles of Australia and were renting a one-million-acre ranch for only $A18 a year.[24] The land rights issue was put firmly on the agenda of the political parties and particularly that of the Australian Labour Party.

Earlier, in 1955, a discovery of massive bauxite deposits in northern Queensland began a series of claims by Australian and foreign companies for mining on Aboriginal land. In 1957 Comalco, a subsidiary of the United States Kaiser Corporation and the British-based Rio Tinto Zinc, was awarded over 5,000 square kilometres of Aboriginal reserve land. The deal struck by Comalco was highly advantageous: the royalty rate was one of the lowest in the world for bauxite extraction; the rent was £2 per square mile whereas elsewhere the average was £320; and the state government agreed to provide aid to build a harbour and townships. There were no legal provisions of any kind for the Aboriginal owners.[25]

In the late 1960s the federal government began to concern itself with the welfare of Aborigines. In 1967 a national referendum seeking amendments to the constitution and allowing the Commonwealth Government to legislate with respect to Aboriginal people was supported by over 90 per cent of the electorate.

In 1972 the Australian Labour Party under Gough Whitlam came to power with a progressive programme for Aborigines. A Department of Aboriginal Affairs was created and provided with substantial funding and a Royal Commission was established under Justice Woodward to make recommendations about future national land rights legislation.

Aboriginal organizations had themselves already become more active prior to Whitlam's victory. The Federal Council for the Advancement of Aboriginals and Torres Strait Islanders founded in 1959 had launched a land rights campaign following the 1967 referendum. Then in 1971 Aborigines played a major role in the opposition to the tour by the Springboks South African rugby team. One year later, in 1972, Aborigines attracted further national as well as international attention for their colonial situation, when they set up an embassy in the grounds of Parliament House in Canberra and won a commitment from Gough Whitlam, then opposition leader, to recognize Aboriginal land rights if he came to office.

The Aboriginal movement was already receiving support from sections of the church, trade unions and other progressive opinion by the 1970s. The Whitlam government responded by rejecting the protectionist and assimilationist policies of the 1950s and 1960s. The report released in 1974 by the Woodward Commission symbolized the new policy of the federal government. It recommended that Aboriginal people should be given freehold title to their reserves, and that other claims to Crown land should be considered where Aborigines could prove traditional ownership or need. On the important matter of mineral rights the report proposed royalty payments and a limited exercise of veto over mining but not full control as demanded by the Aboriginal movement.

On the key issue of land rights the Whitlam government was a disappointment to Aboriginal organizations. Land rights had been promised for the entire country, but only a bill for the Northern Territory was drafted and this became law in the new government of Malcolm Fraser only after modifications. Most importantly, the immediate interests of the mining companies operating on Aboriginal land in the territory were protected.

Yet in many aspects, the short-lived labour government represents, both in comparison to the previous and the subsequent governments, a period of relative advancement for Aboriginal people. Some principles of land rights legislation had been recommended and some limited first steps taken to procure those rights; funding had been significantly increased for Aboriginal welfare and health and support was forthcoming to their own organizations.

The National Aboriginal Consultative Committee, later renamed the National Aboriginal Conference, was established and funded by the federal government to serve as an advisory body. In Northern Territory the first land councils representing Aboriginal communities were formed to assist with land claims and negotiations with mining companies. Land councils spread to many Aboriginal communities and in 1981 a national federation was formed.

On the funding side the Whitlam government created a Department of Aboriginal Affairs both to advise on social and economic development and to administer grants and loans to Aboriginal communities and individuals. With the fall of the Whitlam government, the budget of the Department was reduced and in 1980 an additional body, the Aboriginal Development Commission with all-Aboriginal control, took over some of its leading functions.

Government actions apart, however, by the 1970s, the Aboriginal movement had acquired a momentum of its own. Health and legal services organized by Aborigines had been established. The two main national Aboriginal organizations – the National Aboriginal Conference and the Federation of Land Councils – increasingly made use of the international arena. Both groups have been active in the World Council of Indigenous Peoples since its inception, at sessions of the United Nations Human Right Commission and especially since 1982 at the UN's Working Group on Indigenous Populations. The land councils of Queensland even set up an Aboriginal Embassy for Europe, temporarily in Britain, to promote Aboriginal affairs and lobby mining companies, such as Rio Tinto Zinc, which have their headquarters in London.

Table 10.2
Major minerals and petroleum projects on/near Aboriginal land, 1984

State/ Territory	Company (and location)	Product	Value ($000)
Northern Territory	Groote Eylandt Mining Company Pty Ltd (Groote Eylandt)	Manganese	58,198
	Nabalco Pty Ltd (Gove/Nhulunbuy)	Bauxite & Alumina	283,237
	Energy Resources of Australia Ltd (Ranger)	Uranium	427,821
	Queensland Mines Ltd (Nabarlek)	Uranium	—
	Magellan Petroleum Australia Ltd (Palm Valley/Mereenie)	Oil and Natural Gas	6,210
Queensland	Comalco Ltd (Weipa)	Bauxite	144,968
Western Australia	Argyle Diamond Mines Joint Venture (CRA Ltd and Ashton Mining Ltd) (Kimberleys area)	Diamonds	39,789

Sources: Northern Territory Department of Mines and Energy (1985); Australian Bureau of Statistics, *Mineral Production, 1983-84*; Company annual reports, in McGill, S. & G.J. Crough, *Indigenous Resource Rights and Mining Companies in North America and Australia* (Department of Aboriginal Affairs, Canberra, 1986).

Aborigines have also been active in publicizing the effects of atomic bomb tests in Australia by the British in the 1950s and 1960s. According to *The Observer* Aboriginal people were doused with radiation from two tests, some were rounded up and sent to camps where they suffered great misery and social disintegration, and others wandered about on the unfenced range, camping in the craters themselves.[26] At the Nuclear Test Royal Commission in October 1984, it emerged that 200 soldiers were threatened with court martial and even a firing squad if they told outsiders about how one Aboriginal family went on to the site.[27] Nor indeed were the authorities unaware of the presence of Aborigines on the test site, and Australia's chief scientist for the project rejected requests for welfare provisions because it was 'placing the affairs of a handful of natives above those of the British Commonwealth of Nations'.[28] However, according to the *Guardian* on 13 December 1985, the Royal Commission declared that Australia received more fall-out from the French nuclear tests in the Pacific than from the 12 British tests combined. It also noted that Britain had offered to clean up the range but that the Australian Safety Committee had declined.

In recent years resistance has centred on the activities of international mining companies. With the fall of the Whitlam government the federal and state governments put up fewer obstacles to indiscriminate exploration and exploitation. From 1976 Amax secured an oil exploration lease on Aboriginal land in Noonkanbah provoking determined resistance. This culminated in 1980 when state and local police had to escort a convoy of lorries for five days through a series of picket lines. Aboriginal leaders and clergymen opposing the drilling were among those arrested and eventually the oil-workers walked off the site in support of a trade union ban.[29]

For the Aboriginal movement the opposition on Noonkanbah was an important moment. Mining companies were discredited by the action and this in turn has led to growing public support for Aboriginal land rights and a demand for stronger controls of foreign mining companies. Furthermore, the confrontation at Noonkanbah fostered a sense of self-reliance among Aboriginal organizations.

Mining companies have not been slow in modifying their public image. They have a great deal to lose; the already realized and potential profits from mining are huge. Australia possesses some of the world's largest and most accessible deposits of bauxite and uranium. The Roxby Downs uranium mine, for example, will be the biggest in the world when it is finished and is valued at $A 66 billion. When Pitjantjatjara and Kokatha peoples protested to an access road being built over a sacred site, the two mining companies involved – British Petroleum and Western Mining – agreed to the alternative proposed by the Aboriginal communities.[30] But real concessions are hard to prise from the mining companies or the vested political interests represented in the federal and state governments. On the Roxby Downs site there has still been no firm commitment not to desecrate sacred sites, even though this would now be against the spirit of the Heritage Act passed in 1984.

Instead, mining companies have been ready to invest in public relations campaigns to influence Australian opinion. According to *The Financial Times*, for example, a subsidiary of Rio Tinto Zinc, mining for diamonds in the Kimberleys in Western Australia, recently hired one of the country's largest public relations firms 'to hold down the proportion of the wealth generated by the mine that would be returned as payments or royalties to the Aboriginals'.[31] During 1984 the Western Australia Chamber of Mines spent $A 1 million on a media campaign to get the Heritage Act, which guaranteed to protect areas of particular significance to Aborigines, repealed. One author has commented:

> Mining companies will do their best to avoid and even subvert Aboriginal land rights. They will offer community services rather than money because it is cheaper; they will offer compensation or benefits to individuals or small groups rather than the community as a whole or even contest that a site is sacred if it is in an area of valuable mineral reserves.[32]

Land rights legislation within the states has faced intense opposition from pastoral and mining interests. The Northern Territory was the first state to introduce legislation, and amendments to weaken its impact continue to be proposed; in New South Wales a Land Rights Act was passed in March 1983 but little transfer of land has actually taken place in favour of Aborigines; in Victoria and South Australia no specific land rights legislation exists, although in the latter large grants of land have been made to Aborigines.[33] In Queensland, where conditions for Aborigines are probably among the worst in Australia, there is no land rights legislation. In 1982 an amendment to the Land Act was drafted which gave no security of tenure to Aborigines on reserves and according to one view actually increased the ambit of ministerial control.[34] The Act which Aborigines and some Queenslanders regarded as racist was the focus of violent protest during the Commonwealth Games which took place in Brisbane that year.

The victory of the Labour Party under the leadership of Prime Minister Bob Hawke in March 1983 brought with it hopes of national land rights legislation for the Aboriginals. Promises had been made prior to the elections, and soon afterwards ministers were confirming their commitment. The Minister of Finance, John Dawkins, stated in a meeting of the United Nations in August 1983 that the government wished 'to see a consistent national approach to land rights', and 'a set of principles to apply in all states and territories'.[35]

The five principles that emerged were:

1. Aboriginal land to be held under inalienable freehold title;
2. protection of Aboriginal sites;
3. Aboriginal control in relation to mining on Aboriginal land;
4. access to mining royalty equivalents; and
5. compensation for lost land to be negotiated.

These objectives were reiterated in a speech by Clyde Holding, the Minister for Aboriginal Affairs, in December 1983, when he recognized Aboriginal and Torres Strait Islander peoples as prior occupants and original owners of Australia, and further that the year 1988, the bicentennial of the invasion of Australia by Europeans, should be set as the date by which measures to ensure real equality and advancement of Aboriginal people should be achieved.

Consultations with the National Aboriginal Conference, the Federation of Land Councils and the Aboriginal Development Commission took place during 1984. Equally the federal government was engaged in negotiations with state governments concerning land rights legislation. In June 1984 the Australian Parliament enacted the Aboriginal and Torres Strait Islander Heritage Act 'to protect and preserve areas and objects of particular significance to Aboriginals and Islanders'. The Act is an interim measure, effective for two years, until comprehensive legislation is introduced. In November 1984, the government had already announced that the Uluru National Park in which Ayers Rock stands – a most important Aboriginal sacred site – would be returned to its original owners. The park was leased back to the government for 99 years and tourism has not been restricted by the new Aboriginal owners. Nevertheless, members of the white community and the Chief Minister of the Northern Territory protested strongly fearing that Aboriginal ownership would jeopardize a $A 200 million tourist complex being built about 20 kilometres away.[36]

Table 10.3
Aboriginal land tenure and population (Australian states)

	Aboriginal Population June 1981*	As % Total Population (%)	Total Land Area (sq km)	Aboriginal Freehold** (sq km) November 1985	As % Total Land (%)	Leasehold*** (sq km)	As % Total Land (%)	Reserve Mission (sq km)	As % Total Land (%)
N.S.W. (incl. A.C.T.)	36,190	0.68	804,000	180	0.02	142	0.02	–	–
Vic.	6,057	0.16	227,600	19	0.01	–	–	–	–
Qld.	44,698	1.95	1,727,200	5	0.00	14,307	0.83	19,671	1.14
S.A.	9,825	0.76	984,000	184,738	18.77	505	0.05	–	–
W.A.	31,351	2.46	2,525,000	36	0.00	40,806	1.62	190,654	7.55
Tas.	2,688	0.64	67,800	1	0.00	–	–	–	–
N.T.	29,088	23.59	1,346,200	458,100	34.02	26,074	1.94	42	0.00
Total	*159,897*	*1.10*	*7,681,800*	*643,079*	*8.37*	*81,834*	*1.06*	*210,367*	*2.74*

*   1981 Census.
** Or in the process of being granted freehold.
*** Includes Pastoral, Special Purposes, and Local Shire Council leases.

Source: Department of Aboriginal Affairs.

Australian state names in full are: New South Wales (including Australian Capital Territory, around Canberra), Victoria, Queensland, South Australia, Western Australia, Tasmania, Northern Territory.

Some of the states had also begun to return land to Aborigines and by mid-1984 the government could claim that about 900,000 square kilometres or 11.5 per cent of the land mass of Australia was held under some form of legal title by them.[37] In individual states Aboriginal land ownership was significant. In Northern Territory, for example, freehold title to land already granted or in the course of being granted amounts to nearly 30 per cent of the total land area of the state, although less than six per cent is pastoral and the rest is arid or waterlogged wetlands.

However, despite the progress made on land rights, Aboriginal peoples continue to have misgivings. The Preferred National Land Rights Model published by the Commonwealth Government in February 1985 states:

> There is to be no veto over exploration or mining on Aboriginal land. The formal decision on whether exploration or mining is to proceed on Aboriginal land to rest with Government (Paragraph 9.1).

Aboriginal people according to the new land rights legislation proposals cannot prevent mining, nor can they expect royalties as would be the entitlement of any other private landowner.

> Aborigines to be entitled to appropriate compensation for actual damage or disturbance to their land, such compensation not to take into account the value of minerals likely to be discovered or mined (i.e. no private royalties) (Paragraph 9.4).

By the end of 1984 the Labour government was in practice conceding to mining and pastoral interests. In October, for example, the Prime Minister, Bob Hawke, endorsed a draft land rights bill for the state of Western Australia which would permit Aboriginal reserve land to be taken without compensation for the purposes of mining.[38] Yet in its July conference the Australian Labour Party resolution was quite specific: 'Aboriginal and Islander people shall have the right to refuse permission for mining on their land or to impose conditions under which mining may proceed.' The Prime Minister at a press conference on 18 October declared in direct contradiction that 'there are other ways of ensuring the proper protection of the rights of Aboriginals than by the exercise of veto.'[39] Hawke's statement was also in contravention of the observation of the Aboriginal Land Rights Commissioner, Paul Seaman QC, who stated that 'there is no compelling economic reason why Aboriginal communities should not have control over mining or petroleum activity on Aboriginal land.'[40] Finally, in 1985 government funds to the main Aboriginal organization, the National Aboriginal Conference, were cut off and the offices closed down.

The major issue for Aborigines remains real land rights which include control over mining. They are not claiming privately owned lands – only title to a part of the land owned by the Crown or already occupied by Aboriginal communities. Considering that most unclaimed land is basically desert, their main rivals are the mining companies which have no wish to have their actions circumscribed. But Aboriginal people have never declared themselves enemies of mining or of cattle or sheep-rearing. They claim only some compensation for nearly 200 years of exploitation and dispossession and the right and the means to determine their own future.

The Maoris of Aotearoa (New Zealand)

No formal treaty was ever negotiated between the British Crown and the Aboriginal people of Australia, but in New Zealand the case was different. The British, through their representative Captain Hobson, received recognition of sovereignty by the Maori people in 1840 with the Treaty of Waitangi and in exchange the indigenous inhabitants of New Zealand were guaranteed full, exclusive and undisturbed rights to their lands, fisheries and forests. The Waitangi Treaty, however, was never ratified and, as far as the Maoris are concerned, has never been honoured. For *pakeha* (white) society the treaty has always been regarded as a symbol of unity between the two peoples, but in recent years Maoris have been campaigning for a radical reassessment of the colonial past and the treaty has become the focus of dissent.

When the Treaty of Waitangi was signed the European settlers numbered only 2,000, one-twentieth of the Maori population. It is certain that the Maori chiefs appending their signatures to the document had no idea that they were effectively giving up their country to a Queen living about as far away from their country as is possible. A Maori version of the treaty was eventually prepared by a missionary, but the concepts of sovereignty and of private ownership of land would have been unknown to them.[41]

In 1848, eight years after the signing of the treaty, the Crown forcibly purchased nearly half of the total land area of New Zealand, about 30 million acres. Then, in the 1860s, settlers began to arrive in their thousands. Between 1858 and 1874 the European population increased five-fold. From approximate parity with the settlers, the Maori people became an overwhelmed minority.

The new settlement brought pressures on land and further dispossession of Maori territory. In 1865 the Maori Land Court and Native Lands Act were established to record titles of customary land. The Act recognized only ownership of land on a shareholding basis. Up to a maximum of ten Maori owners could become the shareholders of a parcel of land. Whereas before land was held by the whole tribe, the new act made individual Maoris absolute owners. This facilitated enormously the acquisition of Maori land by new settlers, as well as undermining the cohesion of indigenous society.

It also brought Maori resistance and land wars. In 1858 Maoris, already disturbed at the growing incursions by settlers, chose themselves a king and created a dual system of government. In North Island the Waikato established a frontier but colonial troops invaded and confiscated a million acres in war compensation.[42] From 1863 until about 1872 there were various serious clashes over land and further confiscations.

The Minister of Justice made no secret about the purposes of the Act:

The object of the Native Lands Act is two fold: to bring the great bulk of the lands in the northern island which belong to the Maori people within the reach of

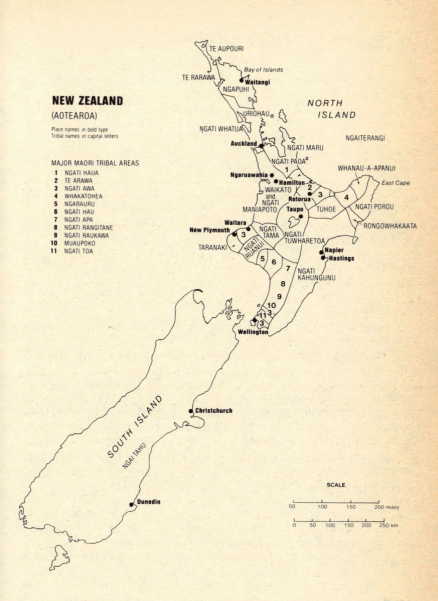

NEW ZEALAND

(AOTEAROA)

Place names in bold type
Tribal names in capital letters

MAJOR MAORI TRIBAL AREAS

1   NGATI HAUA
2   TE ARAWA
3   NGATI AWA
4   WHAKATOHEA
5   NGARAURU
6   NGATI HAU
7   NGATI APA
8   NGATI RANGITANE
9   NGATI RAUKAWA
10 MUAUPOKO
11 NGATI TOA

TE AUPOURI

Bay of Islands

TE RARAWA   ●Waitangi

NGAPUHI

NORTH
ISLAND

URIOHAU

NGATI WHATUA

NGAITERANGI

Auckland

NGATI MARU

NGATI PAOA

Ngaruawahia ●

●Hamilton

WAIKATO
and
NGATI
MANIAPOTO

WHANAU-A-APANUI

East Cape

Rotorua

Taupo

TUHOE

NGATI POROU

RONGOWHAKAATA

Waitara

New Plymouth

NGATI
TAMA

NGATI
RUANUI

NGATI
TUWHARETOA

TARANAKI

Napier

Hastings

NGATI
KAHUNGUNU

Wellington

SOUTH ISLAND

NGAI TAHU

●Christchurch

SCALE

50   100   150   200 miles

0   50   100   150   200   250 km

●Dunedin

Source: Minority Rights Group, *The Maori of New Zealand*

colonization . . . [and] to destroy the principle of communism upon which their social system was based, and which stood as a barrier in the way of all attempts to amalgamate the Maori race into our social system.[43]

Since then the land owned by Maoris has diminished continuously: in 1890 they held eleven million acres and a further 2.5 million acres on lease to the Crown; in 1900 they held seven million acres; in 1919 they held only 1.9 million acres and three million acres on lease to European settlers. Today Maori people have legal title to about four million acres of land of which 500,000 acres are leased to timber companies. In total, Maoris hold approximately four per cent of New Zealand territory and much of that land is of poor quality.[44]

The Maori people have become a disadvantaged minority in their own country. There are now about 300,000 Maoris out of a total New Zealand population of 3.2 million. About 95 per cent of Maoris live on the northern island and the rate of increase of their population is presently 3.7 per cent a year, twice that of whites.[45] One in seven Maoris is unemployed, as compared with one in 30 among *pakehas*.[46] The Maori condition is 'a story of over-representation in prisons; of failure in the education system; of a high unemployment rate; of appalling health statistics; of a shorter life expectancy', one author has written.[47]

The alienation of land and the lack of employment opportunities in the countryside for Maoris have caused a drift to the cities in the last decades. Today over three-quarters of Maoris live in urban areas, often in the most deprived quarters of the city. Many of them are young and without work, and until recently with the revival of Maori consciousness, many had little future to look forward to.

Yet in political terms, Maoris have been active throughout most of this century. They sent delegates to Britain on two occasions at the end of the 19th Century to seek improved conditions and in 1914 and 1924 they returned to present their case again. In the 1920s a political and religious movement to unite Maori people was founded by Wiremu Tanupotil Ratana. The Ratana Church, as it became known, allied itself with the Labour Party, won four seats in Parliament and a number of other concessions. The Maoris, unlike many indigenous peoples, have had full voting rights since 1852.

In the 1960s various urban-based movements developed. One of the first was the Maori Women's Welfare League. Then in the 1970s the Nga Tamatoa (Young Warriors) organization was formed and successfully campaigned for the introduction of the Maori language into schools.

The burgeoning of organizations in the 1960s and early 1970s raised public consciousness about Maori issues. In 1975 about 30,000 people marched the length of North Island in protest at further alienation of Maori land. They established a tent embassy in the grounds of Parliament House, much as the Aborigines of Australia had done in 1972. Then in 1977 and 1978 Maoris occupied land at Bastion Point near Auckland for a total of 507 days in protest at its appropriation by the government for a luxury housing development. They were only removed after a police operation involving 600 men and support from the armed forces.[48]

In the 1980s the Maori movement has grown and has increasingly forged links with progressive opinion in New Zealand. In 1981 there were riots after protests against the tour by the South African rugby team, the Springboks, were ignored by the government. Disturbances have occurred at the Waitangi Day celebrations on 6 February in every year since 1982. In 1984 the Maoris organized a week-long march to petition the government. Maori women have also been active in the peace movement, an issue of importance in the Pacific region.

The Maori Peoples Liberation Movement of Aotearoa, formed in 1980, is campaigning for sovereignty over their own territories as proposed in the Waitangi Treaty. Other organizations, such as the Waitangi Action Committee and the Maori Unity Movement which brings together many of the tribal elders, have headed public demonstrations in support of sovereignty.

The strength of the movement of Maori peoples can be measured by a recent success in halting mining by Conzinc Rio Tinto (CRA), a subsidiary of Rio Tinto Zinc. In 1980 CRA acquired mineral exploration rights on the Coromandel Peninsula. Maoris had four main objections to the mining project. They feared mining activities would destroy the fishing grounds, disrupt lifestyles, interfere with recreational pursuits and desecrate sacred sites. The objections were founded on the idea that mining companies did not share the same spiritual attitudes to land and water as the Maoris, rather than any material preoccupations about royalties. In 1982 CRA withdrew its application after strong protests. But Maori activists were not entirely satisfied because one of their principal objectives had been to amend the Mining Act so that it recognized Maori values about land.[49]

In July 1984 the new Labour government halted the granting of all prospecting licences and announced opposition to all large-scale mining. One year later, in March 1985, the Prime Minister, David Lange, appointed the Anglican Archbishop of New Zealand, Paul Reeves, as Governor-General. He is a member of the Te Atiawa tribe and is the first Maori to hold this most senior, although largely symbolic, public post. As yet the new government has not made any formal proposals for a return of sovereignty to Maori people, but it has taken a number of steps to heal some of the wounds inflicted since the invasion of Aotearoa more than a century ago.

Indian nations of the United States of America

Less than 0.5 per cent of the 230 million people of the United States are indigenous. There are about 1.5 million Native Americans, including Inuit in Alaska, who live in scattered communities throughout the county. The official government body responsible for indigenous peoples, the Bureau of Indian Affairs, recognizes 266 tribes in the United States and a further 216 Eskimo and Indian communities in Alaska. This indigenous population, after suffering heavy losses during the 18th and 19th Centuries, is now increasing at two times the national average.

The Native American peoples have fared differently so it is difficult to describe a general condition. Some, like the Navajo people, have extensive reserves where they are able to retain a degree of tribal homogeneity, while other groups have no land base. Most are now dependent on white society for work. Since the 1950s there has been increasing urbanization and today over half the Indians of the United States live in cities.

Poverty and unemployment, together with inadequate health, education and welfare provisions, are the norm for Native Americans. On the reserves average per capita incomes can be as little as a quarter the national average and unemployment rates can reach 40 per cent.[50] Other social statistics of the reserves are abnormally high: alcoholism and tuberculosis are widespread, the infant mortality rate is four times and the suicide rate two times the national average. In the cities the situation can be just as bad. In Minneapolis, one of the cities with the highest concentration of Native Americans, one study estimated that 57 per cent of all Indian heads of household are unemployed and most of those in work had low-paid, unskilled or semi-skilled jobs. More than half of Native American children in the city dropped out of school.[51]

The drift to the cities and the prevailing deprivation on the reserves is directly related to the continuing alienation of Indian land. At the end of the hostilities between the United States Government and the Indian nations in the 1880s, tribal lands amounted to 138 million acres. But in 1887 the General Allotment Act (also known as the Dawes Act) stipulated that plots of around 160 acres were to be given to each Indian head of household. Some of these lands was held in trust by the government until the rightful owners were deemed competent to hold them without restrictions. However, these lands were often leased for as long as 99 years and many large plots still remain in the hands of non-Indian developers.[52] Land not held in trust but owned outright by Indian families was subject to pressures from settlers seeking to obtain or expand their farms. The Dawes Act led to large areas of collectively held land being disposed of in individual parcels. Often the fragmentation of community land spelt disaster for the social cohesion of the tribe and by 1934 when the Indian Reorganization Act nullified the Dawes Act, the indigenous peoples of the United States had lost nearly two-thirds of their territory.

Although the 1934 Indian Reorganization Act was intended as a means of stopping further alienation of land, it unwittingly created the conditions for continual undermining of collective ownership. The Act recognized the sovereignty of the Indian tribes and recommended the establishment of tribal governments to assume full control over the reserves. The Bureau of Indian Affairs, a body responsible to the Department of the Interior, was empowered to draw up a constitution, see to the elections of the tribal governments and control all contracts between Indian peoples and outsiders. The Bureau was also given an enhanced role in the promotion of welfare, education and housing on the reservation. So long as the Commissioner of Indian Affairs remained sympathetic to the Indian way of life and committed to his independence, the

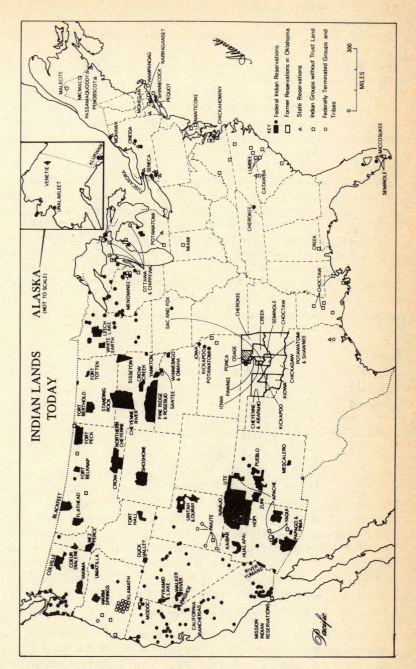

KEY
● Federal Indian Reservations
■ Former Reservations in Oklahoma
▲ State Reservations
□ Indian Groups without Trust Land
○ Federally Terminated Groups and Tribes

ALASKA
(NOT TO SCALE)

VENETIE
UNALAKLEET

INDIAN LANDS TODAY

300
0
MILES

MALECITE
MICMAC
PASSAMAQUODDY & PENOBSCOT
MOHAWK
ST. REGIS
MOHEGAN
WAMPANOAG
SHINNECOCK
NARRAGANSETT
PEQUOT
ONEIDA
NANTICOKE
TUSCARORA
SENECA
CHICKAHOMINY
LUMBEE
CATAWBA
CHEROKEE
CREEK
POTAWATOMI
MIAMI
CHOCTAW
MENOMINEE
OTTAWA & CHIPPEWA
SAC AND FOX
CHEROKEE
CREEK
SEMINOLE
CHOCTAW
WHITE LEECH EARTH LAKE
IOWA
KICKAPOO
POTAWATOMI
OSAGE
PONCA
PAWNEE
POTAWATOMI & SHAWNEE
FORT TOTTEN
SISSETON
CROW CREEK
YANKTON
WINNEBAGO & OMAHA
IOWA
CHICKASAW
KIOWA
FORT BERTHOLD
STANDING ROCK
CHEYENNE RIVER
PINE RIDGE & ROSEBUD
SANTEE
CHEYENNE & ARAPAHO
KICKAPOO
FORT PECK
NORTHERN CHEYENNE
CROW
SHOSHONE
FORT BELKNAP
BLACKFEET
FLATHEAD
COLVILLE
COEUR D'ALENE
YAKIMA
UMATILLA
NEZ PERCE
FORT HALL
UINTAH & OURAY
UTE
PUEBLO
MESCALERO
NAVAJO
PAIUTE
ZUNI
APACHE
YAQUI
DUCK VALLEY
PYRAMID LAKE
WALKER RIVER
KAIBAB
HUALAPAI
HOPI
PAPAGO & PIMA
WARM SPRINGS
KLAMATH
MODOC
MASSACRE
RIVER YUMANS
CALIFORNIA RANCHERIAS
MISSION INDIAN RESERVATIONS
MICCOSUKEE
SEMINOLE
Pacific

Source: Minority Rights Group, *The Original Americans: US Indians*

197

Act could be used to the benefit of Native Americans. However, if a hostile commissioner took over, the Act could be turned against them, as indeed happened. In 1952 the newly appointed commissioner made use of these powers to interfere in tribal elections and sell land without permission. In the six years from 1954 to 1960, 61 Indian tribes were 'terminated', and lost their lands and special federal protection.[53]

The present land base in the form of reservations for Native Americans is 50 million acres or approximately two per cent of the surface area of the country. Much of that land is dispersed in small reserves. The bulk of the indigenous population lives in the western region of the country and there are several large reserves, such as that of the Navajo which covers about 17 million acres and supports about 150,000 people.

Although the total available land owned by the Native Americans appears substantial, it is poor-quality, often desert, land. Three-quarters of reserve land is estimated to be suitable only for grazing and not more intensive farming and only ten per cent has oil or mineral reserves of any kind.[54] Most land left to the Indians was considered useless desert by the European settlers and is rendered ever more vulnerable by restrictions of available water. Today some 95 per cent of water in the dry lands of the west is required by industry or subsequently polluted. 'Without water', one writer has commented, 'western reservations become graveyards.'[55]

Our benefactor, the BIA:
Indian Version of the Lord's Prayer

Our benefactor in Indian Affairs
Hallowed by thy position
Thy downfall comes,
With every election
Thy will be done on this reserve
As will be done on every other reserve.

Give us this day our daily rations
And forgive us our trespasses as we will
Forgive you your trespasses on our land.
Lead us not into integration
But deliver us from exploitation.
For thine is the establishment, the power, and the glory.
For as long as the grass shall grow
And the rivers flow and the sun shines.
Forever and ever – unh!

Source: Shirley Hill Witt and Stan Steiner (eds.), *The Way: an anthology of American Indian literature* (Vintage Books, 1972).

The dilemma for Native Americans is really no different from that of their counterparts elsewhere in the world: their survival as a people will be entirely determined by whether they succeed in keeping hold of the little land they still possess. Recent events, however, indicate that the forces arrayed against them are formidable. The United States Government under President Reagan is fully committed to a free market with as few federal constraints as possible on capitalist enterprise. The transnational corporations which have become increasingly involved in the exploitation of reserve lands can afford to offer substantial incentives to individual Native Americans to encourage them to relinquish their control over the land. By a curious act of fate some of the reserves contain extraordinary quantities of oil, natural gas and minerals.

Studies by the government place as much as 80 per cent of all uranium reserves in the US on Native American land. Reservations occupied by Navajo, Hopi and Oglala Lakota (Sioux) are among those most affected. The US Department of Energy estimate that 33 per cent of all strippable coal reserves are on Indian lands and in some states, like Arizona, virtually all the coal produced is from the reservations. In obtaining permission to exploit these resources, the oil companies have taken the lead.

> A closer examination reveals that not only do 12 oil companies own 76 per cent of uranium and a majority of coal reserves, but also most of the industry, from mines to the processing mills needed to extract the uranium from the ores.[56]

The situation of the Navajo and Hopi peoples provides an example of the manner in which energy companies became involved in mineral extraction on reservation land and the role played by the Bureau of Indian Affairs in facilitating their entry on to that land.[57]

The Navajo nations were guaranteed a reservation in 1868 and the Hopi a homeland in the Black Mesa mountains in 1882. As the Navajo, a mainly sheep-rearing people, grew in number their reservation was extended by executive order until it covered about 17 million acres of northern Arizona and completely surrounded Hopi land. Difficulties and conflicts there certainly were between these two peoples, but in 1923 a new danger menaced. Standard Oil Company struck oil and with the connivance of the Bureau of Indian Affairs signed a lease with the five men of the Navajo Tribal Council. A little over twenty years later, in 1949, Kerr McGee Corporation discovered uranium and once more the Tribal Council and the BIA signed a lease permitting extraction. Then in the 1950s vast coal deposits were uncovered by Peabody Coal and further leases were signed away by the Tribal Councils of the Navajo and Hopi peoples.

The elected Tribal Councils were totally alien forms of organization to the Indians. When the Hopi Tribal Council was formed many of the adult population refused to vote. In one Hopi village only 13 out of 250 voters went to the polls and when the council was finally established it represented only one-fifth of the Hopi people. The Tribal Councils may have seen themselves as progressive organizations, bringing wealth to the tribes by sharing in the exploitation of the mineral resources of their land, but they have been ill-advised and taken decisions detrimental to the long-term interests of their people.

Traditional use of the land as cattle and sheep pasture is being undermined by the increasing area of the reservation being leased for mineral extraction. At the outset, when energy companies first became involved in the reservation, the government imposed sheep reduction programmes with the assistance of the Tribal Council. In 1940, for example, before major extraction had begun, agriculture and livestock made up nearly 60 per cent of total Navajo income, but by 1958 less than ten per cent was derived from this source.

There have been few material rewards for Native Americans emanating from the burgeoning and highly profitable extractive industries on their land. They receive royalties of less than one per cent of the market value of uranium and in 1981 received an average of 25 cents a ton for coal which was sold for about $US 70 a ton.[58]

The health costs of strip coal-mining and especially uranium processing are also high. By 1980 over 700 uranium miners were recorded as suffering from breathing problems caused by the inadequate safety precautions prevailing at the mines; more than 100 of those were seeking compensation either from the government or the companies involved.[59] In 1974, 18 people died from radiation-induced lung cancer. Between 1975 and 1979 over 100 children in one district were born with defects believed to be caused by contaminated water.[60] Today nearly 800,000 acres of Navajo land are leased to uranium-mining companies with little benefit to the people. One writer has commented:

> Energy production on the Navajo Reservation drains large quantities of resources from Navajo lands and leaves little behind for the benefit of Navajo people and tribal government. If present economic trends in energy production persist, the Navajo economy will never achieve self-sustaining development. Nearly 20 per cent of Navajo homes have no electricity, and substandard water, housing, health and educational services are commonplace.[61]

According to the National Academy of Sciences it is virtually impossible to reclaim the land after strip-mining.[62]

Notwithstanding these environmental criticisms of the present mining on Indian land, there has also been desecration of sacred sites. For Navajo and Hopi peoples the Black Mesa mountain is in the centre of a sacred area where herbs and medicines are gathered for healing and ceremonies.

In complying with the policies of federal government and mining companies, the tribal councils have met with opposition from their own constituents. In 1975, for example, when the Navajo Tribal Council approved a lease for a 40,000 acre site for strip coal-mining, the local inhabitants voted against the proposal and many were arrested for occupying their own tribal council headquarters. Since 1982 the Navajo Tribal Council has had a change of leadership signalling a less complacent attitude towards the role of energy companies on the reservation.

It needs to be noted that the tribal councils, together with the Bureau of Indian Affairs, are the main employers on the reservation and provide nearly all the welfare benefits. They are able to exert considerable influence on the community and the bribery of local representatives and other forms of coercion are known to occur. In the past, ambitious chairmen of the tribal councils have made virtual fiefdoms of their office and a generally demoralized indigenous community has done little in practice to prevent them. In recent years the American Indian movement has begun to challenge these unrepresentative councils.

Outside interests have often successfully manipulated these councils and exploited differences within the Indian community. Some 9,500 Navajo and 100 Hopi people are due to lose their homes as they are forcibly relocated elsewhere because of such manipulation. Until 1974 the Hopi and Navajo shared a 1.8 million acre site called the Joint Use Area. The area is known to have extensive coal reserves, possibly as much as 21 billion tons, and probably uranium as well. The nearly 10,000 Native Americans that live there have no wish to move from their land to make way for further destructive development but legislation has paved the way for such an eventuality. In 1974 the Navajo-Hopi Settlement Act was passed by Congress and divided what was once jointly owned land into Hopi and Navajo parcels. The Settlement Act allows the energy companies to negotiate with the Hopi Tribal Council which has agreed to lease their parcel, even though several thousand Navajo people will have to leave their homes.

At the present time mining and other interests are actively involved on Indian land throughout the United States, on the reservations of the Oglala Lakota (Sioux), the Western Shoshone, the Northern Cheyenne, Mohawk and many others.[63] The encroachment on to Indian land over the last decades has been an important spur to action by the indigenous movement. There is now a recognition that further erosion of their land base will leave assimilation into white society as the only option open to Indian peoples.

The American Indian movement began in the 1960s. One of the first organizations to take up wider issues was the National Indian Youth Council, which was formed in 1961. Their style was more campaigning and their position more militant than other Indian organizations. One of the first issues the council raised was that of fishing rights of Native Americans in the north-western states. Fishing was one of the main means of procuring food for the Indians of this region and was under increasing threat from large-scale industries causing pollution and depletion of fish stocks. The states had introduced legislation to conserve stocks from over-fishing and this severely reduced Indian food resources. The NIYC organized a successful campaign to raise public awareness of the threat to fishing rights which were, in fact, guaranteed by treaty.[64]

Further militant action occurred on the border between Canada and New York State when Mohawk Indians seized the Cornwall International Bridge. The Mohawk nation is split in two by the national frontier and the Indians were protesting at the tolls they had to pay each time they crossed. They maintained that a treaty between Great Britain and the United States in 1794 provided for free passage.

A succession of such actions soon forced the public and politicians to take note of Indian demands. Building on the growing political consciousness of Native Americans and the growing awareness of indigenous issues of the public, in July 1968 the American Indian Movement (AIM) was launched. Then in November of that year a group of Indians seized the abandoned island of Alcatraz in San Francisco Bay and occupied it for 18 months. Four years later, in 1972, AIM and other Indian activists marched on Washington in what was termed the Trail of Broken Treaties. In Washington they occupied the offices of the Bureau of Indian Affairs for several days, declared a Native American Embassy and demanded the proper enforcement of treaties.

Then in 1973 a more serious confrontation between the government and Native Americans took place. The village of Wounded Knee, where in 1890 US cavalry massacred 300 unarmed men, women and children of the Sioux nation, was occupied by Indian activists. Although the demonstrators were on their own reserve at Pine Ridge, the government surrounded the camp with troops and police. The siege endured 71 days and the government is estimated to have spent between five and seven million dollars; two Indians were killed and many were wounded.[65]

The immediate cause of the protests was dissatisfaction with the running of the reserve. Virtually the only employment at Pine Ridge was provided by the Tribal Council and the Bureau of Indian Affairs and all other funds were controlled by the former. The tribal chairman, Richard Wilson, elected in 1972 had abused his position, providing jobs for his friends and relatives, sacking people opposed to him and misappropriating funds.[66] Attempts to remove him from his position democratically failed when tribal councillors were bribed and opponents beaten and threatened by hired thugs. After the failure of various attempts at impeachment, direct action was taken up as the only means of removing the tribal chairman from office.

Wounded Knee rapidly became a symbol of the Indian struggle for social justice. Eventually the siege ended with an agreement by the US Government to hold an inquiry and re-examine the terms of the original treaty signed in 1868. However, the agreement was unobserved on the government side and AIM activists in the years following faced arrests and according to one report 40 members and sympathizers were found dead at Pine Ridge in suspicious circumstances between 1973 and 1976.[67]

There have been serious miscarriages of justice against Indian peoples throughout their recent history. At the height of the tension following Pine Ridge, in February 1973, Darold Schmidt, in a bar near the reserve, was heard to announce his intention of killing an Indian. He later stabbed an Indian to death, was indicted for manslaughter and served a one-day sentence. The mother of the murdered man, Sarah Bad Heart Bull, protested publicly at the plea of manslaugher and was charged with incitement to riot and sentenced to one to five years. The perversion of the legal system in this instance was no exception. All-white juries in towns bordering reservations are notoriously racist and prejudiced.

In 1975 the Indian leader, Dennis Banks, for example, found himself prosecuted for rioting by an attorney-general named William Janklow. Janklow had been elected for South Dakota on an anti-American-Indian-Movement ticket and had campaigned on the basis that 'the way to handle the problem of AIM leaders was to put a bullet in the guy's head.'[68] Janklow himself had faced prosecution for the rape of a 15-year-old Indian girl during the time he was legal officer on the Rosebud Sioux Reservation in 1967. Banks had been responsible for the prosecution case and animosity between the two men dated from that time. Janklow refused to answer the summons and was found guilty in his absence by the tribal court. The girl in question was inexplicably found dead on a highway three months after the trial.

Dennis Banks had been one of the AIM leaders who had joined Sarah Bad Heart Bull in demanding that the plea of manslaughter by Darold Schmidt in 1973 be changed to murder. His public protest had been deemed riotous by the newly appointed attorney-general who must also have seen an opportunity to put away an influential Indian leader and old antagonist as too good to miss. Banks was convicted after threats were made against two members of the jury and the defence lawyer, and he fled the court-house when his own life was menaced. He subsequently sought sanctuary on two Indian reservations and was finally extradited through a Federal Grand Jury and is now serving a sentence in a South Dakota prison. If this reads like the script for a cinema portrayal of sordid, small-town American corruption, it should be recognized that it is actually a familiar story for Indian peoples. There are still a number of Indian activists serving prison sentences for crimes for which there is little real evidence of their guilt.[69]

The Indian movement is obliged to fight on two fronts: against the prejudices and ignorance of the dominant white society and culture and against the corruption and vested interests of certain tribal governments which receive benefits by collaborating with white society and its institutions. Some tribal governments and many white Americans would agree that assimilation is inevitable and desirable. This position has been called 'progressive'. The 'traditionalist' view is posited by AIM and other Indian activists. It declares that the Indian peoples of the United States have a distinct and valuable culture, they have a legal and moral right of sovereignty over the land given them by treaty and they have a non-materialist way of life which could benefit the country. But the objectives of the Indian movement are not to return to an imaginary past but to achieve self-awareness, self-sufficiency and self-determination.[70] While upholding age-old traditions, such as government by elders and a deep respect for nature, the American Indian movement has also successfully fought cases in the US courts, negotiated fairer and environmentally safer terms with mining companies and used the United Nations to advance their rights under international law.

Canada's native peoples

Registered Indians, Inuit (Eskimos), Metis and Non-Status Indians make up the indigenous population of Canada. There are approximately 326,000 registered Indians organized in 577 bands. About 230,000 of these, or over two-thirds, live on the 2,200 reserves which cover 2.7 million hectares of land. There are also 25,000 Inuit living in small communities in the Arctic region.

In addition, the last national census indicated that some 90,000 people identified themselves as Metis or half-bloods.[71] However, government figures differ widely from those offered by indigenous organizations. The Association of Metis and Non-Status Indians of Saskatchewan claims to represent 85,000 indigenous peoples in the province and estimates that there are approximately 850,000 Non-Status and Metis Indians nationally.[72] If this is so the total autochthonous population of Canada would number about 1.2 million of which two-thirds are outside the legal responsibility of the federal government.

The Status Indians are those defined as such under the Indian Act of 1880. They are registered on reserves and receive privileges in the form of welfare and exemption from certain taxes. Many of their forefathers had signed over their land in treaties with the Crown in return for their reserves. The first of these treaties was signed in 1871 with the Ojibway and Cree Indian nations who gave up their hunting rights and settled in reserves where they were promised medical services, schools and other benefits.

In all eleven treaties were signed between 1871 and 1921 excluding Indians from virtually all of their traditional lands and confining them to reserves where they would be administered down to the minutest detail by a Ministry of Indian Affairs. The material and spiritual decline on the reserves began in earnest from that moment, so that by the late 1960s Indians were in a state of severe deprivation. Unemployment levels of Indians were more than eight times greater than among Canadians as a whole and in 1969 incomes of at least half all Indian families were less than $C 1,000 in contrast to the national average of nearly $C 9,000. In other respects Indians were demoralized and neglected: they achieved below-average schooling, had comparatively worse health and were more likely to commit suicide, be alcoholics or end up in prison than Canadians.[73] Like the reserves in the United States, those in Canada also effectively undermined the social cohesion and self-esteem of the Indian communities.

Demoralization led a number of Indians to disenfranchize themselves and give up their Indian status so that they could find work and a future as part of Canadian society. Today such peoples are regarded as Non-Status Indians and like the Metis accorded no special protection or privileges and, most importantly, not recognized as having any rights to land and their own system of government. Furthermore, until recently Indian women could lose their special status if they married a non-Indian.

Federal and provincial governments treated Metis differently to status Indians. The treaties signed with the Indian nations provided communal tracts of land and certain other rights, often to hunting and fishing on Crown land, while the Metis were issued scrips for a specific amount of land. Land scrip was a certificate of ownership for a particular individual for a specified number of acres and served to extinguish Indian communal title to land. In fact, the scrip issues were subject to all types of fraud and attracted speculation by banks, clergy and others. According to one study over four million acres of land were distributed in this way to Meti Indians but over 90 per cent of it eventually found its way into the hands of outside speculators. The Metis were left destitute and landless by the scrip system.[74]

The Metis mainly inhabit Saskatchewan, Alberta and Manitoba and consider themselves as Indian nations with rights to self-determination and a homeland. They are demanding amendments to the constitution which would recognize Metis as an aboriginal people and give them ownership and control of natural resources and their own government within Canadian federalism.[75]

How successful the Metis and indeed all indigenous peoples of Canada are in winning self-determination will depend on whether they organize resistance to what has become a major threat: the activities of state and corporate industrial interests. The Dene Nation provides an example of how indigenous peoples in Canada have confronted natural resource companies. The Dene Nation comprises some 15,000 people who inhabit the Mackenzie Valley of North-West Territory and have a long-standing tradition of self-government. In 1899 and 1920 they signed treaties with the Canadian Government by which they relinquished control over their traditional lands. In the 1960s the Dene and Metis living in the area began to reassert their rights to their original homelands, arguing that in their interpretation of the treaties they had never surrendered their lands. In the 1970s the two main Indian organizations, the Indian Brotherhood of the North-West Territory and the Metis Association of the North-West Territory, joined forces and formed the Dene Nation in order to oppose the construction of a pipeline system along the Mackenzie Valley.

The Denes' case was strengthened when in 1973 a Supreme Court Judge, William Morrow, ruled that 450,000 square miles of land were owned by the indigenous peoples of the area and that the two treaties had not extinguished their title. In 1975 the Dene Nation declared that the original peoples of the Mackenzie Valley were a unique culture and a nation within Canada and, as such, were demanding the right to self-determination.[76]

The plan for a pipeline had been discussed secretly by the Canadian Government with foreign oil companies like Exxon, Shell and Gulf. The pipeline, due to carry natural gas, was the largest private enterprise project in Canadian history and in 1983 was costed at $C 8 billion.[77] No consultation took place with the Dene Nation and when the decision was announced by the government to proceed with the project, it brought immediate condemnation from indigenous peoples and Canadian environmentalists. Both groups claimed that the pipeline would lead to massive colonization by outside workers, damage to the Arctic ecosystem and ultimately destroy the Dene way of life.

Widespread opposition resulted in the appointment by the government of a commission of inquiry under Judge Thomas Berger. In 1977 he announced his findings and concluded that no pipeline should be built until all claims to land by the Dene were settled, a period which he considered would take at least ten years. The federal government, however, did not heed the recommendations of the commission and refused to enter into negotiations with the Dene Nation, which now represented Status, Non-Status and Meti Indians living in the Mackenzie Valley. In 1980 permission was granted by the government for a scaled-down pipeline project and for gas, oil and mineral explorations on Dene land.

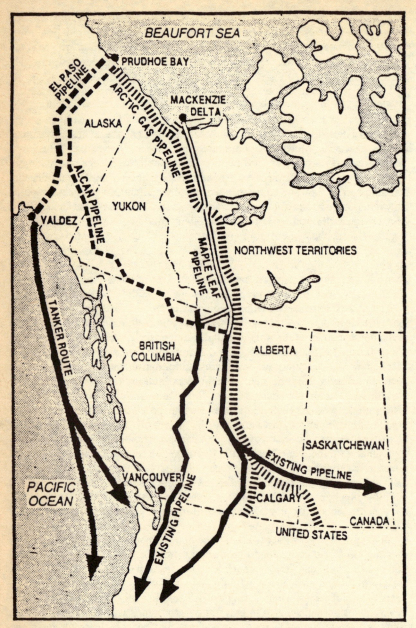

Proposed pipeline routes to bring Alaska (U.S.A.) gas across Dene land in Canada to the mid-western United States markets.

Source: World Council of Churches, *Land Rights for Indigenous Peoples*

Although the resistance offered by the Dene only delayed the pipeline and reduced its full impact, it had other more far-reaching consequences. One observer has commented:

> during the debate over the Mackenzie Valley pipeline and over the inclusion of a clause protecting aboriginal rights in the Constitution, public opinion was mobilized and in the end, played a decisive role in the resolution of these matters to the benefit of the aboriginal nations.[78]

The intervention of non-indigenous pressure groups in Canada has proved vital in the campaigns to protect and enhance indigenous rights.

But to many indigenous peoples the Western model of development appears inexorable. In the James Bay area of northern Quebec where Cree and other Indian peoples opposed a hydro-electric project in the 1970s, one of the signatories explained why the Cree finally entered into an agreement with the government in the following terms:

> We feel that in the long run the hydro project was inevitable. The federal government could simply extinguish rights, claims and interests Native people have within the territory of James Bay. No government was willing to stop the hydro project. The Cree Nation recognised that fact.[79]

Indigenous peoples and national governments have distinct visions of the world and priorities for the future. Nowhere is this more poignantly evident than in the present situation experienced by the Innu people of Labrador. The Innu are enjoying the beginnings of a cultural renaissance after decades of forced assimilation. The culture and semi-nomadic hunting and trapping way of life are being passed on to the new generation, in an as yet fragile experiment to restore traditional values.

Since 1980, however, Innu territory has been used by NATO for low-level high-speed training of fighter bombers. The Canadian, United States, British and West German air forces are based in the region. The flights by pilots, often at heights as low as 100 feet, have distressed small Innu communities and disrupted wildlife populations. Hunting and trapping activities have been upset, and professional field observers attest to the rapid decrease of caribou migration into the area. The Innu are united in their opposition to the flights over their territory and 'do not believe that their economy and the integrity of their system of self-reliance are compatible with the use of their homeland as a training area for the armed forces of foreign countries'.[80]

The numbers of indigenous peoples' organizations in Canada is confusingly high, reflecting the variety of Indian nations in existence at the time of the European invasion. Many of these were able to survive, in part because of their isolation and because Canada still has a relatively low population density, and in the last decades they have endeavoured to assert their rights. They have made effective use of the courts, have entered into renegotiations of treaties with the federal government and forged links with other Indian peoples and sympathetic sectors of Canadian society. But though their organizations are numerous, they share two overriding demands. The first is for the recognition by the Canadian

Government and the international community of the sovereignty of Indian nations. Thus, the Coalition of First Nations states: 'The First Nations of Upper North America are not nor have they been a part of the Canadian Confederation.'[81] An Innu spokesman echoed these words when he wrote to the commanding officer of the West German air force in May 1984:

Ntesinan has never been the object of any transfer of sovereignty from the Innu People to any foreign power and remains legitimately our country. We can see no moral grounds for the Luftwaffe exporting the unwanted problem of high speed low level flight training by military aircraft from West Germany to the countries of Peoples such as ourselves; presumably on the assumption that because of our weak political position as a colonized People, we are not in a position to effectively resist this imposition.[82]

For the more isolated Indian communities in Canada the colonial presence is a relatively recent phenomenon. In a letter to the Premier of Newfoundland and Labrador in 1980 the Naskapi Montagnais Innu Association expressed a commonly held sentiment:

We had never taken seriously the claims made by white officials that they owned our country because we knew that in our travels throughout the interior of Labrador and Northern Quebec we hadn't seen any Europeans nor had our grandfathers or their grandfathers before them. In the settlements all kinds of agencies pretended to have authority over us but as soon as we returned to the country we were free again to exercise our rights as our fathers had before us.[83]

The other demand of Canadian Indians is for the real control of their land: an adequate land base and resource rights. It is on this important issue that the Canadian government shows greatest unwillingness. The federal government has entered on occasion into settlements of comprehensive land claims but there are still as yet few agreements which fully satisfy indigenous demands. Most recently the Inuvialut of the Western Arctic and the Council of Yukon Indians have concluded settlements. The sums of compensatory and support funding involved sound substantial: over $C 50 million for the Inuvialut and $C 200 million for the Yukon Indians. Both the agreements provided the Indian communities with rights to sub-surface resources on part of their territory. In this sense both agreements represent gains of important concessions from the government. However, differences of opinion over the interpretation of settlements of this kind have arisen in the past and may easily do so in the future if resources deemed vital to national development are discovered on indigenous land. It is for this reason that Indians from Canada are increasingly appearing at world fora and seeking the international recognition of their right to nationhood and territorial integrity.

Colonized peoples of the Pacific

Although many of the islands of the Pacific are politically independent, the region generally is regarded as within the sphere of influence of the rich capitalist countries. There continue to be a number of islands and island groups fully or partially administered by the United States: the United Nations Trust Territories, Hawaii (the country's 50th state), Guam and American Samoa which have been non-self-governing territorial possessions since 1898 and 1899 respectively. The French still retain the colonies of New Caledonia, Wallis and Futuna, and French Polynesia. Some islands are nominally independent but in certain respects remain strongly influenced by their former colonial masters, as is the case of Papua New Guinea and Australia, or the Cook Islands and New Zealand. To the French and United States governments these possessions are deemed vital to the maintenance of an enduring military domination of the Pacific. France, for example, has detonated 130 explosions since 1966, 70 of them underground and 40 of them since President Mitterrand came to power.[84]

For the United States, France, Japan and, to a lesser extent, Australia, the ocean is a resource for economic exploitation, a playground for nuclear tests and a dumping ground for radioactive wastes. In the use and future development of the Pacific, the indigenous inhabitants have virtually no influence. The Pacific is like many of the little-understood frontier lands that have been colonized by the rich nations: it is treated as unclaimed and unused by its traditional owners. But this is far from the truth for the ocean has always been fished and the islanders have always travelled and traded across the familiar waters around them. Colonization brought a radical change in the way of life of these peoples and today the growing militarization of the Pacific threatens further, and perhaps more long-lasting, destruction of their cultures.

The peoples of the Pacific may be divided broadly into three groups: Melanesians, Micronesians and Polynesians.[85] The Melanesian peoples live on the islands in the south-west Pacific and the island of Papua whose western half is currently occupied by Indonesia.[86] The islands consist of several former British colonies, now independent nation states and members of the Commonwealth, including the Solomon Islands, Vanuatu (once the Anglo-French Condominium of New Hebrides) and Fiji, which has a mixed Melanesian, Polynesian and Indian population. The total population of the islands is about five million.[87]

To the north of Melanesia lie the numerous islands making up Micronesia. These include Guam, Kiribati and Tuvalu, formerly the Gilbert and Ellice Islands, and the Trust Territories. The Trust Territories are made up of the three archipelagos of the Marshalls, the Marianas and the Carolines, a total of more than 2,000 islands and atolls covering an area the size of continental United States, with a population of about 140,000.[88]

Moving east from Melanesia lie the islands of Polynesia. These include the French overseas territories of the Society Islands, the Marquesas, Gambier and the Tuamota Archipelago, and also American Samoa and Western Samoa and Tonga, these last two being members of the Commonwealth. Hawaii with its highly miscegenated population and large proportion of North Americans, is also normally included within the Polynesian region.[89]

In the last few decades there has grown up a strong movement for political independence among the peoples of the Pacific. It has been particularly

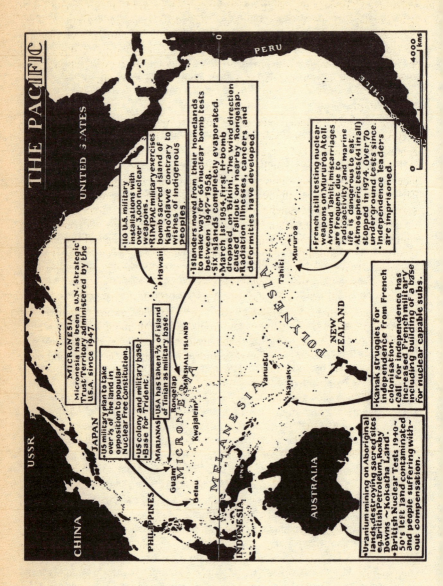

THE PACIFIC

PERU

CHILE

4000 kms

UNITED STATES

MICRONESIA
Micronesia has been a U.N. 'strategic'
Trust Territory administered by the
U.S.A. since 1947.

•110 U.S. military
installations with
over 3,000 nuclear
weapons.
•RIMPAC military exercises
bomb sacred island of
Kaho'olawe contrary to
wishes of indigenous
peoples.

•Hawaii

•Islanders moved from their homelands
to make way for 66 nuclear bomb tests
between 1947~1958.
•Six islands completely evaporated.
•March 1st 1954. First H-bomb
dropped on Bikini. The wind direction
caused fallout on nearby Rongelap.
Radiation illnesses, cancers and
deformities have developed.

•French still testing nuclear
weapons on Mururoa Atoll.
Around Tahiti, miscarriages
are subsequent due to
radio active land and marine
life is danger, and few to eat.
•Atmospheric tests (44 in all)
stopped in 1974. Over 70
underground tests since.
•Independence leaders
are imprisoned.

Mururoa

Tahiti

•US military plan to take
over 2/3 of the land in
opposition to popular
Nuclear Free Constitution.

JAPAN

•US colony and military base.
•Base for Trident.

MARIANAS •USA has taken 2/3 of island
of Tinian as military base.

Guam

Rongelap

MARSHALL ISLANDS

Kwajalein

Belau

POLYNESIA

NEW
ZEALAND

Vanuatu

Kanaky

•Kanak struggles for
independence from French
colonisation.
•Call for independence has
increased French military
including building of a base
for nuclear capable subs.

MICRONESIA

PHILIPPINES

MELANESIA

PNG

USSR

CHINA

INDONESIA

AUSTRALIA

•Uranium mining on Aboriginal
land, destroying sacred sites
eg. British Petroleum, Roxby
Downs ~ Kokatha Land.
•British Nuclear Tests 1940~
50's left land contaminated
and people suffering with~
out compensation.

influential in Melanesia where the peoples, although dispersed over a vast area, now recognize their common ethnic identity and shared colonial experiences. Papua New Guinea achieved independence in 1975 and Vanuatu in 1980, and both countries have offered solidarity and more concrete support to their colonized brothers in West Papua and New Caledonia.[90] Papua New Guinea has hosted meetings of heads of governments of Melanesian countries and leaders of the Kanak Independence Movement of New Caledonia and the opposition groups in West Papua and New Caledonia both have offices in Vanuatu.[91]

New Caledonia

Struggles for political independence are nowhere more acute than in the French-occupied island of New Caledonia. 'Discovered' by Captain Cook in 1774, annexed by France in 1853, New Caledonia is one of the few remaining colonies in French hands in the Pacific. Almost certainly these islands will achieve independence in the near future, but what form it will take is now hotly disputed. The original inhabitants, the Kanaks, are almost united in demanding complete sovereignty, while the French Government under the leadership of the socialist President Mitterrand is willing to concede only independence with association which would mean a continuing involvement by France in internal and external security. The European immigrant community, the Caldoches as they are known, are opposed even to this concession and want to protect their privileged position as virtual masters of New Caledonia.

New Caledonia has a population of about 140,000 of which 62,000 (nearly 45 per cent) are Kanaks, some 38 per cent are European and the remainder are peoples from other Pacific Islands and from Asia. Until about 1960 the Kanak population was in the majority but the development of nickel production – the country has 40 per cent of the world's known reserves and is the second most important source for nickel outside the USSR – led to the immigration of hundreds of workers.[92] The flow of immigration was accelerated in 1972 when Prime Minister Messmer actively encouraged the settlement of non-Pacific peoples on to the island:

> In the long term, the nationalist demands by the autochthonous population can only be avoided if the communities not originating from the Pacific are in the majority . . . the conditions are ripe for New Caledonia becoming a small and prosperous French territory, like Luxembourg [*sic*], within twenty years.[93]

The policy, however, produced the opposite result and as the outsiders flooded to the island, the Kanak people, not merely disadvantaged but now also a minority in their own land, began to unite in a struggle for their liberation. In 1979 the five main Kanak opposition parties joined together to form an Independence Front and won 80 per cent of the Melanesian vote. In the run-up to the French presidential elections in 1981, the socialist candidate promised to support the move towards independence and was rewarded by an uncharacteristic majority of votes from the island.

Even prior to this pledge of support, the Kanaks had much to be concerned about. They were grossly under-represented in the local assembly and in the island's capital Europeans controlled nearly all aspects of administration and economic life and accounted for 86 per cent of employers. Where Kanaks had been given reserves the land was insufficient and of poor quality. Some 30,000 Kanaks were expected to make a living on 165,000 hectares of land, while as few as 200 European families owned 400,000 hectares of prime agricultural land.

The new socialist government introduced a number of reforms to attempt to redress the injustices but these were soon deemed insignificant by the Kanak peoples. The slow rate of restitution of land – about 20,000 hectares of land were being returned each year – was considered inadequate even to keep pace with demographic growth. But it is on the key issue of independence that the indigenous peoples of New Caledonia feel disappointed.

A round table discussion in July 1983 resulted in the government recognizing publicly the legitimacy of the Kanak people to self-determination.[94] But ambiguity lay in the interpretation of who would take part in future decisions about independence. The indigenous inhabitants, a minority within the total population, sought to exclude those who had settled since 1960, the very people forming the backbone of a militant opposition to any withdrawal of the French. A compromise was proposed in February 1984 whereby the French continued to retain all its major functions while the Kanak established its own traditional political system. The Lemoine Statute, as it was known, would be valid for five years and exist as an interim measure while the details of full independence were deliberated. The Kanaks have argued against the proposal because it allows time for further immigration to the island.

The unwillingness of the French Government to grant full independence to the island and seek some form of compromise has not averted violence between the two main communities. Kanaks are now comparing the fight for independence with the bloody decolonization of Algeria. Political killings have been perpetrated by both sides.

The conflict has caused the socialist government, ideologically committed to decolonization, considerable embarrassment. It responded in 1984 by sending special envoy, Edgard Pisani, to find a solution. He subsequently brought forward the date for a referendum on independence. Then in January 1985 President Mitterrand made a flying visit to the island, endorsed the Pisani proposals but made it clear that he would not give up French military involvement on the island.

The strategic implications of full independence are those that most influence the government. The loss of New Caledonia is seen as leading to the eventual independence of French Polynesia and the loss of the nuclear testing centre on Mururoa and, for a country still obsessed with playing a world role, the loss of a presence in the Pacific altogether.[95] The French Government has declared its intention of building a military base on the island which it proposes to lease along similar lines to those of the United States in the Philippines.

For its part, the Kanak Socialist National Liberation Front (FLNKS), the leading organization of Kanaks, has made its position clear. It seeks complete independence and self-determination for the Kanak people. As for those who would vote in any plebiscite, the Kanaks believe they have already made a major concession in agreeing to accept the victims of colonial history as voters, thereby including those who were born or had one parent born in the country. Indeed, support for self-determination has come from the foreign ministers of neighbouring Vanuatu, Papua New Guinea and the Solomon Islands. The ministers have also called for United Nations intervention.

In September 1985 the Melanesian separatists won three out of the four regions in the local elections, leaving the Europeans with only the capital, Noumea. Just the week before the conservative opposition leader, Jacques Chirac, swore that the territory would remain French. In April 1986, after parliamentary elections gave the right wing a majority, Chirac became Prime Minister of France.

In March 1985 a new referendum date was set for the end of 1987 but the future of the island may be determined before any votes are cast.

France not only faces unrest in New Caledonia, but also in its other overseas departments and territories (DOM-TOMs): in Martinique, Guadeloupe, La Réunion and other remnants of its colonies. The growing economic problems – on average 30 per cent of the workforce is unemployed in the DOM-TOMs – is at the heart of the dissatisfaction. Economic difficulties and a cultural awakening among the islands have given rise to new independence movements and in April 1985 the first conference on the future of France's colonies brought together representatives of these movements in Guadeloupe.[96]

Even in French Polynesia the boom, caused by the massive influx of defence-related funds and the presence of the French armed forces, has begun to die down. The armed forces employ 15 per cent of Polynesia's workforce, and defence accounts for about 33 per cent of the economy.[97] However, Polynesia's highly dependent economy has been affected by the recession far away in Europe. Now the indigenous inhabitants are more vocal in their criticisms of the French Government. 'We used to grow anything here, now we import 80 per cent of our food. Ordinary Tahitians cannot afford the price,' one islander has complained.[98] The deteriorating economic situation since militarization of the islands is eloquently stated in these figures: in 1960 food imports cost £1.9 million and in 1980 they cost £370 million; exports now cover less than a quarter of imports, compared with 83 per cent before the nuclear tests. Slums which were non-existent in the 1960s now surround the island of Tahiti's capital, Papeete.[99] As in other French colonies an independence movement – the Polynesian Liberation Front – has been formed. However, French colonial settlers have shown little inclination to negotiate with or even recognize the new independence movements. As one settler commented to Alan Rusbridger of the *Guardian*: 'This is France. If there is any independence movement at all in Tahiti it is because the French, unlike the English, made the mistake of not killing off all the natives when they first arrived.'[100]

The Trust Territories

A politically independent Pacific is now top of the agenda for the indigenous islanders of the Pacific. In the US-administered Trust Territories there is a growing movement for a wider understanding of self-determination than that negotiated to date. The territory now consists of four entities: the Commonwealth of the Northern Mariana Islands, the Federated States of Micronesia, the Marshall Islands and Palau.

In 1975 the Northern Marianas voted to become a 'commonwealth in political union with the United States'. In 1982 and 1983 the other three island groups signed compacts of free association with the United States and their right to full self-government was returned. However, with respect to defence and security matters, the compact provides for the continuation of United States use of the Kwajalein Missile Range in the Marshall Islands and rights to military bases on Palau. For the period of 15 years in the case of the Federated States of Micronesia and the Marshall Islands, and 50 years in the case of Palau, these new governments undertake to refrain from actions which the Government of the United States regards as incompatible with its responsibility to defend the area. In the Northern Marianas the United States has been given 'complete responsibility for and authority with respect to matters relating to foreign affairs and defence.'[101]

A strong stimulus is given to the movement for political independence, as well as growing international support, by the abuses by the rich countries of the land and waters of the Pacific. Since 1946 over 250 atomic and hydrogen bombs have been detonated in the region. The numbers of military bases and nuclear tests are so great that it is little wonder that Pacific islanders believe themselves in a war zone. On Hawaii there are 110 military installations and 3,000 nuclear weapons; on Mururoa the French have exploded over 100 atomic devices; inter-continental ballistic missiles are launched from the United States mainland on to Kwajalein Atoll; on Guam one-third of the land area is covered with bases; on Palau one-third of the land area is destined for bases. In the Marianas Trench to the east of the islands the Japanese plan to dump 60 million gallons of radioactive waste per year from 1985. It is little wonder that Pacific islanders visiting the West to participate in the peace movement should claim that the nuclear war in their homeland has already begun.[102]

Since 1975 when the first conference was held in Fiji, the movement for a nuclear-free Pacific has grown. On Palau the movement has disturbed the uninterrupted militarism of the United States. In 1979 the new constitution of Palau, approved by 92 per cent of voters, specifically banned the storage, testing and disposal of nuclear materials on its territory, making it incompatible with the compact of free association. In view of the military facilities assured by the compact, Palauans are now against the terms of the agreement they negotiated with the United States.[103] On Guam the Organization of People for Indigenous Rights has also recently rejected the continued military occupation of their country and called for a plebiscite of the indigenous Chamorro people to determine the political future of the island. In 1984 the Bikini Islanders, who had been the victims of the first hydrogen bomb test in 1954, took the United States Government to court claiming up to $US 180 million to clean up. The case is still pending.

The people of the Pacific, like many of the colonized indigenous peoples of the rich countries with whom they feel affinities, are comparatively few and dispose of little political and economic power. However, their struggle for self-determination is gaining wider support and greater international recognition. Two decades ago the idea that a few thousand indigenous peoples could defy the governments of the rich nations with their military and economic might would have seemed unthinkable. But there have been enough small, and not so small, victories of indigenous peoples for their demands now to be taken with greater seriousness. As the indigenous movement confronts issues such as nuclear proliferation, the rapacious activities of transnational corporations, the destruction of the ecosystem, the ceaseless and careless exploitation of natural resources, it has found many non-indigenous people who share its goals. For the indigenous peoples of the rich nations more than any other, their future will depend upon the relationship they form with the non-indigenous majority with whom they must co-exist.

Notes

1. Cf. Australian Aboriginal Position Paper, 'Transnational Corporations and their effect on the resources and land of Indigenous People' presented at the International NGO Conference on Indigenous Peoples and the Land, Geneva, Switzerland, 15-18 September 1981.

2. United Nations Economic and Social Council, Commission on Human Rights, *Study of the Problem of Discrimination against Indigenous Populations*, report submitted by the Special Rapporteur José Martinez Cobo, chapter XVII, p.141. Henceforward referred to as the Cobo Report.

3. World Council of Indigenous Peoples, 'Transnational Corporations and their effect on the resources and land of Indigenous People' presented at the International NGO Conference, 15-18 September 1981.

4. George de Vos and William Wetherall, *Japan's Minorities*, Minority Rights Group Report no.3, 1983 edition.

5. On the Sami see: Nils-Aslak Valkeapää, *Greetings from Lappland: the Sami–Europe's forgotten people* (Zed Press, London, 1983); Mervyn Jones, *The Sami of Lapland*, Minority Rights Group Report no.55, 1982; Robert Paine, *Dam a river, damn a people?*, IWGIA Document no.45, 1982; and Lars Ande Baer, 'The Sami– an indigenous people in their own land', *The Sami National Minority in Sweden*, Rattsfonden (the Legal Rights Foundation), 1982.

6. *New Internationalist*, January 1982, pp.26-8.

7. Intervention by Lars Ande Baer, Nordic Sami Council, to the UN Working Group on Indigenous Populations, Second Session, Geneva, 10 August 1983.

8. On Inuit see: Ian Creery, *The Inuit (Eskimo) of Canada*, MRG Report no.60, 1983; Hugh Brody, 'Ecology, politics and change: the case of the Eskimo', *Development and Change*, vol.9, no.1, pp.21-4; and Eric Alden Smith, 'Inuit of the Canadian Eastern Arctic', *Cultural Survival Quarterly*, vol.8, no.3, Fall 1984, pp.32-7.

9. Meic Stephens, 'The Greenlanders', in Georgina Ashworth (ed.), *World Minorities in the Eighties* (Quartermaine, 1980).

10. See chapter 11; also Frances Svensson, 'Aboriginal Peoples of Siberia', Georgina Ashworth (ed.), *Minorities in the Eighties*, pp.1-5.

11. *IWGIA Newsletter*, no.38, July 1984, pp.26-32.

12. *IWGIA Newsletter*, no.37, May 1984, p.51.

13. According to 1981 census the Aboriginal population is 159,897 of whom about 40,000 are full-blooded. Aboriginal organizations believe this is an under-estimate and the true figure is nearer 300,000. The rate of increase of Aboriginals was 3.27 per cent in 1971-81 compared with 1.34 per cent for overall population. The Federal Government defines an Aboriginal or Torres Strait Islander as 'a person of Aboriginal or Islander descent who identifies as an Aboriginal or Islander and is accepted as such by the community with which he is associated'.

14. Department of Aboriginal Affairs, *Aboriginals in Australia today* (Australian Government Publishing Service, Canberra, 1982) p.9.

15. Jan Roberts, *Massacres to mining: the colonisation of Aboriginal Australia* (Dove Communications, Victoria, 1981) p.72.

16. *Asian Times*, 11 January 1984.

17. Roberts, pp.61-6.

18. Ibid., p.72.

19. Ibid., p.75; infant mortality rate among Aborigines is 2.6 times as high as that for the community generally. *The Advertiser* (Adelaide), 24 May 1985.

20. *New Internationalist*, February 1981, p.3.

21. *The Times*, 19 April 1983.

22. Roberts, pp.67-71 and *CARE Newsletter* (South Australia), no.57, March 1984, p.15.

23. *Daily Mirror*, 5 October 1981; cf. also 'Aboriginal Social Indicators, 1984', Department of Foreign Affairs, Government of Australia, 22 May 1985.

24. Roberts, p.62; see also Keith Suter and Kaye Stearman, *Aboriginal Australians*, MRG Report no.35, 1982 edition, p.6.

25. Roberts, pp.96-7.

26. David Leigh and Paul Lashmar, 'Britain's forgotten A-bomb victims', *Observer*, 3 April 1983.

27. *The Age* (Melbourne), 4 October 1984.

28. *Observer*, 12 August 1984.

29. World Council of Churches, *Land Rights for Indigenous Peoples*, Geneva, March 1983, pp.33-9 and *ARC Newsletter* (Boston), vol.4, no.4, December 1980.

30. *Indigenous Peoples Network Emergency Bulletin*, 26 August 1983.

31. *Financial Times*, 23 June 1981.

32. Roberts, pp.186-7.

33. *Survival International Urgent Action Bulletin*, 4 May 1983 and *Survival International Review*, no.43, 1984, pp.117-21.

34. Melbourne barrister Frank T. Brennan prepared a lengthy analysis dated 26 March 1982; see also *The National Times* (Sydney), 11-17 April 1982.

35. Statement by John Dawkins, Minister of Finance, to the UN Working Group on Indigenous Populations, Geneva, August 1983.

36. *New Internationalist*, December 1984, p.23.

37. Information from the Government of Australia to the UN Working Group on Indigenous Populations, Geneva, August 1984 (E/CN.4/Sub.2/AC.4/1984/2/Add.3, 25 July 1984).

38. *IWGIA Newsletter*, no.40, December 1984, pp.3-5.

39. *The Age*, 19 October 1984.

40. Ibid., 5 October 1984.

41. Cf. 'The Treaty of Waitangi', New Zealand Council of Churches, n.d.; see also the publications of the Waitangi Action Committee, address in appendix.

42. *IWGIA Newsletter*, nos.35 and 36, October and December 1983, p.133.

43. Minister of Justice, Henry Sewell, speaking to Parliament in 1870 cited in Betty Whaitiri Williams, *The passage of Maori land into Pakeha ownership: a Maori view* (Cabbage Tree Publications, Christchurch, New Zealand, n.d.) p.5.

44. Ibid., p.14.

45. Harold Wilkinson, 'The Maoris of New Zealand', in Georgina Ashworth (ed.), *World Minorities*, vol.1 (Quartermaine, 1977) p.111; cf. also Robert Macdonald, *The Maori of New Zealand*, Minority Rights Group Report no.70, 1985, p.4, suggests that by the year 2015 Maoris will comprise 30 per cent of the New Zealand population.

46. *New Internationalist*, July 1983, p.5.

47. Martin Maguire, 'Land of the long white cloud', *New Internationalist*, March 1985, p.28.

48. *IWGIA Newsletter*, nos.35 and 36, October and December 1983, p.135.

49. Betty Williams, 'Case study of Maori action against Conzinc Rio Tinto', paper presented to the *Global Meeting on Environment and Development*, 4-8 February 1985, Nairobi, Kenya.

50. James Wilson, *The original Americans: US Indians*, MRG Report no.31, 1976, p.5. The report provides a good introduction to the situation of Native Americans.

51. 'Urban Indians', testimony of Rosemary Ackley Christensen to the *Fourth Russell Tribunal on the Rights of the Indians of the Americas*, Rotterdam, 1980.

52. Roxanne Dunbar Ortiz, *Indians of the Americas* (Zed Press, London, 1984) p.141.

53. Wilson, p.21.

54. Ibid., p.6.

55. Ortiz, p.138.

56. *Akwesasne Notes*, Spring 1984, p.10.

57. Cf. *Akwesasne Notes*, various dates and especially Autumn 1979; Ismaelillo and Robin Wright (eds.), *Native Peoples in struggle* (ERIN Publications, New York, 1982) pp.95-106.

58. Joseph Jorgensen, 'The political economy of the Native American Energy Business', in Jorgensen (ed.), *Native Americans and Energy Development 11* (ARC and Seventh Generation Fund, 1984) p.10.

59. Lynn Robbins, 'Energy developments and the Navajo nation: an update', in Jorgensen (ed.), p.120. For the health hazards caused by uranium-mining on indigenous land see *Akwesasne Notes*, Spring 1984.

60. *Onaway*, Autumn–Winter, 1983, p.29 gives an example of one house which was built with uranium tailings and was radioactive.

61. Robbins, p.117.

62. Cf. Jorgensen, pp.17-20 and 26.

63. See for example the cases presented in Ismaelillo and Robin Wright, and Rex Weyler, *Blood on the land* (Everest House, 1982).

64. Wilson, p.23.

65. *Onaway*, no.30, Spring 1983, p.21.

66. Ibid., p.22.

67. Álys Swan, 'US: Wounded Knee – ten years on', *IWGIA Newsletter*, nos. 35 and 36, October and December 1983, pp.185-9.

68. Information from Dennis Banks Defence Committee, PO Box 881984, San Francisco, CA 94188.

69. E.g. the well-publicized case of Leonard Peltier; cf. *Akwesasne Notes*, Midwinter 1984, pp.14-17.

70. Cf. Discussion by Ward Churchill, 'The situation of Indigenous Populations in the United States', *Akwesasne Notes*, Winter 1985, pp.18-19.

71. Statement of the Canadian Observer Delegation to the Third Session of the UN Working Group on Indigenous Populations, Geneva, 30 July to 3 August 1984.

72. Statement to the International NGO Conference on Indigenous Peoples and the Land, Geneva, September 1981, by the Association of Metis and Non-Status Indians of Saskatchewan; see also James Wilson, *Canada's Indians*, MRG Report no.21, 1977 edition, p.6, which estimates that there are 260,000 Metis.

73. *Left out? The Indians and the Canadian Constitution*, Survival International Document VII, n.d.

74. Clem Chartier, 'Aboriginal rights and land issues: the Metis perspective', Metis National Council, April 1983.

75. Ibid.; see also statement by the Association of Metis and Non-Status Indians of Saskatchewan to International NGO Conference, September 1981.

76. World Council of Churches, *Land rights for Indigenous Peoples*, pp.47-52.

77. Ibid., p.48.

78. Michael Asch, 'Dene political rights', *Cultural Survival Quarterly*, vol.8, no.4, December 1984, p.37.

79. Philip Awashish cited in *Akwesasne Notes*, Late Spring 1982, p.21.

80. Statement by Innu Kanantuapatshet distributed at UN Commission on Human Rights, Geneva, February 1983.

81. *Declaration of the Coalition of First Nations on Sovereignty and Nationhood*, Alberta, Canada.

82. David Nuk, Innu of Sheshatshit, to Major Werner Huhn, Luftwaffe Detachment at Goose Bay, 9 May 1984, cited in 'Low level fighter bomber training over Ntesinan (Labrador) – the issues in the words of Innu people', document of the Naskapi Montagnais Innu Association, Labrador.

84. Letter to Rt. Hon. Brian Peckford, Premier of Newfoundland and Labrador, 1 March 1980, from Naskapi Montagnais Innu Association, from documents presented to the Fourth Russell Tribunal, Rotterdam, 1980.

84. *Guardian*, 10 October 1985.

85. For a brief introduction see 'The Pacific Islanders: an outline', in Ashworth (ed.), *World Minorities in the Eighties*, pp.100-6.

86. For a discussion of the situation of West Papua see chapter 8.

87. The breakdown is as follows:

West Papua	1m Melanesians
PNG	3m
Fiji	640,000 (44 per cent indigenous)
New Caledonia	140,000 (45 per cent indigenous)
Solomon Islands	240,000
Vanuatu	140,000

88. The total population of Micronesia is about 300,000 made up as follows:

Trust Territories	140,000
Guam	100,000 (less than 50 per cent indigenous)
Kiribati	56,000
Tuvalu	7,500

89. The breakdown is as follows:

French Polynesia	164,000 (Polynesian: 114,000; Chinese 30,000; European 20,000)
W. Samoa	32,000
E. Samoa	158,000
Tonga	98,000
Wallis and Futuna	8,500

90. Vanuatu with its Prime Minister Fr. Walter Lini has taken a leading role in the region in recent years. A member of the non-aligned movement, a friend of Cuba, the government has also refused port facilities to US Navy ships.

The literature on Papua New Guinea is massive. Of interest is the fact that PNG is the only country where a predominantly tribal/clan society has an independent government. PNG has about 10,000 tribes speaking some 700 distinct languages. For an analysis of the impact of capitalist agriculture on traditional food production systems see Kenneth Good, *Papua New Guinea: a false economy* (Anti-Slavery Society, 1986).

91. On the growing Melanesian movement see Robin Osborne, 'The island peoples begin to make waves', *Guardian*, 1 February 1985.

92. World Council of Churches, *New Caledonia: towards Kanak independence*, report of the ecumenical visit, 1984, p.19; see also August Siapo, 'New Caledonia: a Kanak view', *IWGIA Newsletter*, no.41, March, 1985, pp.83-105.

93. Letter of PM Messmer to J.F. Deniau, Secretary of State for the Overseas Territories, 19 July 1972, cited in *Bulletin Amérique Indienne*, March/April 1985, nos.49-50, p.28.

94. World Council of Churches, *New Caledonia*, p.14.

95. Cf. Philippe Leymarie, 'Les enjeux stratégiques de la crise néo-calédonienne', *Le Monde Diplomatique*, March 1985, p.13.

96. Cf. Michel Capron and Jean Chesneaux, 'Objectifs communs et grande diversité des mouvements indépendantistes', *Le Monde Diplomatique*, August 1985, pp.2-3 and Thierry Michalon, 'Mayotte et les Comores', *Le Monde Diplomatique*, December 1984, pp.10-11.

97. *Guardian*, 10 October 1985.

98. Alan Rusbridger, 'Palms in French hands', *Guardian*, 14 October 1985.

99. Ibid.

100. Ibid.

101. Article I, Section 104 of the *Covenant to establish a Commonwealth of the Northern Mariana Islands in Political Union with the United States*, p.3; see also Office for Micronesian Status Negotiations, 'The political status negotiations for the trust territory of the Pacific Islands and the compact of free association', November 1984.

102. The economies of the islands are now heavily dependent on imports from the US and the cultures are much demoralized by foreign mass media; there is high

unemployment and high rates of suicide. See, for example, Harold Jackson, 'Victims of the nuclear colonists', *Guardian*, 30 June 1984; also Jane Dibblin, 'Paddling in the nuclear pool', *New Statesman*, 1 March 1985, pp.18-19.

103. Roger Clark and Sue Rabbitt Roff, *Micronesia: the problem of Palau*, MRG Report no.63, 1984; Catherine Lutz (ed.), *Micronesia as strategic colony: The impact of US policy on Micronesian health and culture*, Cultural Survival Occasional Document 12, June 1984.

11. Indigenous Minorities in Socialist Countries

The previous chapters have examined the situations of indigenous peoples in capitalist countries and in countries within the capitalist sphere of influence. In many of those countries the original inhabitants are being removed from their traditional territories to make way for national development projects. The response of indigenous peoples in the face of these incursions has been to organize to uphold their distinctive culture and to maintain their land base. However, in defending their rights to land and their own culture, indigenous peoples in capitalist countries come up against powerful vested interests. Economic development on indigenous land is usually nationally conceived and sponsored and, therefore, has the full authority of the state behind it; more often than not, multinational banks and transnational corporations are involved in investment, extraction and marketing aspects of resource exploitation on indigenous and tribal lands. Furthermore, capitalist notions of private property and ownership of land are in direct contrast to those of indigenous peoples. Much of this book has focused on the ways in which this materialistic culture impinges upon the relatively self-sufficient, self-reliant and self-sustaining economies of indigenous minorities. But, do socialist regimes show greater respect for the lives and cultures of indigenous peoples within their territories? Or must indigenous ways of life be subordinated to the grander objectives of socialism, just as indigenous peoples in capitalist countries must succumb to the might of Mammon?

There are probably nearly 100 million indigenous peoples in the socialist countries, with China alone accounting for 67 million.[1] Yet our knowledge of the conditions of the indigenous peoples in these countries is limited. China has only recently permitted foreign researchers and scholars to work in the country and relatively few have had access to the main concentrations of the national minorities and the USSR has for a long time restricted independent studies of its nationalities. It is only in Nicaragua – whose revolution is anti-imperialist rather than socialist – that outside observers have managed to examine and record the situation of indigenous peoples but even here they are generally divided into two antagonistic camps: those who support the Sandinista government and those who do not.

These peoples, as has been indicated in chapter 2 and elsewhere, are often difficult to define and quantify and in the case of the socialist countries their identity is open to dispute. As one writer has noted, indigenous societies

> may differ from the larger society ethnically and culturally, in their social and political organization, and in their type of land-use. Often several of these characteristics overlap, providing a distinctive identity to the marginal society and a series of focus points for conflict with the larger society. But these different categories rarely if ever cover an identical range of people, and so we cannot refer unequivocally to specific ethnic or cultural identities, or to specific forms of land-use.[2]

This is particularly so in the USSR and China where national minorities are defined and their rights protected, but where the small-scale traditional modes of production, which are the characteristic of most indigenous peoples, are deemed primitive and inappropriate.

This chapter examines the situation of the indigenous peoples of Nicaragua and China, with some brief comments on those peoples still living in a traditional way in the Soviet Union and Mongolia. What has been the experience of these countries' indigenous peoples under socialism and how well have they retained their language, culture, land base and political independence? Are indigenous peoples resisting Russian, Han Chinese or Mestizo Nicaraguan domination and assimilation into the mainstream of the socialist society?

In theory, the socialist regimes offer the most enlightened policies towards minority peoples. Marx argued that the nation and nationalism were constructs of the bourgeoisie to allow them to divide the proletariat of different countries. Lenin maintained the right of nations to self-determination and the present constitution describes the USSR as a 'unitary federal multinational state, formed as a result of the free self-determination of nations and the voluntary union of equal Soviet Socialist Republics'.[3] The constitution declares that 'each Union Republic shall retain the right freely to secede from the USSR'.[4] Both Marx and Lenin believed that the triumph of the proletariat and the creation of Communism would make possible the abolition of oppression of one nation by another. 'The aim of socialism', Lenin wrote, 'is not only to end divisions of mankind into tiny states and the isolation of nations in any form, it is not only to bring the nations closer together, but to integrate them.'[5] Stalin argued for caution and sensitivity in dealing with the non-Russian peoples and advocated the return of minority lands.[6] But, although Soviet leaders have expressed support for the self-determination of peoples, they have in practice regarded any secessionist moves as counter-revolutionary. In Georgia, for example, an insurrection by an independence movement in 1924 was crushed, and today the strongly nationalist sentiments expressed through contemporary literature are discouraged and censored.[7] In other areas the USSR has pursued a policy of Russification and integration of indigenous and tribal minorities into the national socialist programme.

Behind the curtain

In the USSR the Russian peoples constitute a little over 50 per cent of the total population. The rest are made up of European nationalities, such as the Ukrainians, Georgians, Lithuanians and Latvians, and the Asian nationalities east of the Urals, such as the Uzbeks, Kazakhs and Tadzhiks. There is no easy means of measuring the numbers of indigenous peoples in the USSR. In the frozen tundra of the Arctic and forested taiga there are over one million native peoples belonging to more than 25 groups.[8] These peoples are traditionally pastoralists, trappers and fishermen. In the deserts along the southern frontier from the Caspian Sea to Mongolia live mainly Muslim Turkic peoples, some of whom are nomadic pastoralists. There are in the region of six million Kazakhs living on the frontier with China and about 22 million Turkic peoples inhabit the four Central Asian republics.[9]

The revolutionary government inherited a vast empire which had been extended by the Czars eastwards and deep into Central Asia during the 19th Century. The lands colonized were economically exploited and the indigenous peoples subjected to Russian domination. Russians settled in great numbers – some two million in Central Asia – occupied the best lands and displaced the indigenous inhabitants, particularly the nomadic pastoralists in Kazakhstan and Kirghizia. When the revolution broke, nationalists in these subjugated colonies joined forces with the Bolsheviks against their common enemy. Some quarter of a million Muslim Turkic troops fought with the Red Army during the civil war.[10] The Aboriginal peoples of Siberia had been incorporated into the Russian state by the 18th Century and their culture had been steadily eroded by imported disease and alcohol.[11] The Bolsheviks early on provided the indigenous inhabitants, and especially the largest group, the Yakuts, with autonomous districts. These peoples also benefited from improvements in education, health and welfare facilities.[12]

Table 11.1
National minorities in Communist countries

Country	Numbers	% of Pop.
China	67 million (55 minorities)	7
USSR	1 million northern peoples 6 million Kazakhs 22 million Turkic	10
Total	96 million	

The nationalities within the USSR have experienced substantial changes for the better in their social and economic conditions. Most of the indigenous areas had virtually no industrial development and low standards of living before the revolution. Since then progress has been marked and a United Nations

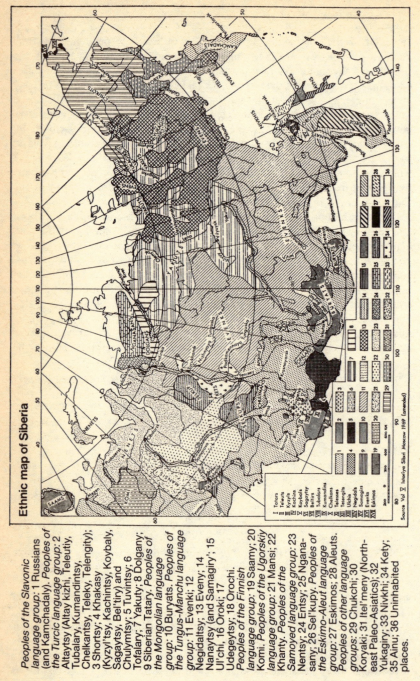

Ethnic map of Siberia

Peoples of the Slavonic language group: 1 Russians (and Kamchadaly). *Peoples of the Turcic language group:* 2 Altaytsy (Altay kizhi, Teleuty, Tubalary, Kumandintsy, Chelkantsy, Teleky, Telengity); 3 Shortsy; 4 Khakasy (Kyzyl'tsy, Kachintsy, Koybaly, Sagaytsy, Bel'tiry) and Chulymtsy; 5 Tuvintsy; 6 Tofalary; 7 Yakuty; 8 Dolgany; 9 Siberian Tatary. *Peoples of the Mongolian language group:* 10 Buryats. *Peoples of the Tungus-Manchu language group:* 11 Evenki; 12 Negidaltsy; 13 Eveny; 14 Nanaytsy (and Samagiry); 15 Ul'chi, 16 Oroki; 17 Udegeytsy; 18 Orochi. *Peoples of the Finnish language group:* 19 Saamy; 20 Komi. *Peoples of the Ugorskiy language group:* 21 Mansi; 22 Khanty. *Peoples of the Samoyed language group:* 23 Nentsy; 24 Entsy; 25 Ngana-sany; 26 Sel'kupy. *Peoples of the Eskimo-Aleut language group:* 27 Eskimos; 28 Aleuts. *Peoples of other language groups:* 29 Chukchi; 30 Koryaki; 31 Itel'meny (North-east Paleo-Asiatics); 32 Yukagiry; 33 Nivkhi; 34 Kety; 35 Ainu; 36 Uninhabited places.

Source: Violet Connolly, *Siberia: today and tomorrow*, Collins, London & Glasgow, 1975, pp. 184–5.

Economic Commision for Europe report from the 1960s declared that the living standards in Central Asia were on 'much higher levels than those of the neighbouring Asian countries, and that they have improved very considerably in the three decades since the end of the Civil War.'[13]

It should be recognized, however, that the Soviet Union measures development in terms of social and economic indicators, such as doctors per head of population and levels of literacy. For Marxists historical development is marked by a progression from pre-capitalist or traditional primitive society to Communism. In its dealings with nomadic pastoralists in the south and trappers and herders in the north, the Soviet regime sought to impose collectivization and bypass what it perceived as the intermediary stage of capitalism. But collectivization brought stock losses in many places, and the disruptions of traditional resource and herd management caused resentment and at times resistance.

In northern Siberia, for example, nomadic reindeer-herding peoples, such as the Chukchi and Eskimo, often preferred to slaughter their animals than have them collectivized.[14] Between 1929 and 1933 the numbers of domesticated reindeer in the country fell by nearly one-third as a consequence of the rigid programme of the government.[15]

The north – the region composed of the coniferous forests of the taiga and the treeless tundra – has experienced a rapid growth of Russian settlement since 1917. Whereas at the turn of the century only some 40,000 to 50,000 Russians were settled in the north, by the 1960s their numbers had risen to nearly two million. In 1926 there had been about 100,000 Russians and 360,000 northern peoples, but by 1959 the Russian population had reached 1.6 million. From a minority in 1926 amounting to less than one-third of the native population, the Russians had become by 1959 a majority more than four times greater than the indigenous inhabitants.[16]

Accompanying the human invasion was a programme of economic exploitation of the north which accelerated rapidly after the Second World War. Nickel, tin, copper and coal mines and aluminium and other processing plants have been opened up in the Siberian landmass. The area is estimated to possess nine-tenths of the Union's coal reserves, two-thirds of its iron ores, four-fifths of its timber, huge oil and natural gas deposits, and substantial quantities of gold and even diamonds.[17] Since the 1950s Siberia and the Soviet Far East have become the main source of vital raw materials for the USSR.

The native peoples have been affected by these changes. There has been a rise in the number of native peoples of the north who consider their own language less important than Russian and a large majority now speak Russian as well as their native language. The successful literacy programmes and education, health and welfare provisions have inevitably led to assimilation of native peoples into the mainstream of Russian society. The landscape and environment are being irrevocably altered by economic development: the Arctic town of Noril'sk – the Republic's main nickel-mining centre – saw its population increase ten times between 1940 and 1970; small fishing villages of 50 years ago have expanded to major towns with port installations to cope with factory fishing boats and transport vessels for locally extracted minerals. A network of railways has spread over Siberia and the Soviet Far East and the rivers have been harnessed for commercial transport.

Furthermore, just as defence considerations have led NATO countries to militarize their northern flanks, so the USSR has developed its own radar defence systems and established military airfields and rocket-launching sites in the north. Nuclear weapons testing is carried out in these comparatively underpopulated regions – Eastern Siberia and the Soviet Far East make up half the land territory of the USSR but contain only ten per cent of the country's population – and put certain areas, such as the island of Novaya Zemlya out of bounds to the native population. The effects of militarization on the nomadic native population of the USSR can only be guessed at, although the impact of Distant Early Warning systems (DEWs) in northern Canada or the test flights of supersonic aeroplanes in Labrador on the indigenous inhabitants is well documented. (A discussion of NATO flights over Innu land in Labrador, for example, is contained in chapter 10.) It is probably reasonable to assume that the native peoples of the USSR have also been removed from their lands in the name of national security.

Mongolia

In mitigation, socialist policy is directed towards ensuring a reasonable standard of living and economic base for its indigenous inhabitants. In the Mongolian People's Republic, for example, the nomadic pastoralists enjoy one of the highest standards of living in Asia.[18] Mongolia has been an independent socialist republic since 1921 and is within the Soviet sphere of influence. It is a country with a land surface some six times greater than the United Kingdom and a population of 1.6 million, of which three-quarters live outside the capital, Ulan Batar, mainly as pastoralists. At the end of the 1950s the herders were collectivized into over 300 large cooperatives (*negdels*) and state farms. However, many pastoralists continue to lead nomadic and semi-nomadic lives and the products and by-products of animal husbandry accounted for nearly 80 per cent of exports in 1976. The rationalization of the pastoral system has eliminated the gross disparities in living standards which existed prior to the revolution. In the 1890s in one area, for example, feudal lords held an average of 230 animals each, while the state and personal serfs possessed only 3.[19] However, the Mongolian economy is increasingly becoming industrialized and in 1978 a joint Mongolian and Soviet copper and molybdenum mine was opened and is one of the largest enterprises in the country. Nevertheless, pastoralism and the way of life of the herders remain central to the social and economic organization of Mongolia and are unlikely to disappear in the foreseeable future.

National minorities in China

There are 55 national minorities in China accounting for about 67 million people or nearly seven per cent of the total population of the country.[20] Nevertheless, they inhabit half of China's land area of 9.6m square kilometres and are spread out along the inland frontiers to the north, west and south. The largest of these peoples is the Zhuang with a population of ten million and there are 12 other nationalities with a population of over one million, including the Hui (6.4 million), the Miao (3.9 million), the Tibetans (3.4 million) and the Uygar (5.4 million).[21] Some indigenous peoples are extremely few in number by comparison, such as the Hezhe with a population of 800. Patterns of population distribution among the minorities are complex and although certain areas may have concentrations of one people, they will also have smaller communities of other nationalities. Thus, in Xinjiang there are 3.9 million Uygars out of a total population of 6.5 million made up of 13 other nationalities.

Size is not the only difference existing among these indigenous peoples. To the north and west, in the regions of Inner Mongolia, Xinjiang and Tibet, the peoples are traditionally animal breeders and nomadic pastoralists; to the south the hill peoples are involved in swidden cultivation and sometimes hunting and gathering.

The minority peoples speak different languages belonging to two main language families: in Tibet and the southern provinces one of the Sino-Tibetan languages and in the northern regions of Inner Mongolia and Xinjiang one of the Ural-Altaic languages. But the language spoken by a national minority may also contain several vernaculars which are mutually unintelligible. This is particularly the case where peoples have lived in dispersed and isolated communities. These peoples use different alphabets – Latin, Arabic, Tibetan or other – and before 1949 and the establishment of the People's Republic of China only 20 of the 50 plus languages had any written form.[22] The minorities have different religious beliefs including Buddhism (Lamaism) among the Tibetans and Mongolians, Islam among the Huis, Uygars and Kazakhs of the north, and animism among the hill tribes of the south. Christianity has also penetrated a number of indigenous communities.

Certain of China's nationalities have a long and resplendent past and have not always been minorities within a unified China. The Manchus and the Mongols both had long dynasties and the Mongol Empire in the 13th Century was one of the most extensive the world has known, stretching across most of Asia, including China, to Western Europe.[23] During the 7th Century the Tibetan Empire reached Turkistan (present-day Xinjiang) in the north and stretched eastwards into China.[24]

The national minorities and the lands they inhabit are of great strategic interest to the majority Han of the People's Republic of China. The minority areas are comparatively underpopulated and contain important mineral resources and the bulk of China's forest reserves. Furthermore, many indigenous minorities live across frontiers. The Shan, for example, are also

Table 11.2
The distribution and population of minority nationalities in China

Nationality	Population	Area
Achang	20,000	Yunnan
Bai	1.13 million	Yunnan
Baoan	9,000	Gansu
Benglong	10,000	Yunnan
Bouyei	2.12 million	Guizhou
Bulang	58,000	Yunnan
Dai	839,000	Yunnan
Daur	94,000	Inner Mongolia, Heilongjiang, Xinjiang
Dong	1.42 million	Guizhou, Hunan, Guangxi
Dongxiang	279,000	Gansu, Xinjiang
Dulong	4,000	Yunnan
Ewenki	19,000	Inner Mongolia, Heilongjiang
Gaoshan	1,000	Taiwan, Fujian
Gelao	53,000	Guizhou, Guangxi, Sichuan, Hunan
Hani	1.05 million	Yunnan
Hezhe	1,400	Heilongjiang
Hui	7.21 million	Ningxia, Gansu, etc.
Jing	10,000	Guangxi
Jingpo	93,000	Yunnan
Jinuo	10,000	Yunnan
Kazak	907,000	Xinjiang, Gansu, Qinghai
Kirghiz	113,000	Xinjiang, Heilongjiang
Korean	1.76 million	Jilin, Heilongjiang, Inner Mongolia
Lahu	300,000	Yunnan
Li	810,000	Guangdong
Lisu	480,000	Yunnan, Sichuan
Luoba	2,000	Tibet
Manchu	4.29 million	Liaoning, Jilin, Heilongjiang, Hebei, Beijing, Inner Mongolia
Maonan	38,000	Guangxi
Menba	6,000	Tibet
Miao	5.03 million	Guizhou, Yunnan, Hunan, etc.
Mongolian	3.41 million	Inner Mongolia, Xinjiang, Liaoning, etc.
Mulao	90,000	Guangxi
Naxi	240,000	Yunnan, Sichuan
Nu	23,000	Yunnan
Oroqen	4,000	Inner Mongolia, Heilongjiang
Pumi	24,000	Yunnan
Qiang	102,000	Sichuan
Russian	2,900	Xinjiang
Sala	69,000	Qinghai, Gansu

Table 11.2 (continued)

Nationality	Population	Area
She	360,000	Fujian, Zhejiang, Jiangxi, Guangdong
Shui	280,000	Guizhou, Guangxi
Tajik	26,000	Xinjiang
Tartar	4,000	Xinjiang
Tibetan	3.87 million	Tibet, Qinghai, Sichuan, Gansu, Yunnan
Tu	150,000	Qinghai, Gansu
Tujia	2.83 million	Hunan, Hubei, Sichuan
Uygur	5.95 million	Xinjiang
Uzbek	12,000	Xinjiang
Wa	290,000	Yunnan
Xibo	83,000	Xinjiang, Liaoning, Jilin
Yao	1.4 million	Guangxi, Hunan, Yunnan, Guangdong, Guizhou
Yi	5.45 million	Sichuan, Yunnan, Guizhou, Guangxi
Yugur	10,000	Gansu
Zhuang	13.37 million	Guangxi, Yunnan, Guangdong, Guizhou

Note: Figures in this table are from statistics reported by the Third National Census, released on 27 October 1982 by the State Statistics Bureau. The population of the Tibet Autonomous Region was calculated according to the figures from areas where the census was carried out. The standard time of the census was zero hour on 1 July 1982.

Source: China's Minority Nationalities, *China Reconstructs*, Beijing, 1984, pp.268-70.

settled in Thailand and Burma and Mongols in the USSR and the Mongolian People's Republic.[25] They have been mobilized in the past against the majority Han peoples, and the present-day regime places importance on their political loyalty.

Prior to the Chinese Revolution, the treatment and conditions of the national minorities were varied. Many peoples were able to remain relatively unaffected by the wider military and political struggles taking place in what was called 'the country of the middle'.[26] According to Chinese sources about four million minority peoples were serfs and one million slaves and at least six million living a precarious existence by slash-and-burn agriculture and hunting-and-gathering.[27] In Tibet about 300 families, only five per cent of the population, owned all the land, forests and most of the livestock, and the peoples were subject to the will of these manorial nobles and lamas.[28] Among the Yi people who live in present-day Yunnan and Sichuan provinces, there were four distinct classes, three of which were types of slave. The hereditary slave-owners or Black Yi were served by *chunuo, achia* and *kahsi*, three ranks of slave with different privileges. Slaves accounted for 93 per cent of the population.[29]

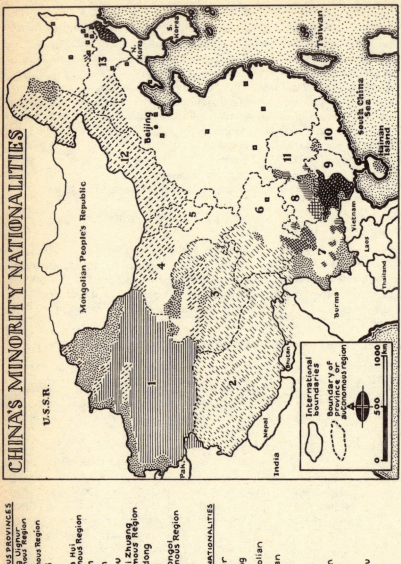

CHINA'S MINORITY NATIONALITIES

AUTONOMOUS PROVINCES

1 Xinjiang Uighur Autonomous Region
2 Tibet Autonomous Region
3 Qinghai
4 Gansu
5 Ningxia Hui Autonomous Region
6 Sichuan
7 Yunnan
8 Guizhou
9 Guangxi Zhuang Autonomous Region
10 Guangdong
11 Hunan
12 Nei Mongol Autonomous Region
13 Jilin

MINORITY NATIONALITIES

Uighur
Chuang
Mongolian
Tibetan
Yi
Miao
Korean
Puyi
Manchu
Other

During the long struggle for power the Chinese Communist Party changed its policy towards the minority peoples. After the founding of the party in 1922, Inner Mongolia, Tibet and Turkistan (subsequently renamed Xinjiang) were accorded autonomous status and in 1930 these three regions were declared to have the right to secede or federate – a right guaranteed the national minorities in the constitution of the USSR. But, as the Communists came closer to power, their attitudes towards the minorities were modified. The principle of self-determination became subordinated to the overriding objective of building a socialist society throughout China.[30] The status of the national minorities was eventually set forth in the Common Programme (1949), the Constitution (1954) and the General Programme for the Implementation of Regional Autonomy for Nationalities in the People's Republic of China (1952). The Common Programme states that:

> All nationalities within the boundaries of the People's Republic of China are equal. They shall establish unity and mutual aid among themselves, and shall oppose imperialism and their own public enemies, so that the People's Republic of China will become a big fraternal and cooperative family composed of all nationalities. Greater nationalism and chauvinism shall be opposed. Acts involving discrimination, oppression, and splitting of the unity of the various nationalities shall be prohibited.
>
> Regional autonomy shall be exercised in areas where national minorities are concentrated and various kinds of autonomous organizations of the different nationalities shall be set up according to the size of the respective populations and regions. In places where different nationalities live together and in the autonomous areas of the national minorities, the different nationalities shall each have an appropriate number of representatives in the local organs of political power.[31]

Institutions of self-government were created at the regional, prefecture and county levels and today there are five autonomous regions – Inner Mongolia, Xinjiang Uygur, Guangxi Zhuang, Ningxia Hui, and Tibet – 30 autonomous prefectures and 72 autonomous counties.

The minority nationalities are guaranteed 150 seats in the National People's Congress, more than twice the number to which they would be entitled on a proportional basis. The Common Programme also makes provision for the protection of indigenous languages, customs, traditions and beliefs.[32] Indeed, early on, Communist cadres were sent into minority areas to help develop a written form for those peoples with only a spoken language.

In pursuing a policy of equality for all nationalities, the People's Republic of China can point to concrete achievements. Food production and living standards have risen in many indigenous communities and the infrastructure – roads, transport, health and educational facilities – has been much improved. In the Yao area, for example, hospital personnel has trebled, the number of schools more than doubled and incomes raised by a factor of three in the 20 years from 1957 to 1977.[33] In Tibet prior to the revolution there was only one hospital for the entire population, but in 1977 there were 7,300 hospital staff, barefoot doctors and midwives.[34]

But if there have been considerable material benefits for the Chinese national minorities, they have been achieved at certain costs. The Chinese Communists maintain that their aim is to eliminate socio-economic differences between peoples, but not destroy the diverse ethnic characteristics.[35] Yet, in practice, the minorities have been persuaded and sometimes forced to change their way of life to suit the interests of the nation and those of the Han majority. During the Great Leap Forward (1956-58) to achieve unity, the Chinese Communist Party began to see certain minority customs as decadent and as an impediment to progress. By this time the party already had developed cadres among the national minorities and increased membership and it felt confident that it could accelerate the rate of change. The ritual slaughter of animals, for example, so important to certain minorities, was discouraged. In Tibet the elaborate headdresses worn by women were thought to prevent efficient work and the cloth was used for other purposes.[36] Among the Naxi these social developments had an impact on women which was retrogressive and permanent. The Naxi inhabit Yunnan province and are traditionally a matrilineal society. Property is passed down through the female side, and heads of household, with a responsibility for planning of farm work, managing expenditure and entertaining guests, were always women; usually, too, the village leaders and arbitrators were women. Both men and women could marry more than once. But, as these communities conformed to the Han model, the privileged position of the women rapidly declined. As monogamy became the norm, the matrilineal household disintegrated and with the introduction of new, paid employment in workshops and in trade, men gained control of income and won greater prestige. Most minority peoples saw the reforms instituted during the Great Leap Forward as assimilative and reacted strongly against them.[37] The Chinese Communist Party for its part modified its policies towards the minorities until a renewed ideologial assault on indigenous culture took place with the Cultural Revolution.

The Cultural Revolution (1966-69), like the Great Leap Forward, was a period in which minority rights to self-determination were denied. Radicals called for the special privileges of minorities to be abolished.[38] In Inner Mongolia the old leadership, including Mongols as well as Han Chinese, was purged and the use of the language curtailed in all urban areas. In Xinjiang clashes between the new radical cadres and the minorities occurred sporadically and during 1967 and 1968 there was an uprising by Uygur nationalists.[39] The Red Guards made a particular attack on the Muslim religion. In Tibet further systematic attacks on temples and Buddhist culture were perpetrated by the Red Guards, and Tibetans responded with guerrilla reprisals or by flight to neighbouring India and Nepal. Following the inflexible years of the Cultural Revolution, the Government of China has pursued a more moderate policy towards the minority nationalities. The aims of the Cultural Revolution, as one author has claimed, were partially achieved:

Minority rights were reduced, their economies brought further into line with that of Han China, and the ethnic cohesiveness of their areas further diluted . . . But the essential differences between radicals and moderates were not on end goals but on timing.[40]

Current policy towards the national minorities in China is characterized by a more liberal appearance. The new Chinese constitution of 1982 has enhanced the rights of the minorities. In the past minority peoples were excluded from power or given important sounding nominal positions while authority lay with the Beijing-appointed members of the Chinese Communist Party. However, in Xinjiang, for example, 68 per cent of key posts are now occupied by natives of the region, compared to 20 per cent prior to 1982, although the power behind the throne remains consistently Chinese.[41] The new constitution also provides for greater education of the minorities, higher investment in national minority areas and further guarantees of cultural freedom, including the right to religion and language. These latter rights have been largely negated in Buddhist Tibet and Muslim Xinjiang in the past. However, for a minority these liberalizing measures neither compensate for the suffering endured at the hands of the Chinese since 1949, nor the occupation of their homelands and the denial of political independence.

The Turkic peoples inhabit a region which currently comprises five republics of the USSR, and the Chinese autonomous region of Xinjiang.[42] The whole area is called by its people Turkistan. Eastern Turkistan had been occupied sporadically by the Chinese but was annexed permanently by the Manchu in 1876. The Turkic peoples are not Han Chinese. They speak a different language, have their own religion and possess a distinctive way of life. Since 1759 they have revolted 42 times in order to achieve independence from Chinese rule.[43] Indeed, the right to self-determination and full independence of the Turkic, Mongolian and Tibetan peoples was recognized by the Chinese Communist Party at its Sixth Congress in 1945. Following the revolution in 1949, however, Eastern Turkistan was earmarked for assimilation. The script was abolished and 370,000 books in Arabic were destroyed.[44] All mosques were closed and the Koran outlawed. Resistance to political and cultural suppression, brought further reprisals from the Chinese and, according to one account, 360,000 Turkic Muslims were executed and over 500,000 have been sent to labour camps since 1949.[45]

The government has also actively pursued a policy of assimilation through large-scale settlement of Han Chinese. Before 1949 there were only 200,000 Han living in Eastern Turkistan, but by 1982 there were over five million, so that now the Han Chinese are the largest ethnic group living in Xinjiang. The region is rich in mineral reserves, especially uranium, coal and petroleum and is a producer of meat, rice and cereal crops. The exploitation of the major mineral resources is controlled by the central government in Beijing and local government has virtually no means of influencing policy. Furthermore, Turkic peoples complain that they are excluded from white collar and other responsible jobs and preference given to Han Chinese. At one textile plant near Urumchi, for example, only ten per cent of employees are Turkic Muslims, the rest are Chinese. Whereas unemployment among Chinese in the region is almost unknown, there are many young Turkic peoples without work.[46]

Tibet, like Turkistan, has suffered at the hands of the Chinese. Until the revolution of 1949, Tibet had enjoyed a history of isolation and independence, occasionally interrupted by the occupations of interested foreign powers. In the 13th Century it fell under Mongol rule and in the 17th Century under the Manchu Dynasty. But Tibet's inaccessibility made such control tenuous and authority lay with the Dalai Lama and the monks.

> Over the centuries Tibetan national identity became indistinguishable from religious identity and every part of Tibetan society, from the highest to the lowest, was saturated by Buddhist folklore and teachings and Buddhism regulated their lives, their festivals and holidays, their work and their family activities.[47]

In 1950 the People's Republic of China declared that Tibet was part of China. An invading force routed the Tibetan Army and imposed Chinese rule. Almost at once the Chinese began to dismantle what it deemed to be the feudal social relations that existed and inevitably this meant the systematic destruction of Buddhist culture. From 1952 until 1959 a series of Tibetan rebellions against Chinese policies took place and more fighting broke out as Red Guards tried to accelerate the establishment of communes in the late 1960s. In 1959 the spiritual leader of Tibet, the Dalai Lama, fled to India followed by thousands of fellow Tibetans. A report by the International Commission of Jurists in the same year charged the Chinese regime with numerous human rights violations, including genocide against the Tibetan people.[48] Buddhist organizations maintain that the destruction of life in Tibet is almost unparalleled in recent times and as many as one million may have perished in the 30 years since 1950.[49]

By their own admission, the Chinese made many serious mistakes in their handling of policy in Tibet. The zealous persecution of Buddhist culture is now regretted and the rigid economic doctrine of communes and collectivization acknowledged as misconceived and insensitively executed.[50] A successful indigenous agricultural system was destroyed to fit in with national economic requirements. Grain-growing was stressed to the detriment of stock-rearing and the Tibetan food staple, chingko or hill barley, was replaced by wheat. The result was an ecological disaster which caused Tibet's first famine in modern times.[51] Huge areas of forest were cut down, grasslands were ploughed up and pasture was overgrazed. Only now are Tibetan farmers beginning to re-establish some of the successful agricultural practices of the past. The Chinese Government for its part has abolished compulsory grain procurement and allowed greater freedom to producers to market their crops.

However, poverty persists in Tibet. A journalist visiting in 1985 commented:

> It is true that per capita income has increased 50 per cent to farmers earning Rmb 317 between 1983 and 1984. Tibet can also boast its share of farmers earning Rmb 10,000 per year. However, those figures obscure the stark poverty in which most Tibetans, particularly those outside the cash economy, still live. Even in Lhasa, living conditions – in particular hygiene and basic sanitation – are appalling. Health care delivery is poor and the literacy rate embarrassingly

low. Beggars, young and old, roam freely in the market place and some are permanent fixtures in popular eating houses.[52]

Despite widespread industrialization elsewhere in China, few factories have been built in Tibet. By 1982 some $US 3 billion worth of subsidies had been poured into Tibet. Yet one-third of the workforce of the regional capital, Lhasa, is employed in the services sector, many of these catering to the 40,000 or so tourists visiting annually.[53]

Any assessment of China's policy towards its national minorities must be a qualified one. Only comparatively recently have outsiders been allowed into minority areas, and even today comprehensive and independent studies are rare. What may be stated is that within China's borders, there are peoples with distinct cultural and historical experiences from the majority population and they have a right to self-determination under international law. The Turkic peoples of Xinjiang and the Tibetans are two such examples and their subjugation has been prolonged and violent. If today they, and several other indigenous peoples, possess some degree of self-government, it does not extend to vital aspects of political life nor to control over the natural wealth of the autonomous region. Nevertheless, few of China's critics would deny that there has been substantial material advancement for many peoples whose standard of living was extremely low before the revolution. Furthermore, since the cultural revolution the rigid political and economic policies have been replaced by a more liberal regime in which the indigenous minorities play a much greater role in their own affairs. Notwithstanding these improvements, Chinese policy towards the minorities remains eventual assimilation through education and Han settlement of indigenous homelands.

The Miskitos of Nicaragua

Thirty years after the victory of the Communist Party in China, Nicaragua experienced a national revolution. On 19 July 1979 the Frente Sandinista de Liberación Nacional (FSLN) marched into the capital, Managua, and President Anastasio Somoza, whose family had ruled for 43 years, fled the country. The triumph of the Sandinistas ended a dictatorship which had brought great misery for the majority of the population.

The revolution has already wrought unprecedented changes in the conditions of life of Nicaraguans. Infant mortality has been cut by one-third of the pre-1979 level, the illiteracy rate which was 50 per cent in 1978 had been reduced to 12 per cent by 1982 and the gross disparities in land ownership – in 1978 just one per cent of landholders owned half the country's land – have been eliminated by agrarian reform.[54] The Sandinista government still faces great political and economic difficulties. The government of the United States of America has been persistently hostile to the Nicaraguan regime, fearing that the revolution will spread to other countries in Central America and thereby weaken North American influence in the region. Since the Sandinistas came to

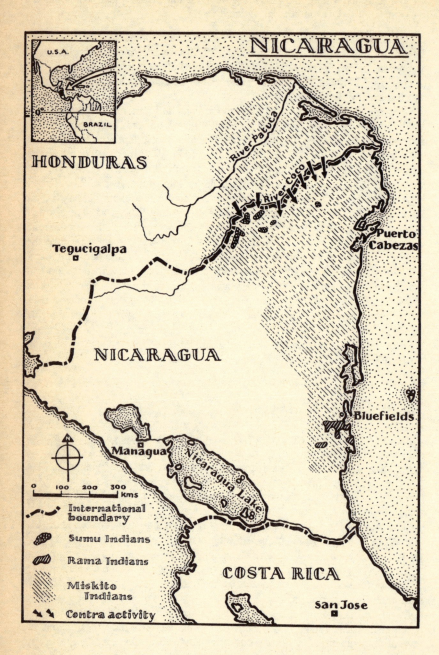

power the United States has supported the activities of the counter-revolutionary forces or contras who are operating along the Honduran border with Nicaragua. In these acts of military aggression, the United States and the contras have identified the small indigenous population of Miskitos, living along the Atlantic Coast, as the Achilles heel of the revolutionary government.

There are approximately 75,000 Miskito, 5,000 Sumu and 570 Rama Indians in Nicaragua, and together they constitute about three per cent of the country's population of 2.5 million. The indigenous peoples are concentrated in the departments of Zelaya and Rio San Juan on the Atlantic Coast, which makes up over half the land area of Nicaragua.[55] The total population of the departments is a little under 300,000, of whom about 27 per cent are indigenous peoples. The majority population on the Atlantic coast is *mestizo* – approximately 62 per cent – and there are also 30,000 Caribbean English-speaking Creoles around the town of Bluefields in the south-east of the department and about 1,000 Garifunas or Black Caribs.[56]

The Miskito peoples live in the north-eastern part of the district along the coast and the rivers where they comprise virtually the total population. A decision by the World Court in 1960 extended the Honduran border from the Patuca to the Coco river and divided the Miskito territory. Today some 45,000 Miskitos also live on the Honduran side. The *mestizos* have settled mainly in the southern half of Zelaya.

The Miskito peoples have retained a high degree of independence despite Spanish and subsequently British colonial involvement. The Spanish conquerors occupied the western half of present-day Nicaragua but did not cross the mountain range to the eastern half of the country in force. Their main interest in the early years of their rule was in the labour rather than the natural resources. An estimated half a million Indians were transported from the region as slaves and the indigenous population of the Pacific region was reduced from close on one million at first contact to about 12,000 by 1548. During the mid-17th Century the British seized several Caribbean islands and began to rival the Spanish in the Gulf of Mexico. Poor whites were brought over as indentured labour to work in the new British colonies and then freed with the inception of the slave trade. Some of the earliest contacts were with those poor white cast-offs who survived as traders and pirates.[57]

During the 18th and 19th Centuries the British strengthened their hold on the Atlantic Coast. Various settlements were established and there began a special relationship with the leading Miskito families. In 1687 a Miskito was crowned King Jeremy I by the British Governor of Jamaica. Jeremy I and subsequent kings became rulers of the British-created Kingdom of Mosquitia and acted as agents for British interests, including the supply of Indian slaves. Although the British did not establish a colony, as they did in Belize (formerly British Honduras), they supported Miskito resistance against the Spanish by supplying arms.[58] For much of this period the eastern half of Nicaragua remained outside the control of the Spanish authorities.

In 1838 Nicaragua gained its independence and in 1860 the Treaty of Managua was signed between Britain and the new republic. Under the terms of the treaty Nicaragua agreed to the creation of a Miskito reserve. The Indians were given the right to govern themselves and all the peoples within their district, according to their customs and rules, provided these were not incompatible with the sovereign rights of Nicaragua. In 1894 the Miskito reserve was abolished by force and the Atlantic Coast reincorporated by decree into Nicaragua as the department of Zelaya. In 1905 a second treaty between Britain and Nicaragua, the Harrison-Altamirano agreement, abrogated the Managua Treaty.[59]

As Spanish influence declined, its place was taken by British and then United States interests. By way of signalling their involvement, US Marines invaded Nicaragua in 1912 and remained there on and off until Somoza came to power in 1936. In the early decades of the 20th Century major US companies began to establish themselves in Nicaragua and on the Atlantic Coast. The former Miskito reserve was subjected to intensive speculation and exploitation by timber, mining and plantation companies. According to one writer, 'in the twentieth century, the US-based companies have extracted more than a billion board feet of wood from the Miskito region of Nicaragua.'[60]

The political and economic independence of the Miskito peoples was effectively destroyed by the declaration of reincorporation and the extensive exploitative activities of foreign companies. The traditional political organizations of Miskito and other indigenous peoples were subordinated to the Managua Government and the self-sufficiency of indigenous communities was disrupted as the region became integrated into the cash economy and the world market. As the economy of the country as a whole was restructured to suit the demands of the world market, many peasants were made landless. After the Second World War poor *mestizos* began to migrate from the Pacific to the Atlantic Coast, until eventually they were in the majority.

The Miskito peoples have, however, retained a strong sense of identity despite these developments. They have their own language and, since they were converted to the Moravian Church in the mid-19th Century, a different religion to the Catholic Nicaraguans. Many Miskitos maintain that they belong to a people distinct from the Nicaraguans, and with a separate history. Their collective way of life, prevailing subsistence economy, communal ownership of land, traditional beliefs and organization of village affairs by elders, mark the Miskito out from mainstream Nicaraguan society. Few Miskitos were members of the FSLN, and Somoza's National Guard, which served as the dictator's private army, were not present in force on the Atlantic Coast. The Miskitos were not in that sense involved in the revolutionary struggle which cost some 50,000 Nicaraguan lives and which brought an end to a dictatorship that even the country's present detractors would agree was one of the most brutal in Latin America.

Until the victory of the Sandinistas, the indigenous peoples of the Atlantic Coast were organized under ALPROMISU, an alliance of Miskitos and Sumus set up with the support of the Moravian Church.[61] The Sandinistas helped establish a new organization MISURASATA, which brought together all three indigenous peoples and in 1980 it put forward its programme and claims in a document entitled General Directions. The document affirmed Nicaraguan sovereignty over the Atlantic Coast:

> We, the indigenous peoples: Miskito, Sumu, and Rama, who have lived, are living and will continue in future in this now liberated fatherland of Nicaragua, raise our voice of life and hope through the manifesto on the General Directions of the organization of our communities (MISURASATA) before peoples of the world and the revolutionary Government of the Sandinist Nation.

It concluded with a series of recommendations:

> For the self-determination and independence of our peoples within the revolutionary process, we present the following recommendations:
> Land: the Agrarian Reform should allow indigenous people to be legitimate owners of their lands without any form of discrimination or subdivision. For this, the full and partial titles possessed by our communities should be recognized and the places we have traditionally occupied should be legally indicated.
> Education: that our children receive instruction in their mother tongue in accordance with our culture and traditions. To do this we want our own people to be trained sufficiently in order to teach our languages and customs and also to teach the Spanish language. We formally propose that our native languages Miskito and Sumu be officially recognized, Miskito as the second official language in the country for it is the most important language after Spanish. Furthermore, we suggest that these native (and national) languages are included within the educational system in the country, at all levels, in order to promote a genuine integration.
> Politics: Our indigenous communities should participate directly in the political and economic tasks facing our new republic so that on this basis they can solve the present political, social, economic, cultural and educational problems. For this, we propose that through our organization MISURASATA there should be representatives at the Council of State which will be constituted next May 4.
> There should be direct participation in the Nicaraguan Institute for the Atlantic Coast (INNICA), a governmental institution created for the development of the Atlantic Coast. We recall that we represent the majority in this area. We understand that in practice, this body is in charge of planning in the Atlantic Coast and we, as indigenous peoples, demand that we are present and participate in a direct and effective manner.
> Finally, we propose the genuine integration of our peoples in the national life. This integration means the development and progress of our communities through the participation of our autochthonous peoples, free from imposition by dominant groups. Our fundamental right should also be guaranteed that we can advance our own means of cultural, linguistic, social, religious, economic and political expression.[62]

In the first year relations between MISURASATA and the Sandinista government were good. The literacy campaign on the Atlantic Coast was carried out in Spanish, Miskito, Sumu and English. MISURASATA was given a seat on the Council of State and negotiations to define the indigenous territories were begun. Although the revolutionary government had nationalized all untitled land, and therefore brought under state control the communally held Miskito homelands, a temporary agreement about the use of indigenous resources was reached with MISURASATA. In July and August 1980 both sides agreed that the village communities would receive 80 per cent of the proceeds from the sale of state-extracted timber for local projects. Implicit in the agreement was the need for rapid demarcation of indigenous land.

In early 1981, however, conflicts began to develop. Certain Miskito communities complained that the government was not complying with the agreement about timber extraction. Then, in February 1981, the government announced that Steadman Fagoth Muller, the representative of the Miskito people in the State Council, was a former agent of Somoza's infamous and hated secret police. The government claimed a separatist plot and arrested the entire leadership of MISURASATA.[63] While trying to arrest one leader in the Moravian Church in the village of Prinzapolka, fighting broke out between the Sandinista army patrol and Miskitos. Eight people were killed. Almost at once Miskitos began to protest and occupy government buildings in the main towns of the Atlantic Coast to demand their release.

The confrontation that developed between the Miskitos and the Sandinista government was rooted in deeper misunderstandings. The Miskito peoples were strongly influenced by the North-American-based Moravian Church, which had provided benefits in the form of education and health care and they received work, wages and consumer goods from foreign, mostly US, companies. The Miskitos viewed North American intervention in the region with different eyes to the Nicaraguans. 'Economically the coast belonged to the big companies. Ideologically, it belonged to the churches', one Catholic priest from the area has stated.[64] The Nicaraguan Government under Somoza had left the coast to its own devices and it was difficult for the Miskito peoples to understand the revolutionary process or that the Sandinistas would behave any differently from previous governments.

Declaration of principles regarding the indigenous communities of the Atlantic Coast.

WHEREAS: It's the responsibility of the Popular Sandinista Revolution to find a just and revolutionary solution to the legitimate claims and grievances of the indigenous population of the Atlantic Coast communities;

WHEREAS: The aspirations of the indigenous population of America, traditionally exploited, oppressed and subjected to the rigours of a brutal internal colonialist system, are now aspirations contained within the Sandinista Revolution; aspirations which must not be betrayed;

WHEREAS: Both internally and externally, imperialism and local counter-revolutionaries are now dedicated to the spreading of confusion, in order to discredit and obstruct the efforts which the Government of National Reconstruction, in conjunction with the genuine indigenous representatives, are now carrying out in order to try to find creative solutions to the difficult and complex problems, inherited from previous administrations:

THE FRENTE SANDINISTA DE LIBERACION NACIONAL (FSLN) AND GOVERNMENT OF NATIONAL RECONSTRUCTION hereby emit the following

Declaration of Principles to serve as guidelines in our dealings with the indigenous minorities of the Atlantic Coast:

(1) Nicaragua is but one nation. Territorially and politically, it cannot be dismembered, divided or deprived of its sovereignty and independence. Spanish is the official language of the country.

(2) All citizens of Nicaragua, regardless of race or religion, shall enjoy equal rights. The Revolution will actively fight and oppose all forms of racial, linguistic and cultural discrimination in the national territory. Wherever racism may sprout this government shall support the fight against it.

(3) The Government of National Reconstruction, convinced of the need to rescue and nurture the different cultural manifestations, present in the national territory, will provide the Miskito, Creole, Sumu and Rama communities of the Atlantic Coast with the means that are required to develop and enhance their cultural traditions, including the preservation of their languages.

(4) The Popular Sandinista Revolution will guarantee and support the participation of the communities of the Atlantic Coast in all social, economic and political matters, which affect them, both regionally and nationally.

(5) THE POPULAR SANDINISTA REVOLUTION WILL NOT ONLY GUARANTEE BUT ALSO LEGALIZE THE OWNERSHIP OF LANDS ON WHICH THE PEOPLE OF THE COMMUNITIES OF THE ATLANTIC COAST HAVE TRADITIONALLY LIVED AND WORKED, EITHER AS COMMUNITIES OR COOPERATIVES. LAND TITLES WILL BE GRANTED TO EACH COMMUNITY.

(6) The natural resources of our territory are the properties of the Nicaraguan people. The Revolutionary State, representative of the popular will, is the only entity empowered to establish a rational and efficient system of utilization of said resources. The Revolutionary State recognizes the right of the indigenous communities to receive a portion of the benefits to be derived from the exploitation of forestal resources of the region. These benefits must be invested in programs of community and municipal development in accordance with national plans.

(7) Because the Government of National Reconstruction is convinced that an improvement in the living conditions of the people can be brought about only through economic development, it will continue to promote all local and national projects that are necessary for the development of the communities of the Atlantic Coast.

(8) In order to ensure the necessary representation in the social, political and economic institutions existing on the Atlantic Coast, the Popular Sandinista Revolution will support all patterns of organizations that are natural to these communities.

Issued in the City of Managua of Free Nicaragua, on the twelfth day of the eighth month of 1981, year dedicated to 'Defense and Production'.

The Sandinista National Liberation Front and the Government of National Reconstruction of Nicaragua.

Free Homeland or Death!

The Sandinistas for their part sought the integration of the Miskito and other indigenous peoples into the revolutionary programme. The revolutionary government had made numerous improvements in the material condition of the peoples of the Atlantic Coast. In March 1982 Luis Carrion, the FSLN representative in the area, claimed that the number of schools had been more than doubled, the number of teachers increased by 84 per cent, and a total of 12,500 indigenous peoples taught to read and write; the number of medical personnel in the area had risen by 348 per cent. The National Development Bank during the period 1981 and 1982 had provided 13 times the amount of credit for agricultural production of that made available in 1978 and 1979.[65] On 20 July 1981 Daniel Ortega, the government junta's coordinator, expressed the concern of the Sandinistas in this way:

> The efforts made by our revolution to deal with the problems of the Atlantic Coast are public knowledge. We have made great efforts. We have invested large amounts of economic resources there to try and integrate the Atlantic region socially, economically and politically into the rest of Nicaragua. We have confidence in this effort now that the fruits are beginning to be seen.
>
> At the same time, however, we cannot ignore the latent danger that exists, because the Somozists have pinpointed the Atlantic region as a favourable zone in which to develop counter-revolutionary activity. They know that if they appear this side, if an ex-National Guard tried to gain support in the districts of Managua, Msaya, Leon or Chinadega, the people would lynch him because they experienced the brutality, the cruelty and the criminality of Somoza's National Guard. But in the Atlantic region this situation does not arise. For this reason, we are obliged to double our efforts to consciously integrate the Atlantic inhabitants into the revolutionary process. We have to compete for them with the counter-revolution, with those who train themselves in Miami, with those who invade our territory and assassinate Nicaraguan citizens.[66]

The Sandinistas were increasingly having to repel the incursions by contras from across the Honduran frontier, as well as counter anti-Communist propaganda from the Somozista radio stations. In mid-1981 Steadman Fagoth and other MISURASATA leaders were released from prison by the Nicaraguan Government. Fagoth travelled to Honduras and Miami, and joined forces with the contras. Since that time Fagoth has called upon Miskitos in Nicaragua to rise up against the Sandinista government and he has managed to attract some younger Miskitos to Honduras to join the rebel struggle.

With the escalation of contra activity along the Coco River on the north-eastern border, and the build-up of US military activity in the region, the Sandinistas began to be deeply concerned about Nicaraguan territorial integrity. The FSLN along the border were often under attack and had suffered numerous casualties. The contras were also involved in harassment of Miskito villagers to make them join their forces.[67] MISURASATA at this juncture was perceived by the Sandinistas as a counter-revolutionary organization and declared defunct. In the light of these difficulties, in January 1982, the Sandinistas decided to evacuate the population living along the Coco River and in direct line of fire. Approximately 8,500 Miskitos were removed to new settlements in the interior on a site covering an area of 54,500 hectares.[68] Criticisms of the relocations were made by the Episcopal Conference of Nicaragua.[69] However, the Sandinista government maintained that such large-scale resettlement could not have been achieved without the cooperation of the Miskitos. Furthermore, they claimed that there were no instances of deaths through illness or accident. In November and December 1982 a further 1,000 Sumu and Miskito peoples from the headwaters of the Coco River were relocated on state-run coffee plantations.

By the end of 1981 and early 1982 the relationship between the Sandinistas and the Miskito leadership had deteriorated considerably. MISURASATA under the leadership of Brooklyn Rivera has taken up arms against the Sandinistas and has an estimated 2,000 armed guerrillas. Rivera himself has lived in exile since mid-1981. Steadman Fagoth's organization, MISURA, claims some 3,000 Miskito guerrillas and is closely tied in with the activities of the contras. While MISURA actively seeks the overthrow of the Sandinistas, MISURASATA's leader Brooklyn Rivera insists he supports the revolutionary government and wants only justice for the indigenous minorities.

Since 1982 an estimated 20,000 indigenous peoples have nevertheless fled to refugee camps in Honduras. Others have been taken forcibly by MISURA guerrillas in their raids into Nicaragua. Once in refugee camps outside the control of the United Nations High Commissioner for Refugees, which under its mandate is not permitted to administer its relief operations within 50 miles of the border, Miskitos are recruited by MISURA by force and face punishment or death if they do not cooperate.[70]

Since the end of 1984 MISURASATA and the Sandinistas have begun to discuss ways of bringing an end to the fighting. On 3 October 1984 Brooklyn Rivera met Nicaragua's head of state, Daniel Ortega, in New York and was invited to Managua. A series of meetings took place: in October 1984 in Nicaragua, in December 1984 and March 1985 in Colombia, in April 1985 in Mexico and in May 1985 in Colombia once again. The Nicaraguan Government has offered to permit the return of refugees from Honduras and has agreed to return those families relocated during 1981 and 1982 to their homelands along the Coco River. Furthermore, the Sandinista government has authorized the drafting of a bill 'guaranteeing recognition of the historical rights of indigenous peoples to their land and natural resources, and self-government through authorities democratically elected by the communities, and ensuring the equal participation of all indigenous peoples and communities in the Atlantic Coast'.[71]

Notwithstanding the conciliatory moves made by the Sandinista government and MISURASATA in 1984 and 1985, there remains an apparent irreconcilability in their two positions. MISURASATA had expressed its position on the question of land and resources in the General Directions in 1980 and in 1981 it had elaborated its programme more fully. The proposal submitted on 28 July 1981 stated that:

> The revolutionary State must recognise the right of our indigenous entities to organize and govern themselves according to their cultural, social, economic and political needs, without this leading to a restriction of our civil rights as citizens. This right includes free organization under the direction of the authentic leaders and representatives of our Miskito, Sumu and Rama peoples.

And that:

> The right of indigenous peoples to land includes the right to the surface and the subsoil, to inland waters and the coast, as well as the right to appropriate them, even including the coastal economic zones. Thus, the indigenous peoples can freely control the land's riches and natural resources. Under no circumstances can a people be deprived of its means of subsistence.[72]

The territory over which the indigenous peoples claimed their rights was virtually the entire Department of Zelaya, an area of 45,407 square kilometres or over one-third of the land surface of Nicaragua. Luis Carrion, the FSLN representative for the Atlantic Coast, was unequivocal in his response:

> Let us compare two proposals made by MISURASATA on the land question, one in 1980, the other in 1981. In 1980 MISURASATA's programme proposed the following: 'Our revolutionary Government must recognize and guarantee each indigenous community ownership of its territory. Titles should be duly registered into collective ownership that is continuous, and inalienable and is geographically large enough to ensure the growth of the communities.' This demand conforms with the traditions and history of the community. But in 1981 they put forward a totally different demand, saying that the 'age-old right of inheritance and possession of our territories is counter to that of property rights on a community basis, which they have always tried to impose upon us. We are not in agreement with this because it is against our interests and beliefs as peoples who possess their own rights.' Within one year already they are not in agreement with the handing over of the lands to the indigenous communities. Instead they claim a portion of 45,000 square kilometres of national territory, which is nearly all the Department of Zelaya, thus passing from a legitimate proposal to a separatist proposal. For the benefit of those who have any doubts about the separatist content of this demand they add the following: 'The right of indigenous peoples to land includes the right to the surface and subsoil, to inland waters and coast.' That is a total and absolute sovereign right over a portion of the nation's territory. Moreover, this territory would be inherited by Miskito, Sumu, Rama and Creoles, but Mestizos, or 'Spaniards' as they are called, would be excluded. In other words, more than 170,000 poor *campesinos* would have to be expelled from this territory who have been settled there for many decades. There is no doubt that apart from being separatist, this project promoted by MISURASATA's leadership is profoundly racist. We see here a resurgence of the values and conceptions that throughout centuries were inculcated in these communities by colonialism. They reappear as a consequence of the conscious actions and plans to attain this end.
>
> All this contains a paradox. Throughout decades the Somoza regime maintained the indigenous population in the utmost misery, but the leaders of ALPROMISU limited themselves – almost shamefacedly – to raising no more than a few timid demands.
>
> Come the revolution, and despite the fact that in one year more is done and greater benefits are attained for the region than throughout all the years of the Somoza dictatorship, a belligerent separatist plan appears.[73]

The disagreements that exist between the indigenous peoples of Nicaragua and their revolutionary government are unlikely to disappear rapidly.

Notwithstanding the manipulation of Miskito peoples by the contras and others hostile to the Sandinista revolution, there are fundamental differences which are not easily reconciled. The demand to have the right to land and its resources recognized by the government is no less a right than that demanded by many indigenous peoples in capitalist countries. In the end the Sandinista government may find it hard to relinquish control, won after so much suffering, to a people who contributed little to the revolution and the creation of conditions which allow such a debate to take place. But the fulfilment of the rights of Nicaragua's indigenous peoples presupposes such a devolution of authority.

West and East

Comparisons of the conditions and rights of indigenous peoples in socialist countries with those of tribal and indigenous minorities elsewhere are likely to be contentious. The West advocates individual civil liberties and the Communist bloc cannot conceive of freedom having any meaning in a society divided by classes. Thus, socialist countries, like the USSR, China and Nicaragua, often point to the great advances in the material conditions of their indigenous peoples – the higher incomes, rises in levels of consumption, improved health and education facilities, better housing and communications – resulting from Communist practices. They point to the exploitative systems in which most indigenous peoples were living prior to the revolutions. There may be little dissension from this viewpoint since most indigenous peoples in socialist countries have seen enormous improvements in their situation. By contrast, as we have seen, the social and economic conditions of the original inhabitants of some of the rich countries are among the worst anywhere.

On the other hand, both the USSR and China are empires and their hegemony extends to peoples, racially and culturally distinct, whose homelands are many thousands of miles from the centres of population of the majority. Just as in capitalist countries, the law may declare equality for all, but racism still persists. The Han Chinese have on numerous occasions since the revolution shown an overriding contempt for the culture of certain of the national minorities and, in the USSR, the Russian majority have oppressed the culture of the minority peoples. In most socialist countries the indigenous peoples are seen as possessing a primitive, pre-capitalist economy which must, if it is to benefit the people, be transformed into Communism, through state farms, cooperatives and other forms of collective organization. The changes forced upon the minorities have often proved inappropriate and destructive and the new organizations, while often allowing some local autonomy, are always subordinate to centralized planning. The socialist ideology, so powerfully promoted and disseminated by revolutionary cadres, coupled with the real improvements brought about by redistribution of wealth, economic development and a certain amount of cultural protection, have meant that the indigenous minorities have been less successful in resisting assimilation than similar peoples in capitalist countries.

The Miskito peoples alone offer an exception to this rule. They are seeking many of the political, economic, social and cultural rights demanded by the indigenous movement. Nicaragua is a small country with a fragile revolution and the Miskito peoples are not demanding complete independence. There are grounds, therefore, for arguing that an accommodation of the two positions has to be reached by negotiation and not by force. This alone will permit the Miskitos to determine their own development within a socialist society.

Notes

1. For the purposes of this chapter the socialist countries are the Union of Soviet Socialist Republics, the People's Republic of China, the Mongolian People's Republic and Nicaragua. The indigenous peoples of Burma, Laos and Vietnam are discussed in chapter 8 and those of Ethiopia in chapter 9.

2. Jeremy Swift, 'Marginal peoples at the modern frontier in Asia and the Arctic', *Development and Change* (SAGE, London and Beverly Hills) vol.9, no.1, January 1978, p.3.

3. Constitution of the USSR, 7 October 1977, section III, article 69.

4. Ibid., article 71.

5. V.I. Lenin, 'The socialist revolution and the rights of nations to self-determination', *Selected Works* (Lawrence & Wishart, London, 1969) p.160.

6. June Teufel Dreyer, *China's forty millions* (Harvard University Press, 1976) p.50.

7. C.J. Peters, 'The Georgians', Bohdan Nahaylo and C.J. Peters, *The Ukrainians and Georgians*, Minority Rights Group Report no.50, pp.16-17.

8. **Table 11.3**

Native peoples of Siberia

	Number of people of given nationality (in thousands) 1970		Number of people of given nationality (in thousands) 1970
Buryaty	313	Koryaki	7.5
Tuvintsy	139	Dolgany	4.9
Yakuty	295	Nivkhi (Gilyaks)	4.4
Khakasy	65	Sel'kupy (Ostyak Samoyeds)	4.3
Altaytsy	55	Ul'chi (Ol'chi)	2.4
Little Peoples of the North, Siberia and Far East of which:		Yaami (Laps) Udegeytsy	1.5
Nentsy (Samoyeds, Yuraks)	28	Itel'meny (Kamchadals)	1.3
Evenki (Tungus)	25	Kety (Yenisey Ostyaks)	1.2
Khanty (Ostyaks)	21	Orochi	1.1
Chukchi	14	Nganasany (Tavgi Samoyeds)	1
Eveny (Lamuts)	12	Yukagiry	.6
Nanaytsy (Golds)	10	Eskimosy (Asiatic Eskimos)	1.3
Mansi (Voguls)	7.7	Aleuty (Aleuts)	.4

Source: Soviet census 1970.

9. Certain of these, like the Uzbeks, are traditionally settled agriculturalists.

10. Albert Szymanski, *Human Rights in the Soviet Union* (Zed Press, London, 1985) p.35. It should also be noted that Turkic peoples were recruited by the White Russians.

11. Frances Svensson, 'Aboriginal Peoples of Siberia'. G. Ashworth (ed.), *Minorities in the eighties* (Quartermaine House, 1980) p.2.

12. Philip Lineton, 'Soviet nationality policy in north western Siberia: an historical perspective', *Development and Change*, vol.9, 1978, pp.87-102.

13. Cited in Szymanski, p.39; cf. also chapter 2 of Szymanski.

14. Violet Conolly, *Siberia Today and Tomorrow: A study of economic resources, problems and achievements* (Collins, London, 1975) p.188.

15. Terence Armstrong, *Russian settlement in the north* (Cambridge University Press, 1965) p.167.

16. Ibid., p.188.

17. Conolly, p.46.

18. Caroline Humphrey, 'Pastoral nomadism in Mongolia: the role of herdsmen's cooperatives in a national economy', *Development and Change*, vol.9, 1978, p.159.

19. Ibid., p.134.

20. In 1970 there were an estimated 40 million national minority peoples.

21. Fei Hsiao Tung, *Toward a people's anthropology* (New World Press, China, 1981) p.23.

22. *Peking Review*, 11 November 1958, pp.16-17 from *China's minority nationalities* (Red Sun Publishers, USA) p.43. About 74 per cent of national minorities speak Sino-Tibetan and 21 per cent the Ural-Altaic languages. See Fei Hsiao Tung, p.28.

23. Wolfram Eberhard, *China's minorities: yesterday and today* (Wadsworth Publishing Co., California, 1982) pp.27-45.

24. Chris Mullin and Phuntsog Wangyal, *The Tibetans: two perspectives on Tibetan–Chinese relations*, Minority Rights Group Report no.49, 1983, p.15.

25. Dreyer, p.3.

26. Eberhard, p.3.

27. Fei Hsiao Tung, pp.44 and 83; Yin Ming, *United and Equal: the progress of China's minority nationalities* (Foreign Languages Press, Peking, 1977) p.42.

28. *Peking Review*, 7 April 1975, pp.27-9 from *China's minority nationalities*, p.167. There is debate about the conditions of the Tibetan peoples; see Heinrich Harrer, *Seven years in Tibet* (Pan, London, 1956) and the two views put forward in Mullin and Wangyal.

29. Fei Hsaio Tung, p.47.

30. Cf. Liu Shao-Ch'i: 'The building of a socialist society is the common objective of all nationalities within our country. Only socialism can guarantee to each and every nationality a high degree of economic and cultural development'. Extract from 'Report on the draft constitution of the People's Republic of China' delivered at the First National People's Congress of the PRC, 15 September 1954, cited in George V.H. Moseley, III, *The consolidation of the south China frontier* (University of California Press, 1973) p.8.

31. Articles 50 and 51 in the Common Programme.

32. Article 15.

33. Fei Hsiao Tung, p.110.

34. Yin Ming, p.84.

35. Fei Hsiao Tung, p.83.

36. Dreyer, p.161; see pp.159-71 for discussion of the Great Leap Forward.

37. Dreyer, p.171.

38. Ibid., p.210.

39. Ibid., p.216.

40. Ibid., p.234.

41. Cf. Erkin Alptekin, 'The new constitution of China and the Chinese Minority Nationalities', unpublished typescript.

42. Uzbekistan, Kazakhstan, Kirghizistan, Turkmenistan and Tajikistan in the USSR.

43. Erkin Alptekin, 'Chinese policy in Eastern Turkistan', unpublished typescript.

44. Ibid.

45. Ibid.

46. Ibid.

47. 'Tibet: the facts', a report prepared by the Scientific Buddhist Association for the United Nations Commission on Human Rights, 1984. The report pointed out that there were 8,000 monasteries and 250,000 monks in Tibet before 1950.

48. Mullin and Wangyal, p.21.

49. 'Tibet: the facts', pp.8-9. This is also the figure of the Dalai Lama's government-in-exile; cf. also *Guardian*, 24 May 1985, which states that ten per cent of the Tibetan population have been interned at some stage during their lives.

50. Cf. for example, 'China's Minority Nationalities (1)', *China Reconstructs* (Beijing, 1984) p.11.

51. Cf. Vaclav Smil, *The bad earth: environmental degradation in China* (Zed Press, London, 1984), who claims that maltreatment of land and resources is so great that it may well be the most serious obstacle to China's future prosperity. Mao's dictum that the guerrilla base must have its grain reserves and the idea that poverty can be alleviated by making new fields, has proved environmentally damaging. An estimated ten per cent of farmland has been lost due to wrong agricultural policies according to a review by the Second National Chinese Environmental Protection Conference.

52. Anthony Shang, 'Lama's lament', *Inside Asia*, September–October 1985. NB. 1 US dollar = 2.6 Rmb; 10,000 Rmb = 3,750 US dollars; cf. also Ewen MacAskill, 'Tibet: China loosens the yoke, but the army remains', *Weekend Scotsman*, 9 March 1985.

53. Ibid.

54. For two good accounts of the Nicaragua revolution see Joseph Collins, *What difference could a revolution make?* (Institute for Food and Development Policy, San Francisco, 1982) and George Black, *Triumph of the people: the Sandinista revolution in Nicaragua* (Zed Press, London, 1981).

55. The Atlantic Coast is also referred to as the Mosquitia Coast and comprises the Department of Zelaya (59,094 sq kms) and Rio San Juan (7,448 sq kms). Together these departments make up 56.2 per cent of Nicaragua.

56. Population figures are from government sources: MISURASATA often refer to 150,000 Miskitos and 15,000 Sumus.

57. Roxanne Dunbar Ortiz, *Indians of the Americas* (Zed Press, London, 1984) p.203.

58. Ibid., pp.202-8; see also Troy S. Floyd, *The Anglo-Spanish struggle for*

Mosquitia (University of New Mexico Press, 1967).

59. Marie-Chantal Barre, 'Le drame des Indiens Miskitos au Nicaragua et son exploitation politique', *Le Monde Diplomatique*, April 1982, p.3.

60. Ortiz, p.215.

61. The Moravian Church is a fundamentalist Protestant organization founded in Germany. The first mission arrived among the Miskitos in 1849. The headquarters of the Church has since moved to the United States.

62. Extract from MISURASATA, *Lineamentos Generales*, 1982 cited in Klaudine Ohland and Robin Schneider (eds.), *National Revolution and indigenous identity: the conflict between Sandinistas and Miskito Indians on Nicaragua's Atlantic Coast*, IWGIA Document 47, November 1983, pp.48-63.

63. Cf. *Patria Libre*, no.11, February 1981 – the monthly magazine of the Sandinista Armed Forces (FAS) – cited in Ohland and Schneider, pp.99-105.

64. Marlene Dixon (ed.), *On trial: Reagan's war against Nicaragua* (Zed Press, London, 1985) p.246.

65. Speech by Luis Carrion, 7 March 1982, to Conference of Latin American Intellectuals, Managua, cited in Ohland and Schneider, pp.252-3.

66. Extract from speech by Daniel Ortega at Second Anniversary of the Revolution, 20 July 1981, cited in Ohland and Schneider, pp.161-3.

67. Statement by Orlando Wayland Waldimar, Miskito leader, in Dixon, pp.84-9. Waldimir recounts how he was tortured in the presence of Fagoth until he agreed to fight for MISURA.

68. Cf. Luis Carrion speech cited in Ohland and Schneider, p.267.

69. Marie-Chantal Barre, p.3.

70. Roxanne Dunbar Ortiz, 'Preliminary observations from a visit to the Department of Gracias a Dios, Honduras, regarding Honduran and Nicaraguan Miskitos', 11-14 November 1984.

71. Statement by Gustavo-Adolfo Vargas, Permanent Representative to the United Nations at Geneva, to the UN Working Group on Indigenous Populations, 14 August 1985.

72. 'Proposal on landholding in the indigenous and Creole communities of the Atlantic Coast', presented by MISURASATA, 28 July 1981, cited in Ohland and Schneider, pp.168-9.

73. Extract from speech by Luis Carrion to Latin American Intellectuals, 7 March 1982, cited in Ohland and Schneider, pp.256-7.

12. Banks and Corporations

In the last two decades large-scale development programmes have caused great damage to the traditional homelands of indigenous peoples. Mining, colonization, agribusiness and hydro-electric schemes have brought about a massive alienation of indigenous land. Vital components of these great enterprises are the multilateral development banks (MDBs) and the transnational corporations (TNCs), but foremost among all the institutions involved in large-scale development projects on indigenous lands is the World Bank.

The World Bank

The World Bank was set up in 1944 and describes its objective as helping raise standards of living in developing countries by channelling financial resources from developed countries to the developing world.[1] It is owned by the 146 participating countries and voting rights are related to the size of subscription. Thus, the United States of America has around 20 per cent of the votes, the United Kingdom about six per cent, and these two countries and West Germany, Canada, Japan and France together hold over half the total votes.[2] In 1985 the Bank provided about $US 13 billion worth of loans and credits and is increasingly drawing in commercial banks to co-finance big projects. Its investment in a project will usually signal the involvement of commercial banks and enterprises which might otherwise not support grandiose and risky ventures in poor countries. The Bank acts as a kind of seal of approval and for approximately every $US 3 it lends to a project more than $US 7 will be raised from other sources.[3] The position the World Bank takes towards projects on indigenous peoples' lands has, therefore, an impact on all its partners in any operation it undertakes.

The World Bank promotes a model of Western development which is almost invariably antithetical to the interests of indigenous peoples. In recent years, however, it has come under fire from the indigenous peoples and pro-Indian groups. This was particularly the case in the Philippines where during the 1970s the Bank became involved in funding dam-building on an unprecedented scale. One of the spin-offs of the programme was designed to benefit small farmers, but, as individual projects got under way, it became clear that they might actually lose the small plots of land they owned or leased. In the Chico River Irrigation Project, for example, smallholdings owned by Kalinga and Bontoc tribal peoples were due to be submerged and land designated for irrigation began to be concentrated in the hands of owners of large plantations. Even Bank officials recognized that the main beneficiaries were likely to be the big landlords and agribusiness interests, many of which were linked to the President and the Defence Minister of the country.[4] Protests grew as it was learned that some 90,000 tribal Filipinos were due to be dislocated by the four dams along the Chico River. In 1977 tribal peoples from the area presented a petition to the then President of the World Bank, Robert McNamara, stating their opposition to the whole dam programme. Eventually the Bank agreed to modify its policy.[5]

The World Bank has attracted a great deal of criticism for its support of development projects on indigenous peoples' land in Brazil. The Polonoroeste project in the west of the country will develop roads, colonies and agriculture over an area of about 400,000 square kilometres and is due to receive a quarter of the total costs from the Bank. More than 8,000 Indians, many unacculturated Nambikwara, inhabit the project area. When the programme was announced, indigenous, church and concerned non-governmental organizations campaigned vigorously to urge the World Bank to withhold its loan subject to satisfactory steps being taken by the government to demarcate Indian land. Some improvements were secured through the Brazilian Indian agency, FUNAI, but the bulk of the Indian land remained unprotected.

In 1983 the consultant anthropologist to the Bank on the Polonoroeste project publicly questioned the sincerity of the institution's commitment to indigenous peoples. At a hearing of the United States House of Representatives he stated that 'one cannot but feel that the World Bank is much more concerned with images than with the welfare of the native minorities.'[6] He complained that the preliminary fact-finding missions by the Bank were too short and too luxurious and that consultation took place exclusively with the local elites. Furthermore, he maintained that the Bank placed great emphasis on the financial gain of the development project, and paid insufficient attention to the likely improvements in the living conditions of the poor or any degradation to the environment and abridgement of human rights.[7] This view was echoed in 1985 by Robert Kasten, a Republican Senator and chairman of the sub-committee dealing with US contributions to multilateral development banks. On the devastating destruction of tropical forest caused by Polonoroeste, he commented:

> What is amazing is that the World Bank continued to fund this project for more than two years after it had identified, through its supervisory missions, that the programme was producing environmental devastation on this scale.[8]

Other critics of the World Bank have protested that officials pay no heed to the political implications of projects. During the 1970s, for example, substantial loans were made by the World Bank and the Inter-American Development Bank to Guatemala. The loans were advanced to finance hydro-electric and infrastructural projects in the northern frontier zone and rural cooperatives in the mainly Indian highlands. But by providing aid to projects which were due to benefit leading members of the ruling armed forces and promoting rural development, the banks created a deep rift between the powerful élites and the poor Mayan Indians. As the cooperatives spread, the armed forces, feeling threatened, began arresting and assassinating cooperative leaders and workers. Shelton Davis, the Director of the Anthropology Resource Center and critic of United States policy in Guatemala, has commented as follows:

> The failure of the multilateral lending institutions to consider these political outcomes before providing assistance to the Guatemalan military results from an extremely narrow, economic conception of the development process. Rather than avoid the political consequences of development aid, under the guise of a neutral economic science, the multilateral lending institutions should be forced to make explicit, in their project documents and annual reports, the probable political consequences of their lending decisions. Otherwise, we will continue to encounter situations like those in Guatemala, where international assistance helps to create a dynamic rural development movement only later to see it destroyed by a highly-repressive, military government.[9]

But it is not only development projects which the World Bank is funding. The massive colonization programme in Indonesia receives finance to the tune of $US 400 million. Transmigration, as it is known, has brought about alienation of indigenous peoples' lands, environmental damage and comparatively few benefits to the new settlers. On Kalimantan, for example, 15 per cent of the population are now transmigrants from Java and the indigenous Dayak and other peoples have been persuaded to sign away their *adat* or communal land. Without land they are forced to settle on special government sites where they become dependent upon state-generated employment. An internal memorandum of the World Bank in 1983 recommended further research on transmigration 'since so little is known of either the agricultural practices of the local people or the problems likely to be encountered while integrating them into the settlement'. The document expresses great concern over the issues of land alienation and customary land rights.[10]

However, these misgivings have not prevented the Bank – with a loan of $US 163 million – from supporting an even more destructive colonization programme in the Indonesian province of Irian Jaya (West Papua). There the government plan to settle about 700,000 transmigrants before 1989, making the indigenous West Papuan population a minority.

The annexation of West Papua by Indonesia in 1969 sparked off a quiet but bloody liberation struggle which continues today. The people of West Papua are culturally, linguistically and ethnically distinct from the Javanese transmigrants and have no desire to be part of Indonesia so the World Bank, by its support of the colonization programme, is making itself an accessory to Indonesian imperialism. Notwithstanding this political criticism, there are growing grounds for concern about the economic benefits of transmigration. One World Bank consultant to the project has complained that there are no proper facilities on many of the new settlements. On some sites the soil is of such poor quality that it requires three times the fertilizer of normal soils and often there are no water sources to sustain the full complement of settlers.[11] According to the United Nations Development Programme (UNDP), only one in ten transmigration sites are considered economically profitable.[12] Even the *Wall Street Journal* was moved to point out that transmigration 'mainly moves poor families from small amounts of good land to large amounts of nearly worthless land'.[13]

The economic viability of projects of this kind and their effect on the local inhabitants seem inadequately investigated. Despite the public hostility to the multi-million dollar dam-building schemes in the Philippines, the bank has nevertheless approved more such loans to similar projects in India. Large dams have become the country's most controversial environmental issue and tribal and other poor people are becoming increasingly active in resisting such projects. One of the largest schemes currently being planned by the Indian Government is the Narmada River Valley Project, where 329 large dams are due to be built and some one million mainly tribal people relocated.[14] The World Bank is providing $US 300 million for part of the project. About 60,000 scheduled tribes are due to be removed from the project area and only the barest compensation paid. As one non-governmental organization has pointed out: 'only one per cent of the project's costs have been allocated to the relocation, less than has been spent housing the few hundred project staff.'[15]

Nor are these disastrous development projects confined to the vulnerable indigenous populations of Asia and South America. At Ouessa in the Congo, for example, a wood-processing plant funded by the World Bank was, according to the consultant anthropologist, not always providing equitable treatment to the 10,000 Pygmies in the catchment area and threatening to have a negative impact on their development.[16]

In 1982, in response to public pressures, the World Bank published its own policy document on tribal peoples and economic development and an operations manual for project workers.[17] The guidelines make assumptions about the inevitability of development on tribal lands and about the eventual integration of indigenous peoples into mainstream society.[18] These assumptions soon came up against criticism from environmentalists and pro-Indian groups, who claimed that there was mounting evidence of the ineffectiveness of large-scale development projects and their potential and actual damage to the ecology. They also argued that the guidelines did not reflect the recent calls – now recognized as legitimate by several international bodies – of indigenous peoples for cultural autonomy and self-determination.[19]

This is not to suggest that the policy guidelines adopted by the World Bank are not a positive first step. The Bank is the first international agency, among those whose work directly impinges upon tribal peoples, to address the issue seriously.

TRIBAL PEOPLES IN BANK-FINANCED PROJECTS

Characteristics of Tribal People

1. The term 'tribal people' refers here to ethnic groups typically with stable, low-energy, sustained-yield economic systems, as exemplified by hunter-gatherers, shifting or semi-permanent farmers, herders, or fishermen. They exhibit in varying degrees many of the following characteristics:

(a) geographically isolated or semi-isolated;
(b) unacculturated or only partially acculturated into the social norms of the dominant society;
(c) non-monetized, or only partially monetized; production largely for subsistence, and independent of the national economic system;
(d) ethnically distinct from the national society;
(e) non-literate and without a written language;
(f) linguistically distinct from the wider society;
(g) identifying closely with one particular territory;
(h) having an economic lifestyle largely dependent on the specific natural environment;
(i) possessing indigenous leadership, but little or no national representation, and few, if any, political rights as individuals or collectively, partly because they do not participate in the political process; and
(j) having loose tenure over their traditional land which for the most part is not accepted by the dominant society nor accommodated by the courts; and having weak enforcement capabilities against encroachers, even when tribal areas have been delineated.

2. Partly as a result of these characteristics, most tribal people do not receive all the national or local social services – particularly health, communication, and education services – normally available to other citizens. The lack reinforces tribal people's low national status and limits their capacity for change and adaptation to new circumstances.

3. Experience has shown that, unless special measures are adopted, tribal people are more likely to be harmed than helped by development projects that are intended for beneficiaries other than themselves. Therefore, whenever tribal peoples may be affected, the design of projects should include measures or components necessary to safeguard their interests and, whenever feasible, to enhance their well-being. Sound project planning and design reduce the risk that tribal people will suffer from the project's consequences or disrupt its implementation. More positively, tribal people may offer opportunities to the wider society, especially by increasing the national society's knowledge of proven adaptation to and utilization of fragile and marginal environments.

General Policies

4. As a general policy, the Bank will not assist development projects that knowingly involve encroachment on traditional territories being used or occupied by tribal people, unless adequate safeguards are provided. In those cases where environmental and/or social change promoted through develop-

ment projects may create undesired effects for tribal people, the project should be designed so as to prevent or mitigate such effects. The Bank will assist projects *only* when satisfied that the Borrower or relevant government agency supports and can implement measures that will effectively safeguard the integrity and well-being of the tribal people. Measures at either extreme should be avoided; either those that perpetuate isolation from the national society and needed social services; or those promoting forced, accelerated acculturation unsuited to the future well-being of the affected tribal people. The Bank would not be prepared to assist with a project if it appears that the project sponsors had forcibly 'cleared' the area of tribal people beforehand.

5. Some practical issues concerning tribal people are difficult to resolve. For example, how can the government harmonize its interest in the development of a rich ore body or a major hydro potential with the need to safeguard the rights of tribal people in the project area? Those are matters for judgements guided by the principle that Bank assistance should help prevent or mitigate harm, and provide adequate time and conditions for acculturation.

The Tribal Component in Development Projects

6. Since successful acculturation is slow and gradual, development projects having tribal people in their zone of influence must provide time and conditions for acculturation. Such projects will require a tribal component or parallel program which includes: (a) the recognition, demarcation and protection of tribal areas containing those resources required to sustain the tribal people's traditional means of livelihood; (b) appropriate social services that are consonant with the tribe's acculturation status, including, especially, protection against diseases and the maintenance of health; (c) the maintenance, to the extent desired by the tribe, of its cultural integrity and embodiments thereof; (d) a forum for the participation of the tribal people in decisions affecting them, and providing for adjudication and redress of grievances. It should be recognized that in some instances the time required for acculturation will extend beyond the period of project oversight by the Bank. A commitment should be sought that this requirement will be honored.

7. The design of an appropriate tribal component depends upon detailed, contemporary knowledge of the peoples to be affected. Tribal societies are complex and information gathered on a particular society amy not necessarily be ascribable even to neighboring tribes. To the extent that project designers are unfamiliar with the affected tribal peoples, pre-investment studies will be necessary, employing qualified indigenists and related disciplines. The Bank, through its Office of Environmental Affairs, is prepared to assist in these endeavors.

(Selected extracts from World Bank Operations Manual Statement, February 1982.)

In practice, however, Bank policy towards indigenous peoples has not been followed. There have been delays in funding the Polonoroeste project in Brazil because of the inadequate protection of Indians, but no withdrawal from those other aspects of the development deemed harmful; and although there are numerous off-the-record criticisms levelled at the transmigration programme in Indonesia, the Bank remains tight-lipped about their misgivings.

Even if the Bank wanted to implement its own guidelines, there is considerable doubt about whether it could do so. Of the Bank's 5,000 or so employees, only five are full-time professionals in the environmental affairs office under which tribal matters are subsumed.[20] Furthermore, of the consultant anthropologists and sociologists employed by the Bank, well over three-quarters are from the developed countries.[21] Under such circumstances it seems doubtful whether the Bank can fulfil its newly adopted protective role. One former employee of the environmental office of the World Bank who assisted in drafting the guidelines has commented:

> When our proposals were accepted it was because they enhanced the progressive image of the Bank and cost the Bank little. When our proposals threatened the future of a project, or had major implications for Bank practice, they and we were dismissed as unrealistic and impractical. Reform was possible, but only insofar as it left the Bank's basis unchanged.[22]

But the World Bank is not the only multilateral development bank to finance projects affecting indigenous peoples. Mention has been made of the Inter-American Development Bank and its involvement in rural development in the highlands of Guatemala. In Brazil the Carajás project has attracted investment from the European Economic Community and various Japanese banks, as well as the World Bank. In the Chittagong Hill Tracts of Bangladesh where some 100,000 tribespeople were forced to leave their land to make way for the construction of a hydro-electric scheme, funding came from the Japanese-dominated Asian Development Bank (ADB). The ADB also made loans available for dam-building on the Chico River in the Philippines.

Transnational corporations

Transnational corporations are often key partners in these major development projects on frontier land. At Carajás in Brazil dozens of companies – Rio Tinto Zinc, ALCOA, Bethlehem Steel, Utah International, British Petroleum, the German firm Korf and two Japanese industries – have already staked a claim to the vast mineral reserves on the 190 million acre site.[23] In West Papua the oil giants – Shell, Agip, Conoco, Petromer Trend owned by Oppenheimer of South Africa, Total Oil, Chevron, Texaco – have carved out profitable concessions in the coastal waters of the western tip of the island; the great copper, gold, nickel, tin and other mineral resources of the highlands are exploited by US Steel, Philips Brothers, Broken Hill Proprietary, Konnecott, ICI, American Smelting, Newport Mining and various others.[24] The US transnational corporation ALCOA, through its subsidiary SURALCO, was involved in bauxite mining in the 1960s in Surinam which led to the forced removal of 5,000 Indians; in Costa Rica in the 1970s the same company became partners in a $400 million aluminium refinery and dam project threatening the homelands of Boruca

Indians.[25] Rio Tinto Zinc has been active in securing mining concessions on Guaymí land in Panama and, through its subsidiary CRA, on Aboriginal land in Australia. In Guatemala the United Brands Corporation came to own some two-thirds of agricultural land in the 1950s; today some 190 US-based companies representing investments of $US 300 million are active in the country.[26]

Table 12.1
Transnational corporations and big businesses in Mindanao, Philippines
(Data as of December 1983)

Regional countdown of corporations in Mindanao			
Location	*Number*	*Location*	*Number*
Agusan del Norte	13	Misamis Occidental	3
Agusan del Sur	11	Misamis Oriental	31
Basilan	3	North Cotabato	5
Bukidnon	32	South Cotabato	19
Davao City	52	Sultan Kudarat	7
Davao del Norte	23	Sulu	5
Davao del Sur	5	Sulu Sea	4
Davao Oriental	6	Surigao del Norte	8
Lanao del Norte	24	Surigao del Sur	17
Lanao del Sur	5	Zamboanga del Norte	6
Maguindanao	7	Zamboanga del Sur	9
		Total	*295*

Big American corporations which control lands in Mindanao
1. Pacific Wood Product Co. (Findlay Miller) – 61,064 hectares
2. Weyerhaeuser – 73,000 hectares
3. Georgia Pacific Corp. (Lianga Bay Logging Corp.) – 96,000 hectares
4. Castle and Cooke (Dole, Stanfilco) – 30,000 hectares
5. United Brands (TADECO) – 6,000 hectares
6. Del Monte (Philippine Packing Corp.) – 24,000 hectares
7. Goodyear – 3,000 hectares
8. B.F. Goodrich – 2,900 hectares
9. Firestone – 2,000 hectares

Source: *Tribal Forum* (Manila), vol.VI, no.5, September–October 1985, p.19.

The expansion of cattle-ranching in Brazil's Amazon region has attracted speculation by numerous foreign companies. Over 100,000 square kilometres of forest were cut down between 1966 and 1983 to make way for large areas of pasture land and the multinationals arrived like wasps round a honey pot. Norman Myers writes:

A US consortium of Brescan-Swift-Armour-King Ranch holds 720 square kilometers in eastern Amazonia, with an investment of some $10 million, while other US corporations with at least part shares in ranching enterprises include Twin Agricultural and Industrial Developers, Caterpillar International, Beltec International, Dow Chemical, International Foods, Massey Ferguson, W.R. Grace, United Brands, Hublein and Sifco Industries, Anderson Clayton, Gulf and Western, and Goodyear. Further foreign enterprises, from countries other than the United States, include Mitsui, Tsuzuki, Marubeni, and Spinning-Nichimen, from Japan; Liquigas, from Italy; Volkswagen, from West Germany; DeBuis Roessingh, from Switzerland; and George Markhof from Austria, among many other well-known companies.

Investment on the part of the twelve largest enterprises totalled $21 million by the end of 1977, except for Volkswagen with $35 million. Volkswagen holds a concession of 1,400 square kilometres in southeastern Para, of which half is eventually to be converted into pastureland, enough for a herd of 120,000 cattle. Large as this Volkswagen enterprise might sound, it is far from the biggest ranch.[27]

Even Barclays Banks has managed to buy itself a small share of the Amazon.[28]

However, indigenous peoples are becoming more successful in obstructing mining and other ventures by TNCs which they deem detrimental to their interests. They have even managed to obtain royalties from mining companies, compensation for lost or damaged land and guarantees of protection of sites of cultural or religious importance. Indigenous organizations, such as the Centre for Alternative Mining Development Policy, and journals like the Multinational Monitor, are strengthening the formal networks of interested people seeking to curtail the power and limit the most harmful activities of the big corporations. But TNCs are not acquiescing easily to any new codes of behaviour which might contribute to an equalization of the relationship they have with indigenous peoples. Any accommodation of indigenous interests is likely to substantially trim their profits. In Australia, as we have already seen, mining companies were ready to spend $A 1 million on public relations to fight federal government policy on Aboriginal land rights.

While international institutions represent formidable threats to indigenous peoples, British public bodies are not untainted by this arrogant interventionism. The Commonwealth Development Corporation, for example, is constituted by Act of Parliament and empowered to assist overseas countries in the development of their economies. The CDC works along broadly commercial lines but is bound to give due regard to the development value of projects it invests in, rather than their profitability.[29] However, CDC investment in a palm oil plantation in the Philippines where indigenous Manobos were forcibly removed from their land and some were beaten and murdered by a paramilitary force employed by their partners, came under criticism in the House of Commons.[30] Since then the CDC has taken a stake in a large palm oil cultivation scheme in Ecuador and there too indigenous peoples are claiming land alienation. The plan of the Government of Ecuador is to develop palm oil on a grand scale in the Amazon region of the country. Already 400,000 hectares have been designated for development. The CDC is investing £6.5 million in the Palmoriente plantation which occupies a site of 10,000 hectares in Napo province. Dozens of Indian communities live within the project area and will be affected. Furthermore, palm oil processing results in considerable pollution and indigenous organizations are already complaining that the Palmoriente plantation has brought pollution to the River Huashito disrupting two Quichua riverine settlements. The Confederation of Amazonian Indians of Ecuador (CONFENIAE) estimates that, if the palm oil project is carried out in full, at least half of the 70,000 Indians of the area will experience a rapid deterioration in their independent way of life; they also claim that the project will cause major deforestation, widespread pollution and eventual desertification.[31]

Indigenous peoples, however, are not antagonistic to all development and most would claim that they have always undergone adaptation to changes in their environment. However, much that is termed development brings poverty, unemployment, pollution, and environmental degradation in its wake. More often than not, it is the indigenous peoples who must give up all they hold dear – land, economic self-reliance, culture and political independence – for the sake of a progress which is defined by others far away and for others' profits. 'We do not seek to stop development,' has said Pat Dodson of the Federation of Land Councils of Australia but he added 'there is no need to commit these crimes in the name of progress.'[32]

Powerful institutions such as the World Bank, the Commonwealth Development Corporation and the transnational corporations take decisions daily which affect the lives of millions of indigenous peoples with little or no consultation with them. The social and environmental impact studies which do now reluctantly get commissioned by some of these bodies, do not carry the same weight as the crucial financial and commercial considerations. If there is a choice required between profits or disruption to man, beast or environment, it is usually the former which takes precedence. Until there is some real transfer of power to indigenous peoples and, therefore, the possibility that these massive bodies must negotiate on equal terms with the owners of the land they seek to develop, the ruthless exploitation of both people and natural resources will continue largely unabated.

Notes

1. Cf. *The World Bank Annual Report 1982* (The World Bank, Washington, 1982) p.3.

2. Teresa Hayter and Catharine Watson, *Aid: rhetoric and reality* (Pluto Press, London, 1985) p.68.

3. Statement of Bruce M. Rich on behalf of the World Wildlife Fund, Friends of the Earth, Natural Resources Defense Council and others, before the Sub-Committee on International Development Institutions and Finance Committee on Banking, Finance and Urban Affairs, United States House of Representatives, Washington, 28 June 1983, p.5.

4. Cf. Walden Bello, David Kinley and Elaine Elinson, *Development debacle:*

The World Bank in the Philippines (Institute for Food and Development Policy, San Francisco, 1982) p.86.

5. Anti-Slavery Society, *The Philippines: authoritarian government, multinationals and ancestral lands* (London, 1983) pp.102-12; on the World Bank in the Philippines see also *Southeast Asia Chronicle*, no.81, December 1981.

6. David Price, 'The World Bank and native peoples: a consultant's view', testimony presented at the hearings on the environmental policies of multilateral development banks, held by the US House of Representatives Subcommittee on International Development Institutions and Finance, 29 June 1983, p.8.

7. Ibid., p.10.

8. Jack Anderson and Dale van Atta, 'The World Bank's watchdog', *Washington Post*, 6 October 1985, p.15; see also Stephen Schwartzman, 'Indigenists, environmentalists and the multilateral development banks', *Cultural Survival Quarterly*, vol.8, no.4, December 1984, pp.74-5.

9. Shelton Davis, 'Rural development programs, indigenous peoples, and multilateral lending institutions in Guatemala', testimony to the Subcommittee on International Development Institutions, US House of Representatives, 29 June 1983, p.12.

10. World Bank office memorandum, *OMS 2.34: Tribal People in Bank-financed Projects*, 11 May 1983.

11. Communication to author.

12. Survival International, 'West Papua transmigration: the invasion of tribal lands', Urgent Action Bulletin, 2 March 1985.

13. *Wall Street Journal*, 30 September 1985.

14. *The state of India's environment, 1984-5* (Centre for Science and Environment, New Delhi, 1985) pp.100-20.

15. Survival International, 'India: World Bank violates international law', Urgent Action Bulletin, 1 October 1985.

16. World Bank office memorandum (see note 10).

17. *Tribal peoples and economic development: human ecological considerations*, World Bank, May 1982.

18. The policy document begins: 'Assuming that tribal cultures will either acculturate or disappear . . .'. Ibid., p.1.

19. Cf. John Bodley, 'The World Bank Tribal Policy: Criticisms and Recommendations', testimony on behalf of the National Congress of American Indians for the House Committee on Banking, Finance and Urban Affairs, 29 June 1983.

20. Correspondence from Bruce Rich, Natural Resources Defense Council with Jerry Paterson, Chairman, Subcommittee on International Development Institutions and Finance, 20 April 1983. At the Asian Development Bank only two of a staff of 1,260 are available for overseeing environmental aspects.

21. Michael Cernea, 'Indigenous anthropologists and development-oriented research', in Hussein Fahim (ed.), *Indigenous Anthropology in Non-Western Cultures*, World Bank Report series, no.208 (Carolina Academic Press, 1982) pp.121-37.

22. Hayter and Watson, p.274.

23. Robin Wright, 'The great Carajás: Brazil's mega-program for the 80s', *Anthropology Resource Center Newsletter*, March 1983, pp.3-6.

24. *West Papua: the obliteration of a people* (Tapol, 1983), pp.33-51.

25. 'Tribal populations and international banking practices: a fundamental

conflict over development goals', testimony of National Congress of American Indians to House Banking Committee, 29 June 1983.

26. Press statement of John Mohawk, *Akwesasne Notes*, at Conference on Native Resource Control and the Multinational Corporate Challenge: Aboriginal Rights in International Perspective, Washington, 12-15 October 1982.

27. Norman Myers, *The primary source: tropical forests and our future* (W.W. Norton, New York, 1985) p.138.

28. Sue Branford and Oriel Glock, *The last frontier* (Zed Press, London, 1985) p.47.

29. *Commonwealth Development Corporation, Report and Accounts, 1984*, p.3.

30. See chapter 8.

31. Correspondence between CONFENIAE and author.

32. *Washington Post*, 16 October 1982.

13. International Action

The previous chapters have told the story, as comprehensively as such a book allows, of the worldwide situation of this loosely titled group, indigenous peoples. They have also described how indigenous and tribal peoples are organizing to defend their rights both at home and internationally. In these actions they are not alone. In the last two decades, as the indigenist movement has grown, so has the concern of international bodies like the United Nations, and individuals in the rich countries. Organizations specifically to support indigenous peoples have been formed by groups of individuals – often anthropologists, lawyers or students – and have established contacts, built up international memberships, and developed networks of media and political sympathizers. These new non-governmental organizations are an essential part of the movement of indigenous peoples and allow not only the communication of indigenous peoples with the outside world, but also make possible on many occasions communications among indigenous peoples themselves.

United Nations

The rights of all peoples and individuals are guarded by provisions in the Universal Declaration of Human Rights and made binding on ratifying governments in the various international covenants, conventions and resolutions. There are no international instruments of the United Nations which explicitly protect the rights of indigenous peoples. However, in the last 15 years the United Nations, often prompted by the vigorous lobbying of indigenous peoples and non-governmental organizations, has begun to take note of the special situation of the world's indigenous peoples and of the need for relevant international laws. It may be expected that in the next decade some new standards will be elaborated by the United Nations which specifically set out to protect indigenous peoples' rights.

Existing international law does already provide a large measure of protection of human rights which can also apply to the situations of indigenous peoples. The Convention on the Prevention and Punishment of the Crime of Genocide (1951), the Supplementary Convention on the Abolition of Slavery, the Slave Trade and Institutions and Practices similar to Slavery (1957) and the International Convention on the Elimination of All Forms of Racial Discrimination (1969) protect all groups and individuals, including indigenous peoples. The International Covenant on Civil and Political Rights (1976) specifically protects the cultural, linguistic and religious rights of minorities (article 27) and both this and the Covenant on Economic, Social and Cultural Rights (1976) declare that 'all peoples have the right of self-determination'. Article 1 of both covenants continues:

> By virtue of that right they freely determine their political status and freely pursue their economic, social and cultural development.

The following paragraph adds:

> All peoples may, for their own ends, freely dispose of their natural wealth and resources without prejudice to any obligations arising out of international economic co-operation, based upon the principle of mutual benefit, and international law. In no case may a people be deprived of its own means of subsistence.

Some 80 member states are signatories to these two principal international instruments. Finally, the Declaration on the Granting of Independence to Colonial Countries and Peoples of 1960, although not legally binding, served as a standard for many millions of peoples who at that time lived in colonial situations. Article 1 states unequivocally that

> the subjection of peoples to alien subjugation, domination and exploitation constitutes a denial of fundamental human rights, is contrary to the Charter of the United Nations and is an impediment to the promotion of world peace and cooperation.

However, although these and other international laws protect the right of self-determination and prevent discrimination, slavery and genocide, they have been largely unsuccessful in providing protection of the human rights of indigenous peoples. From the preceding chapters it will be clear that indigenous peoples are denied the right to self-determination and are the victims of all these violations. It is the very denial of these fundamental rights and freedoms that has led to a world-wide movement of indigenous peoples and non-governmental organizations to achieve very specific protection of their rights in international law as well as effective implementation.

The General Assembly of the United Nations is responsible for the implementation of the Universal Declaration of Human Rights and it acts principally through a subsidiary body, the Economic and Social Council (ECOSOC).[1] ECOSOC is responsible for overall coordination in the United Nations system and is assisted by numerous functional and regional commissions and standing committees. Since its creation in 1946, the Commission on Human Rights has been the main body responsible for submitting proposals, recommendations and reports to ECOSOC on all human rights matters. In general what is submitted by the Commission on Human Rights will be adopted by ECOSOC and the General Assembly. The Commission is made up of 43 representatives of governments who meet for five to six weeks during February and March each year to hear statements from governments and non-governmental organizations and receive reports from subsidiary bodies. It may establish *ad-hoc* committees on special items where there is particular concern, such as the human rights situation in Chile or Afghanistan, and is served also by sub-commissions.

The Sub-Commission on Prevention of Discrimination and Protection of Minorities was created in 1947 expressly to undertake studies and make recommendations 'concerning the prevention of discrimination of any kind relating to human rights and freedoms and the protection of racial, national, religious and linguistic minorities'.[2] Members of the Sub-Commission are independent experts appointed by governments, but not their representatives. There are 26 people appointed for a three-year period representing the geographical and political distributions of the United Nations. The Sub-Commission meets for five to six weeks in August and September each year and prepares its report to the Commission based upon information it has received from its own working groups and special rapporteurs.

In 1971 the Sub-Commission presented a study on racial discrimination including a chapter on indigenous populations in which further research was recommended. The Commission on Human Rights and ECOSOC approved the recommendation to undertake a broad study of the problem of discrimination against indigenous peoples and in 1972 a Special Rapporteur, José R. Martinez Cobo, was appointed. The report, much of whose work was eventually carried out by a member of the Human Rights Centre, Augusto Willemsen-Diaz, was submitted in 24 documents in 1981, 1982 and 1983. The study covered the measures adopted by the United Nations and its specialized agencies and other international action related to indigenous peoples, and contained chapters on health, housing, education, language, culture, religion, employment, land and political rights.[3] The final chapter contained conclusions, proposals and recommendations.

In the meantime other activities by the United Nations included specific items on indigenous peoples. Both the World Conferences to Combat Racism and Racial Discrimination, and two special seminars on racism in Geneva, Switzerland, and Managua, Nicaragua, produced statements of support in which the rights of indigenous peoples to their land, natural resources, traditional economy, language and culture were affirmed.[4]

In 1981 UNESCO held an international meeting on ethnocide and ethno-development in Latin America at San José, Costa Rica. Ethnocide was defined as the condition under which an ethnic group is denied the right to enjoy, develop and transmit its own culture and its own language. Ethnodevelopment, the experts judged, meant that an ethnic group should have, 'authority over its own territory and decision-making powers within the confines of its own development project, in a process of increasing autonomy and self-management.'[5]

The International Court of Justice at the Hague has also been approached by indigenous peoples for advisory opinions. However, no judgements have been made relating to indigenous peoples' rights. Member states of the United

Nations are expected to comply with its decisions and the General Assembly may request non-binding advisory opinions on any legal question.

The other United Nations body whose work bears on the rights of indigenous peoples is the High Commission for Refugees (UNHCR). In recent years the conflicts between governments and their indigenous peoples have grown in certain regions and the High Commission has been directly concerned with the civilian victims of the violence. Tens of thousands of Mayan Indians, West Papuans, Karen from Burma and hill tribes from Bangladesh have been driven from their homelands and are now forced to live in refugee camps in neighbouring countries.

However, the International Labour Organisation (ILO) is the only body within the United Nations system to have taken any specific measures related to indigenous peoples. Its Convention no. 107 concerning the Protection and Integration of Indigenous and other Tribal and Semi-Tribal Populations in Independent Countries and Recommendation no. 104 were adopted in 1957. The ILO had been concerned about the situation of indigenous peoples since its creation in 1919 and had established various panels to investigate native labour. Then in 1953 it published the first comprehensive, world-wide study of the working and living conditions of indigenous peoples.[6] Convention 107, which followed in this major study, was primarily a protective and integrationist measure. It pre-dates the contemporary indigenous movement and does not reflect the present demands for self-determination. The paternalist assumptions of the convention can be judged from its definition of tribal peoples as populations 'whose social and economic conditions are at a less advanced stage than the stage reached by other sections of the national community'. In paragraph 1, article 2 it goes on to state:

> Governments shall have the primary responsibility for developing co-ordinated and systematic action for the protection of the populations concerned and their progressive integration into the life of their respective countries.

While the right of collective ownership of traditional land is protected, removal from that land is permitted on the grounds of national security or in the interests of national economic development provided that there is compensation in equivalent land, employment or money.[7] In 1984 the convention had been ratified by 26 countries.[8]

In the last few years staff at the International Labour Office have been preparing documentation in anticipation of a new draft of the convention which would reflect the goals of the indigenous movement. As one ILO report notes:

> Convention 107 was adopted some three decades ago, long before many states had enacted concrete laws and administrative measures providing for indigenous ownership of the land. In Latin America, for example, the penetration of the Amazon basin for the development of natural resources had barely commenced. Many tribes were uncontacted, many nomadic tribes encompassed truly immense areas within their natural habitat.[9]

The new draft convention is likely to reflect the more assertive international indigenous movement and, of course, the now highly destructive assault on their homelands being made in the name of development. In September 1986 an ILO Meeting of Experts recommended that a revision of the convention be undertaken as soon as possible.

The Working Group on Indigenous Populations

Among the measures resulting from this increased international concern about indigenous peoples was a recommendation that the Economic and Social Council should establish a special Working Group. The special study carried out by the Sub-Commission on Prevention of Discrimination and Protection of Minorities, the UN decade for action to combat racism and the UNESCO meeting on ethnocide all contributed to a raising of consciousness of the international community of the serious situations faced by indigenous peoples. In May 1982 the Council authorized the establishment of the Working Group on Indigenous Populations, which held its first session in July of that year. The Working Group is made up of five members of the Sub-Commission and its first two sessions were chaired by a Norwegian professor of peace studies, Asjborn Eide. Since 1984 they have been chaired by the Greek judge, Mrs Erika-Daes.

ECOSOC mandated the Working Group to:

(a) Review developments pertaining to the promotion and protection of human rights and fundamental freedoms of indigenous populations, including information requested by the Secretary-General annually from Governments, specialized agencies, regional intergovernmental organizations and non-governmental organizations in consultative status, particularly those of indigenous peoples, to analyse such materials, and to submit its conclusions to the Sub-Commission, bearing in mind the report of the Special Rapporteur of the Sub-Commission;

(b) Give special attention to the evolution of standards concerning the rights of indigenous populations, taking account of both the similarities and the differences in the situations and aspirations of indigenous populations throughout the world.[10]

The Working Group is the only forum in the United Nations system which permits representatives of non-governmental organizations not in consultative status and even independent experts to participate freely. In the normal way only listed NGOs of recognized international standing have speaking rights or observer status at official meetings of United Nations bodies.[11] By opening up the Working Group to the victims of human rights violations and allowing them to come face to face with their governments, the meetings have taken on an immediacy and dynamism which other consultative fora lack. It has, however, raised expectations among some indigenous participants that grievances can be dealt with by the UN as in a court of law. The Working Group is not empowered to act as a chamber of complaints. Instead it is authorized to make a report to its superior body, the Sub-Commission on Prevention of Discrimination and Protection of Minorities, which in turn makes recommendations to the Commission on Human Rights. Any action must then receive the authorization of the General Assembly. This lengthy chain of communication requires about a year to run its full cycle, and much of the detail and argument of a case will be lost *en route*. Despite this cumbersome bureaucracy, the Working Group has become a focus for international lobbying on behalf of indigenous peoples and provides an opportunity for dialogue with an officially constituted United Nations body.

By its 1985 session the Working Group had received two draft declarations of principles from the World Council of Indigenous Peoples and a group consisting of the Indian Law Resource Center, Four Directions Council, National Aboriginal and Islander Legal Service, National Indian Youth Council, Inuit Circumpolar Conference and the International Indian Treaty Council (see boxes, pp.270-73). The Working Group had also decided that it should aim to produce, as a first formal step in the fulfilment of its mandate, a draft declaration of indigenous rights which could be proclaimed by the General Assembly.[12]

It appears unlikely at the moment that the Working Group will recommend a declaration based on the principles proposed by the indigenous organizations. In 1983 the then Chairman-Rapporteur pointed out that if self-determination became the primary issue it could hold up the deliberations of the Group; he also added that defining the term 'peoples' and especially determining whether a particular population was a people and possessed a right to self-determination under international law, had in the past given international bodies great difficulties.[13] At the moment the United Nations carefully avoids referring to indigenous groups as peoples.

The question of what is a people is likely to remain a serious stumbling block to the drafting of a declaration. Most states can accept that they have minorities within their boundaries, but none accepts that it has a people with rights to determine its own political status and freely dispose of its natural wealth and resources. At the heart of the matter is the issue of sovereignty. Indigenous peoples are demanding political and economic power in territories they designate as their own and this can only mean that correspondingly states will have to relinquish their own authority over that land. While most governments might readily accede to the less controversial items being recommended for the draft declaration – such as the rights to culture, language or education – they have resisted any unconditional agreement which would commit them to self-determination and full land rights for indigenous peoples.

Yet as the Special Rapporteur in his study states: 'self-determination, in its many forms, must be recognized as the basic precondition for the enjoyment by indigenous peoples of their fundamental rights.' He goes on to say in the same document:

> It must also be recognized that the right to self-determination exists at various levels and includes economic, social, cultural and political, factors. In essence, it constitutes the exercise of free choice by indigenous peoples, who must, to a large extent, create the specific content of this principle, in both its internal and external expressions, which do not necessarily include the right to secede from the State in which they live and to set themselves up as sovereign entities. This

right may in fact be expressed in various forms of autonomy within the State, including the individual and collective right to be different and to be considered different, as recognized in the statement on Race and Racial Prejudice adopted by UNESCO in 1978.[14]

Wisely perhaps, the Special Rapporteur's study recommends further investigation of the right to self-determination as it relates to indigenous peoples.

At the present time indigenous peoples at the Working Group appear to be divided over whether to press for a comprehensive declaration embracing the notion of self-determination, which may not receive the endorsement of governments represented at the Commission on Human Rights and ECOSOC, or reach agreement on the less contentious principles in order to have at least some international instruments for their protection.[15]

The Working Group meetings, although attended by over 50 indigenous organizations, are still dominated by representatives from North America, Australia and to a lesser extent South and Central America.[16] Nearly half the indigenous organizations participating in the 1985 session of the Working Group were from the USA or Canada and to date there have been no participants from India, Burma, Thailand, China, the USSR, anywhere in Africa, Pakistan or the Pacific. Indeed, probably less than one-third of the world's indigenous peoples have been represented. Furthermore, in countries where the governments are engaged in acts of war against the indigenous inhabitants – such as Bangladesh, Indonesia, Guatemala and Burma – there are no means for delegates to leave their homelands to attend the Working Group and present their cases to the international community. This is a serious shortcoming of the Working Group and permits it only a partial and limited view of the conditions experienced by indigenous peoples; it also leads the Working Group along avenues where great attention is paid to the evolution of standards and little to mechanisms to ensure the implementation of any future, or indeed existing, international laws. Indigenous peoples who take personal risks and expend precious resources to bring evidence of their situation to the only United Nations forum open to them will expect, in due course, the Commission on Human Rights to provide unequivocal moral support and bring about real improvements in their conditions. In the field of human rights there is already widespread disillusionment about the United Nations' ability to persuade member states to comply with international standards. After the fall of Idi Amin in 1979, the new President of Uganda, reflecting similar concerns, asked the General Assembly:

> For how long will the United Nations remain silent while Governments represented within this Organization continue to perpetrate atrocities against their own people? Governments come and go, but the peoples of the world remain a permanent constituency of the United Nations. It was for the well-being of the peoples of the world that the United Nations were founded in the first instance. Indeed, it is for their welfare that the United Nations must continue to work. It would be unfortunate if this Organization were reduced to a club of governments afraid to speak out boldly for the rights of the citizens of the world.[17]

Within the Working Group governments have shown varying degrees of willingness to promote the rights of indigenous peoples. A number of governments, including the Australian, Canadian, Mexican, New Zealand, Norwegian and Swedish, have expressed support for the process of evolution of human rights standards for indigenous peoples; several governments have offered to contribute to a UN-administered travel fund to assist delegates of indigenous peoples unable to afford the high costs of travel and subsistence.[18]

Other governments have strongly criticized the world-wide terms of reference of the Working Group and taken issue with the working definition of indigenous populations. The representatives of India and Bangladesh, for example, claim that they have no indigenous populations and the situation of their tribal peoples should remain outside the mandate of the Working Group. Such technical objections are contrary to the spirit in which the Working Group was set up and point clearly to the difficulties that lie ahead. The Working Group can expect considerable obstacles from those governments with poor human rights records in relation to their indigenous and tribal populations. It may be noted that the government of Bangladesh, accused by its tribal inhabitants of genocide, is a signatory of ILO Convention 107 but nonetheless, in 1985, denied independent access to indigenous areas for the purpose of supervising the application of its standards by International Labour Office staff.

Where governments are grossly violating human rights, they pay little heed to the international instruments to which they are signatories. There is no guarantee, therefore, that the declaration of principles or any subsequent convention concerning the rights of indigenous peoples will have any meaningful impact in countries where tribal and indigenous peoples face excessive discrimination, serious deprivation and genocide. However, despite these reservations about the value of further human rights instruments, many indigenous peoples and human rights organizations continue to press for more specific laws and better implementation. The act of advocacy itself can raise public awareness and influence governments conscious of world opinion.

In addition to the United Nations and its specialized agencies, other regional organizations exist which statutorily have concern for indigenous peoples. The Organization of American States' Inter-American Commission on Human Rights has a long history of involvement with indigenous peoples' rights and has heard cases on the Aché Indians of Paraguay and the Yanomami of Brazil, as well as receiving evidence about abuses in Guatemala, Nicaragua and Colombia. The Inter-American Indian Institute has been a specialized agency of the Organization of American States since 1953. The Institute carries out research, provides technical assistance, and publishes and organizes the Inter-American Conferences which are held at roughly five-yearly intervals.

Declarations of principles adopted at the Fourth General Assembly of the World Council of Indigenous Peoples in Panama, September 1984

Principle 1.   All indigenous peoples have the right of self-determination. By virtue of this right they may freely determine their political status and freely pursue their economic, social, religious and cultural development.

Principle 2.   All States within which an indigenous people lives shall recognize the population, territory and institutions of the indigenous people.

Principle 3.   The cultures of the indigenous peoples are part of the cultural heritage of mankind.

Principle 4.   The traditions and customs of indigenous peoples must be respected by the States, and recognized as a fundamental source of law.

Principle 5.   All indigenous peoples have the right to determine the person or group of persons who are included within its population.

Principle 6.   Each indigenous people has the right to determine the form, structure and authority of its institutions.

Principle 7.   The institutions of indigenous peoples and their decisions, like those of States, must be in conformity with internationally accepted human rights, both collective and individual.

Principle 8.   Indigenous peoples and their members are entitled to participate in the political life of the State.

Principle 9.   Indigenous people shall have exclusive rights to their traditional land and its resources; where the lands and resources of the indigenous peoples have been taken away without their free and informed consent such lands and resources shall be returned.

Principle 10.   The land rights of an indigenous people include surface and subsurface rights, full rights to interior and coastal waters and rights to adequate and exclusive coastal economic zones within the limits of international law.

Principle 11.   All indigenous peoples may, for their own needs, freely use their natural wealth and resources in accordance with Principles 9 and 10.

Principle 12.   No action or course of conduct may be undertaken which, directly or indirectly, may result in the destruction of land, air, water, sea ice, wildlife, habitat or natural resources without the free and informed consent of the indigenous peoples affected.

Principle 13.   The original rights to their material culture, including archeological sites, artifacts, designs, technology and works of art, lie with the indigenous people.

Principle 14.   The indigenous peoples have the right to receive education in their own language or to establish their own educational institutions. The languages of the indigenous peoples are to be respected by the States in all dealings between the indigenous people and the State on the basis of equality and non-discrimination.

Principle 15.   Indigenous peoples have the right, in accordance with their traditions, to move and conduct traditional activities and maintain friendship relations across international boundaries.

Principle 16.   The indigenous peoples and their authorities have the right to be previously consulted and to authorize the realization of all technological and scientific investigations to be conducted within their territories and to have full access to the results of the investigation.

Principle 17.   Treaties between indigenous nations or peoples and representatives of States freely entered into, shall be given full effect under national and international law.

These principles constitute the minimum standards which States shall respect and implement.

Draft declaration of principles proposed by the Indian Law Resource Center, Four Directions Council, National Aboriginal and Islander Legal Service, National Indian Youth Council, Inuit Circumpolar Conference, and the International Indian Treaty Council

Declaration of principles

1. Indigenous nations and peoples have, in common with all humanity, the right to life, and to freedom from oppression, discrimination, and aggression.

2. All indigenous nations and peoples have the right to self-determination, by virtue of which they have the right to whatever degree of autonomy or self-government they choose. This includes the right to freely determine their political status, freely pursue their own economic, social, religious and cultural development, and determine their own membership and/or citizenship, without external interference.

3. No State shall assert any jurisdiction over an indigenous nation or people, or its territory, except in accordance with the freely expressed wishes of the nation or people concerned.

4. Indigenous nations and peoples are entitled to the permanent control and enjoyment of their aboriginal ancestral–historical territories. This includes surface and subsurface rights, inland and coastal waters, renewable and non-renewable resources, and the economies based on these resources.

5. Rights to share and use land, subject to the underlying and inalienable title of the indigenous nation or people, may be granted by their free and informed consent, as evidenced in a valid treaty or agreement.

6. Discovery, conquest, settlement on a theory of *terra nullius* and unilateral legislation are never legitimate bases for States to claim or retain the territories of indigenous nations or peoples.

7. In cases where lands taken in violation of these principles have already been settled, the indigenous nation or people concerned is entitled to immediate restitution, including compensation for the loss of use, without extinction of original title. Indigenous peoples' desire to regain possession and control of sacred sites must always be respected.

8. No State shall participate financially or militarily in the involuntary displacement of indigenous populations, or in the subsequent economic exploitation or military use of their territory.

9. The laws and customs of indigenous nations and peoples must be recognized by States' legislative, administrative and judicial institutions and, in case of conflicts with State laws, shall take precedence.

10. No State shall deny an indigenous nation, community, or people residing within its borders the right to participate in the life of the State in whatever manner and to whatever degree they may choose. This includes the right to participate in other forms of collective action and expression.

11. Indigenous nations and peoples continue to own and control their material culture, including archeological, historical and sacred sites, artifacts, designs, knowledge, and works of art. They have the right to regain items of major cultural significance and, in all cases, to the return of the human remains of their ancestors for burial in accordance with their traditions.

12. Indigenous nations and peoples have the right to be educated and conduct business with States in their own languages, and to establish their own educational institutions.

13. No technical, scientific or social investigations, including archeological excavations, shall take place in relation to indigenous nations or peoples, or their lands, without their prior authorization, and their continuing ownership and control.

14. The religious practices of indigenous nations and peoples shall be fully respected and protected by the laws of States and by international law. Indigenous nations and peoples shall always enjoy unrestricted access to, and enjoyment of, sacred sites in accordance with their own laws and customs, including the right of privacy.

15. Indigenous nations and peoples are subjects of international law.

16. Treaties and other agreements freely made with indigenous nations or peoples shall be recognized and applied in the same manner and according to the same international laws and principles as treaties and agreements entered into with other States.

17. Disputes regarding the jurisdiction, territories and institutions of an indigenous nation or people are a proper concern of international law, and must be resolved by mutual agreement or valid treaty.

18. Indigenous nations and peoples may engage in self-defence against State actions in conflict with their right to self-determination.

19. Indigenous nations and peoples have the right freely to travel, and to maintain economic, social, cultural and religious relations with each other across State borders.

> 20. In addition to these rights, indigenous nations and peoples are entitled to the enjoyment of all the human rights and fundamental freedoms enumerated in the International Bill of Human Rights and other United Nations instruments. In no circumstances shall they be subjected to adverse discrimination.

Churches

In recent years the churches, both Catholic and Protestant, have moved away from an essentially evangelizing role to a supportive and even radically committed position. Some reference was made previously to the damaging part the church played in colonization, particularly in Latin America. There are also modern proselytizing organizations such as the Summer Institute of Linguistics which have been criticized by indigenous peoples for trying to destroy their culture and traditional beliefs. However, there are now clear indications that individual priests and even national and international church bodies are ready to provide assistance to indigenous peoples in their struggle for self-determination.

One of the first steps in this process took place in 1971 when the umbrella organization of the main Protestant churches, the World Council of Churches, co-sponsored the Symposium on Inter-ethnic Conflict in South America in Barbados.[19] The meeting brought together anthropologists concerned about indigenous peoples, and the Declaration of Barbados for the Liberation of the Indians, which was drafted by the participants, set forth tasks for governments, religious missions and anthropologists. On land the declaration said:

> The state must recognise and guarantee each Indian society's territory in land, legalizing it as perpetual, inalienable collective property, sufficiently extensive for population growth.

About religious missions it stated:

> We conclude that the suspension of all missionary activity is the most appropriate policy for the good of Indian society and the moral integrity of the churches involved. Until this objective can be realized the missions must support and contribute to Indian legislation.

About anthropologists it declared:

> The anthropology now required in Latin America is not that which relates to Indians as objects of study, but rather that which perceives the colonial situation and commits itself to the struggle for liberation.

The declaration also made this observation:

> Indians must organize and lead their own liberation movement otherwise it ceases to be liberating. When non-Indians pretend to represent Indians, even on occasion, assuming the leadership of the latter's groups, a new colonial situation is established. This is yet another expropriation of the Indian populations' inalienable right to determine their future.[20]

The value of the sponsorship by the World Council of Churches of the symposium cannot be underestimated and, in due course, radical commitments to indigenous land rights and self-determination were endorsed by the Council itself. In 1977 a second meeting was held in Barbados, this time including numerous indigenous representatives, and a declaration was again drafted. The text asserted:

We Indians in America are subjected to domination of two kinds: physical domination and cultural domination.

The main form taken by the physical domination is the expropriation of our land. This plundering began with the European invasion and has continued right up to the present time. Along with our land they also snatched our natural resources – the forests, the water, the minerals, the oil. What land has been left to us has been further divided, national and international frontiers have been drawn, our peoples have been isolated and divided, attempts have been made to sow conflict among us.

The physical domination is economic domination. We are exploited when we work for non-Indians who pay us less than our labour is worth. They also exploit us through trade, because they buy up our products cheaply (crops, crafts, etc.) and sell to us at a high price. This domination is not confined to the local or national level; it is international. The big transnational corporations come seeking our land, our resources, our labour, our goods and are supported in their efforts by powerful and privileged groups in non-Indian society.

Cultural domination can be said to exist when it has been thoroughly implanted in the Indian mind that Western culture, or the culture of the dominators, is the only one and represents the highest level of development, whereas their own culture is not a culture at all, but the lowest level of backwardness out of which they must rise. It follows directly from this that education is a means of dividing our people.

Cultural domination does not permit us our own forms of cultural expression, or else it misinterprets and distorts them.[21]

The World Council of Churches has maintained a high public profile over the issue of indigenous land rights, particularly in the Americas, Australia, New Zealand and recently the Pacific. It has undertaken special studies and supported indigenous organizations and projects. In 1982 its central committee recommended to member churches that they 'commit significant financial and human resources to the struggle of indigenous peoples for land rights' and 'become physically involved on the side of indigenous peoples and join the struggle against those powers and principalities which seek to deny land rights and human rights to indigenous peoples.'[22]

Priests and lay members of the Catholic Church have also been active in the defence of indigenous peoples' rights. Indeed in the predominantly Catholic countries of South America and in the Philippines, they have often been the only voice able to speak out openly. Priests, nuns and church workers are also increasingly the victims of military dictatorships in these countries and the protection from arrest and persecution they once enjoyed is no longer accorded to them by the authorities. In Brazil and Guatemala, most notably, Catholics have been at the forefront of the struggle to save the lives of indigenous peoples and defend their lands. The Indigenist Missionary Council of the Brazilian Catholic Church (CIMI), for example, sponsored most of the early meetings of Indian leaders and supported them in their direct confrontation with the government Indian agency (FUNAI). In the Philippines, Catholic Church workers have endured long periods of imprisonment for their beliefs and one tribal priest has taken up arms and joined the guerrilla forces, the New People's Army.[23]

In countries where Christianity is a minority religion, church workers are often seen by tribal peoples as among the few allies they posses and the official state religions are seen as oppressive because they represent the dominant culture. In India, for example, Hindu organizations are now promoting policies of Sanskritization in order to assimilate the mainly animist scheduled tribes; in Thailand the official Buddhist organizations have recently established a group to try to convert the animist and Christian hill tribes; in Bangladesh's Chittagong Hill Tracts numerous Buddhist temples have been desecrated or destroyed and Muslim mosques built instead.

There is no end yet to the damaging role of assimilation played by the churches. However, many parish level priests and church workers are conscious of the enormous harm done by their institution in the past and the need now to support the indigenous movement in its struggle for self-determination.

Non-governmental organizations (NGOs)

Non-governmental organizations have played a vital part in raising public awareness of indigenous peoples' issues and mobilizing support and providing much-needed funds to sustain their activities. Indigenous peoples and non-governmental organizations lobbied the United Nations over many years to provide a forum and can claim some credit for the establishment of the Working Group on Indigenous Populations in 1982. Until that time there was no direct channel to inter-governmental meetings and the international community remained largely ignorant of the situation of indigenous peoples.

There are now at least a dozen international NGOs specializing in advocacy for indigenous peoples' rights. (These do not include the indigenous peoples' organizations which are discussed in chapter 5.) The oldest is the Anti-Slavery Society which was founded in 1839 by followers of William Wilberforce to fight remnants of the slave trade. Two years earlier, in 1837, the same people concerned at the effect on the indigenous inhabitants of the flood of European settlers to the colonies, set up the Aborigines Protection Society. The Aborigines Protection Society soon became the principal secular pressure group to inform public opinion and provide evidence to Parliament. It could depend upon a world-wide network of correspondents, missionaries, traders, civil servants – sometimes at the most senior level – and members of the local population. For the sake of convenience the Aborigines Protection Society and the Anti-Slavery Society were merged in 1909. The Anti-Slavery Society has a programme of research, publications and international campaigns on issues related to the rights of indigenous peoples; its recent work has been to support indigenous organizations in their efforts to make their situations better known internationally, particularly at the United Nations.

In the last ten to 15 years there has been a proliferation of new organizations established exclusively to promote the rights of indigenous peoples. The British-based Survival International was founded in 1969 and has developed an expertise on the small, unassimilated or partially assimilated, tribal communities of South America which are especially vulnerable to modernization. The organization has a world-wide mandate and describes its aims as helping tribal peoples to exercise their rights to survival and self-determination, and to secure ownership of adequate land and resources.

Another small British-based organization is CIMRA, Colonialism and Indigenous Minorities Research and Action, which has been active since 1976. It has focused its attention particularly on Australian Aborigines and to a lesser extent on North American Indian peoples. Its occasional newspaper, however, covers the situation of indigenous peoples world-wide. Closely associated with CIMRA is Partizans, which was created to research and monitor the activities of the mining corporation Rio Tinto Zinc, and its subsidiaries. The group has collected information on the companies' mining projects on indigenous lands, particularly in Australia, and have publicly protested at shareholders' meetings. There is also a small group – the Onaway Trust – which produces a journal and provides funds exclusively for indigenous peoples' projects, mainly in North America.

Finally, the Minority Rights Group, in common with the Anti-Slavery Society and Survival International, has consultative status with the Economic and Social Council of the United Nations, but is primarily an educational rather than a campaigning and lobbying organization. It is based in London and produces five or so comprehensive reports a year on minorities of all kinds. Of the nearly 70 reports it has published since its creation in 1965, about 15 are on indigenous peoples. The Minority Rights Group aims through its publications to foster understanding of minorities and promote respect for human rights.

Elsewhere in Europe other supporting organizations were set up during the late 1960s and 1970s. In 1968 the International Working Group on Indigenous Affairs (IWGIA) was formed in Denmark and, since that time, has produced a wide-ranging and extensive collection of documents and articles on indigenous peoples, in English and Spanish. In Germany in 1969 the Gesellschaft fur bedrohte Volker (Organization for Endangered Peoples) was founded to publish literature on, and lobby on behalf of, national, ethnic, religious and indigenous minorities. Then in 1977, following the NGO Conference on Indigenous Peoples, the Documentation Centre for Indigenous Peoples (DOCIP) was established. Although DOCIP does no lobbying, it has brought together substantial information on indigenous peoples under one roof. In 1980 in the Netherlands the Workgroup on Indigenous Peoples (WIP) was set up, after the successful Fourth Russell Tribunal on the Indians of the Americas. The Workgroup is run mainly by voluntary staff and has produced educational material, the full documentation of the Russell Tribunal and publishes a regular journal; it also organizes meetings and marches on indigenous peoples' issues in the Netherlands.

In the United States of America two organizations advocating indigenous peoples' rights have been formed. Cultural Survival conducts research on urgent issues, finances projects for indigenous peoples and publishes for both a general audience and policy-makers. Since 1976 it has produced a quarterly magazine of articles written primarily by activist anthropologists. The Anthropology Resource Center (ARC) was also established in the mid-1970s and has focused much of its attention on the indigenous peoples of the western hemisphere, and particularly on the damaging effects of development projects. The ARC has produced special reports and newsletters, and has sponsored seminars and presented testimonies to the US Congress.

In addition to these organizations there are numerous smaller or more specialized groups.[24] Other organizations, such as the American Anthropological Association or broader-based human rights organizations like Amnesty International, have nevertheless undertaken special studies or made specific statements on indigenous peoples. The International Commission of Jurists, environmental groups like Greenpeace and Friends of the Earth, and some of the large development NGOs like Oxfam, have also identified the issues of indigenous peoples as particular areas of concern. There are now few agencies in the human rights, environmental and development fields which do not recognize that tribal and indigenous peoples are a special target for their programmes.

In the last 20 years the organizations of indigenous peoples have multiplied and grown stronger and, as they have done so, many other inter-governmental and non-governmental organizations have developed to support or react to the movement. The expansion of activity on behalf of indigenous peoples' rights, of a more institutional and limited kind, from the United Nations, the International Labour Organisation or the World Bank, and of a more radical kind from the numerous NGOs that have been born since the 1960s, has had mainly positive effects.

Today the international community, the press and the general public are infinitely better informed of the tragedies and violations occurring in what were once deemed insignificant backward areas to peoples considered primitive and harmless. There has been a dawning of consciousness and this had led to the unexpected mobilization of important institutions, such as the churches, as well as committed individuals and solidarity groups. Human rights violations against a dozen Indians in Brazil are likely to draw protest world-wide and considerable press coverage; they may even hold up million-dollar loans or threaten the cancellation of a development project. Of course, no amount of letters of protest or international condemnation can stem the sanguinary violence of military rulers like those of Guatemala. Only the world's most powerful governments can have any influence on those events. But where some concern for public image and a certain social consciousness exist, the NGOs and the appeals of bodies like the United Nations or the International Labour Organisation, can have an impact.

But the proliferation of non-governmental organizations working for the human rights of indigenous peoples has also brought its difficulties. There continues to be a great duplication of research and publications, and there is as yet little pooling of resources and coordination of action. Yet providing the necessary credible countervailing arguments and evidence to successfully call into question powerful institutions like the World Bank and the transnational corporations, with their highly trained professional staff, requires comparable skills and efficiency, and not mere dedication.

Notes

1. The General Assembly also has a Human Rights Committee established in 1977 which communicates directly with member states; ECOSOC operates under Resolution 1503 (XLVIII) an *in camera* work group to consider communications about human rights from individuals and organizations. See *United Nations action in the field of human rights* (United Nations, New York, 1980) pp.282-3; 338-43.

2. For further analysis of the international instruments protecting indigenous peoples, see Robert T. Coulter, 'The evolution of international human rights standards: implications for indigenous populations of the Americas', Indian Law Resource Center, Washington, 11 June 1984; Lee Swepston and Roger Plant, 'International standards and the protection of the land rights of indigenous and tribal populations', *International Labour Review*, vol.124, no.1, January–February 1985, pp.91-106.

3. UN Economic and Social Council, *Study of the problem of discrimination against indigenous peoples* submitted by the Special Rapporteur José R. Martinez Cobo, refs. E/CN.4/Sub.2/476 and Add. 1-6, E/CN.4/Sub.2/1982/2 and Add. 1-7 and E/CN.4/Sub.2/1983/21 and Add. 1-8.

4. E.g. 'The Conference endorses the right of indigenous peoples to maintain their traditional structure of economy and culture, including their own language, and also recognizes the special relationship of indigenous peoples to their land and stresses that their land, land rights and natural resources should not be taken away from them.' World Conference to Combat Racism and Racial Discrimination, Geneva, Switzerland, 14-25 August 1978.

5. *Declaration of San José*, UNESCO meeting of experts on Ethno-development and Ethnocide in Latin America, San José, Costa Rica, 7-11 December 1981.

6. International Labour Office, *Indigenous peoples: living and working conditions of aboriginal populations in independent countries* (Geneva, 1953).

7. Cf. ILO Convention no.107, articles 11 and 12.

8. Ratifying countries are: Angola, Argentina, Bangladesh, Belgium, Bolivia, Brazil, Colombia, Costa Rica, Cuba, Dominican Republic, Ecuador, Egypt, El Salvador, Ghana, Guinea-Bissau, Haiti, India, Malawi, Mexico, Pakistan, Panama, Paraguay, Peru, Portugal, Syrian Arab Republic and Tunisia.

9. International Labour Organisation, 'A note on indigenous peoples and the land' (International Labour Office, Geneva, 1984).

10. ECOSOC Resolution 1982/34 of 7 May 1982.

11. Arrangements for consultation with non-governmental organizations are contained in ECOSOC resolution 1296 (XLIV) of 27 February 1950.

12. Annexe IIa of *Report of the Working Group on Indigenous Populations on its fourth session*, E/CN.4/Sub.2/1985/22, 27 August 1985.

13. Cf. *Report of the Working Group on Indigenous Populations on its second session*, E/CN.4/Sub.2/1983/22, 23 August 1983, para. 100.

14. *Study of the problem of discrimination* (Cobo Report), p.74, paras. 580 and 581.

15. Cf. Coulter, pp.72-4.

16. There are nine indigenous NGOs with consultative status: The Four Nations Council, Indigenous World Association, International Indian Treaty Council, Indian Law Resource Center, Indian Council for South America (CISA), Inuit Circumpolar Conference, National Aboriginal and Islander Legal Service, National Indian Youth Council and World Council of Indigenous Peoples.

17. Cited in Theo von Boven, *People matter: views on international human rights policy* (Meulenhoff, Amsterdam, 1982) p.61.

18. A voluntary fund for indigenous peoples was approved by the Commission on Human Rights and ECOSOC in 1985; an NGO fund to assist indigenous peoples with the travel to Geneva has been operating since 1984 and is administered by the Anti-Slavery Society in cooperation with several European NGOs; other NGOs, such as Oxfam, assist indigenous peoples with travel to the Working Group on an *ad hoc* basis.

19. The symposium took place in Bridgetown, Barbados, 25-30 January 1971.

20. Texts from the Declaration of Barbados, January 1971.

21. Declaration of Barbados, July 1977.

22. *Land Rights for Indigenous People*, statement adopted by the Central Committee of the World Council of Churches, July 1982.

23. E.g. Conrado Balweg, a Bontoc tribal person. In 1979 four Catholic priests joined the New People's Army.

24. E.g. Svensk Indiaski Forbundet (Sweden), Information zentrale fur Nordamerikanische Indianer (Germany), Incomindios Schweiz (Switzerland), Center for World Indigenous Studies (USA), Asociación Diffusion Inti (France), Commission Pro-Indio (Brazil), Comité Belge-Amerique Indienne (Belgium) and many others.

14. Echoes in the West

In the last decades indigenous peoples have faced an apparently inexorable force which has driven them from their lands, pushed them increasingly into the towns and cities and spurned their culture, customs and knowledge. They have reacted by forming organizations and petitioning and even taking up arms against governments. In some places they have had some successes and halted incursions on to their homelands or at least gained a temporary respite. But well-publicized successes disguise the overall weakness of isolated indigenous and tribal minorities confronted by the enormously powerful institutions of governments, banks and transnational corporations. Between the rapacious and short-sighted proponents of Western development and the politically and economically weak indigenous communities whose land and labour are coveted, there is an unequal struggle. The international activities of the indigenous movement, with its notable achievements, belie the generally low level of awareness of many tribal minorities. They, unlike the activists and leaders of the indigenous movement, remain largely uninformed of the discussions and decisions occurring in languages other than their own and in offices and towns far from their homes. Their first knowledge of a hydro-electric dam, a colonization scheme or a massive mining project will often be when construction workers arrive to build the first site offices or when the police come and remove them from their villages or when the stream changes colour and the fish all die. By then, halting the march of national development, arranged in the country's capital, funded in Washington with the cooperation of conglomerates in New York or London, Tokyo or Frankfurt, will be almost impossible. The economic development which spells ruination for the indigenous inhabitants will have been signed, sealed and delivered.

The previous chapters have presented adequate examples of the effects of many development projects on indigenous and tribal peoples. There have been cases where tens of thousands of tribal peoples have been removed from land they have occupied for generations without proper consultation or compensation; there have been occasions when, with great courage, they have refused to move and won the support of people around the world. But probably most of us, while regretting the destruction of tribal societies and the violence which often accompanies development, will regard it as inevitable. After all, most tribal economies have a low productivity, indigenous peoples occupy large tracts of land with abundant natural resources, and their standards of living, health and education are comparatively low. Surely economic development, the apologists might argue, is both inevitable and, in the long run, beneficial.

These assumptions may well be shared by many in the so-called underdeveloped countries. The governments of poor countries are under great pressures to develop underpopulated regions and sometimes the interests of the indigenous minority may well be irreconcilable with those of the poor majority. Furthermore, it certainly should be recognized that not all politicians, bureaucrats and technocrats involved in these processes are completely insensitive to indigenous political and economic systems nor are they malevolently determined to destroy them and merge indigenous peoples into the mainstream at all costs.

There are also plenty of indigenous peoples who are well disposed towards some form of development; very few would deny the benefits of modern medicine or certain advances in science and agriculture and many would want to share in the material fruits of a more productive economy. Nor should it be assumed that indigenous peoples are unwilling to accommodate a development policy which genuinely advanced the interests of the majority poor of the nation. If there is a conflict between indigenous peoples and development, it is because they are hostile to a development which is materialist rather than human, one that brings benefits to the already rich and powerful minorities rather than the poor majority, and one that is dangerously short-sighted since it permanently destroys the environment.

In their critique of materialist development, indigenous peoples now find some echoes in the West. René Dumont, for example, the French agronomist, has commented:

> Development, as it has been viewed by the United Nations for some twenty-five years, consists of bringing the Third World to resemble our civilization, as if the latter were a model of perfection.[1]

It was recognized some years ago that the 'apocalyptic trinity' of population growth, scarcity of resources and environmental destruction were bound to set limits to growth.[2] The burgeoning of non-governmental organizations and political parties addressing themselves to environmental and development issues, and the spread of informal bodies of opinion, all testify to a new consciousness in the West that the growth fetish is misconceived and dangerous for all. Instead a more self-sufficient strategy for development is gaining followers. One writer has stated, perhaps unduly optimistic as yet, that:

> In the wake of the monetary and oil crises of the early 1970s there has now emerged something like a world consensus, not only on the needs for development of the world as a whole, but also on self-reliance as a possible means of bringing about such development. Self-reliant developmentalism is far from the traditional Western European concept of economic development, which is grounded in the belief that development is basically a matter of consistent annual rises in the gross national product and per capita income.[3]

In the West's desire to conquer and civilize, it had assumed that all those who were weaker had somehow got left behind. The aboriginal inhabitants were seen simply as stagnant and unenterprising. But the crisis now affecting the rich countries, and the poor countries anxious to follow their strictures, has given some pause for reflection. Are indigenous peoples perhaps doing something right? Is there something which peoples of capitalist and Communist countries can learn? Are some things already being learned?

Of course, it is not possible for the complex, urbanized and industrialized societies prevalent in so many parts of the world, to return to a state of nature. Nor is the land capable of absorbing this large population. But these are not the messages coming from indigenous peoples. In claiming their rights to the land, they demand territorial integrity and a respect for the sacred quality of nature. Chief Seattle in a speech over a century ago makes this point:

> You must teach your children that the ground under their feet is the ashes of your grandfathers. So that they will respect the land, tell your children that the earth is rich with the lives of our kin. Teach the children what we have taught our children, that the earth is our mother. Whatever befalls the earth befalls the sons of the earth. If men spit upon the ground, they spit upon themselves. This we know: the earth does not belong to man; man belongs to the earth.[4]

The thought was echoed by Petra Kelly, a spokesperson for the Green Party in Germany:

> Humankind must not consider the land and what it supports in terms of property or real estate. We are all temporary custodians of the land – entrusted to us for passing unimpaired to future generations.[5]

For the future there is little likelihood of the vulnerable communities described in this book being left unchanged by the powerful political and economic forces sweeping over them. Nor would indigenous peoples welcome any paternalist intervention to protect them in artificially maintained human zoos in which they survive at the behest of the dominant society and not as a right. What must be hoped and worked for is the realization that there are common interests between indigenous peoples and other individuals and organizations critical of the present model of development.

Notes

1. René Dumont, 'For a moral economy in Bangladesh', *Reports*, vol.13, no.4, January 1985, p.23.
2. The Club of Rome's *The limits to growth* (1972) is one of several such reports.
3. Monica Weregah, 'Self-reliance and the search for an alternative life-style in industrial countries', in J. Galtung *et al., Self-reliance: a strategy for development* (Institute of Development Studies, Geneva, 1980).
4. Speech made by Chief Seattle in 1854 in reply to an offer from the United

States Government for a large area of Indian land.

5. Petra Kelly cited in *International Foundation for Development Alternatives Dossier*, no.35, April/May 1983.

Appendix A:

Select List of Indigenous Peoples' Organizations and Non-governmental Organizations with a Special Concern for Indigenous and Tribal People

There are many hundreds of indigenous peoples' organizations in the world, some representing single communities and others wider national or regional groupings. In certain countries, such as the United States of America, there are a great many organizations; in others – in the Asian countries for example – there are fewer formal political organizations of indigenous and tribal peoples.

The ensuing list of indigenous peoples' organizations is highly selective and indicates only some of the main groups actively working for self-determination, land rights and a greater participation in national development. The names and addresses of the organizations are correct at the time of going to print.

A select list of non-governmental organizations especially or exclusively concerned with indigenous peoples is also given. However, non-governmental organizations specializing in development or environmental issues, such as Christian Aid, the Catholic aid agencies, Oxfam, Friends of the Earth, Greenpeace and many others, are increasingly directing their programmes towards indigenous peoples. The addresses of these organizations are omitted.

INDIGENOUS PEOPLES' ORGANIZATIONS

World Council of Indigenous Peoples
(International Secretariat)
555 King Edward Avenue
Ottawa, Ontario
Canada K1N 6NS

Central/South America

Consejo Regional de Pueblos Indigenas (CORPI)
Apartado 6979–1000
San José
Costa Rica

Alianza Nacional de Profesionales Indigenas Bilingues AC
Madero 67–60 piso
Despacho 611
Mexico 1D.G.
CP 06000

MISURASATA
Apartado 437
Paras
San José
Costa Rica

MISATAN
Puerto Cabezas
Costa Atlantica
Nicaragua

Consejo Indio de Sur America (CISA)
Apartado 2054
Correo Central
Lima
Peru

Movimiento Indio Tupac Katavi (MITKA)
Chitakolla Centre
Casilla 20214
Correo Central
La Paz
Bolivia

Comite de Pueblos y Communidades Indigenas del Oriente Boliviano (CIDOB)
Casilla 4213
Santa Cruz
Bolivia

União dos Naçoes Indigenas (UNI)
C.P. 70880
70.000 Brasilia DF
Brazil

ADMAPU
Casilla 1676
Temuco
Chile

Asociación Regional Mapuche Nehuen-Mapu
Bulnes 699
Oficinas 309–310
Temuco
Chile

Consejo Regional Indigena del Cauca (CRIC)
Apartado Aereo 516
Popayan
Colombia

Confederación de Nacionalidades Indigenas de la Amazonia Ecuatoriana
(CONFENIAE)
Apartado Postal 4180
Quito
Ecuador

Consejo Nacional de Coordinación de las Nacionalidades Indigenas del Ecuador
(CONACNIE)
Apartado 4180
Quito
Ecuador

Movimiento Indio Tupac Amaru (MITA)
Apartado 1831
Lima 100
Peru

Asociación Interetnica para el Desarrollo de la Selva Peruana (AIDESEP)
San Eugenio 981
Sra. Catalina
Lima 13
Peru

North America

Committee for Original Peoples Entitlement (COPE)
Box 2000
Innuvik, N.W.T.
Canada

Indigenous Survival International
Dene National Office
PO Box 2338
Yellowknife N.W.T.
Canada X1A 2P7

Inuit Tapirisat of Canada
176 Gloucester St (3rd Floor)
Ottawa
Ontario
Canada

Innu Kanatuapatshet
Sheshatshit
Labrador (Ntesinan)
Canada AOP IMO

Metis National Council
116 Middleton Crescent
Saskatoon
Saskatchewan
Canada S75 2W4

Native Council of Canada
72 Metcalf St
Suite 200
Ottawa
Ontario
Canada N6A 3N1

National Indian Brotherhood Assembly of First Nations
222 Queen St. Ste 500
Capital Square Building
Ottawa
Ontario
Canada K1P 5V9

Native Women's Association of Canada
195a Bank St
Ottawa
Ontario
Canada K29 1W7

Union of New Brunswick Indians
35 Dedham St
Fredericton
New Brunswick
Canada E3A 2U2

Four Directions Council
4733 no.17th Avenue
NE 37 Seattle
Washington 98105
USA

Indian Law Resource Center
601 E Street, SE
Washington DC 20003
USA

Indigenous Peoples Network Research Center
PO Box 364
Rochester VT 05767
USA

International Indian Treaty Council
777 United Nations Plaza
New York, NY 10017
USA

Mohawk Nation/Akwesasne Notes
via Rooseveltown
NY 13683
USA

National Indian Youth Council
201 Hermosa Drive NE
Albuquerque NM87108
USA

Asia

Burma
Human Rights Committee for Non-Burman Nationalities
PO Box 118
Chiang Mai 50000
Thailand

India
Centre for Tribal Conscientisation
4 Shantadurga
41/5 Karve Rd
Pune 411 038, Maharashtra
India

Indonesia
OPM (Free Papua Movement)
PO Box 11582
The Hague
Netherlands

Republic of South Moluccas
PO Box 9841
1006 Amsterdam
Netherlands

Japan
Ainu Kyokai,
Asahikawa
Sapporo
Hokkaido
Japan

Philippines
Cordillera Peoples' Alliance
Room 304, Laperal Building
Session Rd
Baguio City, 02021
Philippines

Mindanao Tribal Resource Center
PO Box 98
Butuan City 8001
Philippines

Oceania/(Australasia and the Pacific Islands)

Australia and New Zealand
Aboriginal Mining Information Centre
PO Box 237
Healesville 3777
Victoria
Australia

National Federation of Land Councils
PO Box 3620
Alice Springs
N.T. 5750
Australia

National Organization of Aboriginal and Islander Legal Services
PO Box 143
Chippendale 2008
N.S.W. Australia

Waitangi Action Committee
PO Box 61140
Otara
Aotearoa
(New Zealand)

Europe

Inuit Circumpolar Conference
PO Box 204 DK 3900
Nuuk
Greenland

Nordic Sami Council
99980 Utsjoki
Finland

Norske Reindrifssamers Landsforbund
PO Box 508
9001 Tromsö
Norway

Sami Institit'ta
PO Box 93
9520 Kantokeiro
Norway

Svenska Samers Riksforbund
Brogaten 5
90248 Umea
Sweden

NON-GOVERNMENTAL ORGANIZATIONS SUPPORTING INDIGENOUS PEOPLES

Europe

Anti-Slavery Society
180 Brixton Road
London SW9 6AT
UK

Committee for Indigenous Minority Research (CIMRA)
5 Caledonian Road
London N1
UK

Documentation Centre for Indigenous Peoples (DOCIP)
PO Box 59
CH 1211-Geneva 21
Switzerland

Gesellschaft fur Bedrohte Völker
Postfach 2024
D–3400 Gottingen
West Germany

International Work Group for Indigenous Affairs (IWGIA)
Fiolstraede 10
DK–1171 Copenhagen K
Denmark

Minority Rights Group
29 Craven Street
London WC2N 5NG
UK

Onaway Trust
275 Main Street
Shadwell
Leeds LS17 8LH
UK

Survival International
310 Edgware Road
London W2 1DY
UK

Svensk-Indianska Forbundet
Box–9113
S-10272 Stockholm
Sweden

Workgroup for Indigenous Peoples (WIP)
PO Box 4098
1009 AB Amsterdam
Netherlands

South America

Centro Ecumenico de Documentação e Informação (CEDI)
Av. Higienopolis 983
CEP 01238,m São Paulo
Brazil

Comissão Pela Criação do Parqui Yanomami (CCPY)
Rua São Carlos do Pinhal 345
01333 São Paulo
Brazil

USA

Anthropology Resource Center
PO Box 15266
Washington DC 20003–0266
USA

Center for Alternative Mining Development Policy
1121 University Avenue
Madison
Wisconsin 53715
USA

Cultural Survival
11 Divinity Avenue
Cambridge
MA 02138
USA

Asia

Sahabat Alam Malaysia
(Friends of the Earth)
37 Lorong Birch
10250 Penang
Malaysia

Select Bibliography

The following list of books, articles and special reports is a small selection of what is a growing literature on indigenous peoples' issues. Organizations of indigenous peoples are now also producing newspapers and journals about matters of concern, not only to inform their own people but the wider indigenous movement. Special NGOs supporting indigenous peoples publish documentation in English for their subscribers and members. For people wishing to keep informed about the situation of indigenous peoples the following organizations may be contacted:

Anti-Slavery Society: *The Reporter* (annual) and *Anti-Slavery Newsletter* (quarterly)
Cultural Survival: *Cultural Survival Quarterly* and *Occasional Papers* series
International Work Group on Indigenous Affairs: *IWGIA Newsletter* (quarterly) and *IWGIA documents*
Onaway Trust: *Onaway* (quarterly)
Survival International: *Annual Review* and *SINews* (quarterly) *Urgent Action Bulletins*

Adams, Patricia, and Solomon, L., *In the name of progress* (Energy Probe Research Foundation, Toronto, 1985).
Americas Watch, *Human Rights in Guatemala: no neutrals allowed* (Washington, 1982).
Amnesty International, *Guatemala: a government program of political murder* (1981).
Anti-Slavery Society, 'Incidences of slavery and abuses against rural workers in Guatemala, 1976-1978', report for the United Nations Working Group on Slavery, 1978.
—— 'Paraguay: enslavement of Indians and the servile condition of peasants', report to the United Nations Commission on Human Rights, 1978.
—— 'Incidence of slavery and abuses against rural workers in Guatemala, 1976-1978', report to the United Nations Commission on Human Rights, 1978.
—— 'The land rights of Latin American Indians', report to the International NGO Conference on Indigenous Peoples and the Land, 15-18 September 1981.
—— 'Bonded labour in India', statement to the United Nations Sub-Commission on Prevention of Discrimination and Protection of Minorities, August 1982.
—— *The Philippines: authoritarian government multinationals and ancestral lands* (1983).

——— *Guatemala: UN whitewash?*, Special Bulletin, August 1984.

——— 'Bonded and forced labour in Peru and India', report to the United Nations Working Group on Slavery, 1984.

——— *The Chittagong Hill Tracts: militarization, oppression and the hill tribes* (1984).

Arens, R., *Genocide in Paraguay* (Temple University Press, 1976).

Armstrong, Terence, *Russian settlement in the north* (Cambridge University Press, 1965).

Arnhem, Kaj, *The Maasai and the state: the impact of rural development policies on a pastoral people in Tanzania*, IWGIA document 52, 1985.

Aronson, Dan R., 'Pastoralists: losing ground in Somalia', *ARC Newsletter*, Boston, vol.6, no.1, March 1982.

Asch, Michael, 'Dene political rights', *Cultural Survival Quarterly*, vol.8, no.4, December 1984, pp.33-7.

Ashworth, Georgina (ed.), *World Minorities*, vol.I (Quartermaine House, 1977).

——— *World Minorities*, vol.II (Quartermaine House, 1978).

——— *World Minorities in the Eighties* (Quartermaine House, 1980).

Aspelin, Paul, and Santos, Silvio Coelho dos, *Indian areas threatened by hydro-electric projects in Brazil*, IWGIA document 44, 1981.

Baer, Lars Ande, 'The Sami – an indigenous people in their own land', *The Sami National Minority in Sweden* (Rattsfonden (Legal Rights Foundation), Stockholm, 1982).

Bailey, Robert, 'Development in the Ituri forest of Zaire', *Cultural Survival Quarterly*, vol.6, no.2, Spring 1982, pp.23-4.

Barre, Marie-Chantal, 'De l'indigénisme à l'indianisme', *Le Monde Diplomatique*, March 1982.

——— 'Le drame des Indiens Miskitos au Nicaragua et son exploitation politique', *Le Monde Diplomatique*, April 1982.

Bello, Walden; Kinley, David; and Elinson, Elaine, *Development debacle: The World Bank in the Philippines* (Institute for Food and Development Policy, San Francisco, 1982).

Bennet, Gordon, and Colson, Audrey, *The damned: the plight of the Akawaio Indians of Guyana*, Survival International Document VI, n.d.

Berdichewsky, Bernardo, *The Araucanian Indian in Chile*, IWGIA document 20, 1975.

Berreman, Gerald D., 'The movement to save the Himalayas', *The Global Reporter*, vol.1, no.4, Spring 1984, pp.16-18.

Bodley, John, 'The World Bank Tribal Policy: Criticisms and Recommendations', testimony on behalf of the National Congress of American Indians for the House Committee on Banking, Finance and Urban Affairs, 29 June 1983.

Branford, Sue, and Glock, Oriel, *The last frontier* (Zed Press, London, 1985).

Brody, Hugh, 'Ecology, politics and change: the case of the Eskimo', *Development and Change*, vol.9, no.1, pp.21-40.

Brown, Dee, *Bury my heart at Wounded Knee* (Picador, London, 1975).

Budiardjo, Carmel, and Liong, Liem Soei, *The war against East Timor* (Zed Press, London, 1984).

Catholic Institute for International Relations, *British investment and the use of paramilitary terrorism in plantation agriculture in Agusan del Sur, Philippines* (August 1982).

Caufield, Catherine, *In the rainforest* (Heinemann, London, 1985).

Centre for Science and Environment, *The state of India's environment, 1982* (New Delhi, 1982).

—— *The state of India's environment, 1984-5* (New Delhi, 1985).

Centro de Estudios y Acción Social, *El Pueblo Guaymi y su futura* (Panama, 1982).

Chartier, Clem, 'Aboriginal rights and land issues: the Metis perspective', Metis National Council, April 1983.

Chaumeil, Jean Pierre, *Between zoo and slavery: the Yagua of Eastern Peru in their present situation*, IWGIA document 49, 1984.

Christensen, Rosemary Ackley, 'Urban Indians', testimony to the Fourth Russell Tribunal on the Rights of the Indians of the Americas, Rotterdam, 1980.

Churchill, Ward, 'The situation of the Indigenous Populations in the United States', *Akwesasne notes* (Rooseveltown, NY), vol. 17, no.1, Winter 1985, pp.18-19.

Clark, Roger, and Roff, Sue, *Micronesia: the problem of Palau* (Minority Rights Group, 1984).

Colchester, Marcus (ed.), *The health and survival of the Venezuelan Yanoama*, ARC/SI/IWGIA document 53, 1985.

Conolly, Violet, *Siberia today and tomorrow: a study of economic resources, problems and achievements* (Collins, London, 1975).

Coppens, Walter, *The anatomy of a land invasion scheme in Yekuana territory, Venezuela*, IWGIA document 9, 1972.

Corry, Stephen, 'Cycles of dispossession: Amazonian Indians and government in Peru', *Survival International Review*, no.43, 1984, pp.45-70.

Coulter, Robert T., 'The evolution of international human rights standards: implications for indigenous populations of the Americas', Indian Law Resource Center, Washington, June 1984.

Creery, *The Inuit (Eskimo) of Canada* (Minority Rights Group, 1983).

Cultural Survival, *Brazilian Indians and the law*, Occasional Paper 5, October 1981.

—— *In the paths of Polonoroeste: endangered peoples of western Brazil*, Occasional Paper 6, October 1981.

Davis, Shelton, *Victims of the miracle* (Cambridge University Press, 1977).

—— 'The social roots of political violence in Guatemala', *Cultural Survival Quarterly*, vol.7, no.1, Spring 1983, pp.4-11.

Dines, Mary, 'Eritrea's War for Liberation', *Cultural Survival Quarterly*, vol.8, no.4, December 1984, pp.54-7.

Dixon, Marlene (ed.), *On trial: Reagan's war against Nicaragua* (Zed Press, London, 1985).

Dreyer, June Teufel, *China's forty millions* (Harvard University Press, 1976).

Dyson-Hudson, Neville and Rada, 'The structure of East African herds and the future of East African herders, *Development and Change*, vol.13, no.2, April 1982, pp.213-38.

Eberhard, Wolfram, *China's minorities: yesterday and today* (Wadsworth Publishing Co., California, 1982).

Eglin, Jean, and Théry, Hervé, *Le pillage de l'Amazonie* (Maspero, Paris, 1982).

Fourth Russell Tribunal on the Rights of the Indians of the Americas, *Non-selected cases: Central America* (Amsterdam, 1980).

Gedicks, Al, 'Lands for dreaming or mining?', *The Global Reporter*, vol.1, no.3, Fall 1983, p.13.

Gjording, Chris N., *The Cerro Colorado copper project and the Guaymi Indians of Panama*, Cultural Survival Occasional Paper 3, March 1981.

Goldsmith, E., and Hildyard, N., *The social and environmental effect of large dams* (Wadebridge Ecological Centre, 1984).

Good, Kenneth, *Papua New Guinea: a false economy* (Anti-Slavery Society, 1986).

Goodland, R., and Irwin, H., *Amazon jungle: green hell to red desert?* (Elsevier, New York, 1975).

Gordon, Robert, and Schire, Carmel (eds.), *The future of former foragers: Australia and Southern Africa*, Cultural Survival Occasional Paper 18, October 1985.

Government of India, *Report of the Commissioner for Scheduled Castes and Scheduled Tribes, July 1978–March 1979*, Twenty-Sixth Report, New Delhi, 1979.

—— *Report of the Commissioner for Scheduled Castes and Scheduled Tribes, 1979–1981*, part 1, Twenty-Seventh Report, New Delhi, 1981.

Grainger, Alan, *Desertification* (Earthscan, London, 1984).

Gretton, John, *Western Sahara: the fight for self-determination* (Anti-Slavery Society, London, 1976).

Harrer, Heinrich, *Seven years in Tibet* (Pan, London, 1956).

Hayter, Teresa, and Watson, Catharine, *Aid: rhetoric and reality* (Pluto Press, London, 1985).

Henningsgaard, William, *The Akawaio, the Upper Mazaruni hydro-electric project and national development in Guyana*, Cultural Survival Occasional Paper 4, June 1981.

Hickey, Gerald C., 'Some aspects of hill tribe life in Vietnam', Peter Kunstadter (ed.), *Southeast Asian tribes, minorities and nations*, vol.II (Princeton University Press, 1967), pp.745-69.

Hickey, Gerald C., and Wright, Jesse, *The hill people of northern Thailand: social and economic development* (USAID, 1978).

Hitchcock, Robert K., 'Foragers on the move', *Cultural Survival Quarterly*, vol.9, no.1, February 1985, pp.31-6.

Hodges, Tony, *The Western Sahara* (Minority Rights Group, London, 1984).

Holland, Luke, 'Holy smoke: Protestant missions and the Indians of Paraguay', *Survival International Review*, no.43, 1984, pp.36-44.

Howe, James, 'Kindling self-determination among the Kuna', *Cultural Survival Quarterly*, vol.6, no.3, Summer 1982, pp.15-17.

Humphrey, Caroline, 'Pastoral nomadism in Mongolia: the role of herdmen's cooperatives in a national economy', *Development and Change*, vol.9, no.1, January 1978, pp.133-60.

Hvalkof, Soren, and Aaby, Peter (eds.), *Is God an American?* (IWGIA/Survival International, 1981).

International Labour Organisation, 'Indigenous and tribal peoples and land rights' (International Labour Office, 1984).

IWGIA, *Guatemala 1978: the massacre at Panzos*, document 33, 1978.

Jiménez, Nelly, *The dynamics of the Yecuana political system*, IWGIA document 12, 1973.

Jones, Mervyn, *The Sami of Lapland* (Minority Rights Group, 1982).

Jones, Steve, 'Tribal underdevelopment in India', *Development and Change*, vol.9, no.1, January 1978, pp.41-70.

Jorgensen, J. (ed.), *Native Americans and energy development II* (Anthropology Resource Center and Seventh Generation Fund, 1984).

Kloos, Peter, *The Akuriyo of Surinam: a case of emergence from isolation*, IWGIA document 27, 1977.

Lewis, I.M. (ed.), *Nationalism and self-determination in the horn of Africa* (Ithaca Press, London, 1981).

Leymarie, Philippe, 'Les enjeux stratégiques de las crise néo-calédonienne', *Le Monde Diplomatique*, March 1985, p.13.

Lineton, Philip, 'Soviet nationality policy in north western Siberia: an historical perspective', *Development and Change*, vol.9, 1978, pp.87-102.

Lutz, Catherine (ed.), *Micronesia as strategic colony: the impact of US policy on Micronesian health and culture,* Cultural Survival Occasional Paper 12, June 1984.

McClintock, Michael, *The American Connection Volume Two: State Terror and Popular Resistance in Guatemala* (Zed Press, London, 1985).

Macdonald, Robert, *The Maori of New Zealand* (Minority Rights Group, 1985).

Marnham, Patrick, *Nomads of the Sahel* (Minority Rights Group, 1979).

Marroquin, Alejandro, 'El problema Indigena en El Salvador', *America Latina*, 35(4), 1975, pp.747-71.

Materne, Yves (ed.), *The Indian awakening in Latin America* (Friendship Press, New York, 1980).

Maxwell, Neville, *India and the Nagas* (Minority Rights Group, 1973).

Means, Russell, 'Indictment on industrial society', statement to the International NGO Conference on Indigenous Peoples and the Land, Geneva, 15-18 September 1981.

Ming, Yin, *United and equal: the progress of China's minority nationalities* (Foreign Languages Press, Peking, 1977).

Mosonyi, Esteban, 'The situation of the Indians of Venezuela. Perspectives and solutions', *The situation of the Indian in South America* (World Council of Churches, Geneva, 1972) pp.43-55.

Mullin, Chris, and Wangyal, Phuntsog, *The Tibetans: two perspectives on Tibetan–Chinese relations* (Minority Rights Group, 1983).

Munzel, Mark, *The Achè Indians: genocide in Paraguay*, IWGIA document 11, 1973.

Myers, Norman, *The primary source: tropical forests and our future* (W.W. Norton, New York, 1985).

Navet, Eric, *Camopi, commune Indienne? La politique 'Indienne' de la France en Guyane en 1984* (Diffusion Inti et Geria, Paris, June 1984).

Nelson, C.W., and Taylor, K., *Witness to genocide: the present situation of Indians in Guatemala* (Survival International, 1983).

Ohland, Klaudine, and Schneider, Robin (eds.), *National revolution and indigenous identity: the conflict between Sandinistas and Miskito Indians in Nicaragua's Atlantic Coast*, IWGIA document 47, November 1983.

Ortiz, Roxanne Dunbar, *Indians of the Americas* (Zed Press, London, 1984).

Oxfam, 'Lessons to be learned: drought and famine in Ethiopia', Public Affairs Unit, July 1984.

Paine, Robert, *Dam a river, damn a people?*, IWGIA document 45, 1982.

Parliamentary Human Rights Group, *The CDC and Mindanao*, report of a visit to the Philippines by Alf Dubs MP and Colin Moynihan MP, 21 September–1 October 1983.

Peacock, Nadine, 'The Mbuti of Northeast Zaire: women and subsistence exchange', *Cultural Survival Quarterly*, vol.8, no.2, Summer 1984, pp.15-17.

People's Union for Civil Liberties and Democratic Rights, *Repression in Singhbhum* (New Delhi, March 1979).

Plant, Roger, *Guatemala: unnatural disaster* (Latin American Bureau, London, 1978).

Plant, Roger, and Swepston, Lee, 'International standards and the protection of the land rights of indigenous and tribal populations', *International Labour Review*, vol.124, no.1, January–February 1985, pp.91-106.

Pool, David, *Eritrea: Africa's longest war* (Anti-Slavery Society, London, 1982).

Price, David, 'The World Bank and native peoples: a consultant's view', testimony presented at the hearings on the environmental policies of multilateral development banks, held by the US House of Representatives Sub-committee on International Development Institutions and Finance, 29 June 1983.

Ramos, Alcida, and Taylor, Kenneth, *The Yanoama in Brazil, 1979*, ARC/ IWGIA/SI document 37, 1979.

Reynolds, Henry, *The other side of the frontier* (Penguin, Harmondsworth, 1982).

Ribeiro, Darcy, *Os Indios e a civilização*, Editora Civilização (Brasileira, Rio de Janeiro, 1970).

Rich, Bruce, 'Time running out for Mexico's last tropical forest', *Cultural Survival Quarterly*, vol.6, no.2, Spring 1982, pp.13-14.

Riester, Jurgen, *Indians of Eastern Bolivia: aspects of their present situation*, IWGIA document 18, Copenhagen, 1975.

Roberts, Jan, *Massacres to mining: the colonisation of Aboriginal Australia* (Dove Communications, Victoria, 1981).

Rodriguez, Nemesio, *Oppression in Argentina: the Mataco case*, IWGIA document 21, 1975.

Salazar, Ernesto, *An Indian Federation in lowland Ecuador*, IWGIA document 28, 1977.

Sanders, Douglas, *The formation of the World Council of Indigenous Peoples*, IWGIA document 29, 1977.

Schwartzman, Stephen, 'Indigenists, environmentalists and the multilateral development banks', *Cultural Survival Quarterly*, vol.8, no.4, December 1984, pp.74-5.

Scientific Buddhist Association (UK), 'Tibet: the facts', report to the United Nations Commission on Human Rights, 1984.

Seagrove, Sterling, 'Karen rebels in Burma', *Soldiers of Fortune*, April 1984, pp.58-102.

Smith, Eric Alden, 'Inuit of the Canadian Eastern Arctic', *Cultural Survival Quarterly*, vol.8, no.3, Fall 1984, pp.32-7.

Smith, Martin, 'Politics of opium', *Inside Asia*, London, no.5, September–October 1985, pp.7-9.

Smith, Richard Chase, *The dialectics of domination in Peru: native communities and the myth of the vast Amazonian emptiness*, Cultural Survival Occasional Paper 8, October 1982.

——— 'A search for unity within diversity', *Cultural Survival Quarterly*, vol.8, no.4, December 1984, pp.6-13.

Souindola, Simao, 'Angola: genocide of the Bosquimanos', *IWGIA Newsletter*, nos.31-2, June–October 1982, pp.66-8.

Southeast Asia Chronicle, '400 year war – Moro struggle in the Philippines', no.82, February 1982.

Stavenhagen, Rodolfo, 'The indigenous problematique', *International Foundation for Development Alternatives*, Nyon, Switzerland, dossier 50, November/December 1985, pp.4-14.

Stegeborn, Wiveca, 'Sri Lanka: the Veddas – a people under threat', *IWGIA Newsletter*, 42, June 1985, pp.166-80.

Stephen, David, *The San of the Kalahari* (Minority Rights Group, 1982).

Stephen, D., and Wearne, P., *Central America's Indians* (Minority Rights Group, 1984).

Stoll, David, *Fishers of men or founders of empire?* (Zed Press, London, 1982).

Survival International, *Ethiopia's bitter medicine* (London, 1986).

Swift, Jeremy, 'Marginal peoples at the modern frontier in Asia and the Arctic', *Development and Change* (Sage, London and Beverly Hills) vol.9, no.1, January 1978, pp.3-19.

———— 'The future of the African hunter-gatherer and pastoral peoples', *Development and Change*, vol.13, no.2, April 1982, pp.159-81.

Szymanski, Albert, *Human Rights in the Soviet Union* (Zed Press, London, 1985).

TAPOL, *West Papua: the obliteration of a people* (London, 1983).

Tapp, Nic, *The Hmong of Thailand – opium people of the Golden Triangle* (Anti-Slavery Society, 1986).

Taylor, I., 'A report on the situation of the Mapuche Indians of Chile', *An end to laughter? Tribal peoples and economic development*, Survival International Review no.44, 1985, pp.125-35.

Thomas, Elizabeth Marshall, *The harmless people* (Secker & Warburg, London, 1959).

Triana, Adolfo, 'Indian groups in Colombia', *Survival International Review*, vol.6, nos.3 and 4, Autumn 1981, pp.8-9.

Tung, Fei Hsiao, *Toward a people's anthropology* (New World Press, China, 1981).

Turnbull, Colin, *The forest people* (Book Club Associates, London, 1974).

UNESCO, *Declaration of San José*, meeting of experts on Ethno-development and Ethnocide in Latin America, San José, Costa Rica, 7-11 December 1981.

United Nations, Economic and Social Council, Commission on Human Rights, *Preliminary report on the study of the problem of discrimination against indigenous populations* (E/CN.4/Sub.2/L.566).

———— *Study of the Problem of Discrimation against Indigenous Populations*, report submitted by the Special Rapporteur José Martinez Cobo, refs.E/CN.4/Sub.2/476 and Add.1-6, E/CN.4/Sub.2/1982/2 and Add.1-7 and E/CN.4/Sub.2/1983/21 and Add.1-8.

Valkeapaa, Nils-Aslak, *Greetings from Lappland: the Sami – Europe's forgotten people* (Zed Press, London, 1983).

Varese, Stefano, *The forest Indians in the present political situation of Peru*, IWGIA document 8, 1972.

Vos, George de, and Wetherall, William, *Japan's minorities* (Minority Rights Group, 1983).

Whitten, Norman, *Amazonian Ecuador: an ethnic interface in ecological, social and ideological perspectives*, IWGIA document 34, 1978.

Williams, Betty, 'Case study of Maori action against Conzinc Rio Tinto', paper presented to the Global Meeting on Environment and Development, Nairobi, Kenya, 4-8 February 1985.

Williams, Betty Whaitiri, *The passage of Maori land into Pakeha ownership: a Maori view* (Cabbage Tree Publications, Christchurch, New Zealand, n.d.).

Wilson, James, *The original Americans: US Indians* (Minority Rights Group, 1976).

—— *Canada's Indians* (Minority Rights Group, 1977).

Wily, Liz, 'A strategy of self-determination for the Kalahari San', *Development and Change*, vol.13, no.2, April 1982, pp.291-308.

Wirsing, Robert, G. *The Baluchis and Pathans* (Minority Rights Group, 1981).

World Bank, *Tribal Peoples and economic development: human ecological considerations* (Washington, May 1982).

World Council of Churches, *Land rights for indigenous people*, statement adopted by the Central Committee of the World Council of Churches, July 1982.

—— *Land rights for indigenous peoples* (Geneva, March 1983).

—— *New Caledonia: towards Kanak independence*, report of ecumenical visit, Geneva, 1984.

Wright, Robin, 'The Yanomami saga', *Cultural Survival Quarterly*, vol.5, no.2, Spring 1982, pp.27-9.

—— 'The great Carajás: Brazil's mega-program for the 80s', *The Global Reporter*, vol.1, no.1, March 1983, pp.3-6.

Index

SALF	Somali Aboriginal Liberation Front
SIL	Summer Institute of Linguistics
SPI	Indian Protection Service (Brazil)
TNC(s)	Transnational Corporation(s)
TPLF	Tigray People's Liberation Front
UN	United Nations
UNECE	UN Economic Commission for Europe
UNI	Union of Indian Nations (Brazil)
WCC	World Council of Churches
WCIP	World Council of Indigenous People
WIP	Workgroups on Indigenous People
WSLF	Western Somali Liberation Front
WWF	World Wildlife Fund

Act/Dawes Act 196; in Guam 214;
health 23-4, 200; Hopi 199; Indian
Reorganization Act 196; malnutrition
23; military domination 209; minerals
178, 199-201; mining & land loss 200;
Navajo-Hopi Settlement Act 201;
Navajos 25, 196, 199-200; nuclear tests
49, 52; Office of Indian Rights 29;
Oglala Lakota Sioux 199, 201; in
Philippines 148; Tribal Council 200,
202
USAID 96-7, 107, 140, 151
USSR: 211, 221-3, 268; Inuit 59-60, 181;
militarization 226; minerals 225-6;
Mongols 229; national minorities 222;
population 225; Russification 222;
UNECE, Central Asia 225
US Steel 106, 146, 256
Utah International 47, 256
Uygur, China 227, 232

Vanuatu 209, 211, 213
Vedda peoples 122-3
Velasco, General 91, 97
Venezuela (general) 24, 28, 98, 102
Vietnam 118, 119, 121
Volkswagen, Brazil 106

Waitangi Action Committee (Maori) 195
Waitangi Treaty 195
Wallis & Futuna 209
water: contaminated, USA 200; Maori
Peoples 195; Pacific 214; polluted by
mining and industry 198; pollution,
USA 201; *see also* ecological factors
Wave Hill Station (Australia) 185
WCC 273-4
WCIP 8, 58, 60-61, 178, 180, 186, 267
Western Shoshone 201
West Papua (general) 119, 141-7, 157, 164,
211, 252, 256
Whitlam, Gough 185-6
WIP 276
WSLF 165
World Bank 7, 47, 96, 107, 146, 151-2,
253, 250-56, 259, 277-8
World Conference to Combat Racism and
Racial Discrimination 264
World Court, Nicaragua 237
World Vision, Ecuador 52
World War II: 118, 121, 130, 140, 157,
238; Africa 163; Philippines 148, 157;
USSR 225; West Papua 143
Wounded Knee 38, 202
WWF 123

Xavante Indians 111

Xingu Indians 24
Xingu Park 106, 109, 111
Xinjiang 227, 231, 233, 235

Yagua Indians 99, 100
Yanomami 3, 24, 28, 106, 108, 269
Yanomami Park 108, 111
Yao: China 231; Thailand 136-7
Yaruro 98
Yekuana 28
Yucatan Mayans 75
Yukon Indians 208

Zaire 170, 173-4
Zambia 164
Zelaya, department of, Nicaragua 237,
238, 243
Zimbabwe 164
Zulu nation 34, 163

The Anti-Slavery Society
for the Protection of Human Rights

Our aims are in accordance with the principles of the Universal Declaration of Human Rights, 1948.

They are:

1 The elimination of all forms of slavery including forced labour.
2 The defence of the interests of both oppressed and threatened indigenous peoples.
3 The promotion of human rights in accordance with the principles of the Universal Declaration of Human Rights, 1948, and of the International Covenants on Civil and Political Rights and on Economic, Social and Cultural Rights.

If you are in sympathy with these aims you are invited
to become a member of the Society.

For further information please write to:

The Anti-Slavery Society,
180 Brixton Road,
London SW9 6AT
UK

Tel: 01-582 4040

Cultural Survival Inc.

Cultural Survival Inc., a non-profit organization founded in 1972, is dedicated to the physical and cultural survival of indigenous peoples. Many cultures have vanished already and with them their irreplaceable knowledge and wisdom.

In the name of civilization and development, indigenous peoples are often deprived of their belief systems and their lands. Contact with industrial societies often causes social destruction through disease, destitution and despair. Cultural survival for indigenous peoples means the possibility of adapting in their own way, at their own pace, to the outside world.

Through projects on five continents, research and publications, Cultural Survival works with indigenous peoples to help them retain control over their own destinies. Indigenous peoples design and implement many of their own projects, while Cultural Survival supports and records them. Project evaluations serve as models for other indigenous peoples in similar circumstances.

Cultural Survival's activities are based on the premise that culture is a set of mechanisms which permit a group to have a sense of itself, to comprehend its situation, and to adapt to changing circumstances. Indigenous people do not want to be kept in 'human zoos'; they want control over their lives. Cultural Survival therefore does not work to preserve 'traditional' societies, but rather to maintain those mechanisms which permit a group to successfully adapt to change. Central among these is a positive self-image – respect for one's history and pride in one's self.

For further information on Cultural Survival Programs and activities or for a complete list of the more than 350 titles distributed by Cultural Survival write to:

Cultural Survival
11 Divinity Avenue
Cambridge
Mass. 02138
USA
(617) 495-2562